FRANK J. NORTH

The second son of the North family was six feet two and one-half inches tall. He always appeared as he was — a natural but unassuming commander and leader of men. His walk was confident, without swagger or emphasis of authority. Major North always looked straight into the faces of all with whom he talked, and his actions were equally open, leaving no one apprehensive or in doubt.

Pawnee Scout Commander and Pioneer

RUBY E^{sther} WILSON

 Swallow Press • Athens, Ohio • Chicago • London

Title page drawing by Elizabeth Wolgamott

Swallow Press books
are published by
Ohio University Press
Athens, Ohio 45701

Library of Congress Cataloging in Publication Data

Wilson, Ruby Esther, 1902-
    Frank J. North, Pawnee scout commander and pioneer.

    1. North, Frank (Frank Joshua), 1840-1884. 2. Frontier and pioneer life—
Nebraska. 3. Nebraska—History. 4. Pawnee Indians—Biography. 5. Scouts and
scouting—Nebraska—Biography. 6. Pioneers—Nebraska—Biography. I. Title.
E99.P3N678 1984   978.2'031'0924 [B]   83-4797
ISBN 0-8040-0767-5

CONTENTS

ILLUSTRATIONS

PREFACE

More than forty years ago I interviewed several hundred Nebraska pioneers, many of whom were of the old Fort McPherson region of central western Nebraska. Individuals from the first three families who settled near Cottonwood Spring in the years 1858-60 contributed much firsthand history and lore of merchandising with Indians of various Plains tribes and later with travelers on the Great Westward Trail.

When I first conceived the urge to blend those old interviews into a story, I began to realize how often the name of Frank North had come up, until finally the man's own story emerged preponderate. Frank North was the man who first pioneered cattle ranching in Nebraska's Great Sandhill Grassland and earlier had been the organizer and commander of the renowned Pawnee Scouts of the regular U.S. Army. The Pawnees of Nebraska Territory, serving under North's command variously as a battalion of four companies and in smaller numbers of companies, were the first Indians to be regimented by the government.

Frank North, in contrast to his longtime friend, William "Buffalo Bill" Cody, was unassuming and reticent by nature. After extensive search and research, it is my conclusion that North granted but two personal interviews during his life, and none while in active Scout service. Furthermore, North's early scouting was in a land far west of the few civilized settlements bordering the Missouri River; thus, his activities largely preceded news-gathering in the almost unmapped, unmeasured, newly designated Territory. Raw and wild as it was, the country was yet too forbidding, the risks evidently not worth a firsthand story from a lone scout leader of his young Pawnee Indian friends.

In Columbus, Nebraska, during the early 1940s, I made acquaintance with Mrs. Stella North Chambers, Frank North's only child, born in the spring of 1869. She responded to my interest in her father's military activity, showing me the small black tin box in which were the two booklets containing diaries of two of Frank North's campaigns, both written in the field. Esteeming the diaries as treasures, and seeing Mrs.

Chambers was aging, this writer implored Miss Margaret Burke, a granddaughter of a Columbus founder, John Rickley, and of John Burke (who built the first bridge across the Platte River, near the early fort now known as Fort McPherson National Veterans Cemetery), to induce Mrs. Chambers to place those items in the Nebraska State Historical Society in Lincoln, Nebraska. This she did. The items are now on display there with other North souvenirs. Mrs. Chambers died in 1960.

In addition to the reminiscences of Nebraska pioneers, I have pieced together Frank North's story from his letters and accounts, plus the two handwritten diaries. I found no trace of his having written other diaries. Other sources include newspaper accounts, the diaries of his brothers Luther and James, and military records. I have couched the life and events in the first person, and used the form of a journal to recount events. The speech idiom of Frank North, raised in Ohio, is very similar to that of my parents from across the river in Indiana; thus, I have made an effort to capture its flavor. The events in this book are true; readers may distinguish between the journal form I created to tell the story and verbatim excerpts from North's diaries by noting that the latter are reproduced in indented block quotation.

SOURCES

MANUSCRIPTS. *Unpublished manuscripts of interviews* made by this writer during the 1930s. Those interviewed were contemporaries, friends, and acquaintances of Maj. Frank North. Copies of these are in possession of the writer; of Lincoln County Historical Society, North Platte, Nebraska; and Nebraska State Historical Society, Lincoln, Nebraska. One manuscript, probably written by Maj. Lester Walker, is possessed by Mrs. Nellie Yost, North Platte, Nebraska. Another, by A. Sorenson, is a poorly done interview of Frank North, 1880.

DIARIES. *Maj. Frank North's two diaries* possessed by his daughter, Mrs. Stella North Chambers, Columbus, Nebraska. (These are now deposited with the Nebraska State Historical Society.) *Mrs. Jane Townley North's (partial) diary* now with the two above.

PAWNEE. Proper nouns presented in Pawnee are from Frank North's translation and spelling, which varies occasionally, while pronunciation remains about the same. Frank North was believed, according to statements of George B. Grinnell, to be the authority most conversant with the unwritten Pawnee tongue. He accepted the North translations with some scholarly adaptation and refinement of spelling. Pawnee words herein are by this authority.

ADDITIONAL SOURCES. *The Maj. Frank North Collection:* letters, papers, mementos, including an autograph book of signatures and greetings of his fellow legislators of 1883, manuscript of Frank North interview by A. Sorenson, a scrapbook, and so on, found at Nebraska State Historical Society.

The Luther North Collection: letters, papers, etc., and manuscripts of his own reminiscences, also in the Nebraska State Historical Society Museum, Lincoln, Nebraska.

ACKNOWLEDGMENTS

I wish to acknowledge with gratitude these people, no longer living, who were especially important in discovering and making known the history of the Nebraska plains.

Mr. A. T. Hill was the person who first introduced me to, then fostered, the fascinating pursuit of a measure of Pawnee Indian lore. Mr. Hill as an amateur pioneered the search for historical and prehistorical ethnology of Nebraska, particularly of the plains dwellers. He excavated some sites himself, and financed and equipped a number of University of Nebraska archeology field expeditions. He served on the board and in various offices of the Nebraska State Historical Society, became Director and Curator of the Society's museum in Lincoln, and was the recipient of the Nebraska Builder Award from the University of Nebraska in 1948. A. T. Hill was designated the "father of systematic archeology in Nebraska" for his unflagging zeal, interest and financial aid that contributed for more than fifty years to an extensive recovery of the story of Nebraska's past.

Dr. Allan Swallow—a man of literary stature well known as a critic, poet and educator affiliated with Denver University—published many valuable works in pursuing his objective of preserving in print much that was being forgotten of genuine Western history.

Dr. Leo Jacks, an admired and beloved writer, critic and educator at Creighton University in Omaha, encouraged many other writers in his twenty-five years as chairman and guiding light of Omaha Writers.

I also appreciatively acknowledge the assistance of the librarians and personnel of the Denver Public Library Western Collections Division and of the Omaha Public Library; personnel of North Platte Public Library; director Marvin F. Kivett, the Board and personnel of the Nebraska State Historical Society; the Colorado State Historical Society; and the Union Pacific Museums in Chicago and Omaha.

FRANK J. NORTH
*Pawnee Scout Commander
and Pioneer*

Photo courtesy Nebraska State Historical Society

White Eagle, Chief of the Skeedee band

Born on the western Nebraska plains 1830 or before, and died after 1930.
Served as La-kit-tah-we La Shar in the short 1864 enlistment. In 1865, as
La-tah-Cots tah Kah, he became the Pawnee Scouts' first corporal.

1

Thomas Jefferson North, born April 5, 1813, near Ludlow, New York. Jane Almira Townley, born February 7, 1820, in Tompkins County, New York. Of British ancestry, the above-named couple were married in January 1835, immediately moving to Ohio. To them were born three sons and two daughters: James E., 1838; Frank Joshua, March 10, 1840; Luther Hedden, 1846; Sarah Elizabeth, 1848; and Alphonsine, 1850.

The English North's coat of arms bore the motto, *ANIMO et FIDEY,* loosely translated: By Courage and Faith; or, With Resolution And Fidelity; or, In Spirit And In Trust.

Whether the boy Frank North gave a thought or not to the motto and his ancestral history, that motto was proved prophetic of the man. Never in any generation of the family were the words so well exemplified as in Frank North's life.

Under the eaves of their Rome, Ohio, home, the North brothers slept side by side in their trundle beds. Brought in early age to the middle frontier of Nebraska Territory, their bones and flesh have long since mixed with Nebraska elements. Though each, when his time came, was laid away in sorrow and with tears, yet they live on here, their lives and work unforgotten. By singular courage and fidelity they contributed enduring foundation rocks to state-building.

In his general merchandise and groceries store, Frank's father and his friends frequently gathered to talk. Thomas North was also a practical surveyor. In his wider associations, he gathered information on politics and business, which the men discussed frequently whenever they got together.

"Long-headed thinking men," the boy heard his father comment. "The salt of the earth."

Frank never tired of hearing the oft-told tales of brave adventurers and mighty discoverers. Everything else was forgotten as he listened. In his imagining he was the explorer they told of. It was he who crossed the

1

Great Plains and shot the buffalo and roasted the hump meat at the camp fire. It was he who slept under the stars on the prairie. Alone under the open sky or sheltered by granite folds of the Rocky Mountains, it was he who stood guard over a sleeping camp, or forded unnamed streams where beaver played. In the boy's mind, images of the Plains mixed with the frontier tales heard from his grandfather, a Revolutionary War Minuteman who later joined the push to extend the American frontier toward the Mississippi River.

"Wouldn't you think a boy of fourteen, and about big enough for long breeches, ought to keep his mind on his work, whether or not his Pa does?" Frank's father questioned his friends, teasing the boy, seeing he was as wrapped up in their conversation as himself.

Frank snapped to the here and now. Looking sheepish, he went to put blind Barney between the shafts of the spring wagon and hurried to make his after-school deliveries. This done and Barney stabled again, he set about his barn chores, taking away manure and placing new bedding-straw, and fetching hay and oats. Frank filled large woodboxes that fed the huge potbellied stoves to heat the store, carried out ashes, and emptied the spittoons.

After supper he came back to the store to sweep up while his father waited on evening trade, then put things under cover and set the store to rights. James, sixteen months older than Frank and finished with academy schooling, worked every day at the store, toted up the ledger and closed the day's business. The fires in the heaters were banked, and the cats closed in for the night, to discourage the mice.

*   *   *

"Tell me a sleep time story about out west, Frank," Luther always asks of me before we go to sleep. He likes best for me to tell of what I learn at school and hear at the store about the frontier country, and that's my favorite subject too.

"Lute, I'm thinking some day I might be a hunter 'way out west on the Plains. Want'a come along with me?"

"Oh Frank, I expect squirrels there are great big ones?" (My little brother always tags along when Jim and I go a-squirreling.)

"Big for sure," I say, "but not squirrels—buffalo, my geography book says the animals on the Plains are really bison. Wouldn't it be grand to hunt them from horseback like the Indians do? They say the prairie is black with so many buffalo. I hope they won't all be killed as the beaver were all trapped from the Rocky's streams.

"I'll wait if you'll hurry and grow up. Then maybe we'll go exploring, like the French and Englishmen that followed Indians northwest and stayed to trap and trade." (With my little brother I feel tall, and talk that way to him, because he thinks I'm nearly as big as our brother Jim. You see, I'm not growing much. Since I was two and had lung fever, the tissic bothers me—keeps me small. I can't play Ante-Over and One-Ol'-Cat with the other boys when it's bad—just can't get enough breath to run.)

"Then I'll eat a whole lot so I can grow big quick, and go to trap and hunt and explore with you, Frank."

*   *   *

Nebraska Territory is organizing. Though it is Indian country, the Oregon Trail lies westward across its plains, and on through the Rocky Mountains.

Hundreds and thousands in covered wagons, mule, ox, and horse drawn, travel that Big Trace west to Oregon.

From conversations you can't be sure anyone east of the Mississippi River isn't coming down with "going west fever," and about to tie the chicken's legs together, getting ready to pull out, heading west.

A river man told in the store that he sees a pile of people go from St. Louis on every steamboat, up river as far as it goes into the northwest. He mentioned river ports with western and Indian sounding names: Westport, Nebraska Town, DeRoin, Bellevue, Omaha, Council Bluffs, Point Lisa, Dakota, and the like.

September 1855. James turns seventeen.

Whenever two or three men get together, talk turns to the railroads a-building.

I hear that someday an overland railroad will run west across the prairie and plains to the Great Rockies, then right up and over—who ever heard of a railroad climbing a mountain?

Well, I'm not saying it can't happen. Right now a bridge is a-building across the greatest river in this country, the Mississippi.

October 2, 1855. Men are going from our community to the frontier. A few are veterans of the Mexican War, others have already been across the mountains to California. One, John Day, went and came back in a year with enough gold to buy a sizable bunch of cattle. He herded them all the way to California and sold them to feed the miners, and fetched back bags of gold!

"Came back to the State to light and stay put," John Day said, but he has the "going west fever" again. I look at him and wonder what it is that pulls him west. Since he's rich with all that gold, it must be something else that's so mighty grand away out west.

James is more fidgety every day.

"Looks as though James is straining his halter rope," Father says.

"You are almost a grown man, James," Pa tells him. "Business is falling off at the store—I hope there isn't a money panic in the offing. We can get along without you, if you're wanting to go west. You may as well go with friends you know, while you can.

"I'll ask you not to wander about, adventuring. You are to find yourself a position—you have experience in merchandising and bookkeeping. As often as you can, send word home of yourself."

Mother tucks a New Testament into Jim's breast pocket, lays her head on his shoulder and cries.

Jim shakes my hand and gives me a hard thump, saying good-bye. They'll ride the train to Chicago, or further, before they will have to change to a stage where the railroad ends.

"Little brother," I remind him, "I'm waiting so we can go out west when you are big enough." Luther digs his fists into his tears—they stop, and we speculate more and more on what we hear of the frontier.

Fall in Ohio is a good feeling. Under a bright blue, sunny sky the old apple trees bow with loads of fresh, fragrant red and russet apples: Black Twigs and Winesaps, Winter Russets and Yellow Pippins. We pick bushels of all of them to store in our cellars for winter eating.

We help our grandparents make sweet cider, and take our turns to stir the apple butter with long hickory paddles, while it cooks all day in the big copper kettle hanging over an outdoor fire. Mother turns out of the oven a batch of bread.

Grandmother dips hot apple butter from the kettle to cool. We eat it with fresh-churned butter on the new bread, and drink a pitcher of cold milk.

It's fun to gather hickory nuts and walnuts after a hard frost loosens them. Yellow and brown leaves flutter from the trees and rustle underfoot.

Fox and grey squirrels scold and fuss, objecting to divvying up with the nuts, but there are plenty.

Thanksgiving is a long table heaped with turkey, geese, hams, pies, and puddings. Sometimes Pa misses parts of conversations among all the relatives while he's off woolgathering, but I've a notion of what he's thinking.

By Christmas Pa's eyes show the same look Jim's did when he was daydreaming of the West. Pa grumbles about "the shape the country's business is getting into.

"People aren't spending any money—most folk don't have any money. Prices are higher than Ben's kite. It looks real certain," Pa says, "that a money panic is at hand."

In a few weeks that panic is as good as upon us, at least in Pa's estimation.

"I believe, Jane, I had better go on out west—try to find us a new beginning on the frontier," Father says.

February 2, 1856. Ground-hog Day. Father sold the store and businesses, arranged for me to collect accounts owing us, and I am to help Mother get ready to come when he sends us word.

Father joined Jim at Des Moines, Iowa; together, they went on out to the Nebraska Territory frontier where they are employed to survey. They likely won't run out of work, with all the uncharted land between them and the Pacific Ocean.

2

April 1856. We are taking the cars to Chicago, on our way to Nebraska Territory—Mother, our two little sisters, Luther, and me.

Changing in Chicago to the Mississippi and Missouri line, we go on west across the "Father of Waters" on the long bridge recently built. A steamboat passes under our train, and its whistle sounds like the "coo" of a gigantic mourning dove. Shrieking an answering hair-raiser, our train minces, suspenseful and slow, the length of the timbered trestle and onto solid ground. I wasn't sure the big bridge would hold up under the heavy train, and so I breathe easy again.

At Iowa City the rails end. So many are waiting to ride. Mother doesn't get promise of seats in a stage before ten days.

Lute and I go among the men at the stage barns, and around blacksmith shops. There is talk of wide new lands, of unmeasured territories, of new gold fields, and rich strikes of gold ore and pure gold nuggets. Men tell of grizzly-bear attacks and torture by savages. They talk of impassable mountain ranges and fords of wild rivers.

We hear another kind of talk too: that new territories will be unable to settle without admitting slaveholders. When talk of slavery comes up, there is separation of men. Their no longer friendly eyes are watchful, chill. Words, hateful and ugly, slash and lash between men in boiling anger, and there's much swearing.

Not relishing such talk, I take my younger brother away and we go back to Mother. But we had gathered that since Secretary of War Davis's proposed appropriation was granted, a survey is underway for building a military overland road, and bridging of streams too deep for fording, from the Missouri River west to Fort Kearny.

For the sake of Mother and our little sisters, a stage man manages to get us earlier passage. We are again on our way after only five days wait. It has rained steadily three days and nights. The earth is soggy and still the rain pours. The damp air makes my tissic bother, and I can hardly breathe in or out in the close-packed coach.

The stage stops. It is stuck, caught fast in a bog. Men get out to help. They push, the horses are lashed, forced to pull harder. The coach moves out. The passengers, wetter and muddier, settle into their seats and we joggle on.

Again, the stage is stuck, and men get out to lighten the load and help get us going. In only a little while, it's the same thing all over again. The stage is so often stuck the men take turns walking to poke heavy mud packs from between wheel spokes to prevent miring the stage in every bog.

A fat man, the loudest, cussingest, proslavery talker in Iowa City, is even louder here in the stage. He sits through his turn to walk unless others half drag him out. I see him sneaking long draws from a flask while some walk and others doze until their turn to walk again.

At a stage rest station our horses are changed, and the driver and hands reload us while the fat man harangues the station cook. We drive away leaving the noisy and now angry man to cool his heels, and no one objects.

The stage bumps hard into and out of every chuckhole. We ford rivers too deep to be taken lightly. No one expects comfort while traveling, with stage stations few, and rest stops too far apart. Mother sits cramped and crowded. Our little sisters are cold and fretful.

Enduring the struggle to breathe, I don't take turns at walking, though Luther slogs along as many turns as Mother permits, helping clear the mud-balled wheels. Small for his age, he only weighs about sixty pounds, but he is dragging close to his own weight in mud on his boots.

Nearing the frontier, many trails join. Our stage passes slower wagons and canvas topped schooners. We see horseback riders, and there are men going afoot, some carrying packs on their backs. We draw even with, then pass, a large train of oxen-pulled freighting wagons lumbering toward the Missouri.

All the travelers have stopped along a great stretch of flat, widely rutted prairie. Many are taking their noonings until the wheels roll again. Our stage and many rigs struggle to move on, though wagons and coaches are bunched as far as I can see ahead.

A man clothed in buckskin leather, surely a frontiersman, says this crowd of wagons, teams, and herded animals has waited, some, for many days, even a week or more, to be ferried across the Missouri River. Men exchange help so that each can graze his stock, yet hold his place in line and move along.

As our coach is not to cross the river, it skirts the immense jam. Coming down a slope I catch a flash, between woods, of a sun-shot, coffee-colored expanse of water. Looking down along the broad, twisting river we see bluffs to our right and ahead, facing us from across the stream.

A swing of our stage to right angle, a crack of the driver's blacksnake whip, and the horses rush at the fastest gait of the whole trip, this, after averaging, in long stretches of heavy going, three and four, instead of the usual six, miles an hour.

The fast dash comes to a scrambling halt. We have arrived at the stage terminal station house in a small village that Father's letter directs us to. Here we settle to wait for Pa and Jim.

My tissic has almost cleared, I feel well and the weather is fine. Being eager to see more of the bedlam along the riverside, with Mother's consent, we boys go out.

I'll never forget this teeming river front. With the day's warming sun, the stink grows stout, rising from waste, refuse, and human and animal dung and urine, decaying in marshy ponds along the water margins. Wrenching odor grabs our stomach muscles and lends wings to our heels. Sometimes we retch, then we hold our noses and run fast past the worst.

Sunlight flashes from the water's waves, as the steam ferry shuttles over the rolling brown surface, to and from landings where the bluffs allow footing space. Here men hold their place in line by patience and peace, and if need be, by threat and fist. Seeing their animals go with lessened grazing, and hungrier every day, men wait and swear. With their turn, finally, to be ferried they work and sweat at hard, quick labor as mules and horses, or oxen, strain taut tugs pulling wagons onto the ferry.

A wagon next in line comes on. The horses are excited; they get scared and go to crowding. One horse rears—they're about to bolt. A horse squeals—goes down. Men push forward—grab bridles at bits—yank fear-crazed heads down, subduing them.

The downed horse's leg is broken. Too bad! Quickly, for the ferry cannot dally, harness is stripped from the animal. A shot sounds, and the horse is rolled into midstream and carried away by strong current.

Dodging about, we find blacksmiths and farriers busy at forges and anvils. Men squat heel to thigh around lean-to or canvas makeshift shops, as their wagon wheel rims are put through heating, tempering, and shrinking to a tight fit on the wheel. Others manage their animals for farrier's convenience, for fitting and nailing iron shoes through nerveless hoof edges.

Father comes and takes me as a surveyor's helper of the General Land Office Company. I replace Jim, and say "Stick" followed by "Stuck" over and over, as the wagon rolls along; eighty chains counting as a mile.

Jim has a position upriver six miles, at the larger town of Florence[1] working for Mitchell's, outfitters of immigrants and travelers. Father moves the family across the river and now we're all in Nebraska Territory on the frontier.

Back across the river, Pa and I go to Council Bluffs village. There he consults on surveying matters with the civil engineer who was chief assistant in surveying for building of the Mississippi railroad, G. M. Dodge.[2]

"A gentleman of tremendous energy with a compelling personality, if I ever met such a one," Pa says.

During the conversation, the engineer mentions that a span of the Mississippi bridge has burned. Pa fixes the time as a week after we rode across it. Mr. Dodge explains a steamboat hit a pier and burst into flames, setting the bridge to burning.

He says a country lawyer in Illinois is defending[3] the railroad against the steamship company. It seems the suit rests upon rights and usefulness of the one against the other.

Doesn't it go without saying that steamboats and waterways are more useful and will always be? Dodge doesn't think so, and he says this country lawyer puts up the argument: "The railroad's future usefulness, and therefore its rights, are equal to that of boats."

3

January 1857. Winter closes down and stops survey work. It is terribly
cold, a frozen land. Father contracts with Mr. Pierce at Florence to cut
cord wood and dimension stuff out of his timber, so Pa's crew of men can
earn their living until spring. I go to school though I had nearly finished
academy in Ohio. After hours I help Pa keep track of wood cutters' work
and business of the wood yards and hauling.

February 1857. The sun shines warm, and the ground hog will see his
shadow. Now there'll be a month and a half more of winter. Chinook
winds hike the temperature like a day in May. Drifts of snow melt into
little streams running toward the river. Since the ground is mostly bare,
surveying will begin, and I will soon leave school to help.

March 1857. Father and a crew work about ten miles west of Omaha
village, surveying section lines and laying out a town site on Butterfly
Creek (renamed Papillion). Late in the afternoon temperatures drop fast as
a storm comes on. Thick fog rolls into the valleys, then sleet and snow
begin. Father sends the men and teams to a settler's place while he
finishes a task.

When Pa didn't come into the farmer's place, his men lit a fire of hay
to guide him in. They called him and went out into the storm as far as
they dared. The short, sharp storm broke away, clearing with daylight.
Then they found Father. He had lost his bearings and frozen to death.
They brought him home to us for burial.

Our mother is a widow in this raw, new country. No kin is nearer than
Ohio, other than our two little sisters and we three sons. Having but scant
money and no special means, Mother shows us how to stand against
disaster, and we surely learn about courage from her.

I carry out the wood contract, keeping our thirty head of oxen and the
woodcutters busy until spring breaks. Mr. Pierce settles up with me then,
and we sell off thirteen yoke of oxen with yokes, bows, wagons, and sleds
to new settlers.

Jim and I put up a two-room log house in the woods near Florence, on eighty acres bought in Mother's name. (Recorded, July 1857. Jane North purchased the w-2 N.W. ¼ of Section 28, T.15,R. 13 E., paid for by negotiable military bounty land warrant.) Mother moves into our own house and puts the kettle on.

With the two yoke of oxen we kept, Josephus and Bohunkus and Roudy and Buck, I hire out for spring plowing, breaking ground for garden and corn planting. Between jobs I scythe a lot of prairie grasses to stack for next winter. Luther helps me though he's not very big.

I'm nearly as tall as Jim. What's more, I'm strong—put together to last a lifetime if my puckerin' string don't give. I'm well here—tissic never bothers my breathing anymore.

Summer jobs are finished. Mr. Pierce hires me again to measure cord wood and keep general track of the wordyard's business. Another task I like is hauling wood to the yards where steamboats take it on for stocking.

I've learned to recognize a few of the different riverboats' whistles. Every captain of a steamboat has his own signal. Every boat's name, usually a girl's, is painted along the boat hull: North Star, Home Bessie, Samantha Jane, and Suzanna. I think this Silver Heels is probably the last to make it upriver and back down before freeze-up this fall.

October 1857. Autumn valleys are full of ripe wild grapes, and thickets are fragrant with frost-ripened sloe plums, yellow meated and juicy sweet. Lute and I stir up a flock of large white owls (snowy owls, *Nydea scaudraca*) to pick plenty of fruit that Mother dries to stew up for sauce when the snow flies.

As Jim must take grocery staples in part pay, Mother is boarding the wood choppers to turn it all to good use. My pay is part in wood, too. I manage to cut and shock corn for a nice share, besides what I raised of our own.

Nights frost hard and bright fall days get nippier. In certain hours, skies are blackened by waterfowl flying south. Luther supplies Mother with geese and ducks, bunnies and lots of fish. He's a good shot. A rugged, forlorn dog, lost from some wagon, cottoned to Lute—goes with him on every hunt and fetches in his downed game as if he wants to earn his keep.

I kill deer as we need meat. Later, when there is no thawing, I will butcher and hang enough deer meat to last through winter.

After the first heavy snow, another follows, and snow is piling up. I have to keep the oxen going and coming every day with sleds loaded with firewood—scarce and hard to get in Omaha, keeping the trail packed for hauling over it.

Two families move into Mr. Pierce's woods for shelter, with a bad blizzard tailing them. I see them hustling hide tents up as I come from a haul. After seeing to the needs of our oxen, I go to tell Mother the news.

Concerned that anyone would have to be moving in such weather, she wraps up two slabs of hot cornbread in dishcloths, and divides a pot of venison and bean stew for me to take to them.

They've snugged down pretty well. Wood-smelling smoke curls from smoke holes in their tepee tops, mixing with the swirling snow. There is no door to knock on, so I yell.

An edge of hide is drawn back from inside, and a night-black eye peeps at me. I thrust the kettles forward. I hear voices inside, mingling with howling of the wind. A flap is opened and I duck low, taking my offerings in with me.

Opposite the entrance a man sits back of fire going in the fire-hole. I step past a couple of women and small children, toward him.

"How do you do?" I smile as well as my chill-stiffened face lets me.

"Loo-ah," he replies. I take it for "Hello."

"My mother sends hot vittles for your supper," I say, placing a kettle and bread on it, near the fire.

While surveying with Father I grew used to Omaha, Otoe, and even Yutan Indians being around, going or coming from missions[1] and schools that eastern churches maintain for them in the river country around Bellevue, to the southeast.

I know, too, that many people hate, fear, and mistrust red folk. A trapper working for Pa cautioned me, "Yonker, le'me put a bug in yer ear. When them red varmints is around—and fur sure when they ain't cause that's when they are, keep yer back behind you. Don't never, no time, turn yer back to a Injun—er yer daid. Cain't trust 'em, no-how, none of 'em. Jest fiercer 'n animals—worser'n wolves."

"Just the same, red men are humans, too," Pa always said, "and Christian men will not do less than practice the Golden Rule with Indians."

In this hide-dressed man I see natural, quiet self-respect. Neither old nor young, his face is as open as the prairie, and his eyes look not only at, but also straight into me. He gives me ease and I sense in him the extraordinary. His moccasins, leggings, and shirt tunic shimmer and glow in the firelight, reflecting finely beaded and worked quill embroidery.

When the man speaks to the women, they take up the bundle of bread and the kettle. I shift things to pull off a mitten and reach to unsnap the spring-held lid, opening the kettle.

You never saw ice melt as fast as the women's reserve when they smell the steam rolling from the kettle. Though I cannot understand a thing they say, their gratefulness is unmistakable, as, emptying the kettle into their own, they hand it and the cloth back to me.

A boy squatting a few feet from the Chief comes to stand nearer to me. I feel his eyes watching me, especially looking at my warm, thick-knitted mittens. He is as tall as me. Meeting his eyes, I smile. A flicker lights his. Bidding goodbye, I point to the other kettle and bundle, and toward the other tent.

In the second family are two boys, older and younger than me, other children, and one woman with a fine-looking man.

Gradually Luther and I make friends with the boy called La-Roo Chucka La Shar, Sun Chief,[2] son of Peta La Shar,[3] the dignified head chief and counselor of the Grand, or Chaui band, and of the entire Pawnee Nation.

We are friends, too, with the sons of Ke-We Kan La Shar, Buffalo Bill Chief; and older Aru-Saw Kit-toy and his brother, Cot-te-ra-tet Goots. Rough and tumble snow play gives us a level of understanding. Neither La-Roo Chucka La Shar nor Aru-Saw Kit-toy can best me, nor I them, in our snow tussles and wrestling.

The Indians' sign language looks direct and simple enough, but it will take a lot of practice. The Pawnee tongue really stickles Lute and me.[4] We're catching on, though, because we are anxious to learn enough that we can talk with our friends. But we can't write notes to them unless we draw pictures, as there is no alphabet to the unwritten Pawnee language.

Our tongue clumsiness must be funny as the Pawnee boys laugh a lot, but are willing to show us again and again, and we are teaching them our language, too. As we come to understand, they explain that their fathers and families with other chiefs and subchiefs were called by the Great White Father to the Table Creek conference in October to treaty.

We finally learn that Peta La Shar, or Man Chief, in spite of his own disapproval of the treaty, but because he was overruled by the fifteen other chieftains of the Pawnee Nation (four chiefs to each of four Pawnee bands), was the first chief to make his mark on that treaty. Buffalo Bill Chief signed for the Pit-a-hau-rats. I believe they say Commanche Chief signed for the Skeedees, and NaSharo Sed-e-ta Rado for the Kit-ke-haki.

In the conference, presided over by Commissioner J. W. Denver, the Pawnee were induced to sign away their last acre of native land in return for big, bright promises of a reservation on the Loup River that is to be theirs *"forever."*

Promised, too, are schools and teachers for Pawnee children; grist and wood mills; farming equipment; tools, seed, and stock; farm teachers and certain monies to be paid to the Pawnee Nation annually, *"in perpetuity."*

"Pa-ni [Pawnee] remember how that our Grandfather's blood, and another time our Father's blood, and some snows back, our own blood, was spilled on that ground. *Cha-hik si Cha-hik* [Men or Men] shall not sit like *uti-hur-i* [little prairie chicks], under eyes of *La-kot-a* [Sioux] *ur-ik-ta* [hawk]."

Objecting to the place government men decided on for the reservation, knowing it too handy to their old-time enemy, now grown strong; Pawnee objections were squelched by government promise to supply soldiers to guard and defend the reservation.

While buying at Mitchell's Outfitter store last fall, a hunter who works as a guide told Jim that about twenty-seven years ago, in the 1830s, the Delawares, many times uprooted along with other Indian tribes, and crowded west away from settlement, crossed the Missouri River and had gone into country between Kansas and Platte rivers.

Pawnee, along with allied tribes, fought the eastern tribes out of the hunting ground they believed was their own, according to governmental word. That fetched the government's hand into the dispute, and Harry Ellsworth was commissioned to pacify the Pawnee and Otoe tribes, to get them to peaceably accept incoming Indians.

This is a terrible winter. Snow is four to six feet deep on the level and drifts more than three times as high. Men here when the Mormons wintered at this site ten years ago tell of that awful winter that filled a cemetery. They're saying this winter is worse.

Our Pawnee friends tell us this is the "winter of white owls" and I'm reminded of those we disturbed in the trees last fall where the wild grapes vined near the plum thickets.

I've seen no game in several weeks and surmise a lot of animals and turkeys, quail, grouse, and prairie chickens have starved and smothered to death under snow.

As our oxen have fodder, we share their corn with the Pawnee families. That is all the Indians have to live on. For ourselves, Mother makes good lye hominy from shelled corn and we have cornmeal. A mess of fried mush with sorghum brought up on a steamer last fall sticks to our ribs these cold days.

Starvation seems not far from anyone here this winter, but it is much nearer the Indian families. I hope the corn lasts for them. If only they had gotten home to their eastern lodges before the blizzards caught them. There they have corn, beans, and dried vegetables stored underground[5] and dried meats that frontiersmen call "jerky" or pemmican, meat pieces tied in lengths of intestine and boiled. In Ohio we stuffed sausage into intestines that had been stripped from the interlining and washed and scraped on a board with the edgeless side of a knife until they were transparent, but I wonder—do you suppose the delicious taste the boys tell us of came from digestive substances in the intestines? Besides these meats, they have that prepared with bull berries, buffalo berries gathered when sloe plums are, after the first frost, and pounded with meat to a mincemeat pulp and preserved in tallow.

*   *   *

February 1858. The majority of legislators of the fourth territorial legislature adjourned from Omaha's Capital Hill Territorial Capital to Florence. A committee appointed last year by the third legislature reported Omaha would never become the population center needed as permanent capital; and since they could not agree on any other capital, it should be established by laying out a new paper town.

Chester was proposed, but Douglas was approved by both houses after survey and plotting. Governor Izzard, said to favor Omaha, vetoed the bill. The unofficial session offered still another town to be called Neapolis.[6] The squabble goes on.

4

Spring thaw is cracking up the river ice, and it breaks with loud booms to move, grinding and roaring, downstream. The docks are rigging for unloading freight from boats that soon will be coming upriver.

Mother plans to return east with Luther and our sisters this spring on the first steamer downriver. She will settle some business in Ohio and visit our grandparents for awhile.

Overland travelers come through by greenup time, fewer than last season. That means travelers outfitting or restocking at Mitchell Outfitters, where Jim works, aren't bringing much money along. Men say the whole country back in the states is in doldrums—has been for months.[1]

It's seldom now that a man has two coins to jingle together, though brother Jim says gold and silver pieces, eagles and doubles, halves and quarters show up at the store, and he thinks people are digging deeper into their sock.

There is plenty of paper money[2] issued by new banks chartered by the territorial legislature but who wants it unless the named bank is known?

The Florence Bank is the oldest, and, I think, the strongest. The Kountz Bank, started in Omaha village the year we came, was the first west of the Missouri River to get a national bank charter, and it's said to be reliable; upriver, DeSota's Waubeck Bank is said to be dependable. Downriver, one at Brownville and a bank at the big port of Alexander Major's[3] freight terminal are supposed to be as stout as any in the Territory.

Jim and I aren't doing much good for ourselves, having to take our small earnings in stuff we mostly can't use. Our village is dwindling.

People are talking of taking up land by pre-emption. Our friends, the Arnold family, have decided to go west to a new settlement. We should find better opportunities in that new Coleville,[4] so we load the family belongings, leaving our place to a renter.

Heading out with our friends in a rainy season, we slog through rainsoft earth that the wagon wheels cut deep into, with heavy pulling. Soaked clothes are the least of our troubles, though none can get dry at our sputtering, green, and wet wood campfires, and we're lucky to get something cooked to eat.

Wallowing through bogs that have no bottoms, our wagons are stuck time and again. It usually takes Josephus and Bohunkus, doubled on with the teams, to move stuck wagons, as they're extra big, strong oxen. They never back off from their yoke—just stay with it and haul it on.

A stream we must ford has a lot of water, a cloudburst or heavier rain in its upper watershed besides the snow runoff. Testing here and there for depth and bottom, we conclude it can be forded. I take my oxen down and in. Water covers them and sloshes into the wagon. I think I've lost my oxen. I'm about to jump in to get them unhitched. Just then ears and muzzles break water—they're still pulling for the other side.

Hauling to shallow water, they stop on a sandbar for a breather. We are sinking—we're in quicksand! Let's get out of here. Hay-up!

The beasts strain—time measures a labored forward placing of each large splayed hoof; we're barely moving ahead with all the oxen's weight against their yoke. This is a bad sink. It's an even draw—out, or under. Take us out, boys, I urge, and tails twist, necks stretch, muzzles reach out, and eyes bulge from mighty strain as they bawl and heave, inching ahead.

Get out they do, quicksand caked to the briskets, tongues lolling out of open maws, flanks heaving—panting hard and fast after that pull—the hardest they've ever been up against. I'm glad my team isn't horses, apt to get skittish—lose their heads and go to frantic flouncing. That would have churned up the quicksand and got the whole outfit sucked under, fast.

I scrape the sand coat off and blanket my work beasts. After they blow awhile, I move them—lead them or else they will stiffen, lame up, like a foundered horse and be ruined for work. I cool them down, then I can sleep.

The next morning we locate a fording place where the water runs even all the way across, and cross the other wagons over. Clouds of buffalo gnats come with sunshine, and ball up on our animals' noses and eyes. Mosquitos, "big enough to eat a jack rabbit at one gulp," Al Arnold says, torment us day and night, sunshine or clouds. Deerflys through the valleys stab burning hurt like a hornet's sting.

Luther's old dog comes along, swims the streams and looks out for himself. He harangues after sundown at yapping coyotes—warns them to keep away from the oxen and wagon he *owns*. The old dog hollers himself hoarse trying to get the last howl every night, until someone chucks a stick of wood or a boot in his general direction. We find him in the morning, a right brave camp guard, snug asleep between the oxen!

After ten tough-pulling days we come to the new community. The village has about twenty buildings of log and sod, with thatched roofs and a few of shingles from a sawmill by the river. The one large building, not yet completed, is a frame hotel.[5] Being more than we expected, it looks good to us.

Germans from Columbus, Ohio, picked this spot for the town site at junction of the Loup and Platte rivers. West and on either side the Great Plains spread in a grand, wide sweep. From the Omaha and Florence river ports, west a hundred miles, Columbus, Nebraska Territory, is about midway to Fort Kearny. Water is good, soil is rich.

May 1858. The Arnolds find a location to their liking, and we help put up a house for them. I plow to plant a patch of sod corn for our use, then hire out to plow for other settlers.

Jim takes a pre-emption next to mine, and we build our house on our line. He works at the new ferry hauling emigrants' wagons and teams across the Loup.

September 1858. Newspapers brought to Columbus pass through the settlement until the print wears off. We read reports of debates between the "Little Giant" Douglas—once a congressman, a state supreme court judge (it looks like he may be our next President)—and Abraham Lincoln. The country lawyer, ex-congressman, not much known outside of Illinois, challenges the senator to a string of debates around his home state.

Along with other national questions they argue slavery up one side and down the other. "'A house divided against itself can not stand,'" the homespun lawyer quotes the Bible to back up his claim that our government can't exist half free and half slave.

Later September, 1858. "Hey, Frank, there's a gold strike! They've struck gold. Gold—lots of gold. The richest strike that's ever been found." Jim comes from our little town yelling as far as he sees me. "I brought you a paper—a new one, only eight days since it was printed."

THE OMAHA TIMES, *September 9, 1858*—. . . rich diggings discovered, twelve days travel from Omaha . . . great excitement on the plains. . . . From here to Fort Kearny . . . one hundred and eighty miles . . . on a good traveled road . . . principal streams, except Loup Fork, excellently bridged by the United States Government . . . crosses Platte River at Fort Kearny . . . follows . . . to mining district . . . best part of the gold diggings. . . .

All those bridges and good roads around here? Somehow I've been missing them. If the report of striking gold is no truer than this about roads and bridges, then there's no more gold in the Territory than my three dollar gold piece.

"Everybody's starting out for the gold fields," Jim says.

"Are you going, Jim?"

"Sure, wouldn't miss a chance at a Pikes Peak gold mine."

"I don't want to miss anything, but we just could miss our places when we come home. You know, Jim, in spite of our claim club, a man hardly turns his back if he's got a livable place and a crop, until a claim jumper grabs onto it. We'd both lose our pre-emptions, going that far away. You go ahead, if you want to. I'll stay, cut and shock my corn, and hold what we do have."

These days, gold hunters pull along the Omaha to Fort Kearny military road bound for the diggings. Two weeks ago, the first went through here. Now an army of prospectors passes every day, afoot, or on horseback, or by wagon and any way at all.

Grass is cured—no longer green. Immigrant schooners and bull trains that must depend on grazing have quit the trail. Mule trains carrying their own grain feed, and the speedy stages that hook a fresh team on at every swing station, and the gold hunters go on.

Men with gold fever left here in a group. Jim stayed—couldn't tear himself away from an interest he has here, with a pretty smile in her eyes.

October 5, 1858. Today, Friday, the first of Western Stage Company's four-mule, post and passenger carrying stages from Council Bluffs to Fort Kearny came through Columbus, bringing mail right to our town.

"By next spring Western Stage will be carrying people to the Cherry Creek gold fields. We'll make the Omaha to Fort Kearny run in two-and-a-half to three days." Charley Hagerty[6] drives the stage and brags it up like a banty rooster crowing atop an Ohio stake and rider fence.

November 13, 1858. The first of the annuity promised the Pawnee in their last treaty is brought by Maj. W. W. Dennison, the United States Indian agent, under escort of Lieutenant Cunningham, and a posse with United States Marshall H. Z. Ludington. The officers stop at the hotel, just finished, ready to open for business this month. Jim and I go to pay our respects and get acquainted.

Fifteen tons, supposedly, of blankets, calicos, and other dry goods, groceries, coffee, sugar, and staples will be handed out to the Indians. They were promised $40,000 a year for the first five years, and, I believe, it was to be $30,000 annually after that.[7]

The monies are paid to them, minus payments for a passel of claims, said to be for Pawnee-committed wrongs and damages. Charges are made and sworn to by a few settlers and a raft of strangers—though drifters that got wind of the annuity wagons and got here ahead, or followed them up from Nebraska City to trade lies for a fistful of the Indians' money. The claims are allowed.

All I've got to say is the Pawnee are sure more industrious than I thought if they managed to commit all those misdeeds they've just paid for.

THE NEBRASKA CITY NEWS, *November 6, 1858.* "No gold at Pikes Peak, west Kansas Territory," it reads; and describes the best route to the gold mines of Cherry Creek, whether or not it knows.

November (late) 1858. Prairie grass is afire between here and the fort, and on west along the Big Trace, though we don't know how far. Gold seekers fear to go on. Probably, beyond the burn, forage is under deep snow. Many are turning back toward the Missouri, and a few hole up here, scratch up quick dugouts, but some do go on.

I'm husking out my last shock of corn, a right fair crop for first season sod. Three hunters look me up to proposition that I join them in a wolf hunt; me, to furnish everything else needed. As Jim will stay, and I have nothing more profitable to do, I take my gun and throw in with them.

We drive three days to the southwest and there make a dugout with a fireplace in the back and a stovepipe stuck up through the top.

Killing a couple of old buffalo loners, fought out of a herd by young bulls, we hook the team on to pull them to camp and skin and quarter them. The man with the team, and another—a smithy from Columbus—drive away. The oldest and oddest man stays. I guess he's been a hunter all his life. He doesn't talk, doesn't do much of anything but sit and smoke his pipe and stare. I think he's as much of a loner as these old bulls we killed. The upshot is that I have everything to do.

So the wolves can't make off with it, I stake out a portion of carcass of the meat, well seasoned with strychnine.[8] Cutting all the rest into small chunks, I insert a killing dose of poison in each. These I scatter nightly, else crows pick them up.

Circling wide around the staked-down carcass, I drop the single chunks at a distance that will allow for the wolf gulping it to die by the time he reaches the center teaser that draws him by scent. As they die before getting away, I don't have to trail them, so can skin them out faster in the mornings.

These crows are the earliest early birds. Unless it's storming, when they stay on their roosts, I have to get out ahead of the first crack of light to beat them. There's no market for a wolf hide picked full of holes.

A wolf, sometimes wolves, stalk me on my early evening circle. I don't carry my Kentuck, just don't have enough hands, and don't need it. Wolves fear man's scent—won't attack, nor I them.

A varmint is more interested in the chunks I carry than in the frozen carcass. He gets too close to suit me. I hit for the dugout. He tails me right along. Besides his wolfish hunger, he's got a big bump of curiosity.

As I get closer to the dugout, so he will fall near, I drop him a chunk, and he gets a lifetime lesson.

Working steadily, I have plenty to do accumulating hides these six weeks. The Columbus man, Mr. Glass, walks in while I'm out, and tells me the older man left. (It all seems a bit odd, the old man going just after the other came, and not claiming his share of the pelts, nor their worth.)

A large band of Indians sets up a camp neighboring our dugout. Careful to keep hidden, I study them, trying to decide what tribe they belong to. Seeing signs of preparation for a big hunt, I think they are getting ready for a buffalo surround.

Hurrying my morning skinning, and finishing the job, I go to watch the Indians. The whole camp is on the move. Rolled up hide tepees, cook pots, puppies, and the babies just out of cradle boards are packed upon backs of the squaws' old nags, and loaded onto the cross-tied tepee pole travois. One end is dragged, the other end is hitched at both sides of the pony's Pawnee saddle or pack harness. Some women with baby boards on their backs ride on top of the loads on the ponies. Even dogs carry packs. When a jack rabbit jumps up and the dogs take off after it, scattering their packs, the squaws call them everything but pet names.

The men are riding at a fair clip now. I keep low and run on, hoping I can see a buffalo surround. The Indians take advantage of a draw to ride unseen until it half circles a string of hills. I run slantwise from the riders and begin again to see them and their extra horses—I wonder why they bother with fetching along about as many more ponies as they're riding.

Two breech-clout men rise up from hiding and stop the hunters, Buffalo spotters, I think. All strip off leggings and hide shirts, and tie them around necks of the ridden horses. These are shooed back toward the slower traveling women and children. The men mount the led ponies which have been kept fresh for the surround.

I reach the first low butte as the riders go out from either side of a low hill. Some few carry what appear to be fish poles with bright-colored calico banners flying. They are running abreast toward a big herd of buffalo, loosely scattered, from four or five hundred rods distant. Now I see horses at the outer ends are running faster, necks stretching and muzzles reaching, the riders pushing the ponies hard.

The level plain looks like a solid buffalo rug. There is a sudden flash of the banner poles and the ponies all along the line spurt away, soon outdistancing some few slower ones; and I understand the use of the signaling poles is to allow all an even chance—the slow and the quick alike.

Those furthest ahead at the far ends ride to the head of the main bunch and start them circling like a log in an eddy. Now all are riding hard, circling and sending arrows into the big beasts faster than my eyes can follow. Pressure of the rider's knees controls his trained partner, and his hands are free to work his archery while everything churns around and around. The humped beasts run faster and faster to escape the too skillful Indians riding at their flanks. Shaggy humps plunge out of spirals of buff clay dust and disappear as curtains of dust rise and blot the whole thing from my sight.

The dust thins as the wild whirl slackens. I see numerous huge beasts lying over the prairie. After killing as many as they want, the men ride out, allowing the remaining herd to gallop on, followed by a high dust cloud. I watch the skinning and butchering. A thin wisp of blue smoke from a buffalo chip fire rises from where the draw forms. The squaws have put up camp. Moving to the end of the butte, I can see women putting up meat-drying frames of tepee-travois poles. Most of the women are working at butchering, cutting the skinned meat into red slabs. Others tend fires and children.

Bundled into the hide, the meat is lashed onto old pack animals and brought to the drying frames. There it is slashed into thin sheets and spread out to dry.

Bending their backs (there are no work tables), the Indians are working hard and fast. Everybody, down to the cradle-board babies, seems to be busy. Reminded of my own work, I back down and skedaddle, still unseen.

We are visited by a bunch of roistering young Pawnee warriors, curious about our dugout, discovered but minutes ago. Seeing our wolf pelts, they start to help themselves. I give them a few, but I bar them from taking the choice hides. Angered, some lunge and start grabbing. This is when I bring old Kentuck from behind my bunk. I tell them in plain Pawnee to drop the hides and *git.* I speak it well enough that their surprised ears stand out about a foot from their heads. They understand and shake a leg on out.

From their talk, I pick up that they think I'm alone. Mr. Glass happens to be out, maybe fishing at the creek. They talk of coming back to get the pelts.

Late in the afternoon we build up a good fire and bank it to last several hours to convince the Indians, if they do come back, that I am inside, and we set a pot of meat to simmer by the fire.

I hurry my evening circling, and we hide out in the brush. Before long, we see forms sneaking close. They come in on all fours, edging nearer and wearing wolf skins.

The bodies amble here and there like investigating wolves, but all the time all are sneaking closer to the dugout. They watch and wait, inching nearer and nearer. A couple of them go back and make a good imitation of a wolf howl.

These fellows aren't after a fight, coming like this. But if I come a-running out to blaze away at their *wolf,* I have no doubt they would try to overpower me, and take what they want from the dugout.

This is their kind of game, a contest—their cunning against me—a challenge, possibly dangerous enough to sharpen their wits and senses and, they hope, to grab something. They enjoy a joke, too, even if the joke is on themselves; and they'll chance it.

Now they slink in closer to the doorway—only a buffalo hide hung up there. It looks like they've decided to come in and try their luck. We let them get bunched and about ready to barge in, then we scatter some shots close to them. That straightens them up like jackknives. They suddenly think of a spot more to their liking; and all want to get there at once.

Next day, we are honored by a visit of a few Pawnee chieftains. "Old Pete," Peta La Shar, is happy to find me, and I to see him; and Chief Buffalo Bull, Spotted Horse, and two or three others. They are concerned with whether we might cause the buffalo herd to leave. I explain we are doing no shooting among the buffalo and only poison wolves that follow the herd, and that we are leaving soon.

I don't believe the chiefs knew of the young fellows' prank, and we don't tell them. Mr. Glass agrees to make them a present of some pelts. This pleases them and they ride away.

A day or so later the teamster comes. We load the pelts, take them to Dobeytown, and leave them until the fur company's agent arrives. Crossing the team on the still-frozen river, we go back to Columbus.

5

Jim married Nellie Arnold while I was away. Mother and the rest of the family will need another house. We cut logs and build a cabin on my pre-emption.

January 1859. The *Omaha Times* newspapers Jim had saved for me tell of the first gold brought in wild goose quills to Omaha from territory mines. With warming spring sun and green-up time, men around here make ready to light out for the gold fields.

Mother returns and Jim leaves, heading for the Cherry Creek diggings. Luther, only thirteen, substitutes on Jim's United States Mail contract, carrying mail to the new village of Monroe three times a week, twenty-four miles round trip.

The earthy odor of spring-mellowed fields starts me to plowing for a new crop. Gulls fly in to search for bugs and grubs turned up in the furrow. For a few days the gulls are lively field company, then they're suddenly gone. The field seems empty without them. We will not see another sign of them until we begin to stir the ground next spring.

Pawnees camp near our place on the river bank. After the day's work is done, Luther and I go to see if our friends are with them. We are pleased to find Ke-We Kan La Shar, Buffalo Bull Chief, his family and son, Aru-Saw La-Kit-Toy, and Cot-ta-ra-tet Goots. They tell us Peta La Shar and La-Roo Chucka La Shar, Sun Chief, are not with them.

We play the stick game of chance, *Stasa-wi-Kah-Tush,* with the Pawnee boys. Lute sometimes brings his pony for racing, which the Pawnees love. They bet pots of small value. We contest the boys in running and throwing, and manage to get our share of wins.

Unfriendly Indians, Sioux and some Cheyenne, lurk about our settlement. They work their *magic* of our belongings disappearing: a wash hung on a clothesline is taken; a cow, horses or pigs, chickens, and even a hunting dog go and leave no trace; a farm left unguarded is burned.

I sow early spring wheat, plant potatoes on Good Friday, then plow for corn planting. Luther drops seed corn on the days he is not on his mail run. We allow one kernel for the gopher, one for the cow, one for the bluejay, and two to grow for each hill.

The Pawnees had gone two days on their summer hunt when they looked back and saw the smoke of their two burning villages. Runners hustled back and found most of their old folk and young children murdered. The Pawnee blame the Sioux and Cheyenne.

This time the Sioux may be innocent. After looking into the matter, the Indian Supervisor from Bellevue, E. B. Branch,[1] tells me he is morally certain that white men squatting near, and being several notches less civilized than the Pawnee, had a hand in the bloody deed. Branch just could be right.

In Rickley's[2] General Merchandise store to talk with him about doing his freight hauling, I pick up the *Omaha Times*. I perch on a bale of blankets to read, but talk, low and guarded from the other side of the rafter-high stock of goods, pulls me from the newsprint.

"You reckon that damned Indian Superintendent's liable to find out anything?"

The voice is secretive, the question more than interests me.

"No-o, if you're sure the fire burned everything behind you? Nothing you used overlooked—forgotten—left around?"

That's Eb Toole's voice. He's been around a couple of months, looks like a riverboat gambler—fine broadcloth clothes and dress-up hat.

"Yeah, it all went up in smoke, it's ashes now, left nary a track nor trace about, only—"

I'm dead certain that's Zeke Shaw, a sort of besotted fellow, worked at Rickley's sawmill a little.

"Then just sit tight and keep your head closed. The only chance he has to get anything on anybody would be by your telling it. He'll have to lay it to the Sioux."

"I'll kill you, you Injun lover." I didn't see Zeke coming until he lunged at me like a rabid coyote.

I fling the paper into his face and dive from his mauling fists. He takes a kick at my groin. I get away from it, though hurt. He comes at me like a mad bear. I duck, then trade fists with him. He goes wild and I rush him—hammer his nose to juice. I note Eb eyeing Zeke's ruckus from behind the corner. Zeke plasters me and I hit him hard but take a blow to the pit of my stomach that doubles me. Zeke's fingers snatch at my throat —he'll kill me if he can. I twist away, wiser by the minute and learning caution. I have to dodge about until I can take a full breath again. Fighting hard, hitting hard, I hammer him back. My last blow misses as he sinks down, and I follow my fist, off balance.

Eb streaks in, his fist clutching a knife. He slams himself forward to

drive it into me. Off centered, I can only lunge aside, but I manage to trip
Eb. He tumbles onto Zeke, and falling, rips my arm and gashes his own
face.

John Rickley throws the door open—sizes things up—grits "Get out!
Go, Toole. Take that," touches Zeke's foot with his boot toe. The ruff of
white beard under his chin trembles with anger, "—and don't ever let me
catch you in my place again." He slams the door after them, kicks Zeke's
hat toward the woodbox, tramps around cooling his temper, and lets his
hauling to me.

*   *   *

Since crops are planted and garden is up, I put my big wagon in shape,
repair my harness, and drive to Omaha. Looking up Branch, I tell him
about Eb and Zeke. He says it won't get help for the Pawnee—without
witnesses nothing could be proved.

Buying a load of flour, bacon, beans, and some tools, I haul it home
and rest my teams. In a few days, with Al Arnold going along, we head
the outfit for Pikes Peak, following the military trail north of the river. At
Big Island[3] we see the settlement Germans are making.

Just east of Fort Kearny, we ford the Platte River to travel up the
Oregon Trail. Meadowlarks warble, "bright-happy-shining-sweet-day-in-
spring-time." When we veer nearer the river bank, cardinals' red feathers
flash high in willows and cottonwoods.

We come to the new Cottonwood Spring[4] trading post, started last year
by the Boyer Brothers, Ike E. and Nelson and his wife, with their uncle
Robideaux, a Frenchman. We camp near the spring. They are doing a
good business with Indians, trading goods for hides. A son named Felix[5]
was born to the Nelson Boyers here in December, last winter (1859).

A lot of people are going our way. The road is just many paralleling
grooves—ruts in the low places, cut by wagon wheels. We are better off
camping near others. Each wagon or family has its own cooking fire. After
supper, men repair harnesses, and grease the axles. Often a fiddle is tuned
up; there is singing, and usually someone lines out a hymn to wind up the
evening.

Many wagons come from the direction we are heading. They've been
out around the diggings and are going back east. We hear from them
about the lay of the country ahead, road and travel conditions and camp
places—meaning water, grass, and wood or buffalo chips. Most of these
east-bound people are going back broke and disappointed.

Passing Lodge Pole Creek Fork, we part with the Oregon Trail,
continuing to follow the river until it bends north where we take the
Cherry Creek cut-off southwest. In another day we begin to raise the
mountains—just a pearly seashell among pearlized clouds low on the

horizon rim. You would think them wisps of low cloud puffs. Every day they grow larger. But we aren't there yet. Distances fool us in this high, thin air. We skirt prairie dog towns, and hop cactus and rattlesnakes.

At Denver City I sell my load to a dealer. In a busy trade mart a strong, tall man wearing a big hat is the center of attention. I ask an old man with the group who the large-boned impressive man with the long beard is.

"Kit Carson," the man says.

"Yes, Dick?" the man in the big hat turns.

"Young feller here asked who you be."

"I'm Kit Carson," he comes toward me. "From down Taos[6] way, and this old mountain man you're talking to is Dick Wooten."

"Howdy, Howdy!" Both shake hands with me.

"H're you?" I manage, so excited I hardly remember my name. "I'm Frank North, out from east Nebraska Territory way. I heard of you when I was a little nib—never thought I'd get to shake hands with you."

We find Jim, after considerable inquiry, mining over in Leavenworth Gulch.

"A dollar's worth of gold is as much as I've been able to pick up in a day, not that much, most days," Jim says. "With grub at such a price here, I'm not gaining anything."

I can see Jim is discouraged. After a few days digging with him, I believe I'll do better to get back home, cultivate our corn, cut some prairie grass to put up hay.

I turn my back on the Rocky Mountains and head into the sunrise. If I learned anything around the mountains, it is that I like getting back on the plains. Here I can see all the way to the earth's curve—and that moves back to give me room with every step I take.

Summer, 1859. I freight from Omaha to Fort Kearny, ten days to two weeks for a round trip. By Independence Day our corn is knee-high. With two cultivations I lay it by, and start making hay. The cradle on my scythe lays the grass as it is cut into windrows to dry. Lute rakes the rows into haycocks that we haul to stack near the barn.

The Omaha Nebraskian, *August 1859.* The secretary of the Columbus Ferry Company at Loupe Fork informs the *Omaha Nebraskian:*

Emigration across the plains up to June 25 was: 807 wagons; 20 hand carts; 5,401 men; 424 women; 430 children; 1,619 horses; 406 mules; 6,010 oxen; 6,000 sheep crossed westward. No . . . Mormon emigration . . . accounted for.

The returning emigration crosses at Shinn's Ferry,[7] fifteen miles below confluence of the Loupe Fork with the Platte. Many . . . outward bound westward emigrants also crossed at this point. So, . . . probably not less than 4,000 wagons have passed over the Military road from this city since March.

6

Wasn't it a bossy-cow out west along the Oregon Trail about three years ago that, bored with the Mormons' long trek, wandered off from camp right into the Indians' stew pot, causing the Grattan massacre?

Now a settler here complains: Indians killed his cow. Though our responsible men lose no time in looking into it, others are quicker, forestalling telling the elected officials.

Coupling tales of the incident with rumors that Indians are doing bloody devilment, their stories are spread, embroidered to horrendous proportion. Mother tries to talk sense into the settlement women, but they're scared deaf.

Eb Toole with his silk hat and smooth-tongue orating of his ". . . grave concern for safety of settlers in the face of the Indian uprising—murderers, attacking with scalping knives . . . bloody, merciless killing of little children . . . at the very fringe of our fine community.

"Why, just any day—any hour, who knows whether tonight, or tomorrow he may fall victim to a savage's tommyhawk?

"Who knows when the red devils will fall upon us and scalp us all? I am frankly alarmed, ladies and gentlemen, in dread of certain death . . . or worse for poor defenseless women—yes, fates worse than death . . ."

Eb's game is as plain as the fancy scarlet scar across his face that his growing beard cannot hide. His object, of course, is to grab for profitable speculation the corn growing land, mostly river bottom, that the Pawnees still use. Now, I understand his secretive talk with Zeke Shaw.

Before the sham can be exposed, a rider is hustled off to officials in Omaha. "Our community is in dire danger . . . uprising Indians. We ask protection . . . immediate action . . . Territorial Militia, [Signed], The Honorable Ebenezer J. Toole, Esquire."

Territorial publications pounce on the report. In boldface type they cry: "Pawnee Indians Make War on White Settlers," and "Blood Lusting Vicious Rampaging Savages Are Out On A Hair Harvest, with Scalping Knives and Tomahawks."

Gen. John M. Thayer[1] brings the militia from Omaha and Florence, and is joined by a small detachment of dragoons from Fort Kearny. Also, forty-six men here form a company, elect officers, and join the General.

The Pawnee, knowing swarms of Sioux eager for Pawnee scalp-locks infest the buffalo hunting grounds along the Republican Valley, had sent a runner to arrange a hunting pact with the Omaha Nation, and went northeast to the Elkhorn River.

Upon realizing they are being chased, the red men and youths jerk off what little covering is worn in warm weather, as is the Pawnee way of preparing for battle; and take up stances to assure escape for the women and children.

Peta La Shar is the most astonishing figure ever seen on this prairie, when he carries an American flag, given him and treasured since the Table Creek treaty, about his naked dignity, alone, to confront the general.

I'm sure not a soul of the ragtag, bobtail militia realize how narrow is the ledge of life they walk this day.

Pawnee warriors are in an ugly mood; goaded by the burning of the villages, most of their lodges, robes, and stored foods; and mourning death of so many old folk and young children. Many warriors believe white men are responsible. It is touch-and-go whether the warriors will overrun Peta's determined keeping of the peace. Should the braves break down the Chief's restrictions and elect to fight the La chi Kuts (Long Knives or Americans), the foolish little army of about two hundred men under General Thayer most certainly will be wiped out by warriors that can shoot twenty killing arrows into a man while he reloads his mule loader.

Brother Jim is present, the fourth name from the end of the company list, James North, Company 5, Columbus Infantry. Jim says Lt. B. H. Robinson[2] of the dragoons, possibly excited by the chief's steady advance, fires at the chief, misses, hitting the horse instead.

Two hundred silent men "hold fire," watch, see the chief's firm hand guide his wounded pony. No Indian returns the lieutenant's shot.

"Loo-ah! Why does the White Father chase my people?"

General Thayer informs the Pawnee head chief that the tribe is accused of theft, destruction of property and livestock,[3] and of molesting and harming settlers.

Chief Peta La Shar convinces the General nothing is known among his people of such crimes, though he admits a boy once killed a pig belonging to some settler, and their ponies may have picked along the edges of growing crops. However, the chiefs agree to pay, the monies to be taken from their annuities.

Jim says, "We sure fixed those Indians. Two hundred of us brought back one boy!"

I know the Pawnee do some pilfering, and considerable begging of settlers and especially of immigrants along the trails—are nuisances sometimes. I, myself, had to deal with some of the mischievous young bucks and know that, just like young white fellows, they get out of hand. Still, the Pawnee Nation's record of thirty years dealing with us is peaceable.

Yet the Pawnee are accused in every press of the Territory. There is little mention of the really treacherous Sioux. Pawnees are unable to defend themselves before general opinion.[4]

Mid-October 1859. Sumac flames on hillsides. Heads of goldenrod, turned hoar-frost white, nod in fall-crisp sunshine. Woodpecker flickers and blue jays dispute with fat, hoarding squirrels. Corn is harvested and bound in shocks while from under their sere-leaved flounces peep ripe pumpkins and yellow-meated hubbard squash.

I must soon haul the fodder and bring the melons to store in the vegetable cave for winter use. Topping off my load with firewood logs, I hear a strange, chattering sound. I drive my load onto the clearing. Then I see what I've been hearing—Pawnees. Many of the young fellows know me, and I them. Greeting me with "poor minds" (low spirits), they do not stop to visit. Mounted soldiers herd the tribe along. The entire Pawnee Nation, with everything they still possess, is on the move. Under the Table Creek treaty, the government expected the Pawnees to move at once to the reservation. Action, under the excuse of last summer's "Pawnee War," is forcing the Pawnee to the Loup River Reservation.[5]

Peta La Shar rides over to me. He can speak some English, having grown up under the teaching of the missionaries, John Dunbar and Samuel Allis, who lived eleven years among them.

"*Loo-ah, Pi rau!*" he greets me. "*La Shar ta-ka tak-we la—*" His syllables spill out, "Hello, Son. Great White Father moves all Pawnee people upland to that which is bad, this day, today."

Understanding his concern only too well, I'm unable to meet his searching gaze, knowing of no shred of consoling I might offer him.

Long lines of Pawnee people pass, about thirty-five hundred. Once they were the mightiest tribe, most powerful in war, holding the entire central high plains against all enemy tribes.

Continual warfare with other tribes, plus scourges of smallpox and cholera, and other ills more deadly to Indians than to whites, shrank and weakened the tribe.

The Pawnee go along, heads bowed, eyes on the ground. The women wail a melancholy dirge, a shrill "*Ki de de de de . . .*"

In a few days, Jim and I ride to the reservation to see how it is with the Pawnee people. The government had bought and taken possession of most of the buildings put up about ten years ago by Mormons to form Genoa as a trail rest.

The first agent, Judge G. L. Gillis, lives in one house, and agency helpers in another. Orders to Mormons to vacate the village are still only half obeyed, there are no preparations for wintering the tribe nor any assistance for them.

They can scarcely, with their primitive tools, prepare the heavy timbers and dig the deep holes required to build earthen lodge. Nobody told them they couldn't do it and somehow they hack out and set timbers, join them with large framing logs overlaid by piles, brush, and twigs that hold thatching grass, then mound it over with earth.

Agent Gillis permits the Pawnee a brief buffalo hunt, vital to them after the poor summer hunt, and the fact that most of their corn and beans were stolen from their patches. They succeed in making a good surround, coming in with their ponies loaded with meats and hides.

My friend, Co-te-ra-tet Goots, tells me, "Lakota Sioux will be quick to find their Pawnee enemy, moved by the Great White Father. Where are the soldiers the Great White Father promised would defend Pawnee?"

Still self-reliant, in spite of treaties, the Pawnee fight off Sioux that approach the new village from behind near north bluffs.

7

October 28, 1859. Jim is taking a load of wheat we raised and flailed out, and some corn, to a grist mill[1] on the Missouri River, north of Florence. He can't get home in much less than two weeks, at the rate the oxen travel.

Grinding corn for meal would be handier the Indian's way, if we had a rock mortar hollowed out through generations of use, and a round pestle to fit. The kitchen coffee mill makes a poor substitute. By grinding corn through the mill several times, we get a scant bit of coarse meal.

November 28, 1859. Jim is home. So many were waiting their turn that he had to wait ten days. Winter storm caught him near the Elkhorn River. He stayed through the blizzard, at a settler's cabin, and gave flour and meal for the hay our oxen ate.

Freighting from Omaha to Columbus and the fort keeps Jim and me busy. The November blizzard is the only storm we've had.

April 4, 1860. Hauled a load of corn to Fort Kearny. While the soldiers scoop the load into the fort's grainery, I go to town to see the first Pony Express rider streak in. We hear his "Hi-o-o-o!" before he comes in sight. He hits the ground before his pony's last jump, and snatches off the mochila[2] as helpers remove the saddle and swing it over a fresh horse. In less than two minutes the rider is gone again.

April 25, 1860. Ice hasn't all gone out of the rivers. This is a cold, late spring but the sun is warming the ground. Today, I'll broadcast early grain into soil already tilled. I'm seeding a patch of oats and the spring rye for stock feed, and spring wheat for flour.[3]

May 2, 1860. Five wagons of immigrants are here ahead of green-up time this slow spring. There's nothing for their horses and mules to pick on but last year's dead, bleached-out grass. The wagons wait for the Loup ferry, not yet out of winter lay-by and repair.

This sunny morning Jim and I look across the stream and see men

hitching teams to wagons. The first team leads out to the river bank, as
we look on in amazement. What is the man thinking of? He surely won't
try to ford the river here. It's in flood stage. Always a treacherous ford,
the stream is swollen to eighteen or twenty rods across. A big river now,
running fast. The river doesn't divide exactly at the upper end of Buck
Island, which is three miles long. Two main channels course down either
side, passing the island's lower end a couple of miles above the Loup's
confluence with the marl and limestone roiled Platte River.[4]

We run down, wave and yell, "Go upriver to ford. Go upriver, we'll
show you where to cross. Don't try to ford here." If they hear, they pay no
heed. The foolish men drive to the bank, pick the likeliest place, drive
down into the stream, and head into the current. One team is swimming
—they're in deep water.

A second wagon pulls up to the river bank's edge. We still yell, trying
to warn him back. He comes down a steeper bank.

Men working in a sawmill yard hear us yelling and come to join us. A
third wagon goes down where the first came. This man's horses get excited
coming down. They start wild plunging in the water, soon collide with the
second wagon's teams in frightened struggle, the harnesses all in a snarl.

The animals hitched to the last wagon are out of control—are
floundering, completely unmanageable. A wagon capsizes! I see a woman
with a baby in her arms fall from the tumbling wagon.

Jerking off my coat, boots, and buckskins, I run to jump clear of the
bank into the river. I hit for center with all the speed I can muster. If the
woman is swept past the tangle of wagons and horses, I should catch her
about here, midway between the first wagon and the others. My eyes try
to penetrate the water, roiled by the struggling horses, but fail to find her.

Other men have come in and try to cut tugs loose to free frantic
animals. The team on the upset wagon and one horse of the other are
drowned.

The first wagon is unable to pull out of the current. His horses are
under water, barely keeping their noses above the surface. The man,
woman, and two children jump as the wagon settles. The family is swept
into the Platte where we reach and save them.

The wagons are pulled out by hitching multiple teams. As one of the
wagons is righted, we find the other woman's body. I don't think she had
ever loosened her hold on the baby. We lay them on the riverbank.

May 27, 1860. We finished planting corn today—too cold and dry to
sprout corn earlier. A newspaper reports: "The Republican Party's national
convention in Chicago nominated Abe Lincoln over Senator Seward, as
its candidate for the Presidency!"

A July paper reports that the Democrats are squabbling. It says: "The

Democratic Party divided when Southern Democrats bolted their party convention, and put forth Kentuckian John C. Breckenridge, now Vice President, and Oregon's Joseph Lane as his running mate. They adopted virtually the entire platform of Senator Jefferson Davis.

"Senator Stephen A. Douglas of Illinois was nominated by the regular Democratic session on a middle of the stream platform."

The newspaper says both representatives and senators have taken to wearing guns. Southern men challenge Northerners to duels. One Southern "gentleman" was flabbergasted when a challenged man selected Bowie knives as weapons.

A bill was passed to subsidize a telegraph line, to be built from the Missouri River to the Pacific coast. Hauling for construction is to start right away. However, President Buchanan put a crimp in Territorial settlement when he vetoed the homestead bill.

Every summer day, we see an endless string of wagons snaking along the trails. Sometimes travelers stay to turn back or settle here; a wagon breaks down, or one of their team dies. Too often there are drownings of animals, of people, or they are sick, discouraged, or just too tired to go on.

July 16, 1860. We read, "The Methodist Episcopal, North, General Conference resolves: 'Slavery is a great evil . . . selling or holding of human beings as chattels . . . inconsistent with Christianity.' "

NEBRASKA TERRITORY TIDINGS, *July 23, 1860*—We copy for our esteemed readers' contemplation, a widely requested article originating in the New Orleans journal: "Mobile Bay has received and sent to this city a shipment of fresh Negroes, contrabanded direct from Africa. They will be sold as usual at the Public Market Place on Monday of next week. These sound, young blacks will be very useful in the cotton picking season, when we never have enough negroes.

"In spite of ever stiffening penalties and hazards for apprehended traffickers, some audacious Captains dare to bring us valuable stock for our plantation needs and farming."

August 7, 1860. "President Buchanan reports to Congress that five hundred and sixty Negroes were found in holds of a captured slaver."

October 17, 1860. Lute rides with me to take a load of squash and potatoes to the fort. We go on over to Dobeytown and get there in time to watch the Pony Express come in. Lute is interested, as he carried mail to Monroe from the opening of that run until it closed last spring.

"Frank, I want to ride for the Pony Express. Don't you think we could get me a job?"

"You know Mother cried about you going on the Monroe run, after the horse fell with you and hurt your foot. You had to have help on and off your horse at both ends of your run. You might have frozen to death last winter if you had to get off your horse for any reason, with nobody within miles on the prairie to help you."

"Yes, I know. But I got the mail through, anyhow."

I'd like to ride the Pony Express, too, but I can't qualify. I am twenty-one years old and taller than six feet.

When we go to see the agent, he takes a look at Lute, who is only fifteen and stands hardly breast high to me.

"A man has to be twenty years old and hairy chested to hire on with the Pony Express, son," he explains.

"But Mister, I've already carried mail eighteen months," Lute declares, but he doesn't get things changed.

We watch workmen installing machinery in the fort's magnetic telegraph station awhile, then hitch up and drive toward home.

"How will the words come through that machine, Frank?" Lute asks.

"I can't rightly explain, Lute. How do you suppose Ed Creighton built that electric wire line from St. Joseph, on the Missouri River, to within forty miles from the fort in ten weeks? They say they'll be ready to telegraph the election returns to the fort. Pony Express will relay the message to Placerville, California."

Talk around the fort is that, if Lincoln is elected President, South Carolina and other slave states will secede from the Union.

8

November 25, 1860. Jim and I ride to the Genoa Pawnee reservation today. I hire on with the agent, Judge Gillis.[1] We move Mother, little sisters, and Lute to Florence for the winter, where there is a school.

The saw and grist mills are at the reservation, readied for use. I am to lead and teach the Pawnee men how to prepare wood and use the saw. We build a large grainery and bridge across Beaver Creek. Next we haul a load of saw wood. The Indians are good-natured about it all, nod their heads, approve everything we show them. When we get busy, we find they've been just as good-natured about fading away in the brush behind trees. I round them up and try it all over again. A few take hold of ax handles. After a few trial swings, they seem to find the handle of an ax too long and awkward to make a good tomahawk. However, others seem to think the crosscut saw could be fun, until I get a couple of warriors on the push-pull handles. The humor peters out with the first pull-push. They nod and jabber about my demonstrations with shovels and spades—these look like right handy tools for their squaws to use.

"You see, Judge," I explain, "work is beneath a male Indian. His job is to be a warrior, a protector, and a hunter. It is, and has always been, necessary to their way of life."

"Do you mean to tell me that they actually let their women do all the work?"

"No, they do work hard, actually. A self-respecting Pawnee continually practices his skills, sharpens his abilities, and toughens his endurance. Safety and welfare of family and tribe are his first and greatest duty. He is never relieved of that care until old age blinds or slows him.

"A Pawnee woman's work is hard. But her man's life is always at risk, so things balance. And, the Pawnees need all their fighting skill right now, with the Sioux lurking about."

37

"I see," Judge Gillis says, "however, these red men must learn to work."
For the eighth time this year, the Sioux raid the Pawnee reservation.
The Pawnee tell me that Cheyenne and Arapaho at times join in the
attacks. There is always killing, sometimes on both sides, and the Sioux
usually succeed in driving away some of the Pawnee ponies.

Early December, 1860. I'm sent with a party of Pawnee on their late fall
hunt to protect them from white men who might not know them from
wild Indians.

Again, Sioux raid the reservation. With the strong warriors out
hunting, the enemy do some damage.

The Pawnee tell me how the old judge led in the defense. His white
hair flying, waving his pistols, he ran yelling, "Kill them! Kill them!" He
and some of the Pawnee got mounted and managed to rout the Sioux.
The soldiers stationed on the reservation joined in the chase.

Since August, a few soldiers have billeted here under Capt. Alfred
Sully. He was off trying to interest the Sioux in smoking a peace pipe with
the Pawnee when the Sioux raiders came this time. Later, we learn that
Captain Sully was at Fort Kearny assuring the commanding officer that he
had made certain there would be no more attacks on the Pawnee
reservation, when a messenger arrived with news of the raid.

The steam sawmill is fired up and ready to operate. We pull up with a
load of logs. I unhook tugs and assign a couple of Pawnee to stable the
horses. Just then, the judge yanks down on the whistle.

It's the gosh-awfullest war-whoop ever heard on the Plains!

Indians dive for the bush. The team gets away in terror and rips for the
barn. There's not an Indian in sight, though the judge lets up on his
whistle.

After a few days the Indians begin to come around, cautious, but
curious about the monster that chomps wood and terrifyingly blows out
steam and smoke with sparks.

They still involuntarily jump when the whistle blows, then laugh in
wild glee at each other, or titter and giggle like schoolchildren.

By the time enough wood is gotten out to fire the engine, we come up
with logs to saw into boards, for building the reservation's schoolhouse.[2]

An errand runner from Fort Kearny says: "Free Soilers with their
Wyandotte Constitution forbidding slavery won out. President Buchanan
signed the bill making Kansas the thirty-fourth state."

January 12, 1861. "Secretary of War, John B. Floyd, is threatened with
indictment on a million dollar theft, as is W. H. Russell, a partner of the
freighting company of Majors, Russell and Waddell of Nebraska Territory.
It is charged that Floyd endorsed nearly a million dollars of notes bearing
Russell's signature without security, and that Russell managed to trade

these off for government bonds."

Will the Pawnee be paid their annuity this spring? Is it the Indians' money in the Department of the Interior that is stolen?

Believing the earliest spring thunder means their gods are back from far wandering, the Pawnee hold a thunder rite[3] at beginning of the growing season. It is hoped to please the gods, to assure they will grant abundance of grass, corn, and buffalo, health, tribal welfare and lucky warfare.

It was in this rite the Skidi (Skeedee) Pawnee sacrificed annually a virgin captive. That ended when the first Peta La Shar, eighteen, snatched up the girl and squired her home.[4]

I'm invited to see the thunder ceremony to "Paruxti," an earth god— the first of many rites during the three warm seasons. The priest takes from the sacred bundles dried heads of hawks and eagles and rattlesnake rattles, placing these reverently. He then brings out small animal skulls containing little stones that rattle, and gives one to each of the four direction priests who sit in tradition-assigned places in the four quarters, northeast, southeast, southwest, and northwest.

Singing a long chant, they change one word in each repetition, and the whole story is finally changed. Priests and laymen go out of the medicine lodge to the east side where a hillock is scraped up and a small fire laid ready for a spark. A live coal is brought from the lodge firehole in a handful of earth and the earliest green blades of grass. On this fire are placed offerings from the sacred bundle: dried bird hides, toad skins, and a dried scalp. This the priest cuts into bits for his offerings.

The Pawnees' sacred bundles have two ears of "Mother Corn," the seed corn to be shelled and parceled out for planting.

Each of the direction priests takes a strong draw on the big ceremonial pipe, and blows smoke to his direction. Offering of a dried tongue and heart of a buffalo is made to the highest God, Tirawa. All is done with rigid exactness, in intense solemnity. Speaking and chanting, the priests go into the lodge.

After the meeting, the Pawnees set to work preparing ground along the river and creek for their planting.

March 10, 1861. Lincoln is inaugurated president. A detachment of horse soldiers stopping at the agency tells us that news came over the electric telegraph at the fort, and the Pony Boys raced west with it.

April 2, 1861. The newspapers report, "Fort Sumter falls! After being under siege nearly two weeks by seceded South Carolina's militia, the fort capitulated."

April 5, 1861. Wild geese are flying north, their far-up calls quaver back with a spring equinox message of natural laws and flyways.

Mid-May 1861. President Lincoln is vacating many Indian Agency offices to put in Republicans. The old judge goes. The Pawnee respect and like him. It's too bad, just when he is making good headway. He is replaced by a Mr. DuPuy. Appointment of trader for the Indians goes to a Mr. Rood, related to the Commissioner of Indian Affairs. He is hiring me as Pawnee interpreter.

We hear from horse soldiers that the Butterfield Overland stage owner, Ben Holiday, stopped all his coaches running on the southwest road after Texas seceded.

9

June 1, 1861. The new trader, deciding there is no suitable place for his family, hires me to take entire charge of his business. He is going back to the states on the next stage, intending to return in spring and fall when the annuities are paid the Indians.

Jim brought Mother and the family home, and Luther is planting the fields on my place, with Jim near to lend him a hand. Finishing the planting, Lute comes to work on the reservation as a haying crew teamster, later to haul logs.

I'm convinced our new Indian agent is a politician of the worst kind. The Pawnees mistrust him, too. He is jockeying around to hire only people he can depend on to wink at his peculiar ways with business.

Still, it looks to me like he has already hung himself. He induced quite a number of people to leave their eastern homes, and come here under his promise of employment. He keeps them cooling their heels, unemployed. Advantageous bargains are easier made with more or less desperate people. I'm glad my employment doesn't depend on him.

The Pawnees prepared their ground and finished planting, under daily attack by Sioux, even by Cheyenne, and some Arapaho Indians. The Sioux will take no wealth from the Pawnee. Yet they raid, because any Indian who can count coup on his enemy and take scalps, even of women and children, wins tribal esteem.

As I open the trading post, the early summer morning erupts with yelling. Glancing out the window, I see warriors stripping as they run for their ponies—a sure sign enemy Indians are raiding the reservation again.

Grabbing Kentuck, I lock the door and run for my horse. Where is Luther? Throwing a hackamore and saddle on my horse, I jerk up the cinches and ride out.

To my right, women on their way to work in the cornfields, seeing the enemy, turn back, running for their village. Ponies of the Sioux fast overtake them. One after another the warriors swing their tomahawks.

41

A woman, heavy with child and slower, turns back to hide in the corn field when a warrior overtakes her, grabs her by her hair. With a knife in the other hand, he makes a single slash. The woman drops alive and unhurt except for the wound. Not as large as the inside of your palm.

Lute rides up on a little mouse-colored mule, with a reservation neighbor, Mr. Hudson. With the Pawnee warriors, we take out after the Sioux in a running battle, and try to even the score, but can't count coup on as many as the nine women they killed.

Lute tells me the tardy warrior who scalped the woman had chased him a long way. The Indian turned back toward the rest of his band after his horse tripped in a hole and dumped him.

"Ki de de de de . . ." The Pawnee's shrill chant mourns their dead.

After the spilled blood and split heads of yesterday's raid, this morning's peace is ruptured by shrill shrieks.

I run out. On the footpath at the near end of the cemetery used by one Pawnee band, I see Mrs. Elmira Platt, teacher of the Indian school, screaming. She sounds like Judge Gillis's stuck saw-mill whistle. You can hear her beller for a prairie mile!

I see nothing the matter with the woman, but she goes on screeching. She babbles, ". . . its head is out—head out of grave—"

Looking about, I finally see what set Elmira off! It's the Pawnee woman —the scalped one, buried to her chin!

The Pawnee put away their dead, enclosed by a blanket, or, in a fresh hide, smoke saturated. Until reservation life, Pawnee didn't always bury, but often carried the corpse to a lofty place where it returns to the elements.

The whole Pawnee tribe comes up to learn what disturbs their dead.

But who can figure the Pawnee's mind? If they must put away the woman, doesn't it seem reasonable that they would have buried the wounded end of her, too? Lucky for her, they didn't. She still lives!

We ignore black scowls and protests of fear of offended gods. Brushing aside trinkets and food offerings left near to sustain a spirit on its long journey, we dig the earth away and lift her up. Mrs. Platt, quiet now, but still pale, is given charge of the Pawnee woman.

Again, the woman disappears, and we do not find her this time. I corner braves I've known and ask what is going on.

"Enemy count coup on Pawnee; Pawnee die. The scalped woman is becoming a spirit. She is going on a far journey. Our people must help her. The gods might be angry with us if we do not help."

I guess dropping her in the mill pond, weighted with rocks, "helped" her spirit on its journey.

Work has come to a standstill on the agency farm, and the teams stand in the bars. Hired white men, fearful for their lives, no longer will work away from the shelter of buildings. Agent DuPuy stays in Genoa Village in the agency house, and has scarcely seen the reservation.

With start of the rebellion in the South, soldiers stationed here and most of those at Fort Kearny are pulled away. The Pawnee must defend themselves against marauding Indians. We are all under siege, pinned down by the threat of attack. Mr. DuPuy is pleading that soldiers be sent to guard the agency. Lute rides with the message. A few soldiers hustle over from Fort Kearny.

August 1, 1861. After two days, the soldiers are recalled.

These eastern people, after waiting two months for employment by DuPuy, reach the end of their patience. Electing a spokesman, they subscribe the cost of a fare and send him off to the Bureau of Indian Affairs at Washington City. A few days later, DuPuy gets wind of what is going on. He, too, hustles off on the stage. The upshot of the rush to Washington is that DuPuy put his head in his own noose. The Indian Bureau has closed the gate on him and every man on both sides, barring all from further employment or presence on the reservation.

Little hoeing or tending of corn and vegetables is being done. The women no longer dare go into their fields. Drought and grasshoppers finish off the poor growth.

August 10, 1861. We received muskets and ammunition for the Pawnee's defense. Today the Sioux found a different welcome. Seeing every Pawnee warrior armed with a gun, the Sioux pull up short—switch directions, and scoot for the hills.

When we can catch the Sioux within shooting range, Pawnee had better rely on their bows and arrows. These muskets are unreliable and not very effective.

Crops around Columbus are fair to poor this dry, hot summer. The Pawnee have raised little. Most of that little was stolen by Sioux and some white men.

January 5, 1862. All fall the Pawnee had only scant food; so little was raised. They couldn't get more than two months' supply of meat on their fall hunt. Their old enemy pounced on them near the buffalo grounds— kept after them, getting a few of their horses every day, killing some of the hunters, until they must leave the hunt and come home.

The government's fall provision for Pawnees, allotted semiannually, was not more than a third of the usual, and not half enough. The annuity payment was omitted.

Dogs, usually plentiful, have almost disappeared. Of course, puppy (dog) stew, or any other four-legged animal is welcome in pots that are empty. The Sioux have succeeded in stealing nearly all the horses.

I send a runner, Black Eagle, to the supervising Indian agent at

Bellevue, telling him how things are with the Indians—that they have no
food, are suffering and not far from starving.

The agent's reply seems lame; that he will do the best he can for the
Pawnee. I'm guessing he may be without any funds.

The Indians are cutting their robes into strips for their cook pots! The
children's suffering is terrible. With little flesh on their bodies, eyes
shrunken, hands scrawny as claws, they are pathetic.

The oldest of Pawnee old folk now *ha Kah Ka loos* (close their mouths),
the Pawnee way in time of severe famine, a self-imposed sparing of scant
food to assure tribal survival, that the young may live. The old Indian
wraps himself in a robe to "turn away," to sit in an out of the way place,
alone, withdrawn to a near coma. He wills himself to quit the plains that
fail to nourish him. Willing it, death comes amazingly soon.

January 7, 1862. A desperate band of hunters is going up the Loup,
hoping to find elk in the timber. I tried to persuade them to come with
me to my farm at Columbus, each to bring back a small poke of corn.
Even ten kernels to each, a day, might eke the tribe through.

The Indians refuse, saying their head Medicine Man, Lark Ta-hure
Sharu, tells them only red meat will stop starvation. My guess is, he
doesn't like corn.

Priests and medicine men are doing their best to soothe Atius Tirawa,
and all gods, hoping for success for the hunters.

"Medicine is good." Word comes from the ritual, and the men, about a
hundred, start at daybreak.

February 2, 1862. Ground-hog day in Ohio. It's blizzard day here,
twenty-five below zero, and the air is full of fine, hard-driven snow,
heaped into drifts up to twenty feet deep.

None of the Pawnee hunters are back and no message from them.

February 15, 1862. Pawnee people are starving to death. How many
have already died?

March 10, 1862. Winter has broken. The country is a loblolly from
melting snow. Waterfowl go over. Flocks of them settle on melting ponds
and streams and the Indians' arrows will take them, so the Pawnee can
eat.

Not one of the hunters that left in January has returned, nor have we
had a sign from them! Their "good" medicine must have gone bad.

The Sioux sometimes kidnap Pawnees and other Indians and carry them
into Canada to trade off as slaves. Considering weather conditions, it isn't
reasonable to suppose Sioux would bother to take prisoners, but would
have killed them and left them to the wolves.

Some trace should have been found by the search group, sent up the

Loup last week by the Bellevue Indian supervising agent, but they found nothing.

One of the investigators suggested the men left the reservation to stay out. If he knows anything about Pawnee, he would know better. Survival of the tribe is their most sacred responsibility. They wouldn't fail their people.

Pawnees mystically account for the entire thing by saying, "God's magic is in many places, hunters go to Happy Hunting Ground."[1]

10

Three months' newspapers come in a bunch. We'll catch up with the latest on the rebellion!

February 27, 1862. Brig. Gen. U.S. Grant and twenty thousand volunteers capture Forts Henry and Donelson, taking nearly as many prisoners as the victorious command numbered. President Lincoln commissions Grant as Major-General of volunteers.

President Lincoln signed the income tax bill into law, with maximum set at ten percent—calculated to bring in about seven million dollars to finance the war.

A bill outlawing polygamy was also signed into law by President Lincoln. Since by law, Pawnee are not people, I guess that bill won't affect them, though a good time-tested way of life for them is the household of two—sometimes more—women.

A man marries and lives with his wife's people. If there are younger sisters, he marries them, as they get old enough. He must take responsibility for the family. Rugged labor is shared by the women, usually closely related. Their children are better off being double mothered, and it makes a more contented life for the females. Too, the tribe could not increase above losses in warfare if a man didn't raise families by more than one woman, their children usually being few.

Spring 1862. Emerging from a winter of famine, the Indians bury their dead and prepare for a surround. Priests and medicine men fast about sixty hours—not a great change from their winter fare, and offer sacrifices and sincere prayer.

It is as if I had come into a Quaker meeting when I first go into the big medicine lodge. Heads are bowed. Everyone stands silent. A low voiced, indistinct prayer begins, to the Supreme God, the Pawnee's Atius Tirawa. They say He is a spirit, that He lives in the far heavens, and all people are His children.

Priests and medicine men stand near ten or twelve buffalo skulls placed in a quarter circle on the ground. Each holds a sacred tool of the hunt: bows, quivers of arrows, even the colorful signal poles used for silent giving of orders when surrounding buffalo.

I am moved, seeing these respected oldsters humbly acknowledging Atius Tirawa, and imploring his favor toward them, with intense fervency. Though the day carries raw, spring chill, sweat glistens on the beseechers' foreheads, and stress of deep sincerity shakes their gaunt bodies.

"Atius we-tus tai-we . . ." ("Father, you are the ruler"), they say. They place the sacred objects on the earth floor of the lodge, then raise their hands and eyes toward heaven at the finish of their prayers. It is a benediction that I share.

This time, needing their strength for the hunt, the Indians skip the Buffalo Dance that usually follows the religious rite, except that a few dancers, painted and awesomely impressive, wearing the big buffalo's horned heads and robes, come and make certain gestures, I suppose as apologies to their lesser gods, then leave.

Jim and Al Arnold stay on the reservation while I go with the hunters.

The stodgiest Pawnee, once again out on the open grassland, is a new creature. His shoulders square up, he lifts his head, his eyes sharpen. He comes alive.

The Indians are afoot. The few ladder-sided horses are led. They have picked up a little strength, but will not be used to make a surround. Pawnee legends tell of hunting buffalo afoot, before they had horses. They'll have to do it that way, this time. The ponies can pack the meat in, I hope.

It's mid-afternoon when our scouts come back. They've located buffalo. We are led into a valley where they had dropped two animals, so we feast. Tomorrow we'll be too busy for eating.

The Indians skin and butcher the animals, opening the belly to the liver which they slash into chunks and eat warm. Everyone dips knife or fingers into the bile, when the duct is opened, to taste a few drops. They break the bag of waters about the unborn calf, to lick the fluid from their fingers, not wasting any.

My stomach churns violently, followed by their laughter. Though used to seeing Indians relishing parts little used in our own civilization, I am still squeamish.

Soon there is hump and ribs roasting over a fire. The Indians are in high spirits, with meat before them. We hurry the feasting to get out of this valley before dark. Spreading apart, we go in various ways to a second rise, east and south, where we can better prevent Sioux surprises.

Coming from the northwest, I figure the Sioux would be too intent on the buffalo to come further. That might mean a fight tomorrow, but no surprise tonight.

Morning breaks with heavy hoarfrost wooling the prairie. A gentle west breeze comes up with the sun. That is "good medicine" as we are downwind of the herd, and will not have to get around them.

Starting early, we may catch part of the herd still bedded down. The scouts are sent ahead to spot them and to scan for enemy. We follow about a mile behind.

A pattern perfected through ages and generations exacts absolute holding to their customs on a buffalo hunt. It is one of the few times, with this tribe, when great policing power is held by a few highly honored men of sound judgment. These mature hunters plot the surround and signal their orders. They have full authority, may punish, will kill if necessary to prevent a man's error or disobedience from stampeding the herd and possibly robbing the tribe of food. Though they have such power, I have only heard of such extreme action taken once, and that a long time ago.

Lacking the winter-lost hunters, boys younger than would ordinarily be used have to help. They carry bows that seem large. I wonder if their thin, young arms are strong enough to draw those big bows to an arrow's head, to send it into vitals of a tough-hided buffalo.

Steeped in tradition, ways, and manners of the *Ti-ra-hah* (buffalo surround) since cradle-board days, they get final instructions to strictly obey signaled orders. This day they make a long step toward earning their manhood and warrior rights. If they are unfortunate, or if they muff their chance, they could be hurt or killed, or, worse, to their way of thinking, could bring disgrace upon themselves.

No man may glorify himself by running out on a fast horse to kill the first or finest, possibly starting the animals to running so that many would get no chance of bringing down any meat. Every man extends himself to do his best, not alone for his own family, but to provide for all.

A scout signals "buffalo," and by signs directs our approach to take advantage of depressions, ravines, and folds or gullies for concealment. We come up as close as we can, not to chance disturbing the herd, which might stampede.

Now the Indians strip. Color bearers take over, sending all not having horses to creeping low, on all fours, to get near enough for bow shots before the herd is alarmed. We mounted hunters swing forward, wide of the herd. Our marshals coordinate all action.

The signal is flashed from the poles to turn toward the herd for a rush altogether with all the speed the horses are capable of. Our ponies being weak, we dare not chance getting in front of a forward stampede of the buffalo that seldom turn from a straight line when running. We try to hold and confuse the herd leaders, to give the unmounted a few extra minutes to kill buffalo.

The colors are struck! Every man is on his own. All shoot as fast as arrows can be fitted to bows. Most of the Indians jump from their spent horses, letting them escape from the fringe of the herd. I think it best not to risk using my pistols, because of the Sioux.

Time stands still, while crystal light of early forenoon etches the swift drawn bows, flying arrows, bronze-skin bodies in fluid motion. Here and there a great animal crumples to the ground, as the herd takes alarm. Heaving, rolling, the mass begins to untangle. Hundreds of buffalo thunder away, tails up and making time!

In a few minutes, the Indians dropped all the meat the ponies can possibly pack back to the reservation.

I wish the butchering job could go as fast. With lookouts posted against a Sioux surprise, everybody sets to work. We are in luck with still freezing nights and may be able to cache any meat the ponies can't carry.

11

June, 1862. We have a new Pawnee agent, Benjamin Lushbaugh. *"Chara ra-wata!"* Enemies are coming again! It's an eye-opener for the agent and a blood-spilling fight for the Pawnee.

June 25, 1862. The Columbus to Genoa mail carrier tells me President Lincoln's homestead act is drawing homesteaders. Now, the country will settle in a hurry.

July 10, 1862. President Lincoln signed the railroad bill, which means the government will subsidize building the Union Pacific Railroad west from Omaha. Central Pacific will build east from San Francisco, the roads to join somewhere north of Salt Lake before 1872.

I am relieved that Mother, Phonsie, and Lizzie are living here at the agency. Mother is employed as housekeeper for Mrs. Platt's Indian school. Lute was often away from home, working or freighting, and Jim, land agent and surveyor, moved into Columbus.

August 10, 1862. The supervisor of Indian agencies, Mr. Branch, of Bellevue, stops here between stages. He says, "We have caught white traders swindling Indians of their annuities—allowing cheat claims, adding ciphers and defrauding in a dozen different ways. By the time the remainder of the annuity was credited to the Indians, they got less than a third of the payment."

August 30, 1862. "Fort Ridgley, in western Minnesota is besieged by Sioux tribes. Interpreter-scout Antoine Frenier got away from the fort after dark, bringing word of the attack. Hundreds of women and children are reported killed or taken prisoners in scattered settlements. New Ulm has been destroyed.

"Ex-governor Henry Hastings Sibley, with a force of volunteers, is marching toward the fort. Gov. Alexander Ramsey called the state legislature into special session, and also wired Washington for military assistance."[1]

September 30, 1862. The newspapers tell that near Woodlake, Minnesota, a force under Brigadier General Sibley routed the warring Sioux, inflicting heavy losses, taking many hundred of prisoners. The Indians under Chiefs Little Crow and Red Middle Voice wiped out many small communities, and at least five hundred settlers have been killed. Maj. Gen. John Pope has taken over management of offensive.

THE OMAHA TIMES, *September 30, 1862.* "Volunteers for the Second Nebraska Volunteers Regiment are urged to enlist. Many Santee Sioux left their reservation on the Minnesota River and come across the Missouri River . . . believed to be bringing their warfare into the Territory of Dakota."

Autumn of '62. Lute and other young fellows are on their way to Omaha to enlist and muster into the second Nebraska Cavalry.

The Indians, captured in Minnesota in September, were tried by a military court. Each prisoner, of the three hundred and six, had five minutes of hearing before being sentenced to death.

President Lincoln will examine the evidence and has ordered stays of executions of the Indian prisoners.

November 20, 1862. Lute came back, and brought half of the second Volunteer Regiment with him, to be stationed on this reservation.

December 22, 1862. President Lincoln found evidence against thirty-nine of the defendants conclusive as to guilt. He authorized their execution. The others will be sentenced to terms of imprisonment or confinements on their reservations.

March, 1862. While on a hunt in the Republican Valley, the Pawnee fought Sioux and escaped southward, after heavy loss to the Pawnee.

Finding no buffalo, they turned back. Some of the warriors went to settlers along the Solomon River, and forced or frightened them to give them food.

From this, they went to stealing horses, and butchered a cow or two. A company of cavalry from Fort Riley or Leavenworth caught up with the Pawnee, but made no attack.

The Indians came on home, and no one asked any questions. We have no word of any Pawnee misbehavior. Some of the boys I have known several years tell the story when I am the only white man with them.

"If the *La-chi-kuts* (Big Knives, cavalry) came to fight, the Pawnee were too handicapped to hinder, and had no intention of resisting. Then why did they run? Were the brave soldiers afraid?"

This could be only a good story, perhaps may become a legend. But I fear the Pawnee may catch the echo of it to their sorrow, before long.

Mr. Lushbaugh's report on "Progress of the Pawnee" went in, all custard and cream. His clerk, Charley Small, says he wrote a flowery to-do about his farm, a hundred-acre patch to teach the Indians how farming should be done. It was plowed and planted, after a fashion. Indian boys of Mrs. Elmira Platt's reservation school are assigned to weed and tend these acres. Being male Indians, they won't do field work unless forced to do it. Mrs. Platt has already cut off all the Indian boys' scalp locks, and as there is no greater punishment to their mind, her forcing power is no longer feared.

There was a cost and claims report of ten thousand dollars a year to "help the Indians in their farming." Part of this was supposed to be for seven hundred acres plowed for the Indians by the agent's supervisors and help.

The agent reports the Pawnee have fourteen hundred acres planted to corn, beans, and other crops. Will the Indian Bureau think the women clawed up the other seven hundred acres with their bone hoes?

In spite of the Sioux, the Indians' crops, about three hundred and fifty acres in small patches, are thriving.

June 22, 1863. Out of the north hills sweep the Sioux, right through the Pawnee villages, cutting a bloody swath as they go. A small detachment of regular soldiers are here, but seem to be rooted at sight of war-club carrying scalpers. Before I can get to my horse, the wild fellows turn into the hills. We chase, but can't catch them.

Mr. Lushbaugh is very agitated. "Dreadful murderers—I didn't contract to fight redskins." He is terribly afraid of them. All the agency white laborers left us right after the raid.

If nothing else grows here, the tribe's cemeteries do; one for each band. A lot of Indians are planted there, mostly with split skulls and arrow punctures.

Unknown to Mr. Lushbaugh, the Indians' pony herd has made unnatural increase. Young warriors can be most skillful at stealing into Sioux camps and getting away with horses.

I guess the agent hasn't wondered about the Indians' considerable horse trading to immigrants and settlers. Often the Sioux filch the horses back and take them north. The Pawnees go and steal them to barter off again. The Sioux have fairly good guns and ammunition, while the Pawnee rely on their bows and arrows, having few guns.

Mr. Lushbaugh is talking about another glorious, hair-brained idea. He proposes to engineer peace between the Pawnee and their enemies. Everybody in this country knows there can't be such a thing as a peace agreement made, much less kept, between tribes that have always fought. He sells the idea to Branch, the territorial Indian superintendent at Bellevue, and Branch convinces the Indian commissioner in Washington.

June 28, 1863. Today, grasshoppers sat down on the Pawnees' patches of growing stuff, and tonight nothing is left standing but ribbons of the coarsest leaf-spines, and stocks. They didn't bother the agency fields much. Nothing had survived the complete neglect of those fields.

Early Fall, 1863. The Indians say Little Thunder and his Brules are the ones that hit the reservation this time. The new Cavalry captain on a fast horse leads the chase. He finds himself among Indians, and discovers they're not Pawnees! He whips around, heads back in a running fight that we come up and into. He got an arrow in his shoulder. A soldier was killed and several Pawnee women and children and two of our warriors.

October, 1863. Since the Pawnee will harvest nothing for winter, they are laying plans to induce the Great and lesser gods to favor them with "Good Medicine" for the fall hunt. Medicine men[2] and priests are outdoing themselves with their *ti-war-uks-ti* and sleight of hand.

After the religious rites, the burnt offerings and prayers, the three-day buffalo dance starts in relays while the tribe's feasting goes on, though I don't know what the main dish of their feast could be unless it is the roots[3] they dig along the Loup, and fish, prairie chicken, and waterfowl.

This affair is all a desperate effort to gain favor and assistance for the coming surround; worshipping and also trying to please both the Supreme *Ti-ra-wah* (God) and all the smaller ones.

12

It's the last month of 1863. Mrs. Elmira Platt is leaving the reservation school, but the Indian children cry no tears.

December 15, 1863. Lute, mustered out of the Second Nebraska Regiment, is moving mother and our sisters back to the farm with him. I intend to be with them at home for Christmas.

February 3, 1864. Agent Lushbaugh hires an odd male person as teacher to replace Mrs. Platt.

One family, back from the winter hunt, takes their son from the school. The teacher, Maxfield, demands that the Indian office rule that an Indian schoolchild belongs to the government until he is grown; that parents shall have no claim nor control of him. Like Elmira, this one also demands a high board schoolyard fence.

Agent Lushbaugh hits on the notion of having Indians he judges of least faulty character to act as reservation police. This would hardly be tolerated were they not clothed as splendiferous as Solomon.

I can't see that it prevents increase of the horse herd; though raiding Sioux, confronted by our "police" in such fine regalia and plainly awed by this show of power, backed off and hit for the hills without collecting either scalp or pony.

Late February 1864. Something's wrong at the school. Measles and diphtheria! Children are dying. Dying in the villages, too.

The Pawnee mourning chant goes on and on in unceasing single-note monotony. There's nothing stoic about Pawnee parents losing a child.

May, 1864. A hot, dry spring! The Pawnee plant their corn and squash patches as usual, and as usual the reservation farm superintendent gives them no help. Meanwhile, agent Lushbaugh is in Washington City, trying to fund his Sioux-Pawnee Peace Council.

In Columbus on business, I found people all excited—"The Yankton Sioux left their reservation! They're coming south and west to attack Fort

Kearny! Two or three thousand of them—they'll massacre everybody—"

A whole community panicked at a far-fetched rumor! It turns out, in replying to Fort Kearny's inquiry, the Yankton agency can strictly account for their Indians, and it's all quiet.

In one week, we count two hundred and forty-six prairie schooners, a family to each wagon, fording the Loup and rolling on west. Over on the old freighter trail, many times as many people travel from river port towns toward Fort Kearny to join the Big Trace, the Oregon-California Trail.

June, 1864. We are having drouth. Hot winds out of the south curl the buffalo grass to the ground, blast the Pawnees' crops before grasshoppers swarm in to finish off the remains.

A small detachment of soldiers go to guard the hunting Pawnee against numerous enemies in the Republican Valley. If our Indians fail to get meat, they'll starve.

Early August, 1864. Indians raid along the Big Trace! Stagecoaches reverse direction, to head hurriedly east, packed with women and children of settlers, terrorized both by fact and rumor of rampaging Indians. Freighting trains and immigrants halt. Clank of chain, crack of blacksnake-mule and bull whips, and all wagon sounds die away along the Big Trace. Small devil-winds, borne of drouth, whirl along abandoned ruts of the trail and pick up the dust, ground to powder by many thousands of westward hurrying feet that passed here, safely enough, through more than three decades.

Two hundred miles south, Smoky Hill River road is still, as is the freighters' road following the Arkansas River.

News of further attacks trickle in. Shadows of a developing pattern suggest that the widespread strikes are too near the same times to be happenstance.

Many bands of warriors struck first on the Colorado plains, along the South Platte Trail. Sweeping east, they killed and burned at every stage station, road ranch, and settlement.

East of Fort Kearny, the Indians go along the Big and Little Blue Rivers and carry off women and children.

Are all these Indians, called from various tribes by runners bearing war-pipes, persuaded to throw in together for an all-out strike? Whether they succeeded in banding together, theirs is a common cause. Certain, far-sighted chiefs know of, and are clever enough to use, the struggles of our Civil War to their advantage.

August 7, 1864. Soldiers rush from Fort Kearny, west to Plum Creek, where a freighting mule train was attacked and destroyed early this morning. Twelve men were killed, a woman and child and the mules taken, the wagons burned.

Soldiers, though ordered here and called there, are too few to prevent assaults.

13

Far horizons of the high plains shimmer in August heat with mirages of woods and lakes, settlements and towns never yet seen. Cicadas and grasshoppers zing among drouth-stunted sunflowers lining the footpath to the trading post porch.

Brass-throated bugle notes salute the detachment of soldiers stationed on the reservation.

Maj. Gen. Samuel B. Curtis, of the Department of Kansas, including Nebraska Territory, comes riding in. The captain greets the general and escorts him to the trading post. Here they find the Pawnee agent talking with me on the porch.

General Curtis says, "As you doubtless are well aware, hostile Indians— South Cheyenne and South Arapahoe, Kiowa, Siouan bands of Brule and Ogalalla and possibly others—are making war; attacking mail stages, travelers, commerce and settlers.

"Stage routes are paralyzed, stations burned or destroyed—ranch hands murdered and the stock stolen by the Indians that struck on August the seventh, beginning up on the Colorado plains.

"The Indians sacked Julesburg, and hit hard all down the line. The Martin homestead was attacked and two sons shot—pinned together by one arrow. Every man of a wagon train was killed, and many settlers on the Big and Little Blue carried away.

"I aim to reopen these plains roads. I must make them safe through the entire hostile Indian country. I need every available horse soldier including the garrison of this post."

"But General, surely you wouldn't take our last soldier—wouldn't leave us without defense?"

"Yes, yes." The general mops his brow. Florid and fussy, he is about five inches below my six-two. Once red, his hair is graying to a dusty rust color. His fifty-seven years sit hard upon him, not at all eased by his late, tough campaign in the South.

"Sparing soldiers from our defense is unthinkable while those untamed tribes are so vicious," Mr. Lushbaugh says.

"I plan an expedition from Fort Kearny to take the hostiles by surprise," says the general. "By maneuvering along their north-south trail, I shall reduce them to a less dangerous state. This uprising should subside with my campaign through their buffalo lands."

"I must remind you, General, that horse soldiers commonly fail to find and intercept marauding Indians. Time after time, the soldiers have proven woefully ineffective." The agent is a persistent gadfly to the general.

I offer a notion that has brewed in my head since I first saw this trouble coming on.

"Well, General, the way to catch the Sioux is with Pawnee Indians," I blurt.

The general bores into me with more than a hint of irony. "Perhaps you are able to tell the army how it is to use Pawnee braves?"

"Well, the Sioux doesn't live that can hide from a Pawnee tracker. Sioux and Pawnee have warred on each other since before their oldest legends. There aren't better horsemen, and there are no braver braves. Here, we fight prairie fire with fire. It takes an Indian to catch an Indian."

"Very interesting! Just why am I to believe your Pawnee warriors wouldn't lift their officers' scalps, or join forces with the enemy?"

"Their dealings with white men have been friendly for forty years or more. I'm sure they would be eager to help the army against their old-time enemy for a chance to count coup on him. They would be fine guides and scouts, and could ride Pawnee ponies, too."

"You know, Frank, it will require a man—a man's man, an Indian's man —to efficiently lead and discipline these aborigines, to exact worthwhile benefit from them as scouts. How old are you?"

"I'm twenty-four years, five months, and five days," I say, from a habit of exact, strict accounting.

"That's counting details," the general laughs. "Now, I am aware a Joe McFadden is here on the reservation, experienced in Indian fighting under General Harney. He should have the captaincy."

Yes, I think to myself. I know Joseph, "Mack," and in busy times I hire him to work around the post, that is, when I can catch him far enough out of the bottle to be worth hiring. He's not a bad sort.

"Are you willing to help recruit these braves as scouts, and to serve as an officer under McFadden; to responsibly lead these Indians in our campaign against the hostiles?"

Since it started from my idea, and I'm concerned about what happens to them, I probably would have asked for a chance to throw in with them, anyhow.

The general's request is a tribal matter, necessitating consent not only of the agent, but also of the nation's chiefs, which can be had only through council.

The officer urges speedy action. I send a runner calling the chiefs.

The chiefs of each of the nation's four bands come to the post's council room. There is Peta La Shar (Old Pete), the wise and acknowledged head chief of the Pawnee Nation. High Eagle Chief Latah Cota La Shar of the Wolf, Skeedee band, is old, and their best historian with his stories on their separation from the "Rees." Us-sah Wuck, Spotted Horse, and Sky Eagle, the able speaker of the Kit-ke-haki band, come in.

Ter-ra-re Caw Wah, as influential as he is old and prudent, and old Kah-hee Kee, almighty chief; Tec La Shar Cod-dic—One Who Strikes the Chiefs First—a subchief; Pa-Hoo Tah-Wah—the entire sixteen chiefs and other honored Indians are present.

The chiefs come hastily, and that is the end of their hurry. But we can take all night so far as I am concerned. I put a clean paper before Peta La Shar and he places a fine big peace pipe on it.

Ritual is strictly observed. Only chiefs are entitled to sit in council, although some who are influential or who have distinguished themselves in battle, such as Crooked Hand, the fighter, here present, are honored by invitation. No youths or females may be present, although legends tell of once having a woman head chief.

I am amused that eager curiosity sticks out all over these chieftains. Yet they hold to their impressive behavior.

Following a meditative silence with heads moderately bowed, the pipe is filled with tobacco I slipped to Peta La Shar. He prays, "Atius Tirawa, you are the Great Chief . . ." Then I hold a match to light the tobacco, and the chief smokes, and hands the pipe around.

General Curtis, sitting opposite the head chief, accepts the pipe and draws deeply. When the pipe reaches Mr. Lushbaugh, he holds it out before him ceremoniously (not being a tobacco user), bows to it, and then to the Indians and passes it to me. I smoke it and pass it to my right. Peta La Shar fondles the returned pipe, and lays it on the paper before him.

In ritualistic stateliness each chief makes a short speech, a gesture to our guest. I interpret.

Agent Lushbaugh then takes the floor. I am sure he is unaware of the general's latest decision.

"My friends, ten days ago our enemies from the north swept down upon us, as they so often do. You know how many of your people have died while you try to defend them. Now, our honored guest is sent by the White Father to take away the soldiers he sent to fight your enemy for you."

Silence follows. Plainly the agent was depending on the chief's vigorous protests to convince General Curtis of the desperate need of the soldiers.

The chiefs readily agree, "It is good. The soldiers can go back to the White Father," in a droll uncompliment to the soldiers whom they had found clumsy and impotent as protection from so worthy a foe as Sioux warriors.

I have a bit of sympathy for the agent. His disappointment is sadly real.

Now, I get up to introduce the general, aware of the respect and honor the chiefs pay me by their presence, at my invitation.

"*Cha-hik si Cha-hik* [Men of Men], Chiefs, *Atiputa* [Grandfathers, a title of esteem], sitting here in a circle; General Curtis of the United States Army; Mr. Lushbaugh, official agent of the Pawnee Nation; Friends: The Pawnee Nation is great. Its chiefs are wise councilors with good medicine in their hearts.

"Pawnee braves are strong, and cunning warriors against Sioux. They are skillful in making the surround.

"Pawnee women are industrious to raise the corn and melons, and preserve the wild fruit and roots, the meats, pemmican, and dried flesh and bladders of marrow and tallow. They work the hides so you have the wearing skins and robes, and tepees to live in when you go on the winter hunt, away from your earthen mound lodges. And they make your trading goods.

"Tirawa smiles with favor upon the Pawnee. Tirawa has given you the Great White Father to help you. Now he needs your help, to help him make war against your old-time enemies, the Sioux and Cheyenne. Their heart is bad, and he says they must be punished.

"The Great White Father is determined to make sure they are hunted down, so they can no longer kill and scalp and cut off the right hands of your papooses. [This is believed an early custom of some enemy nations.] He asks that you permit some of your braves to go with the officer to track down the Sioux—to count the big coup on him.

"Hear now, the Great White Father's chief, General Curtis. I have spoken."

General Curtis talks to them as man to man, and again I interpret for them.

"Fellow men, my red friends. Thank you for the privilege of joining you in your council circle. It is good to know you."

The general isn't missing his mark. Equality is important to and appreciated by Indians.

"The government, the Great White Father, proposes to hire some of your warriors, for as much pay as the white soldier gets, thirteen dollars a month, and will pay twelve dollars a month for him to ride his own pony, and will furnish grain for his horse.

"For this pay, your sons must be obedient to their leader, just as is the white soldier. They will be expected to learn some things we know, and will teach them, about making war. There will be duties—work, he must do just as the white soldier does.

"They must remain with their leader until he tells them they can come back to you, which may be a few months. If a white soldier disobeys, he is corrected and disciplined. Your braves will be reasonably disciplined by their leader if they deserve it. They will be as well treated as the white soldier, the same amount of pay and food. I await your decision. Thank you."

Thoughtful silence after the general sits down is unbroken, while in sign language they ask, "How many braves must we send?" silently querying each other.

Peta La Shar arises and addresses the council and guest.

"Cunning and strong is our old enemy. He is the lightning that rides out of the north. His eye is quick to see if the Pawnee are weak. Quick he is, to learn if our braves ride away. Then we would have no swift arrows sent from big bows pulled by strong warrior's arms to defend us. If our braves leave us, we will be only old men, crones, and children. Then the ancient enemy will find us helpless like the deer when his legs are trapped in deep winter feather [snow].

"Surely the Great White Father remembers his promise to protect us from our enemies? Yet his protection is too few soldiers, whose guns are broken until our braves force the enemy to turn his back. Then they say, 'Where is the enemy?' They look to the four quarters. They can only see the backs of our braves who chase the enemy far."

The general, mellowed by hidden amusement in finding himself, surprisingly, so capably challenged, replies, "My friends, I am glad you tell me of these things. It is true, the government has made mistakes—failures, which it regrets. It cannot send enough soldiers because it must fight all the enemies for all of us. It is ashamed and sorry if the soldiers it trusts are not brave.

"The government does not ask you to send braves if you need all of them for your own protection. It only wants as many as you can spare for pay, say, three or four companies? It intends that your enemy will be made so busy when we fight him, that you will not need so many braves to defend you."

Again, there is a movement of hands and heads, with low mumbling.

Sky Eagle, the Kit-ke-haki speaker, arises and proves himself a finished orator by his brief summary. Freely translated: "Pawnee warriors will help Great White Father search—fight our old, bad enemy. We give White Father some sons. It will be well."

In clear pre-twilight hours, Indian youths and young braves join in games. They jump, run, and throw like all boys. Their competitive contests are real endurance training.

All turn out to watch the games. I see General Curtis and his staff, watching in concentrated interest these skill-sharpening feats, practiced with intent objectivity. The officers satisfy themselves as to heights of vaults. They heft the rock to be thrown, step off distances, and refer to their pocket watches.

Smaller children frolic about, the naked little boys with their small bows and arrows imitating older brothers with an occasional chilling hint of future deadliness.

With horse Indians, there is sooner or later to be horse racing. This evening I sense considerable anticipation among the bands, and discover wagering is fairly heavy.

14

Before General Curtis leaves in the cool of morning, I have eighty Pawnees enlisted to go as scouts.

Joe and I lead the boys to Fort Kearny, and we make camp apart from the post. General Curtis arranges issue of blouses (light jackets) and hats to assure that our Indians will not be mistaken for wild ones.

Never before have I seen such a curious sight as these bucks, naked below the waist excepting breech-cloths and moccasins, wearing hats, holes cut in crowns of some and a horn ("pani") of crown hair, tallowed stiff, sticking out, though most wear hanging braids and tie bandana bands around their heads.

It strikes me that we may not quite look military. Still, if the Pawnee are willing to endure some obliteration of their usual barbaric traits in accepting regulation garments, I have hope.

Well aware of being closely eyed, the boys stiffen, hiding natural shyness under a stone-still front.

Two officers give the scouts a looking-over, and walk away in silence. A boy flaps his hands beside his head, suggesting the officer's large ears relate him to the flop-eared jackass. This moves another to puff out his belly and strut like a drumming sage grouse, imitating the other officer. Then they all laugh like fools.

We drill for ten days from early to late. McFadden explains military customs and procedures and I give the commands.

The Indians struggle willingly in a suddenly strange world.

After ten days we get orders to be ready to move out in the morning. The twelfth and sixteenth Kansas Cavalry and a company of second Nebraska of 180 soldiers are with General Curtis, and our scout company of 76 Pawnee under Captain McFadden and Lieutenant North—myself.[1]

We march out of Fort Kearny. Coming to Plum Creek stage station, we turn into the south country, and camp the first night on Crook Nose Creek. The Indians kill a few buffalo, so we have a feast.

During the march, General Curtis orders McFadden to take twenty men to scout a half mile ahead of the column, for three hills distance. Captain McFadden rides among the Indians, and seems to argue with them.

Finally, eight men ride ahead. The columns come up to find them dismounted and lolling about on the other side of the third hill. McFadden reports to the general they had seen nor found nothing.

"Well, how much looking did they do?" the general demands, then tells him to send six men to scout a circle west and south, and to meet us on a straight line directly ahead in two hours. Twenty-five men rush west.

"By Jove!" Can't that man give a command and get obedience?" the general demands.

"You see, he is a man with a situation," I explain.

"What do you mean—a position?"

"No, it's just a situation. You see, it's his family—a family situation with his in-laws. He is married to a Pawnee woman—he's a squaw man, so he is another Pawnee. They would never give him orders, except on a surround. It just isn't good Pawnee manners. So, living by tribal customs, he must *ask* them if they will go out on scout. In the Pawnees' thinking, McFadden has no more authority than the rest of them. Of course they accept their council's authority, but wouldn't order a brother, nor will they take or accept orders of a brother. They will follow a leader, if the notion happens to strike them favorably and if he is able to induce them by argument or if his known bravery and skill impresses them."

"So! That's what ails the fellow. Why do you suppose the poor fool accepted my appointment of captaincy, knowing his circumstances would prevent his effective fulfillment of the position?"

"I suppose he thought he could bully his tribal brothers into helping him out enough to get by."

"We will have no more of this 'pretty please' pussy-footing. Frank, you speak Pawnee better than McFadden. Hereafter you will take my orders and give commands translated to Pawnee, and see that you do get obedience."

"Yes sir. I'll try. The boys will do their best to carry out anything I explain and tell them to do."

"You will order ten men to swing east and south, and circle to meet us ahead in one and one-half hours."

I explain to the scouts that the Great White Father and his chief, the general, tell me to instruct them, and that I am counting on them to show the white chief they know how to be good soldiers, to take the order I give them, and carry it out just as if I went with them. All listen closely as I call out ten men to line up before me, and speak the command in Pawnee.

As the ten ride out in good form, the general remarks, "Of course the

hour and a half I mentioned was an approximation. I would hardly expect
aborigines like those to be carrying a pocket watch—much less to read
one."

"Well, General, you may be surprised at Indians' awareness of time. I'm
ready to wager on those boys coming in ahead of us in one and a half
hours, and not more than five minutes variance, unless they find hostiles."

The general takes me up on the wager.

Of course the Pawnees don't fail me. The general first sees them coming
—hauls out his watch, "By Jove! You would think they read time!" he
said.

"They do, General," I admit. "Every stem of gramma grass everywhere
soapweed stalk, is the Indian's sun dial. They know a lot about time, even
if the sun doesn't shine. At night and on stormy days—their time is
instinctive and they express its divisions, too.

"Phenomenal!" the general laughs, pleased, and hands me a silver
dollar. Joe's boys come in during the afternoon.

The Indians had spotted buffalo, and ask permission to kill. The general
consents, and we again have a feast of roast ribs and hump.

We cross the divide between the Platte and Republican rivers, and ford
the Republican River where Turkey Creek comes in. Here, Brig. Gen.
Robert B. Mitchell, called "Fighting Bob," meets us with the seventh
Iowa Cavalry, the first Nebraska, and part of the third Nebraska. He takes
over the company of the Second Nebraska from General Curtis, along
with about seventy-five scouts under McFadden, to make a circular
campaign west, north, then eastward back to the fort.

The Sioux are reported along the Solomon and Kansas rivers, east
toward Fort Riley. General Curtis and the Kansas Cavalry and the First
Nebraska under Colonel Livingston, and myself with two Pawnee Scouts
go downriver eastward.

We may be sixty miles from Fort Riley when we come to a settlement
where Indians are expected. People are frantic—scared nearly to death—
the Indians had plundered, burned, and killed near there.

People had thrown up a stockade and all settlers, with their stock,
huddle there for protection. It's a stinking mix of humans and animals,
worse than any Indian village I ever saw.

They try to induce the general to leave a detachment of soldiers for
their defense, but General Curtis compromises by leaving them a new kind
of gun—a rifled piece called a one-pound Parrot gun to use defending the
stockade.

Nearing Fort Riley, the general says, "Frank, your management of the
Scouts is entirely satisfactory. I am convinced these Pawnee, under the
right leadership, can be of inestimable value. You will be detached when
we reach the fort. You are to return to the reservation and recruit a full

company of regularly enlisted Pawnee Scouts. You will be commissioned this time as captain of your company. I will arrange your authorization and orders through General Mitchell."

At Fort Riley, General Curtis and his Kansas Cavalry separate from Colonel Livingston and the First Nebraska, and move down the Kansas River. I hear, a few days later, that General Curtis caught Confederate Gen. Sterling Price heading for the northern country, and trounced him good.

I take special care to choose the most intelligent and best of Pawnee men this time. After enrolling with the full number of recruits, I ride to Columbus, wanting to see my folks.

I send Luther to Fort Kearny, to General Mitchell, with the roll of my enlistees, and to bring back the authorization and orders.

After supper I go to call at the home of Miss Mary L. Smith, a young lady who came recently to our Territory to make her home with her uncle Samuel Smith's family, and to teach school. I take her to a dancing play-party where we have lots of fun.

Next morning, I find half of my boys have deserted me! Joe McFadden is drinking, and shows an ugly peeve against me. The Indians are getting ready to go on their fall buffalo hunt. By noon I run into one of my boys hiding out. I nab him and ask him why they broke their promises. He says he didn't break a promise, but that I deceived him by telling him we would fight his old enemy, when I knew we were going into the warm country to fight black men.

This explains Joe's ugliness and his drunkenness since returning from scouting. I collar him.

"Get on your feet, you sneaking coyote. You tell my boys you lied to them. You tell them that we are going after Sioux and that's north, not south. Tell them the truth before I lift your scalp with you in it, and shuck you out of your hide."

I get it out of him well enough to convince the boys. Lute rides in with directions that I am to take my company to report in Omaha at once. I report two days later to Captain Wilcox, mustering officer. Wilcox sends out word he is too busy to see me just now. Every day he sends out word he is too busy.

November 10, 1864. Lincoln is elected to another presidential term. So there is to be no "changing horses in midstream" this time, is there?

December 2, 1864. I finally get in to see Wilcox. He orders me to take proper muster roll and enlistment papers to the agency, and do the enlisting job all over again on official forms, and then to return the papers to Omaha, immediately.

As I am readying to leave the river town, news comes of a terrible thing

in the new Territory of Colorado, at Sand Creek. Cheyenne under Black
Kettle are shot down by Hundred Day men led by a Colonel Chivington.
Every Cheyenne warrior, as well as Indians of nations friendly to
Cheyenne, will take the warpath.

When I reach the reservation, I find every boy I had enlisted gone with
the tribe on the winter hunt. They may not return until late winter. I was
ordered to report back in Omaha immediately to the mustering officer,
with these papers that I cannot now fill out. I ask Lute to take Red Hawk,
Loot-tah-we Coots-ah-pah (a tall muscular boy),[2] and find the Pawnee
hunters and tell those boys I'm expecting them to get back here quick.

I go to Omaha with papers not filled out. Unless the officer will grant
me time to round up those warriors I enlisted, I have failed. He may not
understand why recruited men leave on an extended buffalo hunt. Not
that I blame the Indians. They've not gotten a cent for their first
enlistment and use of their ponies.

Captain Wilcox does grant me another week. Following the military
road home, I meet up with a storm. Hard-driven snow soon packs the
road, so nearly obliterating it that my good horse, Jinks, puts his nose
down like a trailing hound to keep himself on the road.

Jinks and I put up at a half-way station overnight. Daylight comes very
cold and clear, and we get to Columbus where I catch a few winks at
Mother's. Lute comes in at daybreak. He takes a shovel and starts away
like a sleepwalker. I take it, and Mother takes charge of Lute. He is all in.
Following Lute's footprints, I go to the river where Red Hawk has broken
a hole through the ice and is reaching under to scoop up handfuls of sand
to enable the horses to cross on the ice. Scattering a handful before the
horses, tied head to tail, he urges them along a few steps, while trying to
warm his wet, freezing hand and arm on them. They stop and he goes for
more sand. The boy doesn't stop trying until I reach him.

The boys found no trace of the hunters, suffered through the storm, and
haven't had a bite to eat in four days. Lute says Red Hawk was never lost.
He found sheltering bluffs for them and their horses.

Finding another Pawnee man to go with me to look for the hunting
band, I make another try, judging they must have gone further to the west
or south than the way Lute went. On the fourth day, having only grain
left for two days, and near the bottom of our grub sack, I am forced to
turn back.

At the reservation, I find a telegram. ". . . unless the company
enrollment is promptly executed and ready to be mustered, I shall be
compelled to rescind my order," signed by Captain Wilcox.

I'm three days overdue in Omaha and still have no Indians. Already out
of more pocket money than I can afford without getting a commission, my
dander climbs up in the saddle with me on a hard-ridden trip to Omaha—

less than two days in poor footing!

I am in luck! General Mitchell is in Omaha and I explain my dilemma. The general extends my time to twenty days, and doesn't say it is final. Return from Omaha this time is with some regard for my horse.

Because of the blizzards, the Pawnee hunters come back to the Platte River where there is cottonwood and willow brush for their ponies to chew on, and shelter, and wood for their fireholes.

Soon we have filled the roster once more. Captain Wilcox is obliged to make a dead-of-winter trip to come and muster the Pawnees into the United States Army on January 13, 1865.

15

Commissions come from Nebraska Territorial Governor Saunders: Charles A. Small is first lieutenant, James Murie second, and I have the captaincy.

After camping a few days near Columbus, our orders come. Go to Fort Kearny where uniforms and equipment are issued. Pitching our tents away from the barracks and walling them up with snow, we made our winter quarters.

Feeling about Indians in this country is at a boiling point. Many officers despise them, and refuse to see any difference between the Pawnee and other Indians. Officers, and their women folk, are mistrustful; some are actually terrified by my Scouts camping only a half-mile from the post. Only a few people, usually those fresh from the States, are not prejudiced.

Post Commander Captain Gillette, First Nebraska Cavalry, issues orders that I shall teach the Pawnee, and drill them by the Manual of Arms. I am needing study in it myself.

I soon find the Pawnee unwritten language has no words to fit certain of the manual's meanings.

I talk the thing over with Captain Gillette. Either the Pawnee will have to learn English suddenly—hardly humanly possible—or I will have to invent Pawnee words to teach them these orders.

"You are not to deviate from the original commands," the captain snorts. "They are in the manual to be explicitly obeyed. It is your responsibility to issue the regulation commands and you will enforce obedience."

I'm guessing that this time I've bumped into the genuine stone wall!

"Captain, your order is impossible at present to carry out. My men are enlisted as scouts, with the assigned duties of trailing and spying. As scouts they are obedient and dependable. I must say I will no longer try to make infantrymen of them, as the commands of the manual cannot possibly improve their natural ability as scouts and trackers."

"Very well! If they are scouts, we will set them to scouting. You will detail forty men with an officer to start, not later than tomorrow morning, to scout for enemy Indians, from here to the Running Water [Niobrara]," the captain roars.

"Have the mounts arrived for my men?"

"Do you mean to tell me these Indians cannot scout on foot?"

"No, but we were to wait here for our mounts."

"Indeed! Nevertheless, you will issue my order with ten days' rations."

"Yes, Sir!" I salute and leave. The Pawnees know as well as I that this scout is unnecessary, as no Sioux will be caught far from his tepee in this kind of weather. The men are astonished, but there is no quibbling as they make ready.

At dawn I go to the river to see them across. The boys have to wade the deep and still unfrozen channels where ice floats in chunks broken away by force of current. They strip and carry their clothing, arms, and ammunition, including their bows, arrows, and rations, high above armpit-depth water. Reaching a stretch of solid ice, they hustle across and plunge through another flowing channel, and out. They soon signal they are ready to go on. Snow is fifteen inches deep. The temperature hardly warms up to zero.

On the Loup fork they get caught by a blizzard. Unable to see two feet ahead, they lay up in a makeshift camp three days before they can travel. Out of rations, no game showing, Lieutenant Murie brings them back. Their feet, unused to army boots, are frosted; some digits must be amputated.

The captain isn't through yet. Next, he orders me to detail scouts for picket duty. While the army's picketing is different, it is within the scope of Pawnee understanding.

As pickets, they really set the post on its ear! If we had friends here, we lose them in a hurry. The officers object to waiting when a Pawnee on duty with his muzzle loading musket yells "Halt!" then draws a blank on further English. Sooner or later, most of the officers get to stand there and yell for somebody to fetch me, or one of my lieutenants.

The Scouts are quick to catch essentials of army life. In their earnestness they fill in and mimic to round out gaps of comprehension. Regulations could present impossible problems, but the most awkward procedure is a target for their tongue-in-cheek but sincere approximation. They perform their duty on the picket line, and smartly report to another sentry at the ends of their beats.

They closely imitate regulation military English that is meaningless to them. You will have acknowledged and passed on before you realize that what you heard sounded like "Ha pass late. All's well, go t'hell!" Actually it is a cross of jibberish and profanity for the regulation sentinel's end of beat report, "Half past (the time). All is well." The boys pick up off-color English and cussing quicker than useful words.

The officers often cross the road to the Sutler's store, saloon, and billiard hall. Something is bound to happen, sometime.

When it does, I am deep in a game of checkers. Captain Gillette stops when commanded by the sentry's "Halt!" and waits for the Scout to give the regulation query.

"Confound it, get on with the routine," he fusses. But the Indian is silent.

"Damn it, man, if you can't do anything else, you can get that blasted old musket aimed somewhere else besides at me!"

The Captain flails his arms and blusters. The Indiand stands firm.

"Captain North! Hey, Captain North. Cap-t-ai-n No-r-r-r-th. Oh Captain North! Come and call off your dog, Captain North!"

The captain's insults and rage are lost on Co-rux-ah Kah Wahdee Bear. The Bear stands staunch with never a thought of doing other than his duty, as much of it as he remembers.

So the captain's heels cool quite a while on a very cold day. His suspicion flares out at me as I walk—I do not run—to unsnag the two.

Seeing that the sentry's need is for a bit of prompting, I patiently give Co-rux-ah Kah Wahdee instruction. I speak in Pawnee, from the Official Military Manual. I am reasonably thorough. I cover a number of subjects one by one and bit by bit, to the Bear's complete bewilderment, while the wintry winds blow by.

Eventually I get to the situation at hand. I lead the Bear through regulation procedure in his own tongue, and then translate it to the English version. He recalls and handles it so well that the captain is plainly hit by increased suspicion.

I ignore his bristling and order the Bear to report at 7 A.M. for further instruction—a routine, full-company drill.

We keep the Scouts busy learning to care for and keep up equipment. Though I'm no great shakes as a drillmaster, the daily drill teaches them to know and obey trumpet calls and cavalry commands. We deploy groups to maneuver and skirmish-afoot. Discipline is mainly a matter of showing them how to do, over and over, with encouraging words. It's easy to see the Pawnees' interest and pride grow with every drill and well-done task.

"You're wearing Pawnee britches," Lieutenant Small tells Lieutenant Murie of a rip or tear in his trousers. It's an army saying that began with issue of regulation trousers to the Pawnee. A number of the Scouts at first cut away portions of cloth, fore and aft, to accommodate wearing of their breechclouts.

Mail and passenger stages haven't run since wild Indians' rampaging stopped them last August. Indians west of Fort Laramie hold a grip on

Oregon and California Trail country as far as Salt Lake, where Gen. P. E. Connor and his Second California Calvalry effectively squelch them.

January 10, 1865. Gen. G. M. Dodge, the engineer of my early remembrance, arrives today in Fort Kearny. He is now commander of the Plains and Platte Indian Department of Missouri.

General Dodge is charged with re-establishing the telegraph line, and making the trails safe. His first move is to require that division commanders report conditions.

The Mud Springs (west of Julesburg) report is of attack by two thousand Indians who overpowered the small garrison.

General Mitchell told me when I last saw him that he wasn't able to communicate with Denver or Fort Laramie. The report is that half the telegraph line has been destroyed between here and the mountains. About fifteen miles of line is down between Lodge Pole Station and Fort Laramie.

On January, this year, Julesburg's telegraph and stage station was burned, including warehouses filled with supplies.

The garrison at Camp Rankin (later renamed Fort Sedgwick) near Julesburg, under Capt. Nick O'Brien, was far outnumbered by hundreds of Cheyenne, some Arapahoe and Sioux. Captain O'Brien's small troop held on but buried half of the troop!

A band of four hundred lodges, many large enough for eight warriors and families, are seen moving west up the Republican River, ignoring the small garrison that tried to turn them.

In the opinion of Capt. R. R. Livingston of the "Starvation Trail," western Kansas region, Indians threaten to wipe the Plains clear of white settlement.

Gen. Thomas Moonlight reports from Denver that the Indians intend war to exterminate whites and to clear the country.

Summing up the reports, the general finds a hundred miles of telegraph line down—a thousand yards here, seven hundred yards further on, and so on beyond Fort Laramie. Every military post, telegraph, and stage station is cut off, with little chance of sending messages if attacked.

The general organizes a three-part campaign. He concentrates soldiers to reinforce outposts, to rebuild telegraph lines, and to subdue the hostiles. Some of this force is called from "quiet" posts, other men are called out of winter quarters, where they await discharge after their stint in the Civil War. Talk is that soldiers mutinied at Fort Riley, when ordered out to march to Fort Kearny.

Mounts for my command are at hand. We begin to campaign under General Dodge.

Every mounted man in this part of his district is assigned to build the telegraph line along the South Platte.

After a day of chinook winds, a backlash of cold put a heavy ice crust on twenty inches of snow. Bright sun can't warm to zero.

My command is spread thin to guard two hundred and fifty miles of Platte and South Platte soldier-linesmen against attack.

"You are to attack any body of Indians, large or small. Stay with them, pound them until you capture them, or they move north of the Platte or south of the Arkansas rivers," General Dodge orders.

Our days are full of skirmishes, pursuing bands of snow-ghost warriors, or signaling warnings of approaching bands, to give the laboring soldier a chance to lay down tools and grab guns. Many are the running fights with marauding bands.

The telegraph is up! We have communication again. The soldiers actually out-Creightoned Creighton, the line builder, who did not build lines during mid-winter. The general expects to start stages rolling in early March. Stages will leave the Oregon Trail to bypass the savage tribes of the North Platte River region.

They will go by the South Platte, overland to Fort Lupton, Colorado Territory, turning north by way of the Cache La Poudre, cross Laramie Plains to Fort Halleck and Elk Mountain, then westerly through Bridger Pass, Bitter Creek, and Green River. From here, stages will run north and west around Salt Lake, to rejoin the main California Trail just past the California cut-off juncture.

Immigrants and freighters will again travel, when grass greens up to sustain driving and draft stock, but only in large, well-armed caravans. Every post is ordered to hold travelers until a strong enough number is assembled to discourage Indians.

16

General Dodge winds up his six-week emergency campaign.
Communication and trails are open. Posts are garrisoned by assignment of
a few more soldiers, though still far from enough to insure their safety.
Hostiles are mostly north of the river.

General Dodge had sent for me. "North," he said, "before I leave for
St. Louis, I want to commend you for the excellent work you are doing
with those Pawnee Indians. Your fine control, and the response you
obtain, is most admirable. You, and they, through your leadership, are
rendering a unique invaluable service.

"I am thoroughly convinced of their potential worth, particularly in
subduing the hostiles, and—is it too much to hope?—in spite of the
general hatred the barbarous tribes have incurred, for their eventual
civilizing, comparable to the tribe of your scouts.

"Now, I have another assignment for you. You will move your command
to Camp Rankin [later renamed Fort Sedgwick] for patrol and scout duty
along the new Overland stage trail.[1]

"Gen. P. E. Connor of California succeeds General Mitchell. He will
meet you after mid-May. Under Connor's command, you will then proceed
with your scouts to the Powder River country where punitive action will
be aggressively pursued to subdue the hostile tribes.

"Your primary responsibility is to find and recover white prisoners,
women and children snatched from immigrant wagons, stages, stations,
and homesteads.

"According to information we have, these white people were taken into
the Indians' camps in the vicinity of the Powder River and Bighorn
Mountains. They are to be rescued at any cost. I know of no other unit so
singularly able to effect such rescues; therefore, I entrust the duty to you."

With my command I move along the Big Trace. We've ridden every part
of this stretch of it often during these months of scouting. Reminders jut
from half-melted snowbanks. Iron of burnt wagons mark the site of the

August 7 Plum Creek killing, by Chief Big Crow's Ogalalla Sioux, of thirteen people[2] from a small freight train. A woman and boy were carried off, the draft stock taken away, and the loads burned.

Our family believes this was the same band that threatened Luther last fall, after he had hauled a load to Cottonwood Spring and started back.

The command reaches Cottonwood Spring Trading Post, now grown into a small village. The military post, Cantonment McKean, was established at the regulation forty rods' distance from the trading post. Maj. G. M. O'Brien and his Seventh Iowa Cavalry companies cut logs and built barracks and renamed the post Fort Cottonwood Spring.[3]

Assigning Lieutenants Small and Murie to direct the Pawnee in bivouacking a half mile from the fort, I report to the commanding officer. This evening I call on my friends, the Boyers. I'm told that my friend William Bischoff came back a month ago to rebuild his ruined place. He, along with other settlers out this way, was scared out and went east last fall.

About seven years ago William Bischoff, with a couple of French partners, put up the second building at Cottonwood Spring and commenced trade with three wagonloads of goods. When his partners left, he traded the place to Jack Morrow[4] for a place south and west of the river forks, which he called Eureka Springs. Charles McDonald[5] then acquired it, the third trader to settle permanently here. Charles McDonald has put up buildings, one a story and a half, and a solid stockade. I call at the McDonald ranch and am made acquainted with Maj. G. M. O'Brien, the post commanding officer, and his brother, Capt. Nick O'Brien, Lt. Eugene F. Ware, Corp. Cy Fox,[6] and others.

In early morning we break camp and move westward. Chill, late March winds fail to halt flights of snow geese and trumpeter swans, northbound. Large flocks of meadowlarks thrum up from snow-bared prairie where they were breakfasting on fallen grass seed.

Two or three miles from the fort, a German has settled with his family. He and his young boys stop digging a trench in the half-thawed earth to lean on their shovels while they stare at the Scouts.

"Howdy!" I say, riding near. "You needn't get upset. These fellows are the Pawnee Scouts of the United States Army. I'm Frank North, officer in charge."

"How'd you do, Sir! Burke, Johan [John] is my name."[7] The man speaks with a German accent. His precise, restrained manner and the ghost of a suggestion of click of heels and salute seem a remnant of a Prussian-like military habit.

"Yeh, soldier-Indians I see sometimes before at da fort." One of his boys makes a run to their house, a dugout in a hillside.

"What are you figuring on doing there?" I ask, looking at a line staked to the riverbank.

"Ve irrigate mit vater from da river, and ve vill raise wegetables. Da post buys—und milk—"

There are three cows picketed out, showing the deep print of working under yokes. A horse is near, and in a willow pen are three calves.

The man's wife and family come running out to see the uniformed Indians. I tip my hat to his lady as her husband says, "Dis is Captain North. Mine vife, Margaretta."

I inquire about the little four-or five-year-old Indian boy with her.

"Mine Mister find ven go chop voods. Und de arm schmashed. Ve fix, mit viskey." She imitates taking a drink from a flask. "Und mit strecht, und mit pull, und mit leetle boards, und vrap round und round; five day back."

"It looks to me like a good job, and that you are a mighty fine doctor. He's a real lucky boy to get your kind of care," I tell her, smiling at him.

"But it no eat!" she says, concerned.

I call for Aru-saw Kit-toy, Fine Horse.

"Friend, please do me a favor and ask the small lad why he won't eat."

"Brule!" Fine Horse says it like a curse and turns away. My friend's mind is bitter against Sioux, especially Brules. After a lengthy pause he looks at me.

"My friend, Skiri-taka," (the scouts honor me, calling me "Wolf," accepting me as one of them—a wolf person). "For you I will speak to the young enemy."

The youngster stands unmoving, as though hearing nothing. Though allowing the white family's kindness, surely he feels terror in facing one of his people's enemy. However, if the child knows fear, he hides it.

Fine Horse tries sign talk, known by all Indians. Beginning with his palm out even with his shoulder and rotating his hand a little, he makes other motions, and ends with the cupped hand moving up and down before his mouth.

The small Sioux shows no feeling—makes no response.

Though Fine Horse gets no answer, he assures me, "The young Sioux will eat. Give him a willow stick to hold his meat to the fire, and let him scorch his own."

Riding along the Oregon-California Trail, in the valley of the *Kee-nesh-tah* ("River that Sinks"), the Platte River, we pass between it and high bluffs on the south. These curve northwesterly, the most northerly being the highest, a cusplike peak—the Pawnee's "Lookout Hill"—from which in times past they watched for the Sioux.

The army has evidence that a road rancher, Jack Morrow, on the flats back of the bluffs, posts Indians of his squaw's band who watch for immigrant and small freighting trains they may waylay and rob, taking anything of value through Moran Canyon to the thief's trading post.

Unlucky travelers, trying to recover their stolen stock, will not miss Morrow's two-and-a-half-story cedar log building where they can buy replacement animals.

We come even with the river forks. Southwest I see that William Bischoff is back rebuilding his walls. A few miles further up trail, Louis Baker has come too, to repair the O'Fallon Bluffs stage station and road ranch, now protected by telegraph and a small garrison.

Overtaking an army supply train, we trade insults.

At the road ranch of a Montreal Frechman, "Colonel" G. F. Beauvois, a friendly squaw man who was earlier an American Fur Company agent, is a detachment of First Nebraska Cavalry, billeted here last fall. They are holding freighters to concentrate a number large enough to discourage Indians.

Since the Indian rampages began late last summer, small garrisons put up sod barracks, beginning at John and Judd Gilman's ranch, fifteen miles east of Fort Cottonwood. They're billeting every road ranch westward to maintain a protective cordon along the Big Trail, and to man the telegraph, now in working order since General Dodge's winter campaign.

Alkali [later, Paxton] station was garrisoned, I think, in January. A hired telegrapher named Searle is here.[8]

Up trail eighteen miles from Camp Rankin, the road ranch owned by young Dick Cleve, Pony Express rider at seventeen, has a small garrison.

Jules Station, attacked last August by Indians and burned in January, is rebuilding the stage-telegraph station and the huge freight receiving-forwarding station. The Northwest and Montana gold-mine settlements at the end of the Bozeman Road make this big freight house necessary.

At Camp Rankin, we join Capt. Nick O'Brien and his small garrison of Seventh Iowa Cavalry, veterans of the big Cheyenne winter attack.

My command takes up guard and escort duty along the Overland mail-stage route. This is shared by squads from the Third Colorado Cavalry.

April 10, 1865. News that Lee surrendered at Appomattox Court house came by telegraph. The post fires off a howitzer by way of hurrahs.

April 15, 1865. Lincoln is dead! Our President is dead! Shot in the back of his head at a theater last night, and died three hours ago, according to the electric message.

The flag droops at half-mast.

*   *   *

May 16, 1865. General Connor orders me to bring my command to him at Fort Laramie. Accordingly, we leave Camp Rankin to move west, up Lodgepole Creek about thirty miles, to ford at the upper California crossing. Sometimes it's a stream of quicksand pockets, but we cross without mishap, and bivouac.

In the morning turning north, we go up a long, rising plain called Jules Stretch, a course he laid out to induce Oregon Trail immigrant trade to his blacksmith shop and small store.

There is no water to be had until, after a day's travel, we come over Windlass Hill and reach the divide, watersheds to the two Platte rivers and Pole Creek, a flat table where a spring flows part of the year. A sod barrack is here and a stage and telegraph station, with an *iffy* garrison—*if* there are soldiers to spare for it, and *if* they can survive the hazards to man the post.

Odd rock formations in the distance are Court House, Castle, Jail House, Chimney Rocks, and Scott's Bluff, called Signal Hill. We camp in the sight of Hogback and Wildcat ranges, their colors ever-changing with the light.

In midmorning, traveling west along the Oregon Trail, we come to the base of Signal Hill, now called Scott's Bluff, with the North Platte River water lapping its north base. We fill canteens from a spring in the south side of the bluff. Circling on south and west from the big bluff, along the Old Trail we pass old Fort Mitchell, jerrybuilt of sod to guard Cheyenne Pass, but abandoned as undefendable.

A treeless, sun-bleached, ochre plain—a wedge between the Laramie and North Platte rivers—a high-flying United States flag of thirty-four stars in the blue field, and magnificent, dark Laramie Mountain behind it is the sight that reaches far out to us along the trail.

When yet a mile or more from Fort Laramie, my command passes far right of a cottonwood log scaffold north of the Oregon-Military Road. Still swaying from trace chains are the corpses of Two Face and Black Foot, hanged earlier this spring under command of Col. Thomas Moonlight, by order of General Connor. The story is of a Mrs. Eubank who, with her baby son, were carried away last August by Cheyennes, from settlements on the Little Blue River.[9] The chiefs were found dragging the woman behind their ponies by a horsehair rope around her neck, her hands bound behind her, according to the army grapevine. The woman, hardly half alive, knows nothing of what happened to the baby.

Covering the last mile to the fort, our mounts smell water and hit a brisker pace. Fording the Laramie River above its juncture with the Platte and falling in by twos, the command rides up a mile of flood plain.

It is a good feeling, a stirring one for me, that I'm swinging up before this landmark of boyhood dreams—old Fort Laramie.

17

Fort Laramie! Thirteen years ago, a fine two-story building was erected here from lumber hauled from a Missouri port. It's like a dream to walk into such a building this far from civilization. A porch—double deck veranda—is on the entire south front side of the elegant, white-painted "Bedlam Hall," bachelors' quarters. Barracks, and most buildings, are of adobe, with log reinforcements.

My command goes into camp away from the fort, down the river. I put Corp. White Eagle in charge—a Skeedee Chief, intelligent and not excitable, a powerful man a few years older than the other scouts. He enlisted with the first company last fall as Lah-Kit-Ta-We La Shar, White Eagle Chief; with his second enlistment, I promoted him to corporal. This honor, according to Pawnee custom, entitled him to choose a new name. He is on the rolls now as La-Tah-Cots Tah-Kah, though I still call him White Eagle Chief.

A brother is enlisted as John Box, the name given him in the reservation Indian school's effort to purge Indian out of the children.

In twilight quietness I seem to see, downriver on the Laramie's left bank, the old fur-trading post of Fort William, built by William Sublette; and I see again, as I saw as a boy when Father's friends told of them, those matchless mountain men—and not one whit less in stature, nor will they ever be.

As though I had conjured him, that greatest of all mountain men—Jim Bridger, himself—comes into the fort to talk with General Connor.

From the teamster's camp a voice to match these mighty peaks sings: ". . . Evening is descending, darker night is near . . . Watchman on the mountain . . ."[1]

Gen. P. E. Connor and staff are here. He is working up a campaign of three parts. Under command of Col. Nelson Cole will be: a battery of the colonel's own regiment, twelve companies of the Twelfth Missouri Cavalry and the Second Missouri Artillery, about sixteen hundred men, hired muleskinners (teamsters), farriers, blacksmiths, and packers. One hundred and fifty wagons full of quartermaster goods for ninety days, some hauling ammunition, others, grain for horses; hardtack (cracker-biscuit), sow-belly, coffee, beans, sugar, and salt will be hauled by three and four teams to a wagon (six or eight mules and horses each).

Colonel Cole will leave Omaha early in June, coming west to Columbus. From the mouth of the Loup River, Cole will move northwest. He is to pass around the upper Black Hills to rendezvous with a middle column that is to move north along the west of those mountains.

That outfit, the Sixteenth Kansas under Col. Samuel Walker is readying here, and with a mule pack train will join Colonel Cole west of the Black Hills. Together the two forces will go northwest to the Panther (Wolf) Mountains, where General Connor is arranging to have a cache of supplies, and thence to join Connor at the mouth of the Rosebud River, about September 1.

When our duties allow us time off, Lieutenants Small, Murie, and I go to the fort and play whist or checkers—though chess, with a sharp opponent, is my choice.

In and around the fort is tremendous activity: thousands of "Pilgrims" (immigrants), bullwhackers, muleskinners, soldiers, carpetbaggers, and men but lately mustered out of the North and South armies, bringing their families out to settle.

Not the least of this stir and bustle is the thousands upon thousands of tons of freight—mountains of it, inching up trails to our distant pioneer settlements and new north and western states. Immense freight lots go to maintain the army posts, and to supply the Conner campaign. Three times more tonnage than last year's is going over the Bozeman road to Montana and Idaho gold fields. Thousands of wheels creak, wagon chains clank, draft animals grunt, groan, moo, and bawl, whinny, and squeal. Sharp whip-cracks, yells of curse and command voiced by a swelling stream of migrant people.

June 22, 1865. A large immigrant train, three hundred wagons, passes up the trail.

The mail stage brings me two letters from home. Luther writes that Colonel Cole's soldiers demanded to know where they are going and what they are to do, refusing to go further west than Columbus. The colonel persuaded them to obedience, and the column finally moved out. Lute refused to hire on as army guide; he doesn't know the northwest.

My other letter is from Miss Mary. It's a long time since last I had the pleasure of her company.

June 27, 1865. An immigrant train of one hundred and eighty wagons passes up river along the north side, opposite the main trail—probably

Mormons going to Salt Lake.

July 1, 1865. Colonel Walker's outfit is assembling: six hundred of the Sixteenth Kansas Cavalry, about four battalions of Eleventh Ohio Cavalry, and other United States Infantry, "galvanized" soldiers—captured Confederates who were offered freedom in return for protecting settlements and trails from Indians. Others, soured because they are forced into Indian fighting after finishing the war down south, expect to be mustered out and have had no pay for many months.

They are hardened, tough soldiers, and I'll be glad to see them in the field where busy men will forget their peeves.

July 5, 1865. Colonel Walker's command is formed up, hearing General Connor's orders read. There's a sudden confusion—yells—lines break into rebellious disorder. It looks like that powder keg's fuse is burning mighty short.

The general summons his artillery batteries, positioning them opposite the rioting Walker command. Suddenly the racket dies away. The plains are quiet enough to hear a pin drop.

"Prepare to mount! Mount! Forward by fours, march!"

They "fall in." General Connor orders the buglers to "farewell" them as though nothing had happened.

July 27, 1865. A messenger comes to Fort Laramie, the telegraph being out, telling of a two-day fight at Platte Bridge.[2] Disaster falls to a detachment of the garrison under Lt. Casper Collins, who was killed with eight of his men.

On the second morning a segment of Company H of the Eleventh Kansas, heading for Fort Laramie to be mustered out, was attacked three miles west of the bridge and twenty-six killed. A wagon train was wiped out in sight of Platte Bridge Stockade.

July 30, 1865. General Connor's[3] general field orders are read to his Powder River Indian Expedition, getting under way today. Lastly, he issues the command: "You will not receive overtures of peace or submission from Indians, but will attack and kill every male Indian over twelve years of age."[4] However, in a circular he had ordered "No outrages will be perpetrated upon their women and children, neither will they be killed."

The Powder River campaign moves out from Fort Laramie, heading northwest along the south side of the North Platte River, to ford three days' march ahead at La Bonte.

Gen. Patrick E. Connor moves out with his staff and companies of the Second California Cavalry, Sixth Michigan Cavalry, Seventh Iowa Cavalry, and Eleventh Ohio Cavalry; myself, and my Pawnee command with Lieutenants Small and Murie; a United States signal corps with

Lieutenants Richards and Brown; and seventy Winnebago and Omaha
Indians under Capt. E. W. Nash and Lieutenants Evans and Mitchell.
The Indians came in last night expecting to learn army scouting from my
Pawnees' example. Their officers know nothing about Indians or their
tongue, and mistrust them.

The old mountain man, "Major" Jim Bridger, has hired on as guide;
also Nick Janis and other mountain men—Mich Bouyer, Bordeaux, Tony
(Antoine) LaDeau, and Jim Daugherty.

General Connor started a courier two days ago from the fort, to find
Cole on the Loup River and deliver instructions:[5] his route, information
of the food cache to be placed at the Panther Mountain, and about where
and when Walker will join him; also the schedule and location of
rendezvous with General Connor on the Rosebud River.

Cracking long whips, yelling and swearing, the teamsters drive six-and
eight-horse-mule teams against harness collars. Trace chains jangle, heavy
wagons creek and rumble and axle-grease buckets hanging on the reach
behind the wagons sway as wheels roll. The long columns and nearly two
hundred quartermaster supply wagons with a driven herd of extra horses
and mules stretch out.

Hugging the river, we go west by north to cross the Platte River at
LaBonte where part of our mountain-wise scouts are sent with the Omaha
and Winnebago Indians to proceed to the Platte Bridge stockade and from
there, northwest through the Wind River valley. Moving then toward the
south Big Horns, they are to rejoin this column in three weeks, on Crazy
Woman Creek, a branch of the Powder River.

My striker tells me Pawnee haven't gone into the Black Hills since his
grandfather's time. Weakened in numbers after a scourge of smallpox, the
late 1830s, they got the worst of it in warfare with the Sioux. Another
plague of smallpox in 1849 and periodic warfare and recurring spells of
cholera, further shrank the tribe. Since they've been impoverished, they
have taken to begging and scrounging along the trail.

"You going along to help take this Indian war to their wilderness?"
Capt. Nick O'Brien queries of grizzled Jim Daugherty.

"Yeh, guess we've got to go up there and shake Uncle Sam'l's fist under
noses of Young Man Afraid of His Horses and Red Cloud."

18

A broiling sun over this high, dry and scraggled region discourages the scant vegetation. Parched ground offers only short spears of grass, a smattering of rabbit weed and a low kind of sage—poor grazing for army animals.

Watering places are scarce. Most small streams have gone underground this time of year. White, lacy frills of alkali decorate fast-drying run-off pools.

So far, Jim Bridger leads us to good springs for night camp. I believe he knows and remembers where every watering place is. He predicts we may make dry night camps sometimes, until we cross this high plain and reach the rivers and foothills.

Every day the country gets rougher. We scramble up ravines and down gullies. Sliding and slipping, wagon wheels and reaches splinter, axletrees break, and our blacksmiths work at their forges far into the night, repairing for tomorrow's travel. We are making only eight to twelve miles a day.

The Pawnees report sizable Indian bands, with travois hitched to their ponies, heading northwest a couple of days ahead.

Wishing to talk with somebody wise enough to Indian ways to keep his scalp through forty-some wilderness years, I ride up alongside of Bridger.

"Howdy, Mr. Bridger," I say.

"Howdy," he returns. "Be ye goin' up to play the Indians' game of hide and hunt?" he asks sociably.

"By gar! I'll take th' hide—you can have the hunt," Nick Janis announces, riding up.

"Probably all the hostiles have left these parts, wouldn't you say, Major?" I ask, well aware my scouts are finding traces of many.

"No! I ain't sayin' ary sech a damn fool thing! Ye seein' Injuns abouts?"

"Why no, I haven't seen a hostile so far, excepting the scalps the

Pawnees fetch in every day from scout duty," I admit.

"Yeah, exackly! When you don't see Injuns is when to expect 'em. Passels of Injuns kin come up, right out'n the barest ground where you're seein' nary a one, nor a brush fur him to hide behind."

The old man's sharp eyes never stop in their unhurried probing about this country we are passing through.

"Mind them reports that come into Fort Laramie, 'bout the Platte Bridge fracas—said the Injuns left the ha'r they'd lifted from the wagon sojers layin' 'round on the ground? Them Injuns catched it, bad—had no stummik to keep the scalps around remindin' 'em of the hurtin' they tooken there. They're fetchin' their hurt ones up north'ard, after buryin' of their dead in rocks and trees. You bet'cha thar's Injuns—a passel more here 'bouts than sojers—an' don'cha furgit that."

The wise old man puts his eyes closely on me, and his tight face breaks into a grin, recognizing I had baited him.

"Anyhow, yeh best be downright sure yer Pawnees don't git s'prised one o'these hyar nights by Sioux or Cheyenne tomahawks."

"None but the Pawnee have had scout and sentry duty since we turned north, away from the Platte River. I'll venture to say no other Indian has gotten a close look and got away. They come, but their scalp lock hangs at a Pawnee's belt by sunup!"

"Be it yer lucky, or be it a sharp watchin' eye that don't sleep?" It don't never hurt nothing' to whet 'em up a leetle."

A bit nettled by the old mountain man, I leave him to his own way of thinking.

Before daybreak I waken. A sickening stench fills the air. By the first crack of light everyone stirs, and comes up for air, looking around for a too close little black and white striped animal.

We find the guilty critter just as his long sharp claws slash his way out of a grain sack. Guessing which way he will take out, we move lively, anxious to give him wide clearance.

He heads toward a group. They shift hastily. Cot-te-ra-tet Goots, Struck with a Tomahawk, with other scouts of the night's last watch, had approached behind them, and as they jump aside, he is suddenly face to face with the plume-tailed animal. It whirls around, humps itself and shoots an amber spray over the Pawnee, then ambles away.

We move fast—to windward! Yelling and bellering, Goots claws at his eyes as he dances about, then rushes into the stream we are camped near. The hostlers cuss him for fouling the water.

The varmint's fifteen-foot bull's-eye on the big Pawnee sends the company to howling and rolling with laughter.

I straighten and lift the reeking sack with a willow pole. The bag top is still gathered and loosely wound by a cord. I suspect a trapper, after nearly a half-century in the wilderness, would know how to take a skunk while preventing its defense act. It hadn't lain here long before freeing its legs and slashing its way out, but it was in camp long enough to teach me a lesson I'll not forget, and to realize I'd been done a good turn.

Calling the Scouts together, though glad to excuse Goots, I ask the last watch: "Didn't one of you see somebody bring the skunk into our camp?"

"See no man—see no skunk," they all admit.

No Sioux—no enemy fetched the stinker. But it was brought in, and not any Pawnee eye saw it done! How sharp are the brave's eyes, that he cannot see if friend or enemy sneaks into our camp? Will it next be a Sioux who comes and takes scalps while Pawnee eyes look the other way?

I don't bear down too hard—I figure they get the point. They are a shamefaced bunch.

The old mountain man is already out and gone. I don't see him all day. As light settles down, old Jim's tiny fire flickers at the far side of the camp.

I confide my objective to Loots-Tow-Ooots, Rattlesnake, and Co-rux-ah Kah Wahdee, Traveling Bear, ordering certain preparation. At about three o'clock in the morning we leave our pallets, skirt the camp, and reach the area where I expect Bridger is sleeping.

With painstaking stillness we search. Though I am never far from the two scouts I hear no sound. Yet, in this hour's search they haven't found the mountain man's lair. Another hour gets by us, and dawn is not far away.

We are forced to give it up and get back to our camp. I, for one, am not sorry that Loots-Tow-Ooots parts with the gift—an all-ripe fish intended to perfume Bridger's pillow.

As we come in, a figure rises from his blanket.

"Be yeh lookin' fur me—er maybe it's a polecat yer huntin'," the old fellow says with a chuckle.

He has outfoxed us again! But, there will be another day. The Indians catch the funny side and laugh and whoop at what they figure is a capital joke.

Army animals aren't getting enough good water to stand the heat, nor enough grazing to stand the hard use. Refusing alkali water, they go until we come to the next watering place—too long a stretch sometimes. If it, too, is not acceptable, they still go on. But horses and mules are not like camels. The time comes, alkali or not, that they drink their fill, too often will be out of harness—if they survive colic and indigestion from alkali poisoning. The column is carrying sacked grain, but thirsty animals won't eat.

August 6, 1865. Who would expect a prairie fire, as scant as grass is? It

can happen—and does. A man must have slept while smoking so that his
pipe fell away from his slack hand or jaw, to spill out live sparks, fanned
by the breeze into a spreading flame.

Soldiers flog the fire that is racing toward the ammunition wagons. Men
push and pull the heavy loads to a knoll of shale and loose gravel, bare of
vegetation.

Pawnees on picket duty come in to find what the fire is. They expect
the big blaze will bring the enemy in overpowering numbers.

August 8, 1865. Passing the head of the Cheyenne River, the scouts ask
permission and bag some fine young *adi-kah-tus*, pronghorn antelope.

General Connor fancies use of their soundless archery in enemy
country, and orders them to kill enough game for an army feed. It's a task
to Pawnee taste. They organize a surround, killing enough buffalo for the
troops. The Pawnees show soldiers how to toast the meat, and everybody
has a feast, a real treat after hardtack and sow-belly.

After days of unending sameness, and ceaseless rolling clay and alkali
dust, we pull up on a long divide. Here men and animals come into
cooling breezes off still-distant snowy peaks of the Big Horn Mountains. In
the left distance are Pumpkin Buttes.[1]

Eight golden-sorrel mules of the lead wagon flop long ears to their
Negro driver's voice, "Ten thousand times ten thousand . . . The Armies
(march) . . . Fling wide the golden gates . . . Orphans . . . Widows no
longer desolate. . . ."[2]

Rumor says, a slave boy stopped a runaway horse rig of a crippled youth,
whose father then schooled both boys in Europe. He died before freeing
the boy, who fled north to escape auction with the estate. Dan
Beauregard's trained singing is heard by these soldiers—and his voice
reaches to the mountains.

August 14, 1865. Coming into the land where Powder River rises in
black soil like powdery slack of bituminous or lignite coal, we make camp.
Here is built a stockade to be called Camp Connor (later renamed Fort
Reno). Clay with coarse grass, sun-baked in blocks, or sod cut from root-
matted swales make arrow-proof walls. Timber, even a few poles for frame
and reinforcement, is most wanted. The stockade is of cottonwood, cut
and upended into a ditch and tamped solid.

A supply train was to catch up here. It's overdue, but General Connor
expects it any time.

August 22, 1865. Pawnees on scout come in telling of a band of Indians
driving horses and mules north. I report this to the general who orders my
command, excepting the camp guards, out after the Indians.

Scouts shuck off army clothes preparing for battle. Weird smears
hurriedly streak bronze bodies with war paint; feathers are braided into war

ponies' manes and sacred clay mud colors are daubed in odd patterns on horses' white spots.

I order White Eagle to caution the Scouts they are to surround the band, to surprise them at close range. (I want, this time, to disarm and capture them.)

We hit the band's trail, following northwestward. Though traveling fast, they are dragging a travois. We keep after them through the afternoon. Shortly before sundown they go north and at dark reach the river and follow along it, though I had expected they would camp.

Our horses are lagging, not having recovered strength since the march, as the Pawnee and their mounts are kept scouting and on guard duty. I pare the command to fifty men riding the strongest horses, sending the others back to camp.

Tracking on foot, a couple of Scouts lead through moonless darkness.

I'll never know how the Pawnees, in relays, keep to the trail through the night. I think probably it is by simple concentration sharpening their senses, added to their primitive Indian awareness. Perhaps their keen noses pick up smells from the horses passing ahead along the trail a few hours ago.

The band often crossed windings of the river, slowing the scouts hunting tracks where the band comes out of the stream; but they never lose the trail.

Loots-Tow-Ooots, Rattlesnake, just off from his trailing relay, says we are gaining on the band. We may run onto them any time now. We could be the surprised ones, and have to battle our way out of a trap, though I think this unlikely—the Pawnees would detect any splitting of the band in an effort to trap us.

It's a dark night; a man can't see his horse's ears ahead. We stop and dismount oftener, to give our flagging horses breathers, then push on.

I'm suspicioning that this band may be nearing a main village, though I hope they are still unaware of being trailed. They've no rear guard, the Scouts say.

A runner comes back, "Hold up! Hold up!" The Sioux band and horse herd are camped in a grassy saucer. Stopping now, the band is probably not as near to a large band as I had begun to believe.

I figure we have three quarters of the darkest hour before daybreak, time enough for half of the boys to get around to the other side, to prevent the band's escape.

While they circle around, we edge up, not too close, and pinch our mounts' nostrils down so they can not nicker to the Indians' grazing ponies.

The Indians are alarmed—whether by some of their horses whinnying to the ponies of the boys going into position, or by a sneeze or neigh from the Pawnees' mounts.

In the next few seconds the band grabs up guns or bows, gets on horses, and starts out of there, ending my hopes of a bloodless capture.

We move fast to break cover, myself riding in advance. The Indians see my uniform—it's enough to convince them we are but a few soldiers. Breaking their flight, wheeling aside to take cover on a low hill, they begin shooting down on us from rocks and trees.

The Pawnees rush in from the other side and behind me, beating their chests and howling their shrill war yell, "Ki-de-de-de-de. . .!"

Indians scramble for cover, freeze in their tracks.

"*Pani! Pani!*" They shriek and scatter.

Happenstance favors the Pawnee as they search out every enemy warrior, and start the entire band, the Cheyenne women with them, and the travois rider, to the Happy Hunting Ground. It is not the result I hoped for!

Among the plunder we find scalps taken from white people, and clothing of women and children, probably of some pioneer immigrant train. There are trappings that are unmistakably United States government property, taken from mail stages and army vehicles: harnesses and parts, blankets, ammunition. They were heavily loaded with loot. Many of the horses and mules they were herding show the government brand.

I believe these were among the attackers at Platte Bridge, and of the wagon train that failed to reach the stockade.

For the Scouts, it is a victory, as I'm sure it is from the military view; anyhow, it's a day's work.

As we are on nearly ridden-out mounts, edging country that is the stronghold of thousands of Sioux and Cheyenne, we don't dawdle. The boys catch up horses from the herd we are driving ahead, to shift saddles, though these, too, have had about as much trail as they are good for. Shifting from horse to horse was the secret of the band's long, fast travel and is the method of our return to Camp Connor, though five of our horses fall and die on the way back.

With the last of daylight we ride in. The arms, evidence, and loot we bring along, packed on mules. The Pawnees cut willow poles to carry the scalps. Nearing camp they start yelling and whooping. Nick Janis and Jim Bridger, knowing the whoops tell of victory, explain it to General Connor.

He forms up double lines for us to march between, and the Scouts strut their stuff, whooping and chanting. The general is pleased, and uses some handsome words in saying so.

I turn the evidence over to the general, and make my report. We were in the saddle about thirty-two hours, without eating about thirty-six hours. We had taken no rations on what we supposed would be but a short chase.

We eat, and the boys ask permission to celebrate in their way, which the general gives. I assign my corporals to keep them in line, and I turn into quarters. The Pawnee dance and chant around a big fire almost all night, with most of the soldiers watching.

For the second night the scouts are celebrating, this time with a general name-changing, as Pawnee warriors do after a victory. It reminds me of the party games of "Musical Chairs," and "Fruit Basket Upset."

They invite me to choose a new name for myself, though I'm satisfied with my own as well as those the Pawnee call me. "Ski-ri-Taka"[3] compliments and honors me; "Father" is their term of respect, though the scouts are near my own age; only White Eagle is a few years older.

They insist that I must have a new name; I ask them to choose one for me, and they promote me to Pani La Shar (Pawnee Chief). Declining the chief part, I accept it as Pawnee Leader, feeling honored and proud.

Also, I am indebted, expected to give them a present after receiving the new name.

General Connor and staff officers inspect the captured material. Excepting for evidence of massacres, government articles, and animals wearing the United States brand, he gives the entire lot to the Scouts, with the rest of the captured animals, after giving me my choice of a horse. That horse is my present to the Pawnees.

19

August 17, 1865. Although the expected supply train hasn't come, the general is shoving the command on today. The two companies of the sixth Michigan Cavalry will stay to garrison this new post.[1]

I send three moderately ailing scouts, and my orderly as guard, in a company wagon with the army train. Somehow my orderly gets a pistol ball through his head. Suspicion flares—war threatens between the Pawnee bands. They are closely related and loyal, brotherly to their own band, though the four bands are one nation. The orderly happened to be of the Chaui, or Grand band.

The scout who caused the accident is a Skeedee or Skidi, of the Wolf band, from which the nation takes the symbol and uses the sign: two fingers pointed forward from a fist, imitating wolf ears.

The Chaui all come up bristling, ready to believe the killing was intentional. I question the two groups—put it to them plain and sharp.

I find that no one knows of any bad feeling in recent years between the two bands, and none between the two men. Neither do I find there was any quarreling between the two, no known enmity nor cause for killing. It is a simon-pure accident. While describing the fracas we had a few days ago with the Sioux band, the scout got so excited he accidentally set off his trigger. It was just that, and nothing more. He and all my scouts must have further arms instruction.

After a Christian funeral with military honors, the bands are mollified, plainly seeing through my interpretation for them that white men, too, honor and pray to the "Great Spirit." The burial service, therefore, honors their God, and all Pawnee.

A system of leaders exists, apart from my appointments, within the Pawnees' ancient brotherhoods, secret clubs or lodges in which warriors pass through various periods of service, grazing and grooming ponies of those already in higher warrior rank. I am impressed when these leaders, in talking with their bands, conclude they are punished by Atius Tirawa, the Great Spirit, for not giving honor due Him for victory over the Sioux.

August 25, 1865. Scouts report many Indians, and my command is ordered out after them. We find three sizable groups within a few miles.

During our effort to encircle them, we are discovered. They begin shooting arrows at us. We engage in a running fight, but the Scouts' horses just aren't up to it—are soon tiring, slowing, not a burst of speed left in them.

The lagging end of my command is in trouble! Indians are closing in on them—cutting them off.

We scratch like everything to beat the savages, then run them again. As I am riding a borrowed mount, a good and quite fresh horse, he carries me well up toward the Cheyennes, gaining ground on them, and putting distance between me and my men.

I stop and jump off to take a crack at the closest Indians, then get on and turn back. The minute I turn my back, a flock of Cheyenne race up, letting off a feathered volley as they pass me.

My horse is hit by an arrow. He falters, stumbles, recovers, then falls. I light free and lay low, the horse between me and the Cheyenne, as they come back, whooping. The ground around me looks like a pin cushion full of arrows after they pass this time.

I tear out, aiming my carbine at one and then another, saving my ammunition. Then I remember I left my forty-fours on the saddle. I've got to have my side arms. I turn around and leg it back faster than I ran away.

Getting the horse between me and the Indians again feels right cozy. I urge the poor beast to his feet and we start moving. I don't actually believe I can keep the savages back much longer, I have so little ammunition. I dust the feathers of a couple of Cheyenne braves.

A horse and rider come up on a distant hill. I'm sure he is a soldier. I wave and beckon but he goes away. Again I talk to the horse—coax him on.

Lieutenant Small rides out from behind a low hill. The Indians break off and scoot away.

The Pawnees corner a chief in a ravine, and count coup on him as we come up. Cheyennes are still lurking around, and we soon discover more bands, some edging closer. They run when the scouts dash at them, then follow, gaining on the scouts as they turn back, like coyotes tag a farm dog after he runs them off.

Seeing we can't do much about this many Indians on our ridden-down nags, I send a message to General Connor asking for help.

He sends a courier with word that he is sending Colonel Kidd of the sixth Michigan Cavalry, with a detachment.

We hate to give our job over to this outfit, and when they come I ask the colonel if we may borrow enough of their fresher mounts to go on out and take the Cheyenne.

Nobody is about to get off strong horses, able to make a getaway in hostile Indian land. I offer to send some of my men to show them where the Indians are.

Lieutenant Murie, with a few Scouts, takes the detail. The remaining Scouts get back to the wagon camp, with my injured horse led, and all mounts dragging their tails, muzzles hanging low.

When Murie comes in, he says the colonel sent him and the Scouts ahead to locate the Indians. Upon going back to report, they found the colonel and his cavalry had skipped out and saw them in the distance, running for camp. I order Murie to report it all to General Connor.

After roll call this morning, the general leads all officers, including me, to Camp Connor. Anger flares up as he gives Colonel Kidd a dressing down!

We move with General Connor's force, down Crazy Woman Creek, then northward along the east slope of the Big Horn Mountains. This is the prettiest country a man could ever hope to lay eyes on, with plenty of fish and game, *ore-ka-rahr* (deer), and *wapiti* (elk). The scouts are in a state of awe, though mindful that they are deep in enemy country. Shaded by intertwined leafy twigs around their heads, or lining their hats with leaves, their watchful eyes penetrate the blue haze of distance.

Pawnees, riding along with me near the creek, see chokecherry trees with fruit hanging ripe and shiny black. They turn aside and ride in among the trees to pick and eat the puckery fruit.

"*Pits-u ca-ha! Pits-u ca-ha!*" Hornets! They yell, boiling out of there in a furious rush, flailing their arms with hats, guns, or bows. Some dive into the stream to escape stingers stirred up from an unnoticed hanging nest. Their horses also run from the swarming, buzzing, black hornets.

From a safe distance, I'm laughing. My scouts are a bit slow in rejoining me. Swelling bumps add to their look of ruefulness, but, comparing lumps they too howl and whoop with laughter.

August 28, 1865. We've moved down Tongue River two more days. Finding where a large band of Indians passed, my scouts tell me the trail is a half to three quarters moon old. Jim Bridger agrees the trail was made nearly three weeks ago.

"Arapahoe. Probably Old David and Chief Black Bear, with their bands."

General Connor orders me to investigate. I take ten scouts. About noon the boys see distant riders. I think they may see buffalo, but knowing of the scouts' sure vision, I accept their idea.

Working down a gully opening into the Tongue valley, we see an Indian village, too distant to judge its size or strength. I send Ke-Wuk La Shar, John Box, and Cot-te-ra-tet Goots, Struck with a Tomahawk, to get nearer the village.

We wait until they come back. They had slipped up close enough to count many lodges. When a woman carrying water walked in arm's reach of their hiding place, they held their breath to prevent her finding them.

I hope this is the time we may surprise the village and capture it. I send a note to General Connor, saying: "To be sure of bagging this village, I will need all the Pawnees sent to me, and at least one company of soldiers."

I say to As-San Ta-Ka, White Horse, and Coo-Towy-oots Co-ter ah-oos, Blue Hawk: "You are to take this message to General Connor. Go as fast as you can."

The Pawnees take turns watching the village. Toward dark we pull our horses back to graze, and keep a sharp lookout for the rest of my command.

By daybreak they're coming along the stream. They tell me the Grandfather (their term of respect for the general) asked White Horse and Blue Hawk how big the village is.

When they told him, through Murie, there are more horses than in his army, the general thought it best to come himself, bringing four times the number of horse soldiers I asked for.

Arriving, the general raps out questions like canister shots.

Over-all tactics, he decides, call for encirclement with demand for surrender. I am to get my Scouts around to the far side of the village within a half hour.

Not waiting half the agreed time, General Connor deploys his cavalry and artillery and advances across a half-mile slope from the stream to the village.[2]

Of course the troops are not within contact distance when discovered by Arapahoe. I do not get my Pawnees into position in time to close off the Arapahoe's escape. Every warrior rushes for his horse and takes off into the mountains.

Many rounds are shot into the village, though his general orders called for "No killing of females and children." Smashing into tepees, the fighting is carried into hand-to-hand combat, with women, children, and old men left behind.

Leaving a detail at the village, the general orders "Rally" trumpeted and then "Charge," and into the mountains he rides after the Arapahoe.[3] They just could be leading into a trap up there. When he gives it up and turns back, he's in trouble. Warriors shoot from behind sheltering trees and rocks, riding close on his flanks. It's a race back to the village, where he orders a piece of artillery dragged into place under Captain Nicklos O'Brien. Grapeshot drives the Arapahoe warriors back, yet many on horses circle in to shoot and flit out of range.

General Connor orders the village destroyed. Through the afternoon and half the night soldiers pile up buffalo robes, dried and stored foodstuff, garments worked with beads and quill embroidery, and stores of moccasins.

The one Winnebago scout we lost is wrapped in a hide and placed on the piles and the torch put to everything.

Bringing some twenty captured women away and our wounded on travois fashioned by my Scouts, we march back to the wagon train. The Arapahoe warriors dodge in to nip arrow or shoot at us, try to stampede the seized horses—upwards of a thousand, a good third of the Arapahoe herd—and try to rescue their tied-together women.

They've lost arrows for their bows in the flames, along with ammunition for guns. As the Pawnees get onto strong fresh ponies from the driven herd, they are able to fight off the Arapahoe.

Nick Janis questions the Arapahoe women in Sioux, which a few understand, and relays the general's order to them:

"Tell Black Bear I command him to go, within this month, and take his tribe to Fort Laramie. I send him a letter to carry to the commanding officer of the fort, instructing him to provide for Black Bear's tribe. You are to tell Black Bear if he does not go to the fort as I order him to do, I shall hunt him and all his band down, and kill every one."

Nick says General Connor is sending the women back with rations and a peace offering of tobacco for Black Bear. Each woman is allowed to select a horse from those seized. They prove their horse sense; all ride away on the best sixteen out of the herd.

20

General Connor waited an extra week for the supply train that hasn't come, and has lost more time going after the Arapahoe. He is late in getting to the Rosebud River to rendezvous with Colonels Cole and Walker.

August 30, 1865. We push down Tongue River, the scouts ranging wide, on the lookout for Indians, and, especially, to watch for the Cole column.

September 1, 1865. A sound like a distant shot indicates the other column may be near.[1] General Connor sends out a detachment to meet the Cole-Walker command. They return without finding any sign of it. General Connor continues pushing north toward the rendezvous.

September 8, 1865. We reach the Yellowstone River. The general orders me out to find the lost command. I start with twenty scouts, in a hard rain that doesn't let up all day. We cover about thirty miles. Finding a protecting canyon with shelter for our horses, we make camp.

September 9, 1865. Rain turned in the night to a cold sleet storm that continues today. Sleet belts our faces. Our horses turn away if reins are slackened, and we have to force them along. Unable to see any distance, we travel by pocket compass. We make camp early. Miles today, I guess at ten.

September 10, 1865. Morning sun is bright and warming. Sleet is all melted by noon. We kill enough meat today to last the trip. Lots of Indian signs about. Scouts report a large Indian encampment along the river.

We go into a mountain canyon for cover. With a couple boys, I climb up to have a look around. I see Indians moving down below, and smoke rises from trees, but no trace of the Cole command.

After nightfall, we go to investigate the Indian camp. We cross the river and find the Cole trail—not more than three or four days old. We follow under a dark sky the leading scout tracking on foot. A hundred and fifty rods beyond the Indian camp we come onto dead horses and mules. Exploring around we soon realize there are hundreds of dead horses about.

The Pawnees are bewildered, as am I. The only thing the Scouts can think to say is, "*Ter ad eda! Ti war uks-ti!*" Enemy magic. Pawnee hands search the dead horses and find shots in the head had killed many.

Stumbling onto ash heaps, we kick out harness and wagon irons, bridle bits, and rings of saddles. It looks like Indian work, but we find no bodies, nor trace of burials.

We go back upriver and spy on the Indian camp, a temporary setup that I had thought might be a village. With but fifty men and a sizable hostile Indian camp near, this is no spot for me. I move out toward General Connor's camp on Tongue River. We ride all night and all day, with short rests, reaching the Connor camp by dark.

When I report the weird discoveries, the general fails to piece it together, and Bridger and Janis are just as puzzled.

With the Connor command, we march upriver for several days. Slowed by the wagons, we aren't making near as fast time as I traveled with the scouts.

September 17, 1865. General Connor is convinced the other column must be starving. He commands me, with as many scouts as I think best, to take pack mules with two weeks' rations and try again to find Cole's column. We set out, and come to the Powder River a little past noon. Further on, the scouts find Colonel Cole's trail. Against orders, he's going upriver, instead of down.

I send scouts to carry a message, informing the general the Pawnee think the trail is about three days old, that I expect to find the Cole force within as many days, and will then bring them to meet him at Clear Creek.

We again ride up trail. Twice we pass sites of night camps, where more animals died, starved, weak and exhausted. We see them, too, fallen and dead along the trail. Some look to have been partly skinned with flesh cut away. Now the buzzards and vultures are at work too. It is plain that Cole's force is starving and lost.

Two hours from midnight we camp and picket our horses. I now know the scouts were mistaken in guessing the trail only three days old.

Another day passes, much like yesterday except that we are oftener forced to rest our tiring horses.

After traveling another twenty miles, I sight wavering columns creeping along in the hazy distance. We urge our flagging horses forward and come up to the command before sundown.

As startled as if we had dropped from the sky, they greet us with weak cheers, and hats tossed into the air.

Ah, what a sight! Men, ragged and tottering, lead what horses they have; the scarecrow cavalry is walking! Most of the horses cannot stand under a rider, although the best still carry the sick, wounded, and crippled.

Cavalrymen march in boots not rugged enough for cactus, razor-edged soapwood, and gravel of mountain granite.

The men crowd around us for rations. I order my scouts to give each soldier two crackers of hardtack, and to divide the sugar, coffee, sowbelly, and beans by small handfuls.

Leaving Lieutenant Small with the scouts, I hunt up Colonels Cole and Walker, and tell them they are not far from help. I explain to Colonel Cole, "I sent word to General Connor, when we struck your trail, I would bring you and your command to meet him on Clear Creek. But you're not more than twenty or twenty-five miles from Camp Connor, the new post the general put up, though about forty miles from Clear Creek. In the condition of your command, I think it best to take you to the new post."

Colonel Cole agrees, and decides to send two of the ablest four-mule teams, wagons, and drivers with an officer, carrying a requisition for supplies. I send along thirty scouts with Lieutenant Murie to guard them.

The camp settles down for the night. Thin blue curls of smoke from many small fires drift up as the soldiers prepare their bits of food.

Hauling out tobacco, I offer it to the colonels. We fill our pipes and I ask Colonel Cole: "What has happened to your command, and why are you going upriver when you were expected to travel in the opposite way to cross over to Tongue River and go to Wolf Mountain, where you were supposed to get the cache of rations before going on to rendezvous on the Rosebud?"

The colonel says, "It's an incredible tale. To begin, I'm sure no man responsible for mapping my route knew anything of the topography and geography of the country through which I was directed. I doubt any white man has ever before set eyes on the hellish desert we passed through.[2]

"Week after week traveling northwesterly, the wagons sank deep into sand, dragging heavily on the draft teams. After we crossed the Loup rivers where the courier came bringing me General Connor's orders, conditions worsened. Wagons often sank to the hubs in sand, requiring as many as could get a hand on the drag ropes to help the horses. Water was seldom found, and often brackish, or covered with scum or bitter with alkali.

Dysentery, colic, and scurvy plagued us from bad water, wormy bacon, and molded hardtack, and just exhaustion and dehydration from the merciless sun and wind.

"Gulches had to be bridged. Wagons and animals mired in quicksand.
Cut banks, ravines, and streams upset wagons, resulting in spilled and lost
rations. Once I turned south thinking to find better terrain. Perhaps I was
somewhat confused as to direction. It is a vast desert and weird bad land.
The guides and scouts knew little about the region.[3]

"The beasts would drop in harness and die, from heat exhaustion, from
overwork, from alkali colic, from starvation.

"My men died from like causes and from scurvy and pellagra. I
eventually hesitated to order "Dismount" for rest periods, as men became
so fatigued, starved, and weak that upon getting off the horses, they would
squat in the horses' shade, dazed, and not sufficiently alert to get water for
themselves and mounts. I saw it was imperative to drive hard to move
from the burning sand.

"Passing along the east side of the Black Hills, the perpendicular banks
of the Cheyenne River necessitated letting the wagons down, and helping
them up on the other side by use of drag ropes and manpower, of which
my command was in short supply. But with water and grass the command
revived to some extent. Leaving the upper end of the Black Hills, I
thought our hell was behind us, as we headed toward the Little Missouri.
Colonel Walker's force joined us, ragged and thin, poorly outfitted and
inadequately equipped; but for all that fit and able compared to my own
command.

"Few traces of Indians had been seen, although we had become so
intent on survival that signs may have been overlooked. However, now
many Indian trails were seen, all in the general direction the command
was moving. We passed through a large Indian cemetery of corpses on pole
scaffolds, or lashed to tree branches.

"After crossing the Little Missouri, Little Powder, and Powder rivers,
new courage was felt in approaching the Tongue River and Panther
Mountain, where promised supplies were to have been cached.[4]

"Struggling up the shale slopes, Walker's men and my command found
no way down but by the way we had ascended. I'm sure no cache could
have been deposited at the mountain by the creek. We found nothing.

"I do not understand why the general indicated on his map and wrote
me assurance the cache would be in that place. His map is confusing.[5]

"Considering my command's worsening condition and loss of so much
time, I thought it advisable to turn back (south) to the Powder River. I
hoped to pass on south to the North Platte and the main road to obtain
help at a military post."

I break the silence. "Another mystery which you may clear for me. In
looking for you my scouts found places where hundreds of horses died.
Some had been shot—many showed poor conditions but we saw no cause

for so many dying."

"Yes, when we crossed back to Powder River, small groups of Indians continually harassed the columns. When we tried to repulse them, detachments were trapped in the chase, as our weakening mounts were so slow. We discovered infiltrations of our unhorsed cavalry by Indians in army uniforms, probably taken from dead soldiers. After the discovery, I turned the howitzers on the savages and they disappeared.

"The next day, Indians attacked again. We skirmished four or five hours until a sudden hail storm and a hard rain discouraged the savages. Many of our horses died that day and night.

"The Indians repeated the attack the following day, this time in large numbers—I believe as many as twenty-five hundred or three thousand. Intermittent fighting continued all day despite sleet and rain.

"I ordered withdrawal to a flat area, away from woods which might conceal ambush. Securing the mounts to tie ropes in double rows, they formed a shield against the enemy who withdrew.

"During the night the temperature dropped low, with sleet and snow falling. Many horses, overheated and exhausted during the day, died. Many still standing in the morning were so stiff they could not be moved out of their tracks. I ordered them shot. Flesh was cut off and eaten at once. The men subsisted three weeks on horse meat."

It strikes me there was poor horsemanship, if not poor generalship, through the whole march. Too many hard-driven miles in the early weeks, through the Loup River sand country, sapped, instead of hardening, the strength of horses and men.

More attention to finding springs, and to digging in stream beds to find water underground, could have made the difference for Colonel Cole's expedition.

Colonel Cole had no Jim Bridger to conduct him, and his own information and instruction was too scant and faulty; the Cole-Walker command suffered from more than one man's misjudgment.

We break camp early to move toward Camp Connor. Sighting the relief wagons returning with escort, I send Pawnees to take a note to General Connor, explaining the Cole command is moving to Camp Connor.

September 24, 1865. I ride out from Camp Connor a half day, to meet the general. His command and two hundred wagons loaded with rations and ammunition, follow at a slower rate.

Concerned about the Cole command and its whereabouts as the general was, he's surprised when I tell him in what a sad condition the soldiers are, after living on horse meat for three weeks.

In General Connor's wagons there are few boots or shoes. There is no supply of clothing or blankets. The expected supply train never came into this country.

"By Gar, them's gotta be Red Cloud's Sioux; got their hangout along the Powder river, beyond," Nick Janis declares, and Jim Bridger agrees.[6]

Though wanderers, without permanent villages such as the Pawnee have, the Sioux's stomping ground is the southern Big Horn Mountains and these rivers.[7]

If Colonel Cole had gone further down the Powder River, as was his final plan, his troops most surely would have been killed by Red Cloud's thousands of warriors.

Mail comes in under heavy escort, the first since we came north. It reaches the stockade gate of Camp Connor just as General Connor, with his staff, and Jim Bridger, Nick Janis, and I arrive. The mail sacks are emptied and rolled up—too soon! Many are disappointed.

Word comes from the mail escort, probably picked up from the Fort Laramie grapevine, that General Connor was sent a sharp reprimand by General Pope for the "extermination" order.

21

After morning roll call, General Connor issues surprise orders: "Prepare to return to Fort Laramie." Privately the general commends me for the Scouts' service, saying their work is outstanding. He explains he is ordered to turn his District of the Plains over to General Frank Wheaton at Fort Laramie.

With his staff officers, the general rides in army ambulance to Fort Laramie. Captain Kidd and his force continue to garrison this post. Colonels Cole and Walker are bringing in the combined command. The scouts work as usual, and picket night camps.

More than five hundred ill or crippled soldiers ride in forty or fifty empty ordnance wagons. Many horseless cavalrymen, their feet in grass-padded wraps, as designed by the resourceful Scouts, take turns at walking as they're able, helped by willow poles or hanging alongside the wagons or to a stirrup for support.

My scouts report bands of hostile Indians coming south faster than the troops—after they were punished and shoved north from the Big Trail country before Connor pushed off for the Powder River. But that was months ago. The Indians are smarter now—maybe they believe they can yet throw white people out. The Indian goes to war with not more than a parfleche of corn and dried meat and a full quiver. His horse is strong, durable and able. Its strength is not paid out for its provision, as army horses must drag their grain feed behind them.

In the long miles to Fort Laramie the command follows the deep grooved ruts of Bozeman road south to the Oregon-California Trail where ruts have multiplied and widened.

October 12, 1865. Coming into the fort from wilderness and desert, meeting again the military routine of reveille, stable, retreat, and lights out, brings a feeling of safety and rest.

General Frank Wheaton, regular army, replacing General Connor, informs me he can offer two choices for the Scouts, as their enlistment time is ended. We can muster out and return home, or we can relieve a

101

contingent of the seventh Iowa Cavalry stationed at the Pawnee
Reservation. The last is a lucky break for the Scouts, paying them for
protecting the reservation and living in their own lodges, and so I accept
it. Command of the reservation post falls to me. I also receive a
government license as the Pawnee Reservation trader.

October 16, 1865. The Pawnee and I light a shuck further north than
the Mormon Trail to the reservation, four hundred miles due east. Just
after we leave, we again pass the dried cadavers of Two Face and Black
Foot, hanging from the scaffold.

After a few days' travel we get deeper into the grassland: cured, standing
forage of blue stem and gramma, belly-deep to a horse. Our mounts and
the horse herd we are driving fill up.

Sumac drapes cutbanks and ravine edges with bright, fall reds. Along
the streams, gold cottonwoods and browning willows do their annual
dance of solemn undress. Around the horizon hangs a cobweb haze. In this
gentle mood, the Scouts pick and eat frosted sloe-plums while the horses
graze.

Nights are getting pretty frosty for sleeping on the ground. It's going to
feel mighty good to lie again on a cornshuck-stuffed tick bed, cushioned
by one of Mother's wild-goose feather ticks, and her crazy quilt comforts.

Every scout, except the orderly killed by the accidental shot, is coming
home. None are hurt, other than stings and scratches. They say Tirawa
always protects Pani La Shar (me), and as they are my command, He
protects them, too. "Cha-hik si cha-hiks," Pawnee call themselves, and my
scouts are not less than "men of men."

A half mile from the reservation the scouts begin whooping it up,
imitating attacking Sioux. It brings everybody on the reservation to
attention, and all the warriors and garrison of soldiers mount their horses.

With guidons flying and scalps aloft on willow poles, the scouts chase in
a dead run onto the reservation. They whoop the driven horses (given
them by the general after battles, with some they traded around for) into
pole pens.

Showing off their good government mounts, saddles, gear, and their
trophies, the scouts have a victory parade. They are received by their
home folks with the same wild enthusiasm.

The scouts strut in their uniforms, which are nevertheless much the
worse for wear.

The gleeful, jolly uproar will continue tonight with feasting and dancing
around a big fire. Then the returned warriors will illustrate, to the beat of
drums with gestures and poses, the story of their scouting.

But the scouts happened upon an unfortunate day for their victorious
return. There have been changes on the reservation. Mr. Lushbaugh was
replaced in July by Mr. Wheeler. The new agent has just completed giving

a series of lectures, with Baptiste Behale, a French half-breed, interpreting. These talks are based on Quaker idealism—and ignorance. The object is to break down authority of the sixteen tribal chiefs.

The agent expects in this way to remove any remaining "bars" to speed "civilizing and Christianizing" the tribe.

"Pawnee hunters must have a responsible white caretaker with them," they are told. The Indians readily agree to this, having tested and found it to be advantageous to them.

"Pawnee men must stop stealing horses." The stolen *Kansa* horses must be taken back where they were "found." But Indian take horses back? Besides, didn't the braves bring horses the Great White Father paid them to take?

"Pawnee men must learn to raise crops, must till the land, must do the field work instead of their women." That edict really blows the feathers in the air! For a man to say men must do squaw's work proves his head is wrong.

While the women snicker and titter, the men get madder and madder. The tribal chiefs assemble, gravely ponder, considering what to do about this threat to their traditional way of life.

December 4, 1865. Riding through the Pit-a-hau-rat village of the reservation at sunset, I see young Koot-tah-we-Coots-ah-Pah, Red Hawk, ground tie three ponies before the Pit-a-hau-rat Chief Ter-ra-re-Caw-Wah's lodge. He doesn't speak to me, being intent on more important business. He sits down outside the lodge and pulls his blanket over his head, as indication of his meekness and modesty.

He is declaring himself a suitor for the chief's daughter, Miss Bright Lance—a thrifty-looking lass, with muscles beginning to bulge; a good squaw wife must be strong.

Red Hawk will sit there for some time, with his head covered, speaking to no one, and go away to come back tomorrow, and two or three more days the same, according to Pawnee custom. About the fifth time he returns, he will go inside, still without words, but will not be misunderstood. He will take the same humble pose in the back of the lodge.

If approved as a son-in-law and if he is giving as many ponies as are wanted, the girl's father or some other male relative of the girl invites him to sit up by the fire. The girl then goes out, takes the horses away, and puts them with her father's herd.

With these signs of acceptance, his friends give gifts to the father-in-law-to-be and Koot-tah-we-Coots-ah-Pah becomes a married man, to live with his wife in her father's lodge. He will marry each daughter of the chief (I believe there are three) as she comes to marriageable age, which will cost him a horse for each.

Red Hawk looks man enough, being well over six feet in height, but he is unusually young, not more than seventeen. The old chief is still in fine fettle, so Red Hawk will not have all responsibility of providing meat, robes, and defense. Perhaps there's a bit of social climbing in the lad, marrying the chief's daughter. I wish him success in his courtin', my own being assured.

Miss Mary said "Yes," though if she had known how cowardly I felt she might have decided different. I was worse scared than I've ever been in my life! Miss Mary's not very big, and never very fierce.

She has set our wedding to take place on Christmas day in her uncle's home in Columbus. A preacher is coming to hold meetin's in the schoolhouse, and he will marry us. I've already bought a wedding band that will make Miss Mary L. Smith my wife.

Finishing my errand, I turn Jinks toward his stable. As we jog along, we pass Indian children playing in late twilight this short December day. Pawnee boys, imitating the United States Army Pawnee Scouts, form ranks to drill and march. I linger a while, watching their play. It's a new game since return of the scouts. The boys play it with the same objective as their warrior practice games, and, as in those games, carry small bows and quivers of arrows for killing rabbits, birds, and small game.

I lift the reins and Jinks moves on. Nearby a "sentinel's" voice declares "Hap'ast o-clock! All's well, go tell."

22

January 1, 1866. We are preparing for housekeeping. I dispossess a colony of field mice and a large owl and clear last year's bird nests out of the chimney and chuck cracks between logs of the trader's cabin. Mary puts a sheet against the wall and hangs her dresses beside my clothes.

A military order interrupts things. I am to send fifty scouts to join an expedition going into the Republican River country. James Murie,[1] second lieutenant on the Powder River trip now promoted to first lieutenant, will lead the company. Luther asks me to permit him to go along. He's no tenderfoot. Four years ago he enlisted in the second Nebraska Cavalry and went, under Colonel Furnas and General Sully, against the Sioux in Dakota Territory.[2] I am not authorized to hire him to serve as an officer with the scouts, but he can go with them.

I take them to Fort Kearny where they're in luck. A company is mustering out and I am able to get their Spencer seven-shot rifles.[3] Heading southwest from Fort Kearny with two companies of mounted soldiers and supporting wagons, teamsters, and helpers, they hit for the Republican Valley.[4] I hustle home.

In about a month the expedition returns to Fort Kearny with Lute riding in the ambulance wagon. When he is able to come home he tells the story.

"We hit the Republican River, traveled up about twenty miles and camped to stay until we scouted all around. I usually rode along on the scouts and hunted as I liked.[5] Every plum thicket hides deer and cottontails. Groves of hackberry and ash that grow in the slues and rough breaks are wild turkey roosts, and elk run out of the willow and cottonwood brush along the streams. Red Fox squirrels come out of their hollows in the cottonwoods to lie in the sun on little platforms built of twigs and dry leaves. We didn't see an Indian anywhere.

"One day the C.O. ordered Murie to send scouts south to see if they could find any trace of Indians. I offered to go in Murie's stead and he let me. We rode south until about midafternoon we crossed a dry-wash (dry creek bed) and went on up a hill. Just then we saw a hundred and fifty Indians about the same time they saw us and came at us.

"I didn't feel uneasy. We were riding strong, grain-fed horses, and the scouts carried the best carbines in the world and plenty of rounds for them. I carried my own Ballard rifle.[6] The Indians looked to have mostly bows. I told the scouts we'd gallop back to take cover on the banks of the dry-wash. It was so cold I didn't think the Indians would stay long.

"Halfway back, my horse slipped on a patch of ice and fell and my head hit on the ice—knocked me plumb out. The first thing I knew was that Nick Koots (a scout) was rubbing my face with snow. The next thing I realized was that the Indians had rushed up and surrounded us.

"The scouts were outnumbered about fifteen to one and on good mounts could have got away, but not a one of them ran—stayed by me to a man—dismounted and stood around me and Nick, and from behind their horses fought the Sioux off. I wasn't giving orders and no other white man was there to order them. They did it because they chose to.

"The scouts held the circling, charging Cheyennes until I could sit up, then Nick Koots helped me onto my horse. As we began to withdraw, the Indians charged in; then we would whip around to fight them. During such an attack they pulled a sneak on us and those on the farther flanks closed in and beat us to the dry-wash. When we made the last hitch of running for the creek, the scouts' Spencers scattered them and they left the creek bed. After that, they made a few charges but had learned our Spencers' range. I laid down under the bank while the scouts kept the Indians off. About sunset, the Indians rode off.[7]

"The scouts pulled the arrows out of their horses—four dead, three hurt, had to be shot, then loaded me on a horse and we traveled back to camp. I reported, and the commanding officer ordered pursuit of the Indians. About that time a courier from Fort Kearny came into camp with a dispatch recalling the outfit."

April 1, 1866. My entire scout command, myself, and officers are mustered out. It is just in time, as I hired a man who knows his hides and pelts and how to buy them for my agency store. I can do the freighting, and tend to farming.

Luther is all right again and working for brother James on his contract to get out timbers for bridge piling. The Union Pacific is bridging the Loup. Rails are coming west at a great rate. It had only built forty miles, until they started this spring. They're laying ties and track at the rate of one and a half miles a day. Congress says that by December 1867 the railroad must reach the 100th meridian just west of Fort Kearny. Since Gen. Jack Casement and his brother, Dan, took over, it looks like they just may do it.

When the planting of corn is finished, I grease my wagon wheel axles to do some freighting. One load I bring this far for John P. Becker, one of the first Ohio Germans here. I send Luther to the Platte Forks[8] where Becker is starting another store ahead of the railroad's coming.

On his way back, Lute stops near Brady Island at Boyd and Harper's grading camp, and hires on with the team, moving dirt for grading the roadbed.

"When we finished the one mile grading contract and moved the last slip off, the tie layers were right on our tails," Luther tells us.

I'm swinging the scythe—haying time. Luther works with me, rakes the windrows into haycocks. We find what the meadow larks' chorus is all about—canopies interwoven of taller grass bent and fashioned to hide the nest so well my eye barely detects it ahead of the scythe stroke.

Antelope stalk near as they dare and turn their big ears on us. They never seem to satisfy their curiosity—come back daily to investigate.

We are nooning in the hay-wagon shade. Lute gets to his feet, raises our water jug but doesn't drink.

"Frank, Indians—a bunch—riding this way." He gets his Ballard from the front of the hay wagon.

"Never mind, Lute, they're Pawnee," I tell him, beginning to see them plainer. The tribe's chiefs—all sixteen of them. They're looking very solemn, I see as they ride up.

"Lau! Lau!" We greet them.

"Lau, Lau, Lau," each of the sixteen answers.

We shake hands and sit in the hay-wagon shade. Seeing that Peta La Shar is carrying the stone calumet pipe, my concern grows. He fills it, smokes, and passes it around for each to take a draft.

Ti-ra-wat La Shar, Sky Chief or Spirit Chief, of the Kit-ke-haki band stands up.

"Pani La Shar is a great warrior-brave. He is our white chief. Pawnee chiefs come to him, Pani La Shar will tell us what is right to do."

The chiefs had counseled about a problem, trying to forestall trouble between bands. When they could not reach an agreement, Sha-tah-lah La Shar, suggested they take it to Pani La Shar.

The Skeedees had been out on the hunt three quarters of a moon, and away from other bands. They failed to find buffalo. The hungry people were on the Little Blue River when Ska-dik, Crooked Hand, had run across a hidden store of meat and recognized the cache as belonging to the three other Pawnee bands—the Chaui or Grand, the Pit-a-hau-rat, and the Kit-ke-haki. It was wrapped in partially treated (brain and ash softened) dry hides. Crooked Hand unwrapped the sliced, sun-dried buffalo meat and gave of it to all of his people.

After this the band began to find buffalo and finally were able to make all the meat their ponies could pack home. Getting back to the reserve, their head chief, Eagle Chief, didn't go to the Skeedee village, but went to Peta La Shar's lodge to tell that the cache had been found and used before the other tribes could learn of it. The two agreed to call a council of all the chiefs to decide whether the tribe should pay, and if so, how much.[9]

This is not Pawnee custom. The Nation's way is that those who have what others need, share. It is shared, always, if there are those who need. However, the chiefs are convinced it is necessary now for their people to come to the white man's way. They are asking me to make this a kind of pattern for all the Pawnee.

Ska-dik has a blazing temper that kindled when the suggestion was made that the Skeedees should pay. The chiefs say Crooked Hand[10] says the Skeedees will not pay.

As members of delegations to St. Louis and to Washington, D.C., these men have picked up considerable knowledge of the white man's ways. They have had some schooling in trading pelts and hides. I think Eagle Chief was rejecting the Pawnee way when he crossed the river and went directly to the head chief. Somehow they saw this as a chance to lead their people along the new way they must go. I think there was never any question among them that it is right to pay. Their main concern, while unspoken, is that the chiefs have no wish to offend the old warrior, Crooked Hand.

Their hearts are all good. I cannot fault Ska-dik for sticking to the old custom but I see, too, they must learn to cope with other peoples' ways.

I speak in their form and language: "Man Chief (Peta La Shar) great head chief of the Pawnee Nation; Great Chiefs of each Pawnee band; my brothers; friends. Today your Pani leader is very honored that the Pawnee chiefs, even some aged, ride so far to visit with him about this. You are wise in trying to cure the trouble before it starts and I want to help you. Yes, I will tell you what I think is right. But my word is not your law. You then must still decide among you if this is right and what you want to do.

"No one denies that the meat was taken and used by hungry people. It is no crime. These people then began to find buffalo and made meat and have plenty. Now they can repay the debt of meat they owe the other tribes. It may be that by repaying what is owed to them, none will come to want. Since I do not know how much meat was taken from the cache I will name four men, one from each band,[11] to enquire of the amount taken which the Skeedees owe and which they will then return in good measure."

"*Loo ah! Loo ah!*" Good. Good, all approve. "Pani La Shar speaks the good," they say, then get on their ponies and ride away. I learned of the payoff later. Lone Chief tells me that when Crooked Hand was told Pani

La Shar's decision, he simply agreed to it.

In June the railroad comes, tie by tie and rail by rail, as the frontier moves west with the worktrain. Only ten years ago this settlement began, out by itself on the prairie. Now with the railroad here, and telegraph, Columbus is as well served as anywhere. The rails were laid so fast the "Hell-on-Wheels"[12] tent city hardly had time to light. At this rate the Casement gangs will be beyond the 100th meridian by December, a year ahead of the congressional deadline.[13]

Columbus is all excited, getting ready to welcome the 100th Meridian Pioneer Excursion train. Workmen clear grounds for a one-night tent city, setting up privies and posts for lanterns.

Columbus people have watched all afternoon for the train, but the sun has set and there is still no sight of it. We wait and wait, then at last out of the gathering twilight come two powerful locomotives, each flag and motto-banner draped. The last car, that of the directors, has a porch at the end and carries the Congressmen and the very most important, money and industry-wise, people who want a close look at the Union Pacific road, its bridges and ground structures, depots, water and wood stations, and the country and soil the road runs through.

The second car from the end with the big eagle medallion on the side was built for President Lincoln. It is Mr. Durante's property now, and his close friends and family ride in it. An express car is fitted up for smoking and refreshment. Four passenger coaches made in the Omaha car shops are filled with invited excursionists. The kitchen cook car and two baggage cars also carry equipment and tents.

The tent city grounds are lighted and all the people are going to a big tent where hustling waiters can be seen, and from which we catch wonderful smells, but we are feasting our eyes now.

A harvest moon blooms up. Campfires blaze around the clearing and "entertainment" is announced by a crier. Pawnees, hired and encamped near the bridge, come all painted and feathered to do their war dances. I see the boys are putting some extra yells and quirks into their dance. They're enjoying this, maybe more than the sightseers.

A grand joke is played on the excursionists by General Dodge, Mr. Durante, and Secretary Pollock and some others. Predawn quiet is smashed by hideous howls as the Pawnees go into their scalp dance in the hoarfrost around the dead campfires.

Financiers jump out of their tents in their nightshirts with firearms ready and women poke heads covered with curlers or nightcaps out to see if they have time to put on their stays before being scalped. Hearing the laughter of those responsible, they discover the Indians were the dancers of last night and everyone goes back to their pallets.

After breakfast, the tents, equipment, baggage, and passengers are reloaded and the train moves west. It is stopped on the approach to the Loup River bridge, in sight of the Pawnee encampment. Pawnee warriors seem to be in an excited council, unaware that another band—are they Sioux?—sneak out of the willow thicket downriver and are encircling the Pawnee camp.

Suddenly the Pawnee warriors jump on their ponies and follow their chief to attack, yelling the Pawnee war cry, answered by an inaccurate Sioux cry. Letting off arrows, side arms, and carbines in a great fusillade, the bands engage in collision of rearing horses and grappling warriors. Many excited horses run about. They don't understand that their riders have reverted to boyhood's make-like-war for the benefit of visitors.

Finally the "beaten Sioux" are fetched by the yelling Pawnee to be "tortured" by presents which Mr. Durante distributes liberally. Women and children come out of their tepee village. They wonder at the white ladies' odd dresses, the hoop skirts and polonaise, and little hats.

The photographer, Professor Carbutt, then takes pictures of the mounted warriors before the Lincoln and directors' cars, and the train moves over the bridge, westward.[14]

Lute helped me shuck our corn then went to stay a while with our uncle, J. C. North in Michigan, so he can go to college to learn bookkeeping.

OMAHA WEEKLY HERALD, January 10, 1867.—Report of progress on the Union Pacific railroad, which laid 239 miles of track in 1866, and was 305 miles from Omaha. The temporary winter terminus is North Platte, Nebraska Territory, the new town which with coming of the railroad was laid out by General Dodge between the Platte River forks. . . .

23

January 15, 1867. Robert Wilson and Ransel Grant, hired by John Rickly
to cut and haul wood for the Union Pacific railroad, chew a bone over
cord measurement—Wilson claims Grant took wood from his pile and put
it on his own. This morning Wilson walked up to Grant and shot him in
the lungs! This happened about twenty rods from the office of Speice and
my brother, James North. Wilson went into the Rickly store. Rickly was
busy and didn't look up.

"I shot a man," Wilson said. "I shot a man in Indiana (or Kentucky)
and had $1,400 and got clear. Take me before Judge Bill Little in
Omaha—I don't want to hang here. I've got $1,700, four wagons, and
fourteen yoke of oxen."

Mr. Rickly at first didn't believe him, but took him to a storehouse and
locked the door.

Rickly told Marshal John Brower about it. The two men took Wilson to
where the dead man lay. They placed Grant's body on the wagon.

The dead man's brother bought a coil of rope and with it over his
shoulder walked all over town and as far out as the old brewery block,
calling loud, "Who will help me avenge the blood of my brother?"

On this very day of the murder Leander Gerard went on an errand to
the Grant brothers. The conversation turned to Wilson—his
disagreeableness, his boasting that he had killed a man and that his money
had got him off. It's probable that at the time of the murder George Grant
spoke a good word for Wilson. After the murder George Grant went to
Gerard and tried to induce him to sign the death warrant.

A coroner's inquest was held before Justice Henry James Hudson[1] and a
trial for tomorrow morning.

January 16, 1867. At the trial before Justice Hudson the courtroom
is crowded. Wilson gets word to the Court that five hundred dollars will
be his if he, Wilson, is allowed the privilege of "sloping." But Mr.
Hudson knows what the public feeling is and keeps his eye on the

prisoner. O. T. B. Williams is the prosecuting attorney. C. A. Speice (partner in law with Mr. Williams) and C. C. Strawn are attorneys for the defense. The court decides to hold Wilson for murder in the first degree.

A citizens' "death warrant" has been widely signed, and as soon as the pronouncement is heard, a rush is made for the prisoner. He tries to break away from the sheriff, is grabbed and held, as are the sheriff and his deputy, Wash Fulton. A rope is thrown around Wilson.

The warrant reads: "Columbus, Nebraska Territory, January 16, 1867. We, the undersigned citizens of Columbus and vicinity having become duly informed of all the circumstances concerned with the shooting of Ransel B. Grant by a person calling himself Robert Wilson, and being fully satisfied that the murder was without provocation, and brutal in its character; and knowing the uncertainty of the law in the Territory, there being no safe place of confinement here, therefore we, for these reasons and others which might be mentioned, are firmly of the opinion that justice requires that the said Robert Wilson ought to be executed without delay."[2]

Wilson was dragged along the road toward a large[3] tree a few rods southeast of the courtroom, saying, "Boys, you don't give a fellow any chance." He was hoisted up the tree with help on the other end of the rope. The body was later cut down and dragged to the Loup River. A hole was chopped in the ice and Grant was shoved in, head first. The murderer's property in Butler County goes to the widow of the murdered man, and all his effects in Platte County are to be divided among the court officials.

The murderer's large white bulldog found his hat, jostled off as he was dragged along. The dog stayed with the hat and wouldn't allow anyone to come near. He was there for days but finally disappeared.

On the last day of February a communication came to the Pawnee Agency for me, from Major Litchfield, assistant adjutant general, saying that Maj. Gen. C. C. Augur, commander of the Department of the Platte, had authority to enlist Pawnees and wishes me to buy ponies to mount them.

March 1, 1867. This day Nebraska is a new state, the thirty-seventh star in Old Glory.

General Augur telegraphed for me to come to his office in Omaha. I go down on a worktrain to report to him.

The general speaks of the good work the Pawnee Scouts did under my leadership. "You made of them a valuable branch of the army," he says. "As the railroad projects further west, Indian harassment increases. I believe the Pawnee Scouts are best able to perform service as effective deterrents to the savages. Therefore I ask you to enlist two hundred Pawnees and organize two companies to be ready when spring opens to guard the grading and track laying crews and property, and surveying groups."

"Yes, sir, I think I can do this," I say to him. "But as I've served as a captain I think I deserve something better."

As the two hundred scouts are to be organized into four companies, forming a battalion, the general promises me the rank and pay of major. I telegraph Lute, offering him the fourth captaincy. The trick in selecting and enlisting the Pawnees (and drawing a full company from each band) comes in trying to explain that I cannot take more than a certain number.

Special order number 46, Department of the Platte, March 8, 1867, directs Maj. Lewis Merril to proceed to the Pawnee Agency to muster the Pawnee for service in the department.

Brother James buys my trading stock and takes over the store. Mother is matron at the Indian school again and Lizzie (sister Elizabeth) is teaching, with 'Phonsie assisting.

OMAHA DAILY HERALD, March 12, 1867—. . . Cold as . . . 20 below. Frost, snow and cloudy atmosphere. Readers, look hopeful that this weather don't last till the Fourth of July. . . .

I get my battalion organized and march them to the train at Columbus. A few had ridden the train before but to most it is a new experience. Jerks and bumps in the boxcar cause laughter and banter. The unexpected roar of passing over bridges quiets them for only the moment. We go into camp, near the fort. I found no acceptable horses or ponies at the reservation nor in the country around Columbus, so we await the mounts we lack. I draw clothes and arms, Springfield muzzleloaders and Colt revolvers with some ammunition—paper cartridges for the revolvers. We concentrate on drills and practice—keep the boys busy, and proud.

E. W. (Ed.) Arnold[4] is captain of Company A, the Chaui or Grand band; James Murie[5] captain, with Isaac Davis lieutenant, of B Company, Pit-a-hau-rats or Living Above (upstream) band; C. E. Morse[6] captain, with Fred Matthews[7] lieutenant, of Company C, Skeedee or Wolf band; and L. H. North (my younger brother) captain, with G. G. (Gus) Becher[8] lieutenant of Company D, Kit-ke-hakis, Republican or Noisy band.

April, 1867. Raw drizzle; when it isn't raining, clouds and cold wind. Underfoot the earth is spongy. When our mounts arrive, things liven up. The scouts attempt to gentle and ride their mounts and soon the bucking ponies have pitched half of the scouts so high it looks like birds could build nests in their pockets and raise their young before the boys come down to earth. For one thing, even a saddle-broke pony is likely to resent the left-side mounting of all Indians.

Big Hawk's[9] pony is fighting the cinch. Two scouts clamp their teeth in his ears—ear him down, freeing their hands to get a sack over his eyes, and clamp his nostrils down to limit his wind, while others knee him in the belly to knock the puff out of him, then jerk up the girth.

Big Hawk jumps for the saddle, at the same time signaling the boys to jerk off the sack. The animal kicks at the belly girth, shakes, twists, goes into a spin that gets his hoof into Big Hawk's off-side stirrup before Big Hawk's foot gets there. Instead of plunging into the rear and buck pitching, the horse sits back heavy to one quarter. Big Hawk jumps off, looks the situation over and laughs with us. The men uncinch the saddle, pry the hoof out of the stirrup, and begin all over.

Sun fishing, moon climbing, squealing, bawling, kicking, rolling, backflipping, raring, running ponies are all brought under control within a couple of days, by these able horsemen.

I take my battalion on a three-day shakedown march, to Fort McPherson. There we put up tents and lay over one day for rest and drying out clothes and blankets. Moving on upriver, we camp above and southwest of the Platte River forks and last winter's terminus camptown of the railroad.

The scouts discover that the Sioux chief, Spotted Tail, and eighteen hundred of his band were camped upriver, three or four miles above us. Suddenly they're all excited, eager to attack.

Calling the battalion together, I talk turkey to them. Most of these boys are just beginning to scout, after short training. Discipline is something they must yet learn.

"My friends: Pawnee Scouts, Soldiers of the United States Army. I ask every one of you to give me your two ears to hear what I must say to you. You each wanted your name and mark on my paper, didn't you? I didn't ask you. You asked me. I am glad to have you. I am proud of my battalion of Pawnee Scouts. I think every one of you will obey my orders now, as the Pawnee Scouts have always obeyed.

"Now I know you are wanting to raid the Sioux camp. You must not. I forbid it. The Great White Father, who feeds and pays you, feeds them rations—they now are his children, though they've long been your enemies. You will not go near, nor harm, any of them unless I order you to attack or fight them. If you do, without my order, you can never be a scout again and perhaps I would send you to the reserve or (the very worst punishment and most face-losing) arrest and put you in jail.

"The Sioux under this chief are supposed to be peaceful people. Oh, I see you are doubtful of the Brules peaceableness—you probably distrust their friendship? [I'm not at all sure of it, myself.] Nevertheless, no Pawnee Scout will go near nor in any way molest them at this time. Is that plain enough to you? Also, no scout is to leave this camp from now until I give the marching order tomorrow. That is all."

The south river is almost brim full. We take the whole day fording it. We proceed upriver to end-of-track between Alkali (later, Paxton) and Ogalalla at O'Fallon's Station. The construction gangs are glad to see us. I assign Company A and B to guard the grader gangs, camps, and stock in this vicinity. Companies C and D I send to Ford Sedgwick to trade in their muzzleloaders for Spencer breechloading seven-shot carbines.

We sleep in our camp near the grading camp, when not on guard duty. Our camp moves with the graders a mile or so every day.

June 20, 1867. Just about daylight, on the day after Companies C and D left, a scout slips in to tell me, *"Cha-ra-rat-wata"* (the Sioux are coming). Captains Arnold and Murie, myself, and about forty Pawnee Scouts mount and ride after the Sioux who have started the work animals off. We rush them—give them a surprise. *"Ki-de-de-."* Discovery that Pawnee are after them jerks them up. They abandon the horse herd and streak right out.

It's a running fight for about ten miles.

Baptiste Behale grabbed up his bow and quiver full of arrows instead of his Springfield muzzleloader. A horse is shot from under a Sioux. He lights running and shooting until his quiver is empty. Baptiste rides near enough to fire an arrow into the running Indian. The arrow ranges downward from under the scapula, courses across through him and out above his hip. The Indian grabs the metal point, yanks the arrow out, sets it to his bow and shoots it at the scout. Baptiste ducks to the side of his horse, feels the arrow's whir but is untouched. The Indian falls dead. Baptiste rides up, reaching his bow down to touch—count coup on—his victim, but his horse shies to the side. Another scout rides up and touches the Indian and gets tribal credit for the coup. The rest of the raiders get away. We turn back, gather up the scattered mules and horses and drive them back to do their day's work. The raids let up for a while. There were no killings in camp, and we recovered the work animals. When the two companies get back with their Spencer rifles, Lute and Morse scout ahead, to clear Indians out of the railroad's way, and also trade in their guns at Fort Sedgwick.

A few miles from the Fort, Lute and Morse, looking through field glasses, see a detachment of cavalry under attack by a larger bunch of Indians. The cavalry[10] make a run for the fort. Seeking to reinforce the soldiers, Lute and Morse and the two companies jump their horses into the river. Strong current carries them downstream, rolls some of the horses under—drowns three ponies, the rest wind up on a sandbar.

They didn't get across the first channel. Within two or three minutes they had put themselves in a defenseless position, and fell far short of assisting the cavalry. They saved themselves, so it is not too disastrous. Three are unhorsed. Some lost guns and all their ammunition was wet. My young brother and Morse led all into the river at once, left none to stand guard over those in the water. They got a lesson and deserved it.

Further along but still north of the river Lute camped his company opposite the fort. By morning the water had gone down enough that they waded across.

My captains took two days worth of pains to see that each carbine was good, after seeing the other two companies had got back with some defective arms. Lute says General Emory, the C. O. of Fort Sedgwick, came over to see how they were getting along—probably thinking to hurry the exchange, since Lute and Morse were taking more than usual time to it. Seeing them reject several carbines, he snatched up one they handed back to the sergeant, and yanked down on the lever on a rimfire cartridge that would not go into the chamber. The breechblock hit hard on the rim —the powder charge exploded and blew his glasses into splinters that pierced his face. The blood ran, but his eyes were not harmed. He didn't further challenge my captains on their choice of guns.

They had no more than drawn rations, ammunition, and forage and made camp back across the river when I came in with Generals W. T. Sherman and Augur with several companies of cavalry, going to inspect frontier forts. I am under orders to accompany the generals with the two scout companies I have here.

A soldier on night guard over General Sherman's tent lit out with a horse belonging to one of the general's staff officers. Is the general put out! When the smoke clears, he orders me to detail the Pawnee Scouts to night sentinel duty over his tent and the camp. No more horses are stolen by white or Indian and no soldiers desert camp while the scouts are on night guard. It may be they think getting caught out of place by a Pawnee Scout could be chancy.[11]

From Fort Wardell, renamed Fort Morgan a few months ago, General Sherman, staff, and escort go on to Denver. General Augur continues upriver to the juncture of Crow Creek. This creek we follow north to Cheyenne Pass. Lute and Morse alternate in taking daily advance scout. Today, Lute and half his men, with Murie volunteering to go along, take the advance.

Through my field glasses I see the boys are about three miles ahead. Hey! What's this—going into "Cavalry a-breast formation"—having some trouble keeping their loose horses. Now what?—Buffalo beyond—No. Riders—Indians—twenty or twenty-five and a herd of horses and mules.

I order Company D and the other half of C Company forward and lead at a gallop. The scouts, still holding formation, are nearing the Indians. I understand the strategy of formation—to dupe the Indians and keep them expecting soldiers, whose stiff military tactics they usually find not too hard to by-pass, since they have learned to duck at the warning command, "Fire."

"*Ki-de-de-de,*" the Pawnee war cry carries far. The scouts break, rush to take advantage of the enemy's confusion.

The Indians leave their horse herd. The scouts serve them a running fight as far as my field glasses follow them. After a couple of hours they come back with a prisoner and over fifty horses and mules.

Luther reports they killed four Arapahoe. I am very pleased the scouts will take a prisoner, and praise them. General Augur also says some complimentary things to the scouts.

The captive makes a break and is killed before he gets clear of the camp. I regret the Arapahoe's death while in our custody. So I put some Pawnee Scouts on the carpet and grill them thoroughly—pin them down for facts and no forked-tongue talk. "Did you pretend not to watch the Arapahoe to encourage him to make the break so you could shoot him?" "No," they say, "we watched all the time."

I'm convinced there was no planned purpose to kill the Arapahoe. What is of more importance, it is evident that their training is becoming second nature to the scouts. Their restraint in taking and holding the captive without mistreatment, also in shooting when the prisoner forced the situation, is clearly from training.

The horse herd is driven ahead as we go to Fort Laramie. There, it is learned the horses were taken from an immigrant train a few miles beyond the fort. I detail Pawnee Scouts with Luther and Lieutenant Matthews to deliver the animals to their owners—a good example for the scouts of how ownership is respected.

From Fort Laramie we are ordered back to the Union Pacific right-of-way to guard grading and construction camps now near Granite City.[12] In a few days my command is needing forage and rations. I take Luther with a dozen men and four wagons to Fort Sanders[13] to get supplies. Lute and I ride ahead to the C.O.'s office. He steps out to meet us, laughing.

"Well, Major, Captain, you got here just in time to embarrass Little Crow and those braves going yonder. Little Crow rode up here to complain to me against the Pawnee Scouts. It seems they killed a couple of his Arapahoe warriors over at Cheyenne Pass. Is that so?"

I nod and he goes on, "I intimated I understood his warriors had some mules that were separated from their owners. He dropped that subject— said he wanted to see the white chief of the Pawnees, that he had an arrow marked for him."

"'There comes Major North now,' "I told him. " 'You can go talk to him.' He went as you saw—in the other direction."

24

Work trains fetch newspapers to end of track, which allows me to catch up with the outside world.

OMAHA DAILY HERALD *June 26, 1867.*—The local Editor of the Herald has received a private dispatch from a friend in Denver. ". . . The first coach through since the first of June, on the Smoky Hill route, arrived yesterday. Two coaches coming west were attacked on the 15th by two hundred Indians five miles east of Big Timber. Two soldiers and one passenger were killed; two passengers, one soldier and one of the drivers were severely wounded. Big Timber Station was surrounded by Indians for three days. The route by Omaha is the only safe one. . . ."

One company of scouts is called for grader's camp, and from Granite Canyon we go in early July to Crow Creek, about twenty miles east. Here, General Augur and escort, back from his inspection of frontier forts, join General Dodge, chief engineer of the Union Pacific, with other railroad officials. We escort General Dodge and his surveying party in laying out the town as a railroad division point. The general selects the exact location, three miles east of where the surveyed line crosses Crow Creek. The officers mark this choice with champagne, and call the town Cheyenne, in Dakota Territory. General Dodge had hardly started survey when settlers, three couples and three men, came. Three days later the first town lot is sold.[1]

General Augur decides on a site for Fort D. A. Russell,[2] near the Crow Creek crossing to protect the southward trail to Denver, the immigrant and freighters road west, and the builders of the railroad. Hundreds of workers are scattered over long stretches[3] and more laborers will be scattered out more hundreds of miles, all to be escorted and protected. Surveyors L. L. Hills and Percy T. Brown were killed by Indians along this part of the line earlier this year, and all data lost.[4]

Contractors, like John Burke at Cottonwood Spring,[5] have hired hundreds of men scattered out wherever there is timber suitable for ties. Tie hacks—lumbermen—carry a gun in one hand and axe in the other. A few men busy with crosscut saw or axe or at sawmills, bridge construction, or quarrying rock can easily be surprised.

I shift the companies of my Pawnee battalion about, over a three hundred mile stretch along the Union Pacific, from Plum Creek across the Laramie plains. One day we ford water, high and swift enough to nearly drown us and our ponies, and the next day we chase Indians across the plains and find no water, yet may wind up the day wrapping blankets over our heads to protect us from a hail storm.

Following the immigrant route east through Cheyenne Pass, I drop a company near Pine Bluffs to protect graders. Twelve miles further east, at Point of Rocks, I detail the other company to guard duty with graders. Going on, unescorted, to end of track about four miles east of "Hell on Wheels"—the boom tent-town of Sidney—I find Lute and Company D, sent down a few days ago. "Kit E. Butts," the scouts call him since the fight with the Arapahoes. It means "Little Chief." Company A is here and I sent them to Granite Canyon—"City" the camp is called.

OMAHA DAILY HERALD *July 26, 1867.*—. . . Sudden descent of a band of hostile Indians on settlements along the Blue River, 30 miles east of Fort Kearny. Two men were killed and five captives carried away; two young girls of 17 and 19 years, the Campbell sisters, and twin boys age six, also a Danish girl of 14 years. . . .

A dispatch catches me at end-of-track, seventy-five miles west of North Platte. From Omaha, General Augur states: "Indians, today, ditched handcar and westbound U. P. freight train. West of Plum Creek, cars plundered. Request you hasten, bring company Pawnee Scouts."

My nearest company is twelve miles west. I send a courier to Captain Murie instructing him: "Report to Official there: You and Scout Company will be absent from guard duty, that area. You bring Company, report to me immediate."

I wire for cars to ship our ponies. They come in time for us to get loaded and on our way by midnight. We arrive at Plum Creek in the forenoon.

August 17, 1867. While unloading our horses and gear, smoke drifts up —the Indians have set fire to some of the cars on the derailed and wrecked train. They romped all day yesterday, displaying a naive ingenuity to find uses for items of merchandise they never had seen before. But, like children, they could always play, tying ends of bolts of calico to their horses' tails to run and see what happens.

We have just saddled and taken out the last horse when we see the

Indians crossing the river, their ponies loaded with loot. I send Murie and
his scouts to rush them out of the country and I go to the station and wire
the general about what I've done. I had given Lute a leave of absence to
go home on the train, now coming. Thinking he might decide to join us
here on the chase, I lead an extra saddled horse along, but I explain to
him that it appears to me the Indians have done all the mischief they like
and are hauling across river and out of the country. From the train he sees
them in the river and our boys going toward it, and decides it would only
be a chase, so goes on home.[6]

I ride over to cross the Platte River with my scouts. Near the old stage
station, a bridge crosses Plum Creek. There we discover the Cheyennes. I
lead over the bridge, but most of the scouts cross the creek, which is low
at this time of year. Their horses bog in the mud. The scouts jump off and
run up the bank to fire at fairly close range at the Indians. Seven
Cheyenne drop dead. The rest hustle for the hills.

Gathering the horses out of the mud, we give chase. The Cheyennes
take a stance between us and their women and children, a delaying action
to give the women a chance to get away. It's a running fight until late
evening, and seventeen Cheyenne will fight no more.[7]

We turn back, fetching along three captives, a young woman, a girl
about ten years old, and a younger boy. Crossing the Platte River in the
dark, the little girl manages to slide down her horse's hindquarters and
escape. I'm concerned—she may starve before she finds her people. The
Pawnees, a bit sheepish, seeing a child has outsmarted them, assure me
she can take care of herself and will come to no harm.

Word goes out that the Peace Commission proposes to hold a council at
North Platte in September with the Sioux and Cheyennes, in preparation
for a general council in October, to be somewhere in Kansas.

In the sandy ground south of North Platte, the Indians begin to gather,
pitching their tepees toward the south river. About this time a runner
comes to me from Chief Turkey Leg, a Cheyenne, suggesting that he
might find six white captives he would trade for the boy and young woman
the Pawnees have in custody. The scouts and Murie are willing; I instruct
the messenger to tell the chief to fetch all his captives to the railroad
eating house and we will have our prisoners there for the exchange.[8]

The peace conference convenes. Brule Sioux chiefs present include
Spotted Tail, Pawnee Killer, Man that Walks under the Ground, Standing
Elk, and Man Afraid of His Horses, Spotted Bear, and Black Bear. Others
are said to be Cut Nose, Whistler, Big Mouth, Cold Feet, Crazy Lodge,
Cold Face and Turkey Leg. Turkey Leg knows me from seeing me in the
fight.

The Indians are invited to speak. Government interpreters relay the
talk, the sum of their wants being that all travel and use of roads, most

especially the railroad, must stop; their reason being wildlife, game, particularly buffalo, are running from the locomotives and are "going under ground."⁹ The commissioners assure them that by their acceptance of reservation life, they will be supplied beef meat.

The Indians ask for any and everything they can name, but always return to their basic prayer.

"My Father: should all the buffalo go under ground from where they came a long time ago, the Indian people must follow, for their life will leave them before they can learn to live on the white man's food meat," the Cheyenne chief, Turkey Leg, says. "Ever since I have been born I have eaten wild meat. My father and grandfather ate wild meat before me; we cannot give up quickly the customs of our fathers."

The unknown manner of life they foresee in their future pulls the earth from under their feet.

Generals at the North Platte council are: Sherman, Augur, Terry, Harney, and Sanborn. Others are N. G. Taylor, Senator Henderson and "Colonel" Tappan, assistants, including myself, and interpreters, scribes and reporters.

Turkey Leg brings the prisoners to the appointed place. Reunion between the little boy and the chief is good to see. There is striking resemblance between the two. I speak of this to the interpreter, who relays it to the chief. Turkey Leg tells me through the interpreter that the child is his nephew. The woman is the chief's wife.¹⁰

October 2, 1867. A dispatch orders me to center my scouts at Cheyenne, in preparation for a northward campaign. Striking camp at Plum Creek with Murie and his company, we move to join Lute and Company D at end-of-track. All then march to Cheyenne—already a tent city, boomed from the three couples and four or five men that settled there as Dodge was laying out the town.¹¹

Now there must be at least a thousand here. General Dodge got a peoples' government organized and there's even a half-size newspaper, the *Cheyenne Leader.*¹²

We march on to Fort Laramie, where I draw equipment and supplies for an expedition with cavalry into the Powder River country. But after the Pawnee battalion is seen around the fort, settlers and ranchers along the trails object to the campaign into country so recently handed back to the Indians. They say it would cause an outbreak of the Sioux. General Augur cancels the projected campaign.

I'm ordered back to Pine Bluffs with my command. Following the old road from the North Platte River south, toward the head of Lodge Pole Creek, outriders report Indians approaching. I order: "Halt. Swing (from columns) into Line." A single rider gallops out of the band carrying a white signal. With my two captains I ride forward and meet Nick Janis.[13]

"Major, I take dees people to Fort Laramie, got to make treedy. What are you going to do?"

I see his Sioux band has been on a hunt. Their pack animals are loaded with meat and robes. As I've heard nothing of a treaty in the making, I surmise Old Nick may be coaxing his charges off the hunt to get them under military supervision.

"All right, Nick. Just have your people get off to the side, give us about fifty rods clearance and the Pawnees will march right on by." There are about a hundred and fifty warriors, I estimate, but their women and children are with them. With so little chance to get their families safely out of the way, I figure they aren't spoiling for a fight. They move aside, giving plenty of margin.

"Take Column by fours (form line). Forward March!" I command, knowing this is ticklish business.

The Pawnees strut past their Sioux enemies in good order, though I think not without insulting gestures and smirks from both sides.

The year's first snowstorm is hammering us as we reach Pine Bluffs and end-of-track. I report by telegraph to General Augur at Omaha. He orders me with my command to Fort Kearny and authorizes me to order cars, which come overnight. We ship down and go into camp with the other two companies ordered down just before us.

Luther goes with his Company D to reconnoiter the North Loup. Daily I dispatch groups on scouting details. Lute and company find no hostile Indians, but fetch in plenty of elk and deer. A like report comes in with scouts I sent to the Solomon River. I propose to see that we don't get caught and continue the sorties of scouting groups.

Some of the Union Pacific's moneyed sportsmen desire a buffalo hunt. I am appointed to arrange it and to provide protection from Indian attack, to supply saddle horses, equipment, and all services, to make it a satisfactory hunt for them.[14]

The Union Pacific's president, Sidney Dillion, Vice President Thomas C. Durrant, Oakes Ames, George Francis Train, and C. S. Bushnell, with several newspaper reporters take their choice of riding out to the hunting ground on horseback or in the army ambulances along with my wife and my youngest sister, Alphonsine, visiting our camp for a few days.[15]

I send scouts in advance and the hunting party gets under way. After fifteen or more miles a scout reports a herd of buffalo. He guides us a couple of miles. Here everyone who wants to get his buffalo is provided a horse. (Lute and I scoured the herd to find good buffalo running horses.) The ladies mount up astride, in long riding habits. My wife's fine sidesaddle hangs at home, unused. I insist she is safer seated naturally astride.

The greenhorn dignitaries are assisted up, and we adjust stirrups for each. Revolvers with cartridge belts are provided to all who care to use them. It turns out that only President Dillon, Vice President Durant, and Mr. Train have the spunk to get on a horse for the hunt. The rest watch the hunt from the ambulances.

We ride nearer the herd. A scout signals stop. Last adjustments and directions are given. The scouts lead through a deep ravine and out on a plateau and the buffalo are before us. The sportsmen have their chance to shoot a buffalo. I give the word and we cover ground at a dead run.

Luther's horse is the fastest and he is overtaking the herd. Mary and Alphonsine are in the midst of the chase, riding right up with the Pawnees and having the time of their lives.

There has been no snow in these parts this winter and the ground is dry. Clay dust swirls in clouds. Lute has cut a prime, mature young cow from the herd, running it into the clear where he can shoot from a safe angle. His horse's tail flips into the air as it steps into a hole and takes a somersault, throwing him clear. It scrambles up and runs off. Lute gets up all right. He had given his own buffalo running horse to Mr. Dillon and just now the man and horse fly by, running to overtake the buffalo. While I hadn't expected him to ride like a Pawnee, Mr. Dillon's elbows are flapping and so are his feet, having lost his stirrups. He clings for dear life to the pommel with one hand, the other hand somehow keeps possession of the revolver. Suddenly this horse upsets, too, probably tripped by the same badger hole that Lute's mount hit. Mr. Dillon is all shook up and bruised, but no bones are broken.

Mr. Durant brings down a fine bull while the Pawnee keep the herd milling, then I signal them to kill meat for our camp and for the "hunters." Finally part of the herd is turned past the ambulances and in close view. Co-rux-ah-Kah Wahdee, Traveling Bear, shoots an arrow into a buffalo—buries it the full length of the shaft to its feathers. He strings another arrow to his bow and shoots again. This one passes clear through the bull and drops out on the other side. I've been with the Pawnee killing buffalo many times, but never before saw an arrow driven through one. Traveling Bear is a large, powerful man and his bow is of a different wood; he says it is made of osage orange, which would give it a lot of spring.

Back along the Union Pacific railroad the scouts continue on routine details, until we are mustered out, January 1, 1868.[16]

25

Early February, 1868. A dispatch comes ordering me to recruit two
companies of Pawnee Scouts for railroad guard and patrol. I offer Luther
the first captaincy this time. He jumps at the chance, eager to accept.
The first of the year he went to work for James, clerking in the trader's
post. James doesn't speak Pawnee and objects to Luther's leaving. Maybe
Lute had better stay a while. General Augur says he probably will want
another company or so before long.

The Pawnees are pleased to be enrolled. I assign Company A to Morse,
with Billy Harvey first lieutenant; Fred Matthews is captain of Company B
with G. G. (Gus) Becher as lieutenant. We are quickly afield to patrol
and guard the one hundred mile stretch of railroad, Wood River to Willow
Island, for twenty-five miles on each side of the track.

By detailing four detachments of twenty each, I have two ten-man
detachments for other duties. This is surprisingly effective. The hostiles
respect a uniformed, active Pawnee Scout and give him wide clearance.

A flock of trumpeter swans flies over. Pintail ducks splash in every
buffalo wallow. Spring is on its way.

By mid-July patrols are routine—no hostiles seen along the railroad. I
take half of each company south for a scout along the Republican Valley.
We are to protect a hunting party of four friendly Indian Nations—
Pawnees, Poncas, Winnebagos, and Omahas. I invited two friends along,
J. J. Aldrich[1] and Sumner Oaks. Captain Ogden, in charge of the Indians'
hunt, wishes off on me a pair of tenderfoot adventurers, Magee and Dunn,
out to see the world.

My two half companies (fewer than fifty Pawnee Scouts is a small force)
provide military protection.

About five miles southeast from Wood River are the four camps,
thousands of Indians. The large horse herds graze under the care of
numerous herd boys.

I lead the Indians toward the Republican Valley. Whitening buffalo skeletons spot the prairie—mostly the doings of hide hunters. From small bunches of buffalo, my scouts and other Indians take choice critters and prepare supper.

On this evening, Peta La Shar brings all the chiefs together around the ceremonial pipe. I supply tobacco and each of us takes a draft and passes the pipe on. We council on arrangements for the buffalo hunt.

By daybreak the Indian men are on their way, ignoring their women who are pulling down tepees and loading them with cook pots, camp "traps" (articles), and young children onto travois hitched to old nags no longer able to run in the hunt. Soon all are in motion, with the younger women with baby boards on their backs in the lead. The unused part of the horse herd and young herders trail behind.

Going far ahead of the main body of hunters, spotters scouting for buffalo are led by a pole man of each tribe. Medicine men flank each side of the bearers of staffs, tall poles bedecked with feathers, bright cloth strips and geegaws. The buffalo pole men give signals and police the hunt. No man may move in advance of them.

We are signaled "stop!" Buffalo are ahead. A sacred pipe-tomahawk is lighted, smoked, and handed to another buffalo pole man. Each ceremoniously blows his smoke about his pole, and passes the pipe on.

The medicine men perform a brief ceremony of chanting and prayer. "Medicine is good!" is the word they send out.

We move on at a faster rate, seeing buffalo right and left feeding on low hillsides, and along small streams leading to the Republican Valley.

A signal of the buffalo poles halts the march. The Indians and scouts strip as for combat. All who led a reserve horse now turn loose the ridden horses to start them toward the herd boys. We look to arms, be they bows, revolvers, or rifles. High-strung buffalo-running horses become intolerant of restraint.

The Indians tighten belts to their "gee" strings as we tighten saddle cinches and mount, they riding bareback.

In near quiet 1,500 horses and more men (some without horses) move on, using any possible natural concealment of hills, swales, ravines, or gullies; every man's eye is on the buffalo poles. Tense excitement grips us. Guided by signals relayed from spotters, the pole men hoist the poles, warning that the signal is due any minute.

Down slash the poles in an arc of color!—"Go Surround" signal. Ponies break forward. Now it's every man for himself. The ponies, trained to run the buffalo race alongside the beasts, gradually turning, but not fast enough to get in front of a buffalo's horns. The clever horse keeps out of reach of whirling horns, still running into the whirling melee, while his rider shoots and kills. A lot of meat is on the ground.

A great bull, knocked down by a shot, jumps to his feet, lunges with his

great horns, breaks a pony's rib cage as the Indian jumps away. The
buffalo disembowels the horse, then falls dead.

Hunters skin out the meat and pack it on old horses to take to the
nearby new camp set up by the women. The women slice, dry, and pack
the meat into parfleche cases made from rawhide. It's all hard work—the
Pawnee way—and they're happy, going on the summer outing meatmaking
hunt.

We won't be moving camp for a few days. Drying the meat takes time—
jerky must be drier than an old shoe to keep. Wet meat spoils. Hides, too,
require drying time—even in hot dry air.

Old Peta La Shar doesn't miss an evening of rounding up the rest of the
chiefs for our accustomed smoke—usually kinnikinnick, tobacco being
reserved for special occasions.

A few days of camp life pass while processing of jerky and hides is the
order of the day. When the medicine men judge the sign to be right,
hunting is resumed and change of camps made to be near the newest
slaughter ground.

I move our camp south across the Republican River near a spring where
we have fresh water and less flies, better location than where the Indian
women set up camp for the latest meat-making. (I am to have all the
dried meat for the scouts that they will require.)

Three or four more surrounds bring the time near that we must get back
to the railroad right-of-way.

We go on our last hunt and will get fresh meat for the scouts left on
duty along the railroad. I don't see that our kills, upwards of a thousand,
have made any dent in the number of buffalo in the Republican River
country.

During the chase I wounded a cow off in a small bunch. I marked that
she went up a ravine, and after the surround I ride apart from the three or
four boys with me to find and kill her.

"*Chah ra rat wata!*" A scout rushes up, calling to me that the Sioux are
coming.

"They're our Indians," I say, hardly glancing up.

"No, Sioux, Sioux," he insists.

I take a look. Sure enough, Sioux warriors are riding at us full-tilt. We
run to catch up with two scouts, and from a ravine Captain Morse and
four scouts ride up, calling to us. The Sioux's shots are coming pretty
warm. We back off to a ravine, completely hemmed in.[2]

The Brules split around the end of the ravine as they slam a fusillade at
us. Scouts are wounded and five horses go down. "Fire only when you've
got an Indian in your sights," I caution.

La-Roo-La-Shar-Roo-Cosh, Man that Left His Enemy Lying in the
Water, a Pawnee but never a Scout, who came with Morse, works his way

to me.

"Grandfather" (the scouts and Pawnees call me Grandfather since there are now the company captains), "my horse is faster than all the Pawnees' ponies. He can take me around the Sioux to the Pawnee camp to bring my brothers and ammunition," he offers.

"Then go, my friend," I tell him.

He prepares himself and his pony, a deep-girthed, exceptionally stringy, tall, but gutless looking nag, and chooses a moment when the enemy are farthest from the ravine. Placing his horse between two others, he scrapes soil from the ascending ridge, digging a channel through the cutbank and inches his horse up the grade. Suddenly he springs upon its back, digs his heels into its flanks, works his quirt, and the two rise up out of the ravine. Over the prairie they skim.

Some Sioux leap upon ponies and give chase. Others race to head him from the direction of the Pawnee camp. Yet he skims on, the warriors behind him, and all run over the hill out of sight.

Plainly the Sioux, nearly a half mile distant, are making ready to charge us again. Here they come a-pelting! We tense, our forefingers at trigger. Suddenly they recollect how our Spencers bite. The forward rush falters— breaks at some distance—and we save our lead.

During the charges I spotted one rascal carrying a little American flag. He may be their "Big Medicine," who calls their turns. I believe that if I can put him out of commission, the Indians might lose interest. I hurry along the ravine to get within range of him and rest my carbine on the bank. Howling, the Indians race at us. The Indian with the flag rushes toward a small hill off to the side. I take a crack at him at about two hundred yards. He and his flag tumble from the pony. Two Sioux warriors sweep up between them the "commander"—a dead one, I think.[3]

Breaking off, the Sioux turn short. They go behind the hills and we see little of them. I find that I can do little for my two wounded men; we give them the warm water in our canteens. The gear is taken off the dead horses. We wait and watch under a baking July sun. If we can hold off until dark, we might stand a chance. I've never heard of Sioux fighting at night.

Some Indians show up among the hills, run a halfhearted circle beyond our Spencer's range. Yet some braves dare to dash in on fast horses to throw a shot at us. Our carbines take care of them.

Little motion is seen among the Indians. Mostly they just watch and wait too. I didn't know a summer afternoon could be so long. There is little chance that La-Roo-Cosh made it through to bring help. The half of my detachment left with the white sportsmen back in our field camp on Mudd Creek near the hunting tribe have no way of knowing we are under siege and nailed down here. Too, they also may be under attack.

As the sun sinks into a glaring ball for the day's last hour, the Indians mount charge at us but split widely out of range. Only one arrow finds its way to wound one of our horses.

Warriors again are in motion in scattered forward thrust, sweeping toward us, a ragged front, as though shoved from behind. Drumming hooves round our ravine's cutbanks—riders intent only on getting away.

"Ki-de-de-de-de." It's the Pawnee Scouts' prairie-wolf yipping bark, mighty welcome! The Pawnee Scout detachment bolstered by the four tribes of buffalo hunters—Pawnee, Omahas, Poncas and Winnebagos—are driving the Sioux before them.

"Oh my Grandfather," La-Roo La Shar Roo-Cosh explains, "the Na-huo-kac, Tira-wa's animal servants, give my pony wings, and we flew away from the Sioux all right, but I found a large warrior party attacking the camps. I must then ride more to find the hunters to defend the camp—at first it was a pitched battle, then more and more hunters came, then it was a seesaw back and forth until the Sioux began to lose out and we drove them. I went to find the scouts, most were out hunting near their camp, and we joined the Pawnees, making the Sioux run, run, run to get away. He-he-he," he laughs.

The scouts leave the hunting ground to return to the railway patrol. We strike camp, load the meat which the women dried and tramped into packs one and a half feet long by two wide and nearly a foot deep. We head back with our wounded and a fallen scout, shot by the Sioux and scalped, probably about the time we were attacked. We take the corpse back, wrapped in a buffalo robe, and will make his grave in the Fort Kearny cemetery.

Everything is quiet, so I take the train to Columbus. It seems a year since I last saw Mary, but is only about five weeks.

OMAHA DAILY HERALD, August 20, 1868.—To the Editor: The late Indian Commission who worked so long to bring the Sioux and Cheyenne to terms of peace, guaranteed them that no armed bodies of citizens or soldiers should penetrate their immediate hunting grounds and interfere with the buffalo.

Not long ago a large body of Pawnee and Omaha Indians, accompanied by a large number of Whites, including an officer of the army, left the Platte at some point not far from Fort Kearny, going south on a grand hunt. They had arrived at a point between the Republican and North Solomon Rivers when discovered by the Sioux and Cheyenne. A fight ensued. The south Indians discovered that whites were conspicious in the battle. They knew to a certainty that the "Pawnee Scouts" were there, headed by their officers. It was taken as a declaration of war, and looked upon as a violation of the late treaty. A raid upon the settlements east of them, on the Solomon and tributaries was decided upon. We know what followed. [Signed] Blue Cloud.

It's plain enough to me what the man is trying to write, but his bag of half-facts hardly makes a truth with all of the mess.

Mary's glad to see me, and I'm mighty glad to see her. After while I hitch to the buggy and we go to the reserve to see the folks. Mother and the girls come to Jim's and we visit. They cook Sunday dinner.

Monday morning I run around town on business, then go back to Mary. Together we look at her garden—she's raised a dandy one. "You are as good a gardener as the Pawnee women," I tell her, and then take to my heels. I go up the line by train.

The corpse of a Mr. Harkins comes through on a train, accompanied by his family on the way to Missouri for burial. The man was killed and scalped not far from Pine Bluffs and his mules taken by Indians while he worked, getting out and hauling stone for Union Pacific bridge and culverts. A detachment of my scouts soon nailed the Indians and fetched the mules back, which were then sold and the money sent to the widow.

OMAHA DAILY HERALD, August 25, 1868.—To the Editor: Permit me to say a few words in answer to a letter in your issue of the 20th over the signature of "Blue Cloud." He must have some private advice from the Peace Commission as to the treaty he says has been brought about with the Indians referred to, inasmuch as the officer of the United States Army who accompanied the hunting expedition has received no notification of such treaty. If he had, it is certain he would not have crossed the Platte nor intruded upon the ground, said by your correspondent to be exclusively belonging to the Indians named.

The . . . purpose of the officer was to kill buffalo for that portion of the Pawnee Scouts who accompanied him and for those left on duty north of the Platte, and in no way or shape to create excitement in the country.

It is quite a case your correspondent, Blue Cloud, lays out. But, if he knows, he does not admit: that the reservation selected for undisturbed possession of the southern Cheyenne and Arapahoe is not in Nebraska and northern Kansas; that the reserve supposed to be for the Sioux is hardly south of the Platte River.

There was no trespassing of forbidden land by the Major, his two officers, the white men—only four, not a large body, with him—nor his Scouts, nor the people of the four hunting tribes who were escorted.

That large body of Indians harried the peaceful tribes, any time the Scouts were out of sight and hearing, killing the hunters, separated into small meat killing and butchering groups, until they must leave the meat to spoil while forced to fight or decamp and run. It was in this way, while getting fresh meat to take back, that the Major with another officer and a small handful of Scouts was attacked and under siege for many hours, successfully holding off the Savages, which he believed finally numbered around five hundred. One Scout, also hunting with only two or three others, was shot and scalped.

This is the first Scout the Major has lost from his Command at the hand of enemies. However this remarkable record is not because the Scouts have not been in the forefront of danger at all times, when enemy were to be confronted. They have always borne the brunt, have protected and saved countless lives and much property which the Savages would have destroyed.

The Indians who jumped the hunting people were out of place; were not hunting buffalo, but were out to make war and to kill as many of the friendly tribes as they could, and incidentally, white men too. [Signed] One of the Whites.[4]

OMAHA DAILY HERALD, August 28, 1868. Editorial.—To set Major Frank North right before authorities and citizens, we wish to retract whatever appeared in a recent article that, even by implication, might reflect upon his official conduct in the matter of the recent conflict with Indians in the Republican Valley. General Augur himself informs that in going there, Major North violated no treaty with the hostile tribes. They are hereditary enemies of the Pawnees, and fight is the word whenever they meet.[5]

September is here with yellow goldenrod, and still we daily patrol, covering every mile along our stretch of the line. At least two times a week we catch sight of Indians, but when they see the scouts, the Indians back off.

General Augur telegraphs orders to take one company of scouts by railway to Potter, to scout the north country after Indians raiding in the Sidney and Bridgeport region.

We get there, and join Major Wells and his detachment of the second Cavalry. Together we proceed to Court House Rock on the old trail near the Platte River. It doesn't take the scouts long to spot the Indians, north of the river. I send Lieutenant Becher and a detachment after the rascals. The Indians show fight and get a couple of themselves killed. The rest are chased north, the scouts behind them, until they turn back to drive the stolen stock, all recovered, and several Indian ponies.

The ranch stock is turned over to Major Wells to give to owners as they return to Sidney. With Lieutenant Becher I lead the company downriver to Ash Hallow, then on to Ogalalla and finally to Fort Kearny, and into winter camp.

Christmas this year is very special in the North family. Sisters Elizabeth and Alphonsine are having a double wedding—Phonsie to Charley Morse and Libby to Sylvanus (Jim) Cushing.

January 1, 1869. A happy new year to all. The scouts are disbanded.

General Augur retains me in service to assure that the scouts' mounts will be cared for, to have them in good shape for spring use.

26

New Year's Day, So I begin to write my diary: *January 1, 1869.* Happy New Year to all. Today I ran around town. After dinner we made some calls and had a good time and a big dance tonight. Mary is sick and I did not dance much.

January 2. This morn Charlie and I hauled one cord of wood to the railroad. This evening Jim Galley[1] and sister were here and we sang with instrumental music. Started for Kearny—too late for train which pleased Mary.

January 3. Started on number 1 to Kearny, arrived at 3:15 A.M. Found a saddle made for me by my friend McCully. . . .

January 4. Spent today in the Fort. Went to Kearny City and danced all night and had a very good time.

January 5. I took the ponies on the Island and left them for the [Pawnee] boys to feed. Came home just in time to go to Adobe Town [Kearny] after Tom Russel. Came home and wrote a letter to Mary.

January 6. Took ponies on the Island again and went over the river to the [Pawnee] Indian camp. Came home and all went to Adobe Town again, came home at 6 o'clock and sat up 'till one, had lots of fun.[2]

January 7. Sat up till 10 o'clock tonight, had lots of fun, Tom full as usual. Had a theatrical play from Tom, very good.

January 8. Day passed very slow as it was my day for going home . . . will go down on passenger train. Tom full as usual.

Saturday, January 9. Arrived home this morn at 5:10, found Mary awake for me at the American House.[3] This afternoon we went over and saw all of the folks. Jim North [eldest brother, James] and the boys came home at dark with wood. I went back to town, traded property with Geo. Clothier today, also leased Ernest my mules.

As George wants possession, we pack up our household goods (we took lease on the hotel with furnishings), and take them to my farm to store there. I get through in time to go on freight train to Omaha. After breakfast, did my business at different stores, in time for west train. Met Mary at Columbus and we came on to Kearny to visit our friends, the J. F. Walkers (telegrapher and station agent). They gave us a bed. After breakfast I leave Mary with them at the station and ride Walkers' horse across the river to the fort.

Thursday, January 14. . . . Today around the Post until afternoon, then I went with an ambulance across the river after Mary and Mrs. Walker. We got back here at sundown and after dinner we went to the Theatre. It was splendid.

Friday, January 15. . . . With the ladies we called on Mrs. Sydenham. . . . Ladies had to get out of the ambulance twice. . . .

Snowdrifts are packed solid and the mules seesaw when we are stuck, so that the rig is threatened with upsetting. I secure the lines counterclockwise around the hub and then tie into the spokes, and help the ladies out upon a snowdrift, then gee-haw the mules into a settled pull that gets us out.

Saturday, January 16, 1869. . . . Mary and I went up the road on No. 1. Mary stopped at Harnards [telegrapher-agent and wife at Plum Creek Station], and I went on to Willow Island[4] . . . came down on No. 6, got Mary at Plum Creek and we arrived at Kearny at 10 P.M., went to bed.

Sunday, January 17. . . . Came from Kearny to Lone Tree[5] on No. 4. Stayed with Joe Adams [station agent], had a good visit. . . .

Monday, January 18. . . . Arrived home 3:15. Found Jim and Lib here and in the evening Ma [Mrs. Jane Townley North], Charlie and Tom came from the Reserve. Lute started today for Fort Randall after his horse.[6]

The folks came to see me before I leave for Ohio in the morning. I've intended to go there to see all the folks we left back home, ever since we came to the frontier, and now I have the privilege, though I can't be gone long. I shall carry all the greetings and messages to them, also hope I may induce some to move here.

Wednesday, January 20. . . . In Omaha at 6:30 A.M. Two hours later after doing my commerce I went to Council Bluffs, got my pass to Chicago. . . .

Thursday, January 21. Today started with Cols. Litchfield and Ransom for Chicago . . . at Boone for supper and . . . went to bed in the sleeping car.

It was a rough stagecoach ride that Mother, our little sisters, and Lute and I had only a little more than a decade ago, coming to the frontier. To think I am riding away from that frontier in a bed on a train! When the Union Pacific is finished, pretty soon, we will see cars as fine as this on trains through Nebraska too.

January, Friday 22, 1869. . . . Took breakfast at Chicton and arrived at Chicago at 1 P.M. Instead of being alone as I expected I found lots of old friends and had a good time until 9 P.M. then started for Toledo.

Saturday, January 23. . . . At Toledo for breakfast, went on to Monroeville and from there to Plymouth. Thence to Shiloh and then to Rome [the North's former home]. Today I met any number of old friends. Did not know any of them. Stayed all night at Dave Aziurs.

Sunday, January 24. This morn, Dave Nelse, George Snapp and myself drove down to Hen Chire's, had a good visit. Came back and Nelse, Joel Pifer and I went to Shiloh. I stayed all night at Shupe's, had a good visit, talked Nebraska strong. [7]

Monday, January 25, 1869. . . . Went to Plymouth, saw Louis North and family. Telegraphed Mary I was starting home. Came to Hillsdale [Michigan] stopped off there six hours. Had a good visit with the Smith's [Mary's relatives] and came on for Chicago in the night.

Tuesday, January 26. . . . At the Sherman House just in time for a good breakfast. Traveled around town until 3 P.M., then started for home, supper at Dixon, took sleeping car.

Wednesday, January 27. . . . Breakfast . . . at Boone and dinner at Dunlap then skedaddled for Omaha. Arrived 8 P.M., bought my lumber and went to Theatre, started home at 12 midnight on the freight train.

Thursday, January 28, 1869. . . . Home at 7:10 A.M. in time for breakfast. Took Mary and went over the river, gave the folks a description of my trip.

Saturday, January 30. . . . After dinner Doddrige [W. B., the Union Pacific station agent], Crucheon, Lieut. George Lehman and myself went skating, had lots of fun. Tonight I started for Kearny.

Wednesday, February 3, 1869. The day is very cold. My carload of lumber is here. I have a carpenter hired to begin building a commercial building when winter breaks. Fred, George Barclay, and I unload the lumber.

Thursday, February 4. Fred Matthews and I go over the river and bring my mules to haul sills for my building over on the lot.

Wednesday, February 10. . . . At one o'clock P.M. I receive orders to recruit one company Pawnee immediately. Tonight I go to Kearny.

Two days ago, I saw two men from the advance guard of returning winter buffalo hunters, at my Pawnees' camp near the fort. I meet the tribe coming to the river crossing. I select and enlist my men. All are eager to be taken, but fifty is my number this time. I recruit, clothe, mount, and equip them all today, and our ponies are shipped for Fort McPherson and hope to arrive there early. The weather is very cold—a storm threatening.

We get to McPherson Station at noon, march to the fort across the frozen river, and I draw pants (I could only get a few at Fort Kearny), guns, ammunition, forage, grub, and two wagons for hauling the company supplies. No tents are to be had. We go into camp and a cold rain starts with sleet.

This morning I lead Company A with Lute as captain, Fred Matthew his lieutenant, and we head for Morrow's ranch in a driving snow. After going about a mile we cannot see two feet ahead. The scouts lead us to the old Holiday Stage Station bought by John Burke after his place was destroyed twice and burned out by the Indians. We get our horses and selves under sheds and in outbuildings and stay the rest of the day and night, a miserable, cold one.

Saturday, February 13, 1869. This morning we get unkinked and Lute and Fred lead out. The company will turn south from Morrow's ranch. Lute is ordered to join Major Noyes, already four days gone toward the Republican River country. The sky is clear but ground wind swirls the snow, still very cold. I turn homeward.

. . . At McPherson Station [now Maxwell][8] I take an "extra" passenger train for Lone Tree. Got down to Grand Island and the train was ordered to stay all night. I slept in the palace car.

Weather too cold for outdoor business. I loaf around home, visit our folks, go to reading circle a time or two.

February, Sunday 21, 1869. Today I stayed in the house all day, weather very cold. Mary popped a lot of corn for me. I eat it in milk.

Monday 22 . . . after dinner took the mules and Mary and I went up to Mullens, spent the afternoon. Had a nice meal. Today the cellar to my outfit building was finished.

Tuesday 23. . . . Took Mary to ride this afternoon. This evening we went to Rev. Samuel Goodales to reading circle. Heard Lute arrived at

McPherson Fort today all right.

Wednesday 24. . . . I have not been out at all today. Had a dispatch from Lute. I telegraphed him to come home tomorrow. Tonight I attended the bridge meeting. We propose to have a bridge.

Thursday 25. . . . Went to the Depot tonight and expected to hear from Lute but nothing from him.

Friday 26. This morn Lute came and we went over the river and visited all day, had a real good time and a good dinner which we enjoyed very much.

Lute says they found no buffalo and no Indians and only killed one antelope. Major Noyes had turned his command back when Lute and company came up to him.

"They were out of rations—hadn't found game. The Republican buffalo are down around the Arkansas River or further and don't start north until the winter begins to break. They had been rationed, calculated on buffalo meat for half their fare. The scouts gave most of their rations to the soldiers and Noyes said we would return to the fort in the morning.

"We started in a new snow storm, got up on the divides into a howling blizzard, couldn't see the trail. By noon it was much colder. We went on a couple more hours. I knew Major Noyes intended to camp on the White Man's Fork (Frenchman) River but when Co-rux-ah Kah Wahdee, Traveling Bear, said he was sure we weren't far from a deep wooded ravine, I told him to lead me to it. He and the rest of the scouts cut lodge poles and took the canvas off the wagons to make tepees. They cut the heavy grass and we spread our robes and blankets around a fire. One of the drivers on a wagon had cut the ice away in the morning so the horses could drink and slipped and wet one foot. When they got his boot off, I thought it was frozen through and I was sure he would lose it. Traveling Bear[9] stuck his foot in a bunch of snow and chewed some kind of pounded root in his mouth and rubbed the foot many times through the night with his spit from the chewed root powder. The foot looked good in the morning and he could walk. The surgeon at McPherson says he will lose one toenail.

"It was crackling cold, and clear as a bell in the morning. We picked up camp and hustled for the Fork [Frenchman]. There the major and troops were, camped without tents on the open prairie. They fired some of the wagons trying to get a little warmth. They're all pretty bad off—bad frostbite, even Noyes is bad with frostbite. I heard before I left the fort that a lot of the men will have amputations.

"Major Noyes really appreciated the scouts and wasn't backward about saying so to them and to me. They chopped ice to move him across the river—his horses were not shod. The Pawnee cut a trail the width of a wagon, then rode ahead to fetch the lead mules to each wagon. The major said he 'didn't know how his men could have done it, they were so badly frozen.' He left more than fifty horses that had frozen to death during the night. We had no rations the last two days."

Strange as it seems, Lute was able to draw tents when they got back to the fort, and he camped his men on the Big Island[10] where there is plenty of shelter.

> *February 27, 1869.* Stormy weather this morn. I took my mules and went over the river after Mother to come and tend [nurse] Frankie, he is very sick. Lute . . . and Jim Allen went to the Reserve. I bought a nice pony today. Had little mules shod.

> *February 28, 1869.* . . . . Went over the river after [bought] some corn . . . Brought Lib, Tom and Olive over to the Hotel. Morse's team broke in through river ice and had a hard time getting out and Jim [Allen, Major North's hired man] hauled the corn [after Morse's team had failed] with my team. Lute went West tonight.

> *Tuesday, March 9.* . . . . At 4:30 took the train for Omaha in company with Gus Becher, Barnum and Hoffman. [11]

Did my trading, my own and lists for others: Phonsie (sister Alphonsine) wants: one bureau, one set chairs, yellow; two rocking chairs, one like Mary's and one like Mrs. Whaly's; one wash stand, nice walnut wood.

For Mary one pair slippers, No. 3. For Ma, one pair cloth gaiters—birds-eye toweling, one bolt. Exchange dishes. One water pitcher, one dozen sauce dishes, one small platter. One case tomatoes, corn, peach preserve and one case jellies, pickles.

For my building: Sixteen lights—glass 19 × 38; two 12 × 25¼; four 28¾ × 21½; one black walnut plant 10 ft. × 20 in. and 2 in. thick for the bar.

For me nineteen small and seven large buttons to finish clothes (military), yellow striping for outside pants seams.

As I've finished my business and the shopping, and wait for the train, I read.

OMAHA DAILY HERALD, March 12, 1869.—Washington—President Grant issued an order appointing Sherman as General of the Army.

Nebraska—There have been more than the usual number of squalid looking Indians on the Omaha streets; as a consequence, chickens roost high or go by the board. Yesterday was pay day for the military. The streets were crowded with soldiers who spent their hard earned gains with reckless prodigality. The 27th Regiment of infantry was strongly represented in police court.

—Rather a serious shooting affray occurred at North Platte as the train was passing that point yesterday. Mr. Landgraber who keeps an eating house was standing on the platform of the depot calling the passengers for meals. The party was ordered off, after which some altercation ensued. A railroad employee then fired at Mr. Landgraber with a revolver. He produced a shotgun and returned the fire. Mr. Landgraber was wounded in the side and fell to the ground. Bullets flew lively for awhile.

At noon yesterday the thermometer certainly marked 50 above zero in the sunshine and at eight o'clock it as certainly marked 10 degrees below freezing. When the thermometer gets to oscillating 28 to 30 degrees in eight hours, it is not healthy nor agreeable. Parasols in the day and furs at night; the poor and ill clad are to be pitied.

Goodby Temporary Bridge—The workmen of the UPRR commenced pulling up the rails yesterday. Great efforts will be made in the coming season to complete the permanent bridge. The ferry boats have commenced crossing. The river below the pile bridge is free from ice.

—A robe at W. D. Hall and Company is made from twelve large beaver skins, lined with crimson broadcloth and ornamented with blue. It weighs twelve or fourteen pounds, valued at $200. It is a present to Dr. Durant, U.P. road vice president.

March 15. . . . Today very cold, my carpenters could not work.

Friday 19. . . . Went [into Omaha] to see Gen. Myers[12] and did not get any money, had to come home with but little cash . . . on No. 3, arrived on time.

Monday 22. . . . Weather beautiful. . . . Drove Winnie [a mare] up to my place, rented it to a farmer. Helped Charlie and Jim get [bring] across river their farming machines. . . . This evening we had a grand council of all the chiefs [a family council].

March 24, 1869. Got Lute's letter saying some of the boys (scouts) had ran off. Mary and I go to Fred's house to see if he's gotten his new-come folks settled in. They are, and he starts with me tonight to McPherson. I stop off at Lone Tree as the westbound train doesn't stop at Silver Creek and at 3:15 this morn I come back, borrow a horse and ride north to the Pawnee village after my boys. I got them, have supper at Kah-Lo-Hah La Shar's house (lodge). Came back at 5 P.M., pretty tired. We go down to McPherson tonight.

The boys have no intention of abandoning scouting, nor Lute and me. It is Pawnee nature to want to be with his family when he isn't making war. They pike off for home, forgetting to get official leave. Too, the railroad carries them free, in gratitude for the lives and property they have protected along the line.

So I rush the boys back, give them a little dressing down, and, for the record, find them some extra duty, and all's well. I spend a couple days at the fort, then go home.

March 31. . . . Started for Omaha with Yost, Murie and Pete. I stopped off at Fremont. Went on, on the freight, arrived at 4 P.M. Done some trading and after supper went to theatre . . . played billiards till 12.

April 1, 1869. This morning, after getting my money, I had a few games of billiards, started for home. . . .

Saturday 3. This morn started for Omaha with four Pawnee Chiefs, expecting to go to Fort Harker[13] in Kansas. Got a dispatch from General Augur stating that he was bringing the prisoners. Came home on the freight, arrived at 2 A.M.

Tuesday 6. . . . Went to Omaha and had a talk with General Augur. Did not get much encouragement. . . .

"Our military force must be strengthened to combat those hostiles committing depredations in northern, central, and western Kansas, southern and western Nebraska and northwestern Colorado," General Augur lays it out to me. "The army has an oversupply of officers, but the rank and file is very depleted and appropriations have decreased."

"Well, General," I say, "one way you might fill your ranks would be to authorize me to enlist every able Pawnee, put them under the white men I have trained, who know and like the Pawnee and speak the tongue, with orders to force the Plains Indians into submission."

"You're a little too late, Major. President Grant has relied for advice on Indian affairs on an eminent educator, Benjamin Hollowell, a Quaker. It appears the Bureau of Indian Affairs will be administered by church groups. If the Quakers take charge of the Pawnee, they probably will not allow enlistment of Pawnees as scouts. I cannot now offer you any encouragement."

April, Saturday 10, 1869. . . . Went over to my Hall with Bowman [J. W., a saloonkeeper]. . . . After dinner made arrangements for a dance and we had a fine one, lots of fun [housewarming for the new hall].

April 12. . . . Went to Omaha and bought the glass for my new front. . . . I got home at 9 P.M., have got to go back to Omaha in the morning.

April, Tuesday 13. . . . In Omaha just in time to meet the prisoners. They came up on the Glasgow.[14] I brought the men up tonight and they have gone on home.

Wednesday 14. . . . Have been sick all day. . . . [15]

Thursday 15. . . . Have been sick today. . . .

Friday 16. . . . Drove Florence [a mare] and the mule down to the bridge, took Lute down and . . . brought Ma back. . . .

April, Saturday 17, 1869. Last night at 11:30 Mary gave birth to a fine girl baby.[16] This morn Lute went over the river and . . . Charlie, Jim, Tom and Lib came over to see the new born. They are all pleased and of course I am. Lute and Jim Cushing went to North Platte tonight.

Sunday 18. . . . Mary seems quite well today.

April, Monday 19, 1869. Was called up this morn at 1 A.M. Mary was real sick and I went for Doc and him and I sat up 'til daylight. We had lots of callers today. Just before dinner I rode up to the bridge, then to my farm, then home.

Mary so sick—in danger—the ground under me sank, my tongue was wooden, my feet, lead. I have to get out under the open sky. Out here, the meadowlarks have a lot to say about life, and they sing it, sweet and ringing, and my ears begin to hear. A wild canary or gold finch alights on a weed's low branch, hangs on, swaying, head down, picking and eating seed from a long-stemmed, whitened dandelion blossom. A bumblebee hums, nosing into dandelions blooming in the low seeps from the river, and I'm ready to go back home.

Tuesday 20. . . . Went to Omaha with Joe Baker, Yost and Negro Henry, the Negro under arrest for selling whiskey to Indians. Had the trial and put the Negro to jail. I got orders today to recruit another Company. Came home tonight and will go to the Reserve in morn.

Wednesday 21. . . . Drove over to Murie's and got Jim Murie and went to Reserve to recruit . . . but the chiefs said they must see their Father, so we brought two of them down (to Columbus) and got Whaley's consent, so we are all right for tomorrow.[17]

April 25, 1869. . . . I drew and issued arms and horse equipment and then we pulled out (from Fort Kearny) for Kearny Station . . . at 5 P.M., got tents up and oh how it rained. Farmers all looked pleased, sure . . . Lieutenant Cushing went down tonight.

April Monday 26. . . . I drove over to the fort to exchange guns and get bayonets for picket pins. Tonight I go home.

Tuesday 27. This morn I voted for Barnum [for commissioner] then went to bed and slept 'til noon. . . . I went up to my place and surveyed out forty acres for Ernest to break. Barnum is elected by a large majority.

April 28. Today I have felt very bad and have been in the house most of the time. Jim and Lib came over after dinner and Lib will stay with Mary, and Jim and I go to Kearny tonight.

Thursday 29. . . . After breakfast took both teams and drove to the Fort [Kearny], drew 31 days rations, came back . . . at 4 P.M., started the company out. They are encamped in sight.

April 30. . . . At North Platte for breakfast. . . . I had the men clean up their arms then had inspection and muster. . . .

Sunday May 2. Arrived home, found Mary and Lib up, had been up all night with the baby, she is real sick. After dinner took Mary out riding. . . . The baby is sick yet tonight, hope she will be better in the morn.

Monday 3. . . . Went to Omaha. After a good deal of running around got through with my business. Came home on No. 3. Found baby all broke out with measles.

May, Tuesday 4, 1869. Today I go to Omaha to interpret Pawnee in U.S. District Court. Pawnees are on trial for the murder of Charles McMurty, a settler found dead on a river island not far from the south side of the reservation. The verdict by a coroner's jury was that he had been shot by an Indian. Since it was near the Pawnees' reserve, they were suspicioned.

Settlers filch pasture, cut hay, take all the wood they want. The Pawnees understand they are not to take wood from land off their reserve. They tried to make that work both ways. They told me of catching men taking choice hardwood. This time the Pawnee barely let them go, peeled off boots, pants, shirts, and coats, cut harness from the team and ran them off and played a lively game of target shooting arrows next to the thieves' feet. Within the last eighteen months more than a dozen Pawnees have been murdered, and no Sioux or Cheyenne anywhere around. At about the time McMurty was missed, a Pawnee man was killed just east of the reservation line. The law never bothered itself about that death.

Eight Pawnee suspected of being on or near the island at the time of the murder have been jailed and held through the winter. When the court got around to the hearings, Yellow Sun, Blue Hawk, Horse Driver, and Little Wolf were held for trial.

The lawyers juggle and bicker with the judge. The courtroom is warm, gets warmer, hot and hotter and paper collars wilt. Not much gets done and it goes over into tomorrow. I go home and find the folks (baby) better.

Wednesday, May 5, 1869. The trial in Omaha is put off and I am excused for a week. I go to see General Augur, who orders me to Grand Island to guide a detachment of the fifth Cavalry, commanded by Maj. E. W. Crittenden. The detachment is ordered to Shell Creek to establish a base camp to protect the Pawnee Reservation and settlements in the region from Sioux raiders.

I catch a train and at Grand Island hire a horse from Mr. Orr, ride to Soldier's Camp and deliver the message from General Augur to Major Crittenden. In an hour I lead the troops north toward the Loup rivers. Overnight the weather changed to chill with cold wind. But meadowlarks perch on clumps of bunch-grass, making nesting talk in musical tones. Lots of antelope are picking greened-up grass on the divides.

About 35 miles above the reserve we bivouac by the Loup, running bank full. By morning, the water hasn't gone down a lot. I lead out to try a ford. This horse, not the best I've ever ridden, is plainly not a water horse. He panics, and force of the current rolls him under. We get out on the same side we started from, my clothes soaked through.

I take the troops to a safer ford more than thirty miles downriver. The wind is cold through my soaked clothes by the time I march the major and his troops to the fording place to camp. I cross over to the Agency and am at Jim's tonight, trying to beat the chills.

May 8. This morning I am sick, but arrange with Jim to see that the detachment will be supplied grocery staples and meat. I ride across and lead them as far as Looking Glass Creek where I leave them and ride home. I'm too sick to go on. I send John Bloomfield to guide the troops to Shell Creek.

May 10. Today the last spike will be driven in Utah at a summit called the Promontory, to join the Union Pacific Railroad, built from Omaha, Nebraska, to the Central Pacific from California. This evening we hear that Mary's cousin, Louie Smith, was shot and killed.

May 12, 1869. I'm going to Omaha, will bring out a casket, have to see when court will convene and need me to interpret for them. Last night I sent Elias Stowe as second sergeant of Company A—haven't heard from the boys for a week. Coming home, Mary's Aunt Clara and grandpa were on the train, coming to the funeral.

May, Thursday 13, 1869. I drove Whaley's team and took Mary and went to Uncle Sam's [Smith] to the funeral.

Friday 14. . . . Mary and I went over the river, had a splendid visit [with the folks] and I came home, left Mary and baby there. Tonight I go to North Platte and . . . Ogalalla to see my men. Two of them deserted a few days ago.

Saturday 15. . . . At North Platte for breakfast, went on to Ogalalla . . . [returned to] Kearny tonight . . . a splendid dinner today, lots of antelope steak.

Sunday 16. . . . Went over the river with Walker [from Kearny Station to] Fort Kearny, got part of my pay . . . went to Plum Creek this afternoon and took supper at Harnards. Mrs. Harnard goes to Omaha tonight and I have to go through to get payrolls.

Monday 17. Hired Wm. D. Farren, teamster, and sent him up the road tonight. . . . Came home. Found Frankie Whaley had died. [One-year-old child, died of measles and complications.] I received money today for Co. "B."

Tuesday 18. . . . I went up to my farm and . . . in afternoon . . . to the funeral of Frankie Whaley. . . . Tonight I started for Plum Creek. No sleep tonight.

Wednesday, May 19, 1869. Arrived at Plum Creek 4 A.M. rode to [Pawnee Scout] camp. After breakfast . . . march[ed] west to Willow at 1:30. Paid off Co. "B" . . . tonight I stay in camp, leave . . . west on No. 3.

Thursday 20. . . . Found Colonel Wright on train. We get off at Brady and went 1 mile to Noyes Company, Col. paid off the men then we got grub and went to Fort McPherson. I drew 4 horses, got my prisoner . . . sent the horses down to Cushing. Came to North Platte tonight.[18]

Friday 21. . . . This morn brought the boy prisoner up. . . . I sent out some men and they killed six antelope, we had lots of meat. The paymaster came this evening. . . .

Saturday 22. This morn the men got their pay . . . are well pleased. I collected all of Jim's money for him. After dinner we pitched horse shoes and raised Ned generally. . . . Fred and I started home, got some grub at old Majors [store].

Sunday 23. . . . We drove to the Reserve and are now at Jim's [North].

Monday 24. . . . Went to the [Pawnee] council[19] . . . Fred went up the line tonight.

Tuesday 25. . . . Fixed up my business with Johnny Bowman. He is to give me $40.00 per month rent for my place. After dinner, went up to my farm and measured off 40 acres for Ernest to break. Eddie [nephew] and [brother] Jim are here.

June 1. . . . George Clothier and I went to Omaha. Geo. bought a lot of goods. I loaned him $200.00 and went his bail for 200 more.

Frank North in 1867

Organizer and Commander of the Pawnee Scouts, he is shown wearing the uniform of a Major of Cavalry, at 27 years of age. (From a tintype loaned by Mrs. Stella North Chambers.)

Photo by William H. Jackson, courtesy Nebraska State Historical Society

Peta La Shar, "Man Chief," head chief of the Pawnee Nation

The chief is about 50 years old in this photo (1868-69). He died in 1874, possibly by accidental discharge of his own pistol.

La-tah-Cots La Shar, "Eagle Chief"

Photographed about 1868 at the Pawnee reservation, Genoa, Nebraska.

Fort Kearny as it looked about 1864.

As-sau-Taw-Ka, "White Horse," a Pit-a-hau-rat

This photo shows several features of the earlier Pawnee Scouts, including the uniform of the United States Army, the tomahawk and revolver.

Photo by William H. Jackson, courtesy Nebraska State Historical Society

Pawnee braves of the Pit-a-hau-rat band, about 1868

Seated: Tuc-ca-rix-te-ta Ru-pe-row, "Coming around with the herd";
standing: Coo-Towy-oots Co-ter-ah-oos, "Blue Hawk." Note the combined
Indian attire and U.S. Army uniform.

Pawnee village of earth-covered lodges on the Loup Fork

Pawnee braves, about 1870

Seated: left to right, La-roo La Shar Roo cosh, "Man that left his enemy lying in the water"; A-haw La Shar, "Night Chief"; Tec La Shar Cod-dic, "One who strikes the chiefs first"; Te Low-a hut La Shar, "Sky Chief."
Standing: Baptiste Behale, a half-Pawnee sometimes used as an interpreter who also served as a Scout one year.

Pawnee women and children in front of Loup Fork dwelling

Hair style of young brave in center is similar to that of some of the adult warriors.

Pawnee House, Indian school built by U.S. government

Erected in 1868 on the reservation at great expense, the school was barely fit for use because of poor construction.

**Buffalo Bill Cody's "Scout's Rest" Ranch,
built near North Platte in the mid-1880s**

Courtesy Nebraska State Historical Society

Home of Frank and Mary North in Columbus, Nebraska

The Norths settled here at 1002 West 14 Street during Frank North's years as a cattle rancher, after his last Indian War campaign. Pictured on the veranda are the late Mrs. Stella North Chambers (daughter of Frank and Mary North), her husband Edwin, and their child Marguerite. The house no longer stands.

Frank North at about 43 years of age, two years before his death

Mary Smith North (1845-1883)

Husband and wife are buried side by side in the old Pioneer's Cemetery of Columbus, Nebraska.

Personal possessions of Frank North on display at Nebraska State Historical Society

Clockwise from top: Spencer 7-shot repeating rifle, known as the "Indian" model. Driving gloves of muskrat fur. Black tin box in which Stella North Chambers kept keepsakes of her father, including the penciled diaries of two Indian War campaigns. One of the pair of Smith-Wesson revolvers carried by North, who was known as a crack shot. Gold-headed cane presented to North by his constituency after his election to Nebraska Legislature.

Luther North revisiting Summit Springs Battleground in 1933

27

"Good Morning, Major," General Augur greets me as I'm shown into his office. "I was thinking of you and your Pawnee Scouts." He shows me a letter, written under the letterhead of the State of Nebraska and having the seal of the governor.

> . . . I have just received news from the Big Sandy and Republican [rivers]. The Indians are in arms again and are again threatening to repeat their former depredations in that region. The news which I have received is no idle rumor . . . I would ask if you can send a company of soldiers to that region. If you can, how soon can you do it? Can you spare them for four months? Or if not, how long can you spare them? If you can not spare them at all can you furnish me with ammunition, subsistence and transportation for one hundred men, immediately? Or if not with all, with what of these can you furnish me? . . .
>
> [Signed] David Butler, Governor.[1]

"The governor is only the latest to report bands of hostile Indians who eluded General Sheridan's winter campaign. This spring they first hit a few hunters on the Saline River; have wreaked death and destruction on settlements and homesteaders, and killed most of a crew of a Kansas Pacific railway train. In a German settlement of Kansas,[2] thirteen were killed and several women and children carried off.

"At the moment I can only offer token assistance. If I detach companies from my command, which is the only mounted force I have to protect all exposed settlements, I will have none to oppose the Indians. To enable settlers to protect themselves, I will send fifty Spencer Carbines and ten thousand rounds of ammunition for them. The only permanent safety to frontier settlements, is to drive the Indians entirely out. This is what I hope to do this summer.[3]

"Brevet Major General Eugene A. Carr, with troops of the 5th Cavalry, was assigned to this district from winter campaign south from Fort Lyon,

Colorado, to Texas. He is now at Fort McPherson preparing for an expedition in the Republican River country.[4] I am assigning you, Major, with your Pawnee Scout Command to General Carr for campaign. You shall be notified when to assemble your companies at Fort McPherson."

June, Wednesday 2, 1869. . . . Went around and paid a lot of debts . . . stayed with Mary . . . until train time. . . .

June, Thursday 3, '69. Arrived at Ogalalla at 9 A.M., at 10 A.M. I received orders to be at McPherson by Sunday night. I move. . . .

Friday 4. Moved . . . at 7 A.M., . . . at Alkali Paxton . . . met Lieut. Wheelen with 2nd Cav. going to Ogalalla. We camped about 3 miles above O'Fallon. I went down to the Station on hand-car and from there to Plum Creek on No. 4, slept with Brown on the floor.

Saturday 5. Returned to North Platte . . . on No. 3. . . . When Lute came with his company . . . I took them down and crossed the South Platte. Lute, Fred and George did not come down till we were all fixed in camp, and George and Fred were pretty tight. Lute, George and I came back to North Platte and I came home on No. 4.

June, Sunday 6, 1869. Arrived home at 5:10 A.M. Stayed with Mary all day and came back to Brady Island on No.3. Jim Cushing came along. . . .

Monday 7. . . . Brady at 4:30 A.M. found Co. "B" waiting for me. Crossed the River after a great deal of hard work and arrived at the fort at noon. I went back to Brady after wild ponies and to ship Indians' [Scouts] horses home. Returned to the fort at 11 P.M. in an awful rainstorm. 1 bay horse struck by lightning.

Tuesday 8. . . . Went up to Post and made arrangements for my outfit-wagons and . . . turned in all my tents. Just as I was ready to go to camp I got orders to go to Pawnee House[5] and enlist another company. Fred and I go down tonight. Gen. Alvord[6] in company. River high.

The stars and stripes on the parade ground flagpole of Fort McPherson sheets out full in a fresh June breeze. At the Pawnee Scouts' camp there's a spirit of mustering-up-for-doing. Tomorrow is the big day—the day for a full dress review.

Five years I've worked toward this. For five years—anyhow the major parts of them—the scouts have watched and practised, learned and tried, and how proud they are to be a part of the army they so admire.

Tomorrow the scouts will have their day. I'm sorry I won't be with them. I got permission for them to drill in the full dress review. Lute and I put them through it once more today. Drill is a natural to them—fits alongside their excellent tribal rituals and exacting dances.

June, Wednesday 9, 1869. . . . At Columbus 5:10 A.M. Mary and baby are over River. . . . Arrive at [Reserve] noon, have filled the company.[7] Skeedees ponies came tonight from Silver Creek.

Thursday 10. . . . Company started for Columbus. . . . Met Col. Litchfield . . . and we mustered the men in this eve. We are to buy horses here tomorrow. Rained tonight.

Friday 11. Today have been very busy buying horses. . . .

Saturday June 12, 1869. Today finished buying ponies and shipped . . . for Kearny. We sat up till 1 o'clock waiting for train . . . a poor sleep of it on the train.

Sunday 13. Took breakfast at Grand Island, at Kearny 9:30 A.M. Saddled all the ponies and took them off the cars and issued arms, clothing, etc. very tired tonight. . . .

Monday 14. Charlie Walker took a team and brought our traps to the river then ferried them over. We swam the River and drowned four ponies.[8] We drew clothing, tents etc. and stayed at Kearny tonight. Fenton and Mac done all they could for us.

June, Tuesday 15, 1869. . . . Started for Republican.[9] Oh what a long dry march, mules, horses and men nearly perished. Marched 35 miles. Camp on Dry Creek, plenty wood and water.

Wednesday 16. . . . Marched to Prairie Dog Creek [variously called Short Nose Creek] came in sight of Carr's outfit. I sent man with request for wagon. It came and we moved 4 miles when a heavy storm sent us into camp . . . lost 1 horse.

Thursday 17. . . . Moved on, overtook Command at 3 P.M.. . . .

I report to General Carr, unsling the oilcloth dispatch case that I carried on my shoulder from the department adjutant (Bvt. Brig.) General G.D. Ruggles, and deliver it. He opens the case and reads the communication.

His hand slashes the air with annoyance. "I am to detach Captain Sweatman and Company B to cover and protect settlements on the Little Blue! A damnable farce! For loading my command with fifty wild aborigines, worse than useless to me, I am bilked of an entire company of veteran cavalrymen!"

I take over my command. Lute tells me the scouts in drill made the officers sit up and open their eyes—that the officers spoke favorably of the scouts and commended "(our) efficiency of leadership, obvious in the development of aborigines to capability of performing so remarkably well."[10]

Luther reports,

Parade drill, and duty was done for the day, expecting to go out after
enemy the next day, the scouts *must* do their tribal war dance. They
stripped off their clothes as if going into battle, and put on breechclouts
and moccasins, and daubed paints on zig zag and every which way, put
on a feather or antler or some other head gear, built up a fire in the
open and put on a war dance. The post officers and their wives came to
watch the boys put on a real good show. When the expedition jumped
off from McPherson the following morning, the flags were flying, everybody was out to see us off, and the band played "Gary-Owen," as we
pulled away.

Wagons were left behind because forage hadn't come. At the last
minute it did come and the sacks of grain were scattered onto the loaded wagons. It was too much. We led down through the big canyon and
wallowed through the sand. Most of the hired teamsters left the post
drunk, got a couple wagons upset. Some broke down and had to stop to
be repaired. They came stringing into first night camp near Medicine
Creek all throughout the night.

Day before yesterday, after sundown, Indians jumped two teamsters
guarding the mules. (The wagon boss overlooked bringing hobbles for
the grazing animals so they have to be herded.) Well the whooping
started, trying to stampede the herd. The Scouts ran for our ponies, me
with them. We jumped on bareback and lit out. I heard "Boots and
Saddles" sounded, calling out the troops. Cody[11] hadn't unsaddled and
he got to the river ahead, but we caught up before he got out, and some
of the Scouts on faster ponies went ahead. Both of the teamsters were
killed.

When the Scouts gave out with their Pawnee war-cry those surprised
Indians left the horses and mules they were driving away, and started
quirting their horses, but we killed two of them.

We chased them until almost dark and I thought there might be a
chance of them dodging around behind us. We turned back, brought all
the horses and mules back and two of theirs. It was near midnight before we got bedded down.[12]

The command trailed the Indians, leaving the wagon train guarded by
one company of cavalry, on the north side of the Prairie Dog River, so
bank-full from recent heavy rains that the wagons could not ford. After
crossing the North Fork of the Solomon and finding the trail split—the
Indians' way to lose pursuers—General Carr turned west, and next day
southwest, when I caught up with him.

June, Friday 18, 1869. . . . I send Gus Becher and ten [Pawnee] men
out on scout down this creek we are on a tributary of the North Solomon. . . . Sent 5 men across to scout south of the Solomon. I scouted

north 'till noon . . . none found anything of importance.

Reveille at three begins morning and day follows day in similar fashion. I daily send the Pawnee out on scouts as the expedition crosses and crisscrosses its trail, working north and west. Pony tracks found are usually too old to hold any interest. A track of ponies, made earlier the Pawnees are sure, was of cavalry, probably from Fort Wallace or Fort Hays.

Fifty-four wagons, including three of my command—forage, supply, ammunition, ration, and two ambulances—string out, overloaded. The sun and wind on the plains dries out the wheel wood and the rims come loose. The wheels are then removed and soaked when camping near streams. Teamsters grease their axles and care for animals with lamed shoulders and neck (collar) galds.

Daily activity includes the constant search for sign of Indians and buffalo hunting. In this the Pawnee shine, and it's often more sport to watch them make a surround than to be in there shooting and running with them. Bill Cody watches with me this day, then proposes that I let him show the Pawnee how he kills buffalo. I motion the scouts back from another bunch they had pretty well surrounded, and Cody rides in and kills thirty-seven buffalo in a run of about a half mile.[13] With thirty they had killed, the Pawnee have a butchering job for the rest of the day. With less than five hundred men, counting teamsters and all to eat the meat, we have plenty.

June 23. Lute's riding a sorrel mare that is unused to running buffalo. She starts bucking when he heads her toward the bunch. He controls her, then discovers his pocketbook has jolted out of his hip pocket. Unable to find it, he asks a scout if he saw the mare start bucking and could find the spot. The Pawnee thinks he can, and does, and we find the pocketbook with ninety-five dollars in it. It's a mystery to me how he spotted the place as he had no reason for remembering it. I've seen this many times with the Pawnee. It must be natural, keen awareness apart from thought.

A company B boy accidentally shot himself today,[14] and another shot himself in the leg yesterday. Few lodgepole trails have been sighted for several days, and those not fresh. We had a false alarm—a scouting detachment of cavalry thought they had seen Indians, but the Pawnees found they were buffalo. The boys found two horses and a mule; one horse I had lost last winter on a hunt. They also captured an old, starving squaw.

June, Sunday 27, 1869. . . . Marched up the Republican valley . . . nearly 29 miles. Lehman [George, second sergeant of Company C] is quite sick. . . . We are camped near where Lute was last winter.

Monday 28. . . . marched 5 miles and camped. I sent Barclay [George, first lieutenant Company B] over to White Man's Fork. He found train supply there. He came back tonight, brought lots of mail, 2 letters from Mary. *Oh ain't I glad to hear from her.* Had several scouts out, killed ten buffalo.

Tuesday 29. . . . Busy all day getting ready to muster. Sam Wallace out on scout. . . . He returned at P.M., found trail pretty fresh. the train supply arrived today. We will live high again for a while.

Major Crittenden and the escorts of the supply wagon train stir up the camp when they report a big band of Indians[15] in the hills along the Fort McPherson trail this morning as they came in at about 2 P.M.

The camp bustles, transferring rations, forage, and materials from supply wagons onto expedition wagons. General Carr readies two companies of cavalry and one of Pawnee Scouts under Gus Becher to strengthen Crittenden's escort for the wagon train returning to McPherson.

In the cooling twilight breeze, officers hold a jollification and singing. Here are some of the songs:[16]

*   *   *

I'm just as fond of beauty as any one can be
With pretty eyes and rosy cheeks I always love to see
But none of us have got them except myself and you
For I know a little fellow and he's got the money too.
    Oh, don't I love my Honey and won't I spend his money
    I am happy as a flower that sips the morning dew
    For I know a little fellow and he's got the money too.

*   *   *

Oh the old home ain't what it used to be
The banjo and the fiddle have gone
And no more you hear the darkies singing
Among the sugar cane and corn.
Great changes have come to the poor old farm
But the changes make me sad and forlorn
For no more we hear the darkies singing
Among the sugar cane and corn.

*   *   *

June, Wednesday 30, 1869. . . . Mustered all the men this morn. Had inspection mounted and had some fun. Gus Becher started out on 3 days scout with Crittenden. I draw 5 days rations today. The train went back . . . I sent our wounded men and the squaw home, pleasant today. I sent mail to Mary. . . .

July, Thursday 1. . . . Today . . . very dull. Gus returned at 2 P.M. found no Indians, brought in a lot of nice calf meat [young buffalo]. Jim Murie is quite sick today. . . . Lute got all the co-wis he wanted tonight. . . . [17]

The Pawnee Scouts found Major Crittenden's "Indians" in the same locality—not Indians, but buffalo—and fetched in the calf meat. It's easy to think we're seeing Indians. We're now in higher country, grass is thinner and shorter. Up away from the stream are the desert plants, cacti and soapweed (Yucca) that can look like the feathers on a Sioux warrior's head. Besides the old woman, not an Indian has been sighted in more than two weeks.

28

Friday 2. . . . At 6 A.M. marched about 15 miles. Camped on the Republican, near Thickwood. Jim Murie is quite sick today. I'm real sorry I did not send him home with the train. The boys killed an antelope today.

July, Saturday 3, 1869. . . . At 5:30 marched up North Fork of the Republican R. I sent Sam Wallace and ten men out on scout. They found trail of 30 lodges. Two white men went with them and one has not returned. Geo. Barclay is out on a little scout. Marched 15 miles, good camp.

Sam and the scouts with him picked up and fetched in several mule shoes from around the Indians' camp, abandoned a day and a half ago. Trails of thirty tepees or lodges show it to be a good-sized band. The mules with the Indians indicate they've been raiding freighters, since the mules were shod, and probably raiding settlements too. I think these are the bad boys we're after.

July, Sunday 4, 1869. . . . At 5:30 marched 25 miles. Camp on same stream as last night. Sent Gus, Barclay, and Wallace with 50 men [Pawnee Scouts], out on scout with Col. Royall[1] to follow Indian trail. Sam came in tonight. Nothing of interest. . . . Killed 5 buffalo today.

July, Monday 5. . . . No excitement, drew 15 days rations. One of Lute's parties came in at 1 P.M. with news from Col. Royall. I think he has found the Indians before this time. Gus writes me that they are nearing the Indian camp. One horse played out.

July, Tuesday 6, 1869. . . . Marched in a half circle[2] about 25 miles. Sand till you can't rest. No news from Royall today. Sam and Bart walked about 10 miles for disobeying the quartermaster. Lute whipped Steve tonight [wrestling]. Killed 8 or 10 buffalo, nice fat meat.

July, Wednesday 7. Here come the scouts on the run, with scalp poles high.[3] The regulars in camp take it to be Indians coming to raid the camp, but the Pawnee here in camp don't get excited—just start whooping in answer. I assure General Carr there has been a fairly successful skirmish, and that if these were wild Indians approaching, the Pawnees in camp would be stripped and out to battle before now. The general knows this to be true. His complaint of the scouts was that the Pawnees precepted his commands when the Cheyenne jumped the teamsters grazing the herd.

Company B under Lieutenant Becher races into camp, in advance of Colonel Royall and the two companies of cavalry. They had discovered, jumped, and chased a dozen or so Cheyenne braves, one on a travois—a litter fetching a disabled one. The boys took three scalps and eight animals, two with the United States brand, which I turn in. Six I give to the men.

Any day they can take a scalp is a great day for the scouts; they're dancing in celebration tonight. I am not much pleased. It is clear enough to me that Lieutenants Becher and Barclay failed to order and instruct the small divisions detailed out on scouting parties that should they find Indians they were not to attack, but to stay hidden, and keep a watch on their find while one of them reports back, and if that one, or others, do not return to the hiding scouts after enough time, they are not to attack but are to come in. The scouts are trained—will do as commanded but are dependent on command, and lacking orders, will naturally go back to Pawnee ways, as they did this time. With able management, the dozen Cheyenne warriors should have been in the bag tonight, captured or killed.

The general, too, is considerably less than happy about the affair. It is, of course, a smell of victory to him. But he knows, as I do, that because hostiles were allowed to escape, the band will be warned in no more time than it takes the warriors to get to them. The possibility of surprise is lost —if a train of army wagons rumbling along over empty plains through ravines and cutbanks, to say nothing of fording streams, tricky with quicksand or treacherous banks, can be a surprise.

Tomorrow we are to turn back—the general isn't giving up. He believes if the Indians, who twice tried to swipe the mule herd, didn't get warning to the band that the army is after them, those that escaped in the attack did. We dare not risk too long a dry stretch. Too, the way for wagons is rougher every mile. So, the expedition will swing around and find a more northerly route where, the Pawnees say, "Cherry" River, as they call Whiteman's Fork (now, Frenchman), leads west.

I order an end to the scouts' victory-short-of-victory dance and the camp beds down.

Thursday 8. . . . At 6 A.M. marched 15 miles back to our old (earlier) camp on North Fork. No game today. I camped on north side of creek opposite the general. Mosquitos very bad. Went to bed at 9 P.M. Was awoke at 11 by firing in camp. Five Cheyennes charged our camp.[4] One of Fred's men was shot by our own men, not bad.

Indians sailed past the sentry and into the mule herd whooping and firing, trying to scare them into breaking loose and running, but all were well tied. They pounded right through camp, shooting into the wagon yard and among the tents and into my tent and Lute's. The scouts on sentry were right on their tails. One of the galloping horses was shot, or stumbled, and fell. Co-rux-to Chodish, Angry or Mad Bear, sergeant of the night guard, ran up to kill the Cheyenne[5] fallen from the horse, and was himself shot from among my command, a flesh wound above the buttock, though not deep.

The commotion ran west out of our camp. To chase them would be like catching feathers in the dark. I've never before known of Indians attacking at night—it's against the superstition, I believe, of all tribes of the Plains. I think this was more to break loose the horses and drive them away than to make war.

July, Friday 9, 1869. In camp on Becher's Battleground.[6] Arrived here 4 P.M. Marched 30 miles without water and oh how hot and dry. The wounded man is doing fine. We have very poor water, nothing but standing rainwater. One antelope today.

July, Saturday 10. . . . Moved at 6 A.M., followed Indian trail. . . .

An hour later we run onto a campsite the Indians left day before yesterday. Here we see white women's shoe prints—captives! These are most surely the Dog Soldiers, raiders of northern Kansas and southern Nebraska settlements for the last two or three years.

About mid-morn the scouts tell me an Indian campsite we are passing was left only yesterday morning. I have the scouts well fanned out to avoid a surprise attack or running onto Indians unprepared.

A hot south wind whips at the blistering clay around the buffalo-grass hillocks on the divides, digging at the tough roots—a battle as old as the grass and I wonder if finally the grass or the wind will lose. The army forces the march, scouts on far point are well ahead of me and the scout advance.

Across the uplands we catch the high plains smell: low sage (not a brush in this region), with rosin weed, short-stemmed sunflowers, occasional clumps of loco and larkspur, bright flowered cacti and the grasses, buffalo, short grama, and weedy plants. Slogging through great regions of sand we see the white poppy thistle, sand-cherry and buffalo beans and others, all an unforgettable plains perfume mixture, apart from the strong ammonia smell of sweating, lathering horses.

Time and again the columns cross the twisting riverbed and its dwindling channel, dragging the wagon train behind. Each step takes us higher into drier land and air. Horizons shimmer in heat waves. Mirages paint pictures of dreams, wonderful make-believe scenes that are no part of the plains. Ahead lies a blue lake of water, silver waves and great cottonwood trees at the far edge, and under them, horses lazily switching mosquitos. Lush pools of water, trees, green shade, and meadows appear. A railroad train runs yet doesn't move but in the wink of an eye it is gone. Mansions stand alone on the empty prairie, cities show up like magic and disappear. In the afternoon's white-hot clarity, unreal human figures dance on the horizon walls in weird, apart-from-earth forms.

We come upon a campsite where a number of heads of antelope, killed not more than a day ago, shows the Indians left only this morning. Strangely, the people seem still, though distantly, present, their furtive forms only a little less than visible.

"*I-tut-war-uks-ti-ca-riks-ta*" ("some magic people"), the Pawnees explain. I'm not sure whether they speak of the dancing images or of the yet unseen Cheyenne, now only a day ahead, as we find a likely place to camp.

[Continued diary entry of July 10, 1869]: Marched 35 miles, passed three Indian camps. Water poor. In the morn, we move early and take 3 days rations on pack mules and light out for the Indians. We will have a fight tomorrow, sure. I hope we may come out victorious. I shall be careful for sake of dear ones at home.

We prepare for forced march tomorrow. Our horses are in poor shape. Hot days and tough going have taken a lot out of men and horses. General Carr selects the best of his cavalry's mounts—finds, among his seven companies, upwards of five hundred men, less than half the horses with enough bottom left in them to depend on going all the way tomorrow.[7]

Although the general fretted about the scouts being poorly mounted, their ponies have seen more continual use and miles than the cavalry horses. The meat hunting and butchering chore just naturally fell to the Pawnees, and after making the surrounds, their ponies packed in tons of buffalo meat for the camp. They've carried the big end of scouting and courier detail. The scouts were not resting nor were their ponies picking like the cavalry horses during the many hours they worked at these extra jobs. They're worked down and thin, every pony is ladder-sided, but they and the scouts are tough, bred to endure this land. I find fifty ponies that, allowing for the extra miles of scouting and courier work they'll be called on to do tomorrow, I'm ready to bet on to do the job, and then some. Most of the rest of the ponies are not too bad off and will have their work in scouting and courier jobs with the wagon train.

How many Cheyenne warriors we may find is anybody's guess, and whether the number of cavalrymen and scouts the general and I have selected will be enough, no one knows. The general's tactics depend on getting up with the Indians as soon as practicable. Then all depends on the element of surprise if we are to save the prisoners from being killed.

The camp quiets and the high plains evening air cools and rests. There is low, indistinct sound of tired men and animals settling to sleep. Distantly, an occasional halter buckle jingles, and blurred voices of sentinels' routine exchanges drift away.

Reveille sounds early and soon we march. Scouts are on far point, flanks and rear. I lead out with the other scouts falling in. Back of us the cavalry and officers come along. Mules packing three days' rations are behind as we pull away from the wagon train, leaving part of cavalry and Pawnees whose mounts could not take pushing, to escort it at a slower pace.

The sun is hot on our backs. Salt rings on our clothes from many yesterdays' dried sweat are already dissolving in perspiration. Along our horses necks dampness begins to show. Their heads bob steadily as we shove them at a running walk, with occasional short stops for relief, when cinches are loosened, saddles lifted, and pads straightened.

The scouts ahead on point are waiting to show me where the trail splits. Each fork will frazzle out—a crafty mislead. The Pawnee trailers find after tracking that plain tracks disappear—probably by careful brushing out, or all scattering widely, or some such of their many tricks.

General Carr orders Colonel Royall, a company or so, and scout Cody to reconnoiter the larger trail. He and remaining troops will follow the small trail as the Pawnee advance lookouts at point, wide flanks and rear.

We skirt soapweed (yucca) and large clumps of low spreading cacti and dog it through loose sand. The sun is nearly straight overhead. Noon passes—an hour past, and I begin to fidget.

Something's not right—there's something missing here. From beside my mount's hoof a jackrabbit jumps from his small hollow under a clump of brushgrass—about startles me out of my saddle!

Not a single scout has reported seeing Cheyenne lookouts covering their back trails!

I mull it over. Were I this band's leader, Tall Bull, I would post lookouts with swift ponies to watch from the vantage points while the tethered ponies graze in ravines or behind a rise, handy but unseen. That's exactly what they've done and that's the reason the scouts haven't seen lookouts! There are none on their back trails.

Of course the army was seen to turn right back in its tracks and continue going away. (Cheyenne warriors may have tailed us through the entire day's march eastward.)

After I, as leader of the band, had daily split the trail, to have my people scatter from a place of hard surface or outcrop that seldom tattles tales (or tracks), to gather at day's end at a prearranged place from so many separate ways; and after I was careful to see that for days not one of my people or horses had shown themselves about the skyline; then I suppose I would believe I had convinced the army that I and my band had completely left the region—if I were an Indian.

Then, if I were an Indian, I would do as they do after the enemy seems to have gone or been disposed of. I would rest with my people. The lower tepee air flaps would be open for circulation. Little children would run free in play. The horse herd would rest and pick, with a few older boys to herd them. Women would do their tasks, while hunting parties would go out to bring in meat. Put out lookouts? Why? To watch the wind after it has blown away?[8]

A scout courier rides up from our left flank saying the scouts with General Carr have seen two horseback riders, Indians, and that the general orders me to come immediately to him. At two o'clock we get to him and find him waiting back of low bluffs. With the general and other officers, I go up on the bluffs of the South Platte valley. We put our field glasses on the river course four or five miles north and the rise of slopes to a center summit and see nothing living in the whole land, not even a jack rabbit.

Securing cinches and mounting up to move on, the scouts say the command should now proceed like the *kirl-uk-u-lah*, the yellow-red fox, with cunning, keeping low between, not over the sand hills and draws, and Carr so orders.

The scouts prowl the vantage points and examine the ravines, ever on the lookout for dividing or crossing trails. Our horses are flagging and the general is saying he believes "the whole thing is turning out to be a humbug," when we see the scouts motion us to come.

As we ride up the Pawnees point out a distant herd of animals as horses.

"Probably are only buffalo grazing on the sand hills. However, as we've came this far, we will go and see," the general says.

The herd looks to be as distant as two or three miles—space, distance fools a man here. Once, four years ago in the Powder River country, I said "buffalo" when the scouts said horses and Indian riders. Well, the general will learn to take the Pawnees' word for what they see.

The boys suddenly scramble to throw saddles off their ponies and most of their clothes off themselves; tying colored bands around their heads to

mark them as Pawnee. This convinces me and impresses the general that
they're sure they've found the Cheyenne village.

The general orders a "Halt." Our horses get a breather, awaiting
Colonel Royall and troops, now coming up. I change the saddle from the
mule I rode this far to the gray mare, led along to be strong for the attack.
After Colonel Royall's report to the general, the order sounds, "Prepare to
mount!" All stand to horse.

"Mount up!" is followed by groans and grunts as tender, raw backsides
settle into sun-hot saddle leather.

"Forward at trot!" With Lute at my elbow I lead my scouts. We proceed
about a mile, as I believe still unseen when the Pawnees on point send
back a courier to warn we are about to ride in sight of the camp.

I relay this message to the general. He again calls a "Halt" to arrange
his plan of attack; dresses his cavalry into two parallel columns of twos.
Major Walker is assigned with a detachment on the left to prevent escapes
from the village. Captain Price with a company goes to right flank. My
Pawnee Scout command with white officers will follow my lead. General
Carr places Major E. W. Crittenden in command, as Bill Cody comes up
to join in.

Again we are mounted up. All are aware *this is it!* The order "Charge!"
sounds. I put my mare at "speed" and see General Carr and escort break
off to command the field from a vantage point.

I glance back, seeing my fast mare has gained two hundred yards ahead
of my nearest scout. Luther lets his mount out and comes up fast. The
cavalry comes up from some distance on "fast gallop."

Lute pulls up even as I gain the ridge that follows the curve of a small
stream below. Beyond in low sand hills a horse herd leaps into motion,
stampeded toward the village. Herd boys have seen us! From behind the
herd shoots a white horse carrying a herd boy—running hard. The race is
on! The white horse streaks for the village—the boy races to warn his
people.

If that horse and boy can outrun the greater distance, can give his
people a half minute or so, the prisoners will be killed and every Indian
armed.

Like a shooting star that white horse pounds direct for the village—
points its location below cutbanks along the stream. We spur our mounts,
do not get half the speed of the desperately racing horse and rider.

Moving so fast the two seem *a'na hur ac'*—a Pawnee spirit. We hear his
cries, but his people do not.[9]

I raise the Pawnee battle cry and charge in as the scouts sound it out.
The village explodes with action and the cavalry sweeps through, shooting
in every direction.

Indians run around like mice in a box. I catch a glimpse of an orange-sorrel horse with silver mane and tail carrying three, running for the open.

A number of horses were tied in the village and some of the herd were caught and now carry a back full of Cheyennes away. Others scuttle for the hills, dodge into ravines and pockets. Those warriors who got mounted draw small squads away into running fights, trying to give the women and children a chance to get away.

That our right flank is open occurs to me—is providing escape through ravines fringing the plain. I wonder why Walker is not blocking the getaway.

A scattering of scouts with two or three soldiers are at the far side of a deep ravine. As Luther and I ride past the near side a bullet whistles past my face. I throw up my hand. Lute thought I was shot. I jump off and throw him the reins.

"Start at a gallop," I say, and drop to my knee, take a knee rest with my Spencer carbine, see a rifle slipped up on the ground from the ravine, then a head as far as the eyes—enough to sight his aim. I squeeze my trigger. The rifle falls back on the ground as the Indian disappears. I'm sure I shot him in the forehead.

Lute only went a few jumps—is back at the crack of my gun. As I wait for another warrior to take the place of the first, a head comes up—a woman. She comes to the top, gets out, then reaches down and pulls up a child, maybe five years old. The scouts on both sides of the ravine again start firing at Indians who knife out steps up the near vertical sides from which to shoot us.

Making "talk" sign the woman comes toward me, passes her hands over me from head to foot—an act of blessing and appeal for mercy—and on her knees asks me by sign to save her and the child.[10] In the same language I tell her to go to the rear, and stay there, out of danger.

Soon no more shots come up from the ravine. Scouts creep up and venture in. I look down. Under the place where the man's head showed up, he lies dead, shot as I thought, through his forehead. I see the bright sorrel horse again, in the ravine, dead, stabbed and shot.[11] I call the scouts out and we ride on.

Cor-ux-ah Kah Wadee, Traveling Bear, jumps four warriors. All run into a ravine and he after them. We are engaged in a running battle of a half mile or more. We make short work of it and turn back. Traveling Bear comes up out of the ravine with four scalps and four guns besides his own.[12]

Lute, Cushing, Wallace, and I stop, seeing a wooden keg of water by the largest hide lodge near the end of the half-mile-long village. Cushing jumps off, picks up the keg and drinks, passes it to me. I drink and give it to Sam Wallace. Dismounting, I pass the keg to Lute. Turning away, I hear a sharp grunt from him.[13]

Cushing looks—goes into the hide lodge after seeing a white woman, and I follow. She is bleeding from a breast wound and scared nearly out of her senses. She crawls to Jim, winds her arms around his legs crying, moaning and talking—a language we don't understand. Jim says something to her, bolsters her a little and we hurry on. Within minutes we find another white woman not far from the big tepee, killed by a shot or tomahawk blow to the skull.

The air is deathly still, sultry, as we are ordered to charge Indians riding about just beyond shooting range. We go at them almost at a walk and they skedaddle for the hills. Going on, we round up the large horse herd. The scouts catch themselves fresh mounts, turning their own loose with the herd to drive all nearer the village. I detail scouts to herd them to prevent escaped Cheyennes from taking horses.

General Carr Reports the Engagement
with Dog Soldier Cheyennes at Sand Springs

[General Carr's statement as recorded in Journal of the March, July 11, 1869, NARS RG 98, is quite revealing of how greatly, toward the end of this campaign, the general relied upon the Pawnee Scouts, in spite of his terse, skeptical statement of opinion of them, just prior to the campaign beginning. Although the white scout, William Cody, whose services the general had specifically requested and obtained, was present in his command, it was the Pawnees who led and advised him at the last and who won his unstinted praise in his report.]

Next day June 10, 1869, we followed the trail which led up the Frenchman Fork, passed two of their Indian camps and encamped on a third. . . .

They had left it that morning, and I determined to leave the wagons and push on for them. I took all available men; that is, all whose horses were fit for Service, and they amounted to two hundred and forty-four (244) officers and soldiers and fifty (50) Pawnee Scouts, out of seven companies of the 5th Cavalry and one hundred and fifty Pawnees. This shows the necessity of having the horses well fed and cared for and of having extra animals on every expedition. . . .

When we reached the breaks of the Platte Bluffs the Pawnees reported seeing two horsemen, and recommended taking the whole command into the ravine which was done. . . .

We galloped about an hour through low sand hills and loose sand and saw no sign of Indians, and I began to think the whole affair was a humbug . . . when some Pawnees beckoned me to come to them, which I did with the command, though I had little hopes of finding anything. . . . The Pawnees pointed out a herd of animals about four miles off in the hills . . . I thought it were possible it might be Buffalo but of course determined to go and see.

The Pawnee stripped themselves for the fight, taking off their saddles and as much of their clothing as could be dispensed with and still have something to distinguish them from the hostiles. . . . When concealment was no longer possible, I placed the three leading companies in parallel columns of two's, directed Major Crittenden, 5th Cavalry, to take command and sounded the charge. We were over a mile from the village and still undiscovered. . . . The Pawnees on their left put their horses at speed while the rest followed at a fast gallop. . . .

They [the hostiles] proved to be Dog soldiers, Cheyennes and Ogalalla Sioux, I had only one man slightly scratched by an arrow. One horse killed, and twelve died in the chase. Fifty-two Indians were killed on the field and seventeen women and children captured.

The Pawnees under Major Frank North were of the greatest service to us throughout the campaign. This has been the first time since coming west that we have been supplied with Indian Scouts and the results have shown their value.

The place where the battle took place is, I believe, called Summit Springs. [The Summit Spring site is located about twelve miles south and five miles east of Sterling, Colorado.] This band proved to be Dog Soldier Cheyennes commanded by Tatonka Haska or "Tall Bull" who was killed in the engagement after a desperate personal defense.

"Journal of the March," July 11, 1869

Property captured, Items invoiced

56 rifles	31 mess pans
22 revolvers	52 water keys
40 sets of bows and arrows	64 brass and iron camp kettles
20 tomahawks	200 rawhide lariats
47 axes	16 bottles strychnine (to bait
150 knives	wolves)
50 lbs of powder	85 lodges complete
20 lbs of bullets	125 travois
14 bullet molds	9300 lbs dried meat
8 bars of lead	160 tin cups
26 boxes percussion caps	180 tin plates
17 war shields	200 dressing knives
17 sabers	8 shovels
9 lances	75 lodge skins (new)
13 war bonnets	40 saddle bags
690 buffalo robes	75 bridles
502 panniers (large baskets) with	28 women's dresses (new)
carrying handles	50 hammers
15 moccasins	9 coats
319 raw hides	100 lbs of tobacco
361 saddles	200 tin coffee pots

1500 dollars in gold and national
bank notes
25 horses and mules killed
In addition, 274 horses and
114 mules were captured.

29

July 12, 1869. Being without a chaplain, a man, Kane, volunteers to read the orthodox burial service as the body of Suzannah Alderdice, the murdered white woman, wrapped in robes, is placed in the grave prepared in the rain-washed earth. " . . . Ashes to ashes, dust to dust . . ."; and this place is named Suzannah Springs.

We turn from the funeral to destroy this village, rich with hand-beaded and dyed porcupine-quill embroidery on buckskin shirts and dresses, finely finished robes, tanned unfinished robes, and many dry, unworked hides. The scouts are permitted to load dried meat, packed in the dry hides, on any pony of the captured horse herd not needed for riding. The harness-marked mules from the captured herd are roped in to replace the fagged, weak, wagon-train animals. So, the near-to-empty wagons carry hides and dried meat for use of the scouts and soldiers. Every buffalo-hide tepee lodge, all articles not wanted, and excess dried meat are piled and burned.

I find that my scouts have gathered up twenty-dollar gold pieces. Surprised at the amount, I speak to the general about them. The wounded woman is asked, through the Swedish soldier who interprets German, if she knows where the Indians had gotten the gold pieces. She says her father had recently come from Germany to the Kansas settlement and brought money with him, which he exchanged for American twenty-dollar gold pieces; about two thousand dollars worth he had in their home in the settlement raided and burned by these Indians. The general orders that all gold and valuables, such as jewelry, are to be turned in for the woman. The Pawnee Scouts do not object; six hundred and forty dollars we turn in. The soldiers only turn in three hundred dollars.

We are glad to turn our backs on this place. At noon we drag out for the Platte, a swollen, cumbersome outfit now. The wounded woman is in the ambulance wagon which Co-rux-to Chodish, Mad Bear, vacated to ride a travois, as do also the small children. The other young captives and

163

the women are riding Cheyenne saddled ponies led by watchful scouts who haven't forgotten the little captive girl who gave them the slip in the dark last year. Going into camp a few miles down the Platte brings up more new problems, the large horse and mule herds to guard; the camp and the prisoners are to be closely guarded.

> July 12, 1869. [The day after the battle.] Invoiced property today and burned what we did not want. Started on the march at 12 noon for the Platte River. Arrived in camp at 4 P.M. Find good grass and water and plenty of wood, such as telephone poles. We are 65 miles from Julesburg. George and ten men [Scouts] went to Julesburg with dispatches.

The second day moves us downriver twenty miles to bivouac at Riverside, the west end of Fred Matthew's stage driving run three or four years ago. The Fifth Cavalry officers select the best ponies from the Cheyenne herd. Cody and myself get the privilege of choosing a horse each. Each of the scouts get to select a horse, and I still have 180 horses left that have to be herded along with the mules and the army's extra animals.

> Wednesday, 14. This day's march gets us to Antelope Station—distance, twenty miles. Gus, with four men, goes to Fort Sedgwick at midnight. I telegraph home, also write—hope I can go home in a few days as I'm scheduled to report in court on the 20th.

> Friday 16. General Augur, after getting General Carr's first dispatch, comes to Fort Sedgwick and General Carr's camp. An interpreter, Leon Palladay,[1] is called in and we quiz the women prisoners. General Augur is taking them to Omaha to send to the Whitestone Agency near Fort Randall. I am to go home tomorrow leaving Lute in command in my absence. We separate the ponies to load them in the morning on freight cars at Julesburg, a couple of miles east.

> July 17. We're leaving Julesburg at 2 P.M. Stop at North Platte for supper. Murie and Jacob Haupt come down with me. Jimmy is not at all well.

> Sunday, July 18. We get lunch this morning at Grand Island. Arrive home and find Mary, Baby, and Lib waiting for me. Mrs. Murie met Jimmy at depot. (I had sent word to Mary for her.)
> We unload horses and materials from the Cheyenne village sent by the scouts to their people. I am waiting for train to go to Omaha—it is nine hours late.

> Tuesday, 20. Omaha at 4 A.M. went to bed at St. Charles Hotel, slept till 7 A.M., then reported, done my business, and home. This morn, I and

my man deliver all the packs to the Pawnee and the horses that are marked for them. Get back from the reserve and Mary and I take a ride on horseback to Aunt Sarah's.

Thursday 22. Al Rose, sheriff, wants me to go with him to the reserve. We serve some warrants and make some arrests on the McMurty murder. Bob White came to the Pawnee village with the wounded sergeant, Mad Bear.

Friday 23. We brought the arrested Pawnees to Columbus, will send them to Omaha on the No. 8 train. I'm not going until on No. 4 at 11 P.M. I traded two ponies for Antelope Horse at the reserve today. I've liked the horse—he's good and runs like an antelope—fast.

Saturday, July 24. This morn we take the witnesses and prisoners (Pawnee) before the judge and have them examined. They are all dismissed when the judge finds not sufficient cause to hold them. I propose to surprise Mary—I'm buying a carriage and double harness today, will have them shipped out.

Got home in time to get a good night's sleep, then get my buggy off the train and drive home to take Mary for a ride. This evening Mary, Baby, and I went to Aunt Sarah's.

Monday 26. Another week begins of shuttling back and forth almost daily. This time United States Marshal Joseph T. Hoile and C. A. Baldwin, the prosecutor in the murder case, come back with me. After breakfast I hitch the team to the carriage and we go to the reserve.

We tell the chiefs we will have to take them to Omaha and keep them until we find the guilty parties. So we came to Columbus in time for supper and the officials go down on the train. I hold the chiefs overnight.

Friday, 30th. No train down until 2:30 P.M. I play billiards and after dinner take Mary for a buggy ride, then start to Omaha on the freight with the Pawnees. Arrived at 11 P.M. and in the morning talk with the chiefs then go home.

Tuesday, August 3, 1869. Back in Omaha we commence the trial and keep it up six hours. The Pawnees are all sent home but six who are indicted. Their trial is set for August 31.

Wednesday 4. I get my payroll matters all fixed up then go to the races until time to catch No. 4 to go home. In the morning Mary and Baby and me drive to Muries to pay Jimmy for July scout service and what I owe him. Back home I prepare to return to my command, to let Luther come home. I take the train for Julesburg at 12:40 P.M. I find the command is at Ogalalla, so I jump on No. 8 to backtrack that far. Lute meets me at the depot with a horse. We cross the river and ride to camp. He reports: "The cavalry laid over a couple of weeks at Sedgwick to rest and recoup the horses. General Carr was notified of his son's death and went to Fort McPherson and east. Colonel Royall, now commanding, moved south to the head of Whiteman's Fork where the Pawnee Scouts found a fresh trail. This was followed to the junction with the Republican. The Indians discovered the troops before being seen, switched directions and kited[2] north. We chased 'em across the divides to the South Platte. They got here and crossed yesterday, just a jump ahead of us. We had to lay over as the wagon train mules were too fagged to pull the river."

Saturday, August 7, 1869. This morn cross the river with the whole command and camped between the rivers. I go with Lute to the depot, pay him, give him a train pass home, and fetch his horse back. The column leaves the South Platte valley, passes into the north hills and over rolling land to the North Platte River. It's a long dry march, one rolling hill looks exactly like the next.[3] We camp at a small slough where the Indians camped and their trail is plain. The wagons won't catch up to us tonight.

Sunday, Monday, Tuesday, Wednesday we march on. I rotate details on far point, at near van, and at flanks, also set night camp sentinels. On Thursday I send Fred with ten men out on a scout. Kisslingbury with part of Company "A" is in advance. Two horses played out today. We bivouac tonight north of the Niobrara (Running Water). Fred has not come in.

Colonel Royall decides to give up the chase. I'm sure the Indians are bee-lining straight for Fort Randall Whetstone Agency for the winter. We've passed only two of their camps. They're running and have no chance to gather food. If any of them got away from the Tall Bull fight with arms, they would have used all the ammunition in the fight. They've none to bring down game, even if they were not being hard pressed. The remnant of the Tall Bull band won't be bothering these parts for a while at least.[4] They've left forty-two raddled-out ponies along the way north.

I send out for Fred. He comes in about 10 A.M. The last of our rations are issued and we turn back. Fourteen miles retraced. Nothing to eat tonight.

August 14. A long, hot march over baked hills today. Our stomachs are caved in. We surely will make the wagons by tonight in order to get something to eat, and we begrudge the time we have to give the horses for breathers. We've nearly starved by nine o'clock when we find the wagons. The cavalry lost ten horses today, gave out and shot.

Sunday 15. Lay in camp all day today. One of Fred's men died and we bury him. He was taken sick the day we left here and nothing could be done to save his life. I don't know what the disease was.

I had left him back with the scouts escorting the wagon train, and expected he would be all right in a day or so. The scouts have had no sickness among them before this—are always able for the day.

Finally reaching the North Platte River we drag down the north side, daily losing horses. By Thursday evening we reach Birdwood Creek,[5] with plenty of grass and good water.

All day and every night in the river valley, men and horses fight mosquitos, and on windless days, clouds of gnats with an occasional deerfly. After another day and a half of marching we arrive at Fort McPherson at noon, the fort band playing a serenade.

The smart Fifth may have marched out of the fort a-stepping snappy on the ninth of June. They're not showing a bit of spit and polish today. Our clothes, sun-faded and sweat-bleached, are under layers of body salts and prairie dust. Every man's face is weathered to about the same color as the Pawnees'.

Below the fort a couple of miles, we make a good camp, but the mosquitos are bad.

Monday 23. Went to fort. I transfer eleven ponies to the AAQM. My officers all draw clothing for their men. At 6:30 I see a horse race between Cody and Doherty, the latter won twenty dollars.

Wednesday 25. With a message from General Augur permitting me to go home, we load all the ponies that Colonel Royall agreed, a week ago last Saturday,[6] the scouts may have on the provision they ship them at their own expense. I got supper at Harnards and we're on the move. Captain Cushing gets off at Silver Creek to see to unloading the ponies, later catches a freight down.

I hire a man to drive the ponies to the reserve. Mary and I drive over in the buggy, in time for dinner at Jim's, got some Pawnees with wagons and mules to help me bring over the bundles for the Indians—the rest of the meat and salvage from the Cheyenne village. Had a rough time, a team got scared, started running and stampeded another team—scattered Pawnees and bundles to kingdom come.

Getting home late, I still have to go across the river and get Cushing to go to McPherson. Mother takes Baby, and Mary comes with me to Omaha to visit a day or so with friends. We put up at the St. Charles and in the afternoon hire a rig and drive up to Florence to visit Zura (Mrs. Mitchell)[7] and the Bigsleys.

Mary and Kate McCausland visit at Purchase and we spend the evening with the McCauslands. This morning I take Mary to the depot and start her for home. I am all day in court, talking Pawnee. After two more days

I go home on No. 7, arrive at 2 A.M.

September 4. Back to Omaha on No. 4. Have further court investigation in the afternoon. Nothing new brought to light. A bill is found by the jury and Yellow Sun and Blue Hawk are asked, "Guilty or not guilty to the charges?" When they plead not guilty they are remanded to jail to await trial, set for the first week of November. I got home on No. 7, in the rain. This afternoon I took my pacing ponies and Mary and Baby and went to the Kelly's. Came back in a heavy downpour. All got wet and were sick in the night.

Wednesday, 8. Before I go I want to get a picture taken of my Baby. We take her to Al's and the first one is good. I leave at 12:40, get to McPherson at 9 P.M. Found horses and wagon waiting for me and came to camp.

After seeing the general this morning Fred and I made a horse race with Cody. I get beat and we wait to see the race between Hays and Mason. Hays wins by big odds. Tomorrow the boys will draw rations and forage enough to last a month.

We are preparing for another campaign through the south country. This evening some officers and ladies visit our camp. A rainstorm is coming up and our visitors soon leave. Lightning crashes and thunder roars. It rains hard all night and turns too cool for comfort. We are all chilled through. There'll be no drilling today. I wrote to Mary yesterday and today get a letter from her.

We play billiards to pass the days after orders to move are countermanded. The day comes, September 15, that we move out as far as Medicine Lake.[8] Everybody is hungry—the teams and wagons are slow and late. Orders come tonight for me to start one company of scouts to Pawnee Reserve to defend against Sioux.

Thursday 16. I send Fred and B Company—and send along a saddle of venison to General Emory. He had hoped to come out on this campaign but had to stay at the fort to conduct a court martial. Four of Fred's boys are staying with me for the campaign.

After a day's lay-over here, getting shook down, Bvt. Brig. Gen. Thomas Duncan's expedition heads south. Three troops of Second Calvary and seven of the Fifth—besides three companies of Pawnee Scouts' A, B, and C—are the expeditionary force. None of the troops are at full strength. Pawnee Scout troops are nearest to full. After eighteen miles we camp among wild plums and have plenty of meat, at the Medicine's big bend, where we camped just about a year ago with General Augur.

September, Sunday 19, 1869. The column moves fourteen miles, the scouts ahead. I take a couple boys and kill two buffalo. The next night bivouac is near the old stockade we discovered four months ago with Carr.[9] It has been here a long while. Perhaps built as a fur-buying agency's subpost. It looks too old to have been put up at the time of the Colorado gold rush.

Buffalo by the thousands hardly stand aside for this mile or more of column to pass. We swing wide around, especially when fording the river.

My Pawnee Scouts call the Republican River *Kiz-ka-tus*—meaning the "river-that-stinks"—of buffalo manure from its forks to its outlet. We daily move downstream; plenty of fresh meat as we just go out and get buffalo as well as antelope, elk, and turkeys in wooded places.

September 22, 1869. This morn crossed the Republican, march to Short Nose (Prairie Dog Creek). Nearing camp time I ride off aside expecting to see buffalo in the next ravine. I do, and as there has been considerable speculation among the officers on possibility of capturing a buffalo calf by lassoing it, I put a loop in my picket rope, take a run up to the bunch, swinging my rope and settle it over a calf's head. He takes off like he was shot. I get rope burn as it sizzles through my hand. Unable to hold it, I chase after him.

My horse is wild, a cavalry horse, not trained to run buffalo and objects to approaching it. A touch of my spurs change his notions and I think we may catch the rope. I pull my horse down on his haunches—he is on the rope. I run to the calf to make a stab with my knife. The calf bucks, the blade strikes a rib, glances off, my rope-scorched hand slips down over the blade. It draws blood—mine, but not much of the calf's. My hand is badly cut. The horse steps off the rope and the calf goes galloping. I bind my right hand with my handkerchief, mount and take after the young beast again. We catch up and I slide off onto him. I discover the calf's got a lot of buffalo bull in him, and he leaves me again.

I climb back in the saddle and chase after the calf. My horse stumbles, flounders, and rights himself. By the time I take a look around the calf has disappeared. Where he could be, beats me. I ride around a while before I find him, lying in a little coarse grass by a shallow buffalo wallow that sometime had held enough water to grow reeds. The calf lies low until I ride near, then jumps up, throws that funny little pig tail straight up and scoots. I catch him quick and with the knife in my left hand I bleed him and drag the veal into camp, no bullet hole in it.

I send out several men to get meat. The army surgeon sees to my hand —thinks the tendons may be cut, treats it and binds it up.

Toward the end of the day's march Cody[10] and I ride ahead to find a campground. He stops at the side of a ridge to guide the train to the site that I ride on over to locate. I dismount, hold my horse, and stretch my legs. Six Indians suddenly ride up a ravine—startles them to see me here as much as I'm surprised. Just as suddenly, they flip down off-side on their ponies and beat it away. I get on my horse and ride back to Cody. The Indians take a second thought—come back and give us a lively chase. We play them along—get them nearer the command, then I ride in circles to call out my scouts. Cpt. George F. Price's engineer corps led by Lieutenant Volkmar advance toward us, but not a scout do I see. I ride on up to the general, ask him the whereabouts of my command—until now in the advance by a half to a mile or more.

"I have assigned them to the rear position," he says, and at my request grants me permission to take them. Some sharp Pawnee eye me circling, and Cushing is bringing them on the fly, shucking off saddles and clothes as they come ready for a fight. It's a gallop of more than a mile up the column.

As the scouts come up we see the Indians, upwards of forty, the entire hunting band going out of the river on the other side. The scouts take out after the band, sounding the Pawnee cry. That speeds them, quirting their ponies furiously. After a chase of six or eight miles and one Indian killed, the scouts turn back about dark with a couple of captured ponies and a mule.

> *September, Sunday 26.* Today we marched 24 miles and I and Cody came ahead to the Creek. Indians got after us and gave us a lively chase you bet. I got my men out and they killed one Indian and got two ponies, a mule and lots of trash.

Monday, 27. The column moves eight miles when the scouts run onto the Indians' abandoned camp. Now I understand the scheme of yesterday's buffalo hunting band. After running onto me, their dash away was to have me chase them away from the direction of their camp. When I didn't take up the chase, but turned back and joined Cody, they probably intended to get near enough to kill us to make their camp safe from white men. They failed, worse yet, learned troops were present on the plains and saw the column. Joining their hunting brethren and showing themselves across the stream they expected the troops to chase them. Real fear struck them when the Pawnee war cry hit their ears.

Terror-struck, the Indians pulled out, abandoned tepees, camp equipment, meat, dried and in the making, robes, garments, and saddles, and—strange enough here—a surveyor's transit, hammering mauls, and other tools.[11] We destroy the tepees—a hint to them to go to the reservation.

General Duncan orders out a company of cavalry and one of Pawnee Scouts to track and follow the Indians, and to return if no Indians are found between here and the Republican River. They came back, report the trail so overrun with buffalo that it is lost.

George and Kis out on scout with small detachments found three horses and one jack, no Indians. Tomorrow, Stowe with six men, Pawnee, will go with "B" and "M" companies of cavalry for Sheridan, Kansas, with Mitchell's mules—some of the animals found at Summit Springs and recaptured from the Cheyenne, brought to Fort McPherson, their brands identified and claimed by Mr. Mitchell for Moore and Company as property taken from them.

September, Thursday 30, 1869. . . . Came up Beaver Creek . . . camped, nice food, wood and water. We are glad to get a little rest. We have been in the saddle every day for two weeks.

Another day we do not move. Our horses needed rest. We expected Major Brown and George Barclay with twelve Scouts to return from scouting Middle Beaver but they did not. We read most of the day, all the old papers in camp.

Saturday 2. This morn we move earlier than usual, come for Republican, *my Scouts in advance* catch an old squaw that strayed from the village.[12] She is nearly starved. We feed her and will take her to the Fort. Arrive at Republican at 2 p.m. Find Brown and George here waiting for us. 25 miles.

Sunday 3. . . . Lay over, I spend the whole day in reading. This evening I read several chapters in the Bible to Clark and Dick, have had an awful headache all day. I take some pills tonight and salts in the morning.

After laying over another day, camp is moved two miles to fresh grass. Scouts kill three antelope and a buffalo—had some good ribs for supper. Today, on general's order, I sent Lieutenant Kisslebury and six Pawnee men to Whiteman's Fork to guide the train to us at Big Timbers, and to bring the mail. Stowe, with his six men and the two cavalry companies, got in tonight from Fort Wallace. They saw three Indians yesterday, no trail.

The mail comes, also the wagon train. We lay over, get our mail ready to send, and draw twenty days' rations. General Emory was for a short while with the expedition and went in with his escort and the wagon train.

Friday 8. I discharge Sinon, teamster on one of my outfit wagons, for his all around general cussedness and, specifically, for his senseless abuse of his team. Co-rux-to-Chodish, Mad Bear, is driving.

Saturday 9. . . . moved for the Forks of the Republican . . . I arrive at the Forks with my Command at 11 A.M., 12 miles. Sent Kis and men on 3 day scout. . . .

October, Sunday 10, 1869. This morn I send Elias Stowe and James Deyo and 15 Pawnees with Lieutenant Wheeler [and B Troop, Second Cavalry, and M troop, Fifth Cavalry] to scout up South Fork of the Republican, had 5 days' rations. Barclay and Hunt and 15 Pawnees, also Major Irwin [and A and I Troops, Fifth Cavalry] scout Arickaree Fork [River], Black Tail Creek and Rock Creek.

Monday 11. For a fresh campground we move up a couple of miles. Kis came in this evening from scouting the Frenchman River in advance of B and E Troops, Fifth Cavalry. He reports no fresh Indian sign, but they found the Indians had crossed the Frenchman and went on in a northwesternly course.

Tuesday, October 12. This morn I take about two miles ride and come back to Camp feeling fine. Sent to Col. Crittenden after some papers and read the balance of the day. Oh, this laying in Camp is fearful dull, am anxious for the days to pass by, so we can go in and go home.

With the valleys alive with game— elk, deer, antelope, and buffalo— and little danger of running into hostile Indians, this expedition would turn an eastern sportsman-hunter green with envy. It's a mighty pleasurable expedition. Its military objective is to sweep the country clear of all hostiles. I think that job is done. Now, I want to get all the scout reports in and have done with this laying in camp.

On Thursday night George Barclay gets in from the scout up the North Fork and the Arickaree; says they found no signs of Indians, but found two horses and a mule. When Stowe comes in on Friday afternoon with good news (which is no news of Indians), nobody is disappointed.

We move in a couple of marches to Big Timbers. Stowe and a couple of scouts were started yesterday for McPherson with mail, and we hope he will bring orders to come in at once. The command separates here, two companies of Second Cavalry and Captain Cushing and his company go downriver to the old stockade while we go across country to the Beaver creek.

October, Tuesday 19, 1869. This morn we got up and found the ground covered with snow. . . .

Thursday 21. . . . General Duncan sends me a turkey. We [the Pawnees] roast it and I think it the best eating I ever had.

October, Friday 22, 1869. . . . Snowed all day. Of course we did not move camp. We hauled up a lot of wood with a mule and sat by the fire all day.

Saturday 23. . . . Move at 8 A.M. The Gen. invites me to take a hunt down the Creek with him. I don't think I have been so tired this trip as I am tonight. Gen. killed two turkeys. Barclay brought us good news tonight, that we are to go for home now, after a forty day trip. I am tired.

Monday I take Kis and the men out hunting all day, kill six turkeys and three buffalo. The command marched 15 miles, rugged, rough traveling. One more day gets us to Medicine Lake. The next day we reach Fort McPherson and camp near the river.

Friday I get special order number 44 from General Augur to move down the road on Sunday next and quarter at the agency. We are all on tiptoe to go home. I receive all my ponies today that we left here. General Augur comes in the night.

Saturday 30. This morn Gen. Augur sent for me, told me to turn in all my company property and go home on the cars. We hurried around pretty lively and got through and over to the station before 10 o'clock. I start down tonight.

October, Sunday 31. Arrived at home 9 A.M. Found Lib, Mary and Stella at Depot waiting for me. I am glad to get home. My baby has grown so I hardly know her. . . .

It's pretty nice to begin this month at home with my own folks, and getting acquainted again with my pacers. In the morning Jim and I go to Omaha and report for the trial. It is postponed until Thursday. With Tom Palmer, a horse dealer, I drive around town and buy some ponies. In the morning I draw the money for my outfit and get Jim started west with the thirteen ponies. I pay Palmer twenty dollars for helping me buy them.

Trial of the Pawnees came up today in United States district court. A jury was called and is being examined. Each is asked if he has any prejudice against Indians and those not prejudiced are few and far between. Some say they've no use for any of the Pawnee tribe and especially these four accused red men. The general idea is about the same as one fellow's answer to the questions:

"Me prejudiced? Why no, of course not—I've been tracked by Indians, and they've chased me; and I've stood battle in the army with them Sividges more'n once. Naw, I'm not prejudiced—leastwise not too much to hang every last one of the red devils—and I'll help jerk 'em up."

This is the first time, I'm told, that a trial like this has been had of Indians. Little Wolf, Horse Driver, Blue Hawk, and Old Yellow Sun hold no faith in the fairness of this legal ritual that is meaningless to them. And I'm morally certain it will not be as just as it would be to a white man. But it's a start in the right pattern. Old Yellow Sun is a wise old medicine man and doing his best to get a pact fashioned through me with the Great White Father and the court to accept his life for whatever the boys are accused of and let them go free. I explain over and over how the law must take its course. None of the Pawnees have caught more than a dim understanding of it, because the long imprisonment coupled with cruel treatment by some jailors is plainer to them. If I could see some men here on trial for murder of Indians I could feel the scales are more balanced.

The court orders a new list of people to appear tomorrow for examination for jury duty. Another day goes in examination of possible jurors.

Saturday, Nov. 6, 1869. Trial continued and no new evidence. I came home on Number 7.

Monday the trial goes on. Four chiefs are in the courtroom; the Pawnees just can't figure why the murder of one white man stirs up so much trouble for them, when fourteen Pawnee men have been killed and no enemy Indians around.

The proceedings drone on. Ti-ra-wat La Shar, Sky Chief,[13] arises, speaks (I translate): "My Father, you have lost one man; recently I have lost fourteen. Let us call it even and let these boys go, Yellow Sun, Blue Hawk, Horse Driver, and Little Wolf."[14]

The court is struck to silence until the astonished judge recovers and continues the case the next day. On Saturday we go at it again and no new evidence is brought in. I go home on No. 7 and come back to Omaha Sunday night.

November, Monday 8. Court in session all day and all four Pawnees are found guilty on mighty poor evidence, and that admitted by all four: they were on the large island in the river at about the day McMurty was believed murdered.

Suddenly there's a lot of commotion. Horse Driver and Yellow Sun try to kill themselves but the guards are too quick for them. Meanwhile, Blue Hawk has managed to escape—gets clear away.

November, Monday 15. I'm called on to help the marshal find Blue Hawk. I went to Lester Platt's lodge and stayed all night. In the morning we got two ponies from him and go over the river and find Blue Hawk. He refuses to go with us and his tribe backs his stand.

We return to the station and report to Hoile. I am nearly dead with asthma.[15] I go home on No. 4.

November, Thursday 18, 1869. Today went down to Uncle Brown's to Thanksgiving dinner and came home this evening; pacers drive fine.

November 24. This morning drove over the river on the new bridge and found I have a niece, born last night to my sister, Alphonsine, and Charlie Morse; all doing fine.

As Mary and I expect to go visiting in the east before long, Lute, Fred, and I work every day we can on getting our reports and stores fixed up.

December 1. I came to Omaha this morning on Number Four—train was late, did not do much business today. Myers[16] [quartermaster of the army district] is not here and I won't get my money. Went to theater tonight, Miss Price played in "Lancashire Lass."

I get up early on account of being nearly frozen. Get my business done and come home on No. 3 with Gus Becher and lady he married in Dakota Territory. We had a good visit, I think Gus done well.

Fred, Lute, Flymer, and I go across the river hunting and shoot some prairie chickens, then get back to get the balance of our papers finished as I must go to Omaha.

This afternoon I came to Omaha, am here at Oak's St. Charles Hotel and very lonesome. I sleep very little but get along fair, and get up early. I do my trading and get payrolls fixed up and paid, then I go to the theater and see Annie Ward as "Fanchon."

Tuesday 14. Came home this afternoon and find our little darling sick, she feels real bad.

We had planned to start east this morning but are far from it. I am sick and the baby is getting no better. I have a high fever tonight— bilious.

Thursday 16. Got up awful sick this morn, hardly able to move suffered all night with my head, and expect the same tonight. I dread it much.

Friday 17. Am some better this morn but very weak, had a hard time again last night. This eve I feel very much better than I have since I took sick.

Saturday, December 18, 1869. Today I am nearly well, feel fine, played some billiards.

Sunday 19. Today is very cold. I tend baby while Ma and Mary go to church. This afternoon we go to Charlie's, Jim's, and down to Brown's, bid them all goodbye. Tomorrow we leave for East.

In Omaha we stop at the St. Charles Hotel, went to the theater.

Tuesday, December 21. Came over the Missouri River this P.M. and got passes and lit out for Chicago—have a section in sleeping car.

Wednesday 22. Got breakfast in Davenport, at Chicago dinner and got passes to Cleveland, and return, took sleeper.

Thursday 23. Arrived at Hillsdale at 7 A.M. Lute met us at Depot. Wrote to Mother today, having a nice time here and took a good sleigh ride.

30

1870 *Spring.* In March I'm thirty years old. Too old to play and not old enough to work, I tell James to answer his argument that I ought to settle down to what he calls a regular occupation, farming or other business.

General Augur orders two companies of Pawnees, which I enlist and place, one at O'Fallon and the other at Plum Creek under white officers who speak some Pawnee and have served with the scouts before. Lute has other employment and is not with the scouts.

As for me, I am detailed, by special order of General Sheridan[1] to guide his friend, Prof. Othniel Charles Marsh,[2] with a group of Yale geology students to northwestern Nebraska's fossil beds. General Cole learned in 1865 that there was no reliable map of the Nebraska Sandhills and the Bad Lands bordering them. I guess I can thank General Sheridan for the prospect of "wet-nursing" a bunch of young city fellows through the Loup Forks and sand waste. I'd rather fight Indians!

The professor and his covey light at McPherson Station, are brought across the river to the fort by ambulances. General Carr orders them outfitted for camp and trail and escorted by a Fifth Cavalry detail including Scout Cody. With two Pawnee Scouts I lead out across the Platte, the south and middle Loups both running bank-full, but we ford all right.

The professor, I soon discover, is not at all the bookish kind of person I was expecting. He and the others ride knee to knee with me. They're all around fine fellows, and mighty interesting—tell me about geology and what they want to do here, and I tell them a little about what I do, and of the Pawnee Scouts. One young man, George B. Grinnell, has made friends with the two scouts and the longest summer day isn't long enough for him to ask all his questions and get them to talk of their "Old Ones" (forefathers), with me interpreting.

June is in flower all over the prairie and especially over the tall-grass

sandhills. The sky is sunny-blue with little white floating sea-like clouds.
Meadowlarks practice their singing-school "do, re, mi's" all day long. I'm
surprised to find likely country up through here—springfed lakes where
waterfowl play and sandhill cranes stalk the shorelines like sentinels on
beat.

Digging like badgers, these hard-working young fellows seem to believe,
is a seldom-come-by privilege. A sixteen-hour day isn't daylight enough for
all the sifting of dirt; or looking into cutbanks of bluffs or old streambeds
and canyons—always writing in their books on the specimen they're taking
for the Peabody Museum of Yale College.

After the supper fires burn down, and the birds have sung their last
note for the day, the young fellows, never tiring, make the camp jolly with
college songs, laughter, and highjinks. The scouts, much the same age, are
invited to sit in. Not understanding a word, they catch the mood with
keen enjoyment, plain to me.

The grass cures and crisps, and the buffalo berries show orange-scarlet
on the bush. Professor Marsh and group invite me to accompany them
into northern Colorado to examine fossils left from, they believe, an
earlier age than seen here. I cannot go as the last courier brought me a
new order from General Augur.

I angle back through the sandhills—get over one and face another just
like it. If a man forgets in what direction the sun comes up, he could be
lost and never find his way out, for there are no landmarks, just sky and
sandhills.

Coming to the head of the Dismal River I follow it as far as Birdwood
Creek and along it to the North Platte River and eastward to Fort
McPherson and home.

Something new is happening in Nebraska, and our little neighboring
village, Schuyler, has given Columbus its what-fors. The Union Pacific
arranged with the Burlington and Rock Island Railroad a uniform rate for
shipping cattle east, a saving to Texas drovers of twenty-five percent. They
are trailing across the Kansas Pacific, past Abilene, and pointing up the
Blue River valley to the Union Pacific's shipping point. Columbus worked
to get the Union Pacific's favor, but our town doesn't happen to sit at the
head of the Blue River valley trail. Between 40,000 and 50,000 head of
Texas cattle came up the trail and into cars this summer.[3]

Herds of cattle are not new in Nebraska. Road ranches along emigrant
trails early learned to turn a nice piece of money by trading for two sore-
footed oxen, one they maybe had taken in trade six weeks before and put
it out on grass to become slick, well muscled, sound hoofed, and able to
work again. Boyd, down by Kearney, the Gillman Brothers, and further
west, Jack Morrow are stock traders.

Creighton's crews used hundreds of oxen, and he left poor and foot-sore cattle in 1859 to shift for themselves on the plains of western Nebraska Territory. When they were rounded up for spring work they were found in generally fine condition, and there had been little loss, though they had gone into the winter very poor "skins and crips."

Two years ago I got acquainted with the man said to know all there is to learn about running cattle on the Plains, John W. Illif.[4] His home ranch is in Colorado on the South Platte at Cedar Creek. He said his cattle range the western Platte Valley and three-state corner, with never, since he turned his first herd loose in 1859, any food or shelter but what they find on the open range; and the loss in winter storms or starvation is small. It is said his range-fattened cattle have made him a rich man. In January last year, 1869, Indians raided and burned one of his cow camps but his friendliness toward Indians has mainly been his protection.

The first big herd of Texas cattle, mostly heifers and cows, was brought up to Nebraska last year, to North Platte. A thousand head was bought by M.C. Keith and partner, Guy C. Barton, at North Platte. Brown and Russell in Lincoln County put their brand on five hundred head. Bratt, ranging on the Birdwood in Lincoln County, bought some and the rest were parceled out in smaller bunches.[5] None are farming or raising feed for their stock—just gambling on the weather.

Lute is out with a company of scouts. General Carr is making a combination scouting and sportsmen's hunting trip in the Republican Valley and south country with his guests, a number of Englishmen and some men from Syracuse, New York.

In December I'm ordered to take charge of a buffalo-hunting party of visiting officers and some from Fort McPherson. My special guest is Congressman James W. Wadsworth of Genesee, New York.[6] Some Union Pacific officials will join us.

I assemble the outfit at the fort and send saddle horses, camp equipment, and supply wagons ahead to O'Fallon. In a couple of days I take the party on the train to that point and Lute comes along. At O'Fallon I take Captain Cushing and half of his scout company, stationed here, and march west as far as the station of Rosco. Here I lead across the river and make camp. The air is still, temperature is dropping. We are glad to settle into stove-heated wall tents for the night.

Morning breaks clear and bright. The river is frozen hard except the swiftest channel. The railroad men get off the train opposite our camp and come over the ice as far as the open channel. I send some Pawnees to carry them piggyback through waist-high, four-rods-wide water.

Con Groner[7] is the first to land on this side, the nearest are in midchannel. One of the smallest Pawnees is carrying a six-foot six-inch man. Con says to me, "Major, tell that boy to fall down," and I call a hint to La Shar loo-Ni-ha. The division superintendent makes a big splash

as he hits the water. The big fellow cusses and wades on across. We hustle
him into a tent where he is soon stripped and wrapped warm while his
clothes dry on a line above the stove. I send ten men out to get enough
game for all, and some to fetch wood from along the river. We stay in
camp and everybody yarns and plays pitch. After a while we have some
good roast ribs before bedtime.

The scouts lead us, in early forenoon, to buffalo and all have a good
hunt. Mr. Wadsworth shot four—says he wants to have some of the
buffalo heads mounted. Cody's cavalry horse is scared of getting near the
animals and he follows a bunch about a mile before he gets his horse to
running parallel with the herd within range of the buffalo. He shoots left
sixteen times and kills as many buffalo. Never a miss! I've seen a lot of
good shooting, and we've all seen excellent marksmanship, but all are
agreed that we have never before seen such an exhibition as Cody put on
today.

I consider myself a pretty fair shot with revolvers on a running horse,[8]
but none of us can mention anyone who is known to have even come
close in rifle shooting from horseback to Cody. He laid his kills on the
prairie as even as corn shocks in a farmer's field!

As most of the sportsmen wish to have their buffalo hides for robes,
they skin out legs and neck and start the hide from a split down the belly.
The scouts make short work of jerking the hides by tying to a bunch of
thick neck skin and hitching it to a chain on the double-tree. A crack of
the whip signals a quick, hard pull and peels the hide, all prime ones now.
The best heads are taken, humps and tongues, too. After quartering, the
meat is loaded and all are glad to start back to camp.

Cody's horse is still skittish, and in some way manages to fall and catch
Bill's leg underneath with the other over it. He is caught close up behind
its front quarters. Bill grabs hold of its legs to keep it from threshing. If it
should, he can't protect his head and face from its hoofs. He's talking
sweet and soft to it, soothing it, when Captain Cushing,[9] the nearest
rider, comes up to the horse's back, bends over its withers (shoulders), and
takes its legs from Cody's hands. Using the horse's shoulders as his
leverage he lifts and pivots the animal onto its back, right up on the
saddle pommel and cantle and off Cody's leg. He is not badly injured.

Late in November, Lute and some of his company stationed at Plum
Creek, while scouting in the south country, ran across a small party of
Indians off the reservation. He chased them several miles, didn't come
within shooting distance, but captured three of their ponies.

In December we are mustered out and I go home to play with my little
daughter. I go to work at putting my farm building in good condition. I
have no expectation of being called back to service, and we have sold out
of the hotel. We are settled into our farm home by Christmas.

Several family men want me to lead and manage a buffalo hunt for them to get meat and robes. I get a wall tent of heavy canvas and a stove and we fix up four wagons and get our outfit together.

Lute and Billy Harvey[10] and myself are experienced buffalo hunters; of the rest some were soldiers in the rebellion, but few have shot big game and not many have a buffalo killing gun. We throw in together, four as teamsters, the rest on horses, and head south to Grand Island, ford the Platte, and gather a couple wagonloads of downed trees to roast some of the meat we're going after. Later in the afternoon, near camp time, Lute rides on with me to find a likely site and Billy Harvey stays to guide the wagons. We happened onto a newly put up sod house—a homesteader— and, wanting to buy some bread, I get off and knock at the door.

A young woman opens it, looks at me and at Luther on his horse holding the reins of my mount. Her eyes sweep back to fasten upon me.

"How-de-do. I wonder if I can buy some bread off you?" I say.

"I believe I know you, aren't you Major North?"

"Yes, I'm Frank North, and this is my brother Luther," I tell her.

"I don't think you remember me. I'm one of the Campbell sisters. You got us away from the Indians when you traded your captives for us at North Platte three years ago."[11]

"Well, well. Of course I didn't recognize you. Is this your home?"

"Yes, I'm married now and we are homesteading here. My husband has gone to a distant neighbor's. He will be back by supper time. Won't you and your brother come in and stay for supper? We can put you up overnight, too. I want so much for my husband to meet you, and I have really never thanked you for what you did for me and my sister."

"I'm well thanked today, in seeing you well and making a home here with your husband. Besides, you know it is the Pawnee Scouts and their officers who took those captives and enabled me to get you freed, and I give them much credit. I would like to meet your husband, but we have a hunting party waiting for us so I can't stay this time."

"Oh, I'm sorry, but wait," she darts from the door, quickly brings out two loaves of bread wrapped in a cloth. Handing it to me she refuses the piece of money I offer.

"No Major. It is little enough but I want to give it to you."

I take the loaves, thank her, and turn away. A thousand (plus or minus) days and nights of scouting and all that has gone with it is balanced today in seeing this nice young woman making a home with her young man in that new, neat little soddy. Now it all seems worthwhile.

A few miles from the homestead we set up camp. In the morning buffalo are found along the Blue River. As Lute is riding a colt he is breaking to buffalo running, I borrow his Zep (Mazeppa), as intelligent a buffalo horse as any on the plains.[12] Zep lets me engineer the gunning

while he manages the taking of us, and what's more, the keeping of us, in
the right shooting distance and angle. As I am shooting my six-shot
revolvers I kill eleven buffalo—had one miss.

Lute's colt high-tailed it the other direction. Harvey got several kills.
We have as much meat down as we can haul in. Saddle girths are
loosened and the riding horses picketed for grazing while everybody starts
skinning. Lute and I ride over to fetch the wagons. Riding a ridge to find
the best crossing of a ravine, we run onto a nearly new wagon.

I had believed the tribes would all be staying around the reservations
through winter, but this, and the horse tracks leading down the ravine,
look like Indian mischief. I give Lute his Zep and send him to trace along
until he can see about this.

The skinning is done and the butchering is progressing. The air is heavy
with storm coming on. Lute gets back to camp as we begin to put the
meat in the wagons. He trailed the tracks a ways then up onto a flat for
eight or nine miles, that brought him to where he could see along the
river with his field glass a good sized encampment of Indian lodges,
guessing them up to two hundred teepees.

This beats me. For that many Indians to be away from a reservation,
some agency must know of it, if they're paying any heed to their charges. I
think likely the Indians are a band of Spotted Tail's Brules, away from the
reservation for a hunt.

For this night we have something else to reckon with. The storm is
blowing in like a blizzard is back of it. We work on. Some get the tent up
and wood ready. Others picket the horses closer to the ravine bank. The
snow and sleet that started about the time Lute came back is howling right
along by the time we finish loading the wagons. Inside, hot food and
drink fixes us up. We are sheltered and warm, and aware of the difference
our thin canvas walls make.

If anything, the blizzard is worse this morning. We drag in wood and
meat chunks that we chop with an axe and tie up to thaw for cooking. No
one is to go out further than the tent pegs without a rope tied to his arm
and the other end around somebody's leg here in the tent. Some play card
games, others just talk.

Lute, a first rate yarner,[13] tells about the greyhounds that General Carr
had along on the Republican Expedition in June-July 1869. (I hadn't
caught up with the column when it happened.) "The general proposed to
give his hounds a run after antelope. 'Well, General, do you think they
can catch antelope?' I asked.

"'Yes, they can catch anything,' General Carr said. We went along,
easy until an antelope was spotted, just one, a big buck. The general
brought his hounds up until they saw the antelope and he turned them
loose pretty close to the critter.

"Antelopes are curious as a coon. Well, the buck came trotting toward the hounds as they ran at him. When they looked to be about six rods apart, the antelope turned tail and lit out, going away.

" 'Oh, they'll catch him before he gets started,' the general told us, and we all rode up the hill after them. They went up and over and out of sight until we got up on top and saw them crossing a two-mile-wide flat. The dogs were about sixteen rods behind the antelope when he ran over a hill, and he must have been clear out of their sight when they got up there. They just looked, turned around and started back and in no hurry. Up to now only the general had done any talking.

" 'General,' Bill Cody said, 'if anything, the antelope is a little bit ahead.'

"Everybody laughed and the general grinned and agreed with Cody, but he wasn't talking very loud."

The blizzard howls on. The stories all are told, discussions run down, and card games lose interest before the third day, when the storm is blowing itself out. We dig the wagons out from under snowdrifts fifteen to twenty-five feet deep in the ravine. We melt snow to water our horses, slow business, and by the time the last one is watered the first is thirsty again.

By double teaming, the wagons are pulled out. The sun comes out, sparkles brilliant against the snow. Lute and I lead; no trails nor landmarks are to be seen until we get to the Platte. After a while my eyes pain. Later the pain is so bad I have to get inside a wagon and tie my bandanna over my eyes. I'm completely snowblind. Lute takes us across the Platte and heads for Columbus, before pain in his eyes drives him into the wagon, snow blinded. I tell the fellows to give the horses their heads. They take us home, load and all, the saddle horses follow along without their riders' guidance.

This winter the Union Pacific is building stock shipping pens at Kearny Station. Next season, Texas drovers will bring their trail drives two hundred miles further to the west, away from settled country. Settlers along last summer's Texas trail in Nebraska demanded and got enforcement of the state's herd law, in effect, a shut-out of the longhorns and, more to the point, of their ticks and tick-carrying Texas fever.[14]

Early March 1871, begins my reactivation as scout and guide, a company each of cavalry and infantry going to establish a post on the North Loup or main Loup River. The country is getting some settlers, homestead colonies near the north-south crossing used by Indians in old times and still traveled by any wilderness bands who dare, and the smaller groups that now and then steal away from reservations to raid the Pawnee. Garrisoned there, this token force may deter trouble. A dozen Pawnee Scouts would be more effective, though no orders for their enlistment are foreseen.[15]

James North and his friend, Jay Paul, and Luther and myself join a
group around Columbus to go west to organize a county and lay out some
town sites. We travel west nearly a hundred miles, locate a survey mark,
and conduct a formal meeting and choose the name of Howard County.
Lute is one of the commissioners and James has an office.

I learn that a contract for putting up hay for the post might be had.
Lute is working with surveyors along the lines between Howard County
and part of the Pawnee reservation. If he's not finished by haying time he
says he will leave that to fulfill the contract. I sign it, knowing I may not
work at much of it, unless my duty here ends soon.

Getting home doesn't come handy—no traincars to get on—just fork a
horse. I had thought I would be farming, but have a hired man tending
the farm. Mother stays with Mary and Stella on the farm while I'm gone.
This post is fearful dull, and I miss the Pawnee Scouts.

In June, Lute runs onto an old-time Pawnee village ruin below Spring
Creek where the Columbus people and our sisters and husbands are
homesteading. He found there had been a round building of more than
seventy yards diameter. He went on down to the Pawnees' reservation to
talk with Eagle Chief about it. Lute says they talked the rest of the day
and he ate supper at the chief's lodge. Eagle Chief told about the village,
and of how the Skeedees got separated after a Sioux beating, when part of
them got away northward along the Missouri River, became friends with
the Mandans, and have lived near the Mandan villages ever since and are
known as Arikarees.[16]

Twice a month a courier with an escort brings mail, dispatches, and, if
we're lucky, newspapers.

Luther and his crews make hay. He has hired some good scythe men
and the grass is thick, as tall as a horse's belly. They wind up the contract
by putting three hundred tons of hay in stacks at the post, a nice profit for
us, and good wages paid the hired men.

General Sheridan, back from Europe where he observed Germany's
maneuvers in the Franco-Prussian War, plans to entertain some high and
mighty officials and friends, military and political, on a buffalo hunt. He
requisitions me to make the arrangements and assemble the necessary
equipment. I'm to have a company or so of Pawnee along for atmosphere.

The Cody's have a newborn son, mother and baby doing well, and
Cody even better! Struts around the fort stepping high and fancy, proud
and happy. Every officer is interested, of course, and Cody is setting them
up generously so that there is jollification and fun. Also some speculation
with free suggestions on a name for the child. Recalling discussions Bill
and I have had of frontiersmen and mountain men, and Cody's high
regard for Kit Carson, I ask: How about Buffalo Bill's first son being

named Kit Carson Cody?[17] Cody mulls it over, likes it, and decides on
the name, and I am honored.

The gentlemen arrive with General Sheridan who reviews the troops.
There are several newspapermen in the group, J. G. Bennet of the *New
York Herald,* and the *Chicago Journal's* editor, Charles Wilson; Frank
Thompson, a railroad man; and the big man of Western Union, Gen.
Anson Stager; Lawrence and Leonard Jerome, and ten officers. Fine fall
weather and along the Republican Valley plenty of buffalo, not many deer
and no elk are bagged, but antelope are taken. Cody isn't satisfied with
being Buffalo Bill. He has got to demonstrate it at every chance—with all
the newspapermen to take note, I would guess he will see his name in
print. He is interesting, likeable, and by far the best rifle shot on a
running horse I've seen. But I wonder why he wants to show off so much.

Over Christmas on the farm, I get my bobsled to going and drive in to
town with bells on the harness. Youngsters run to hitch sleds for a ride.

31

Surgeon Morris Joseph Asch and Gen. George A. Forsyth[1] of General
Sheridan's staff came to Fort McPherson early in January to oversee our
preparations. To insure the comfort and entertainment of Grand Duke
Alexis of Russia, and his traveling staff and aides and the distinguished
guests, the officers add numerous refinements and luxuries particularly of
old vintage and bottled sorts.

The day comes, also the special train, bringing Russia's fair-haired son
to step foot on Nebraska soil, and sample our now gentled "Frontier." Six
or eight army ambulances are drawn up for use of guests who do not
choose to mount the extra saddle horses. Every man, woman, chick, and
child in the region comes to the North Platte station, bundled in their
warmest against January cold, curious to see those "furriners." Everybody
and their cousins close to icicle condition by the time General Sheridan
appears with the young duke, in a rich seal fur coat, towering over "Little
Phil."

Led across the south river and southwestward the party is brought to
Red Willow Creek. There the camp awaits the royal hunting party. Here,
encamped in hide tepees and government issue canvas tents, besides my
Pawnee, are as many Sioux with their families, under Spotted Tail.[2] He
was relocated last fall, his reservation moved from the Little Missouri
River down to the White River, in northwest Nebraska. Being nearer
eases their journey to raid the Pawnee reserve. Red Cloud, too, was
allowed to come south to the Platte River, east of Fort Laramie. Why
these tribes are allowed to leave the reservations, where they were away
from trouble for themselves and others beats me.

Doc Carver[3] is present in fringed buckskins—his sharp marksmanship is
tough competition in the target matches in camp—also W. H. (Paddy)
Miles,[4] pioneer of the region.

The Pawnee do a ritual dance, as exactly as their military drills, and I
interpret its meanings. The Sioux do their war dance.

After the royal and distinguished guests do their daily hunts, a tribe demonstrated its manner of hunting and killing buffalo—the Pawnees' strikingly methodical; the Sioux's wilder, probably more exciting to these spectators, but the helter-skelter, every man for himself, is less efficient.

A Sioux brave chases a bull up near the guests, pulls his bow—sends the arrow through the buffalo which falls dead. Two Lance picks up his dripping arrow as everybody applauds him. This is only the second time I have ever seen an arrow driven clear through a buffalo. The Pawnee Traveling Bear did it and, strangely enough, also before spectators. Both exceed six feet in height, and are magnificent men. With considerable flurry and too much speech and champagne for a cold day, Two Lance's lucky arrow (or another like it—I'll bet he doesn't give away his luck) is presented to the Grand Duke Alexis. He, in turn, presents a gift to Two Lance.

So ends this remarkable three-day hunt in honor of the Grand Duke Alexis.[5] The gathering up to leave is beginning.

"This has been a splendid spectacle, General, most remarkable, and on a superbly grand scale—" Sidney Dillion, superintendent of Union Pacific of Omaha, compliments General Sheridan.

"Who would have thought a buffalo hunt could also be great entertainment—" Russell Watts,[6] a York stater, started cattle ranching two-three years ago south of the Platte Forks, is interrupted by Cody.

"And if the champagne had just held out we'd have cleared the rest of the buffalo off the plains for you cattlemen, eh, General?"

They all chortle including Paddy Miles; Frank Thompson, "trail boss" of the Grand Duke's special train; J. B. Omohundro, also a trail boss who brought the first large herd from Texas to Nebraska, to Lincoln County; General Custer, myself, and others.

My temporary detail in connection with the hunt done, I go home and soon after report to Fort D. A. Russell. Third Cavalry troops arrive at this post from Arizona Territory, ordered to the Red Cloud Agency. I am detailed to guide the troops under General Reynolds. After a few days' layover here, resting from their march, I lead out, north to Fort Laramie, thence, bear northeastward into the northwestern Nebraska-South Dakota bad lands and sand-hill region—a vast, wild and unorganized land given over to, and called, the Sioux's land. The tertiary fossil beds are in another part of this region.

After about three weeks the agents of the Spotted Tail and Red Cloud reservations admit that all is about as usual and that there is no requirement for further presence of the military. General Reynolds pulls up camp, folds up tents and orders, "Forward march—twos!"

I need to get home for some business, so I get a furlough to that end, for a few days. Coming home is the best part of being stationed at

Fort D. A. It's plum easy to just step on the train and step off at
Columbus, no horses to harness and hitch, nor long horseback ride
through any kind of weather.

I'm thinking about moving my family up to Fort D. A. Russell as I'm
not farming. I'm to be occupied as interpreter, guide, and scout for some
time.

I watch through the train window to see our white farm cottage and the
red barn. As the train slows for the Loup River bridge I jump off and I'm
on my farm just north of the bridge. If I let my man know when I'm
coming, he ties a saddle horse to a cottonwood tree for me, but this time I
walk across the fields and come in the back way.

My hired man is working at the anvil, sharpening plow shares, and he
has helpers tending the little forge and tempering the blades. "Howdy-do,"
I say. "Everything all right?"

"Es fur's I know. Say, Major these here young fellers showed up t'other
day. They brang out orchard stuff on the railroad freight. The Missus told
'em you'd be along home in a day or so and to wait around to talk to you
'bout things."

I shake hands with the young chaps.

"I'm Edwin Jaques, and this is my partner, Willis Lawbaugh."[7]

"I'm going to the house now, later on we can talk," I tell them. Mary
and Stella are watching for me at the window. I throw the kitchen door
open and I'm home again.

I get around to talking to the young men.

"Yes, we turned our earthly possessions into about 50,000 root grafts,
apples and other fruits, loaded them on board the cars and headed west.
We arrived at Columbus and our first effort was to find a suitable nursery
location," Edwin explains. Willis snickers, "Word soon spread of what we
are looking for. Who would have believed that everybody is indeed very
interested in the establishment of a nursery, also that each one has the
only suitable site near Columbus? We were just besieged by such people.

"But one after another's interest cooled down when they found we do
not intend to pay in advance on the lease a sum equal to at least twice
the market value of the land.

"We went rambling about the country to find what we wanted. We
chanced upon an ideal site for our enterprise only two miles west of
Columbus on the north bank of the Loup River. Your man at work on the
place told us to inquire at the house. Mrs. North invited us to make our
headquarters here until you should come home, as she expected you in a
few days."

The acreage they selected is a sheltered south slope of deep, black
soil—I wouldn't lease it to them if I was going to be farming, but the only
orchards in Nebraska, that I know of, are those planted by J. S. Morton at

Nebraska City and one or two others in that vicinity, a long way from here. I agree to allow them the acreage and on terms that make them happy. I consent to their building a shanty by the river to live in, and instruct Tom to furnish them horses, plows, and tools when they need them. The boys set to work as soon as the contract is made. By June all the rows of young fruit tree whips are leafed out and the young proprietors tell me their orchard is thriving.

In early June I receive a letter from the young Yale scientist, George B. Grinnell, asking me to guide him and James Russel on a buffalo hunt if arrangement can be made to join the Pawnees, when the tribe hunts to make meat. I can't think of anything I might like better but I am on duty. There is no chance I could have much time away—I'm lucky to get home regularly. I take the letter to Lute. He agrees to take the job and makes arrangements.

Luther tells me the Pawnees' summer hunt was the happiest in years, free of enemy, thousands of buffalo, so they and the Oto and Omaha hunting with them made plenty of meat. Grinnell came to the Pawnee villages in time to see the last of their religious preparations in the medicine lodge, the consecration of the buffalo staves (the slender spruce poles decorated with bright calico, bead ornaments, and hawk and eagle feathers, used to make silent signals during stalking of buffalo). After the last prayer dies away, a drum beat brings young braves in headdress suggestive of buffalo, who do the buffalo dance. In relays of a dozen to twenty or more the dance is performed on three days. Then the tribe moves on.

Lute and his charges traveled with the Pawnees along the Platte, crossed at Kearny and went on south to the Beaver, south of the Republican. Grinnell filled notebooks with what he saw. One evening as the women made camp, some went with the children to gather wood along the river. They ran onto a flock of turkeys coming through the brush to roost in the hackberry trees. The children's efforts to slay or capture the big birds forced them to wing, and the silly fowl attempted to fly lengthwise above the long lines of Pawnee coming into camp. " '—Just like schoolboys.' " Lute quotes Grinnell as saying, upon seeing the hunters let fly with whatever they could throw at the turkeys churning along overhead.[8]

Summer is ending with discouragement for the young orchardists. Grasshoppers raided the acreage, chewed leaves and bark on the tender little trees; bad enough that the boys feel their prospect is set back at least one year. They are unsure how many trees will survive. Crops are fine, and not much damaged by the grasshoppers. Nebraska harvest this year will be a big one—a lot of it from ground broken out by new settlers.

Settlers are coming in all over. Lute, while on the summer hunt, found a settlement started quite a way west of the mouth of Medicine Creek where two men have taken homesteads.[9]

Of late, as sure as I come home, I'm in for a miserable attack of asthma and, oh how I suffer. In Wyoming, if I have it, the bouts aren't as severe. I get a house and will get my family moved before snow flies. Mary is happy, having our home near Russell. We bid the folks good-bye. Lute helps us load and ship up. I bring my horses and the buggy, a few hens and a couple of milk cows, house equipment and furnishings, and grain.

Duty is routine since the tribes all are more or less quiet and supposed to be staying on their reservations, except when they get official leave and then the posts are notified.

Lute gets a job as hunter for workmen putting up telegraph wires from Cheyenne to Rawlins, Wyoming, until it is finished and he goes home for the winter.

In the spring he works for a crew surveying the Pawnee reservation into sections. Since the Friends (Quakers) have taken charge, they intend the Pawnee shall be farmers of wheat for commerce.

I'm willing to credit the Friends with the best intentions. They also can be credited as the most unobservant, least understanding of all who have blundered with the Pawnee! They intend that each family shall leave the villages and live on individual small wheat farms. The Pawnee, in their villages, have some chance to protect themselves from the Brules and Ogalallas, both now moved much nearer. I think old Pete (Peta La Shar) and most of the head chiefs are smart enough to balk at scattering the families all over the reservation. Lute writes the Pawnees' "Grandfather" (Friend Troth, their agent) teaches they should love their enemy and not be suspicious that they intend harm![10]

George B. Grinnell of New York is spending his summer vacation elk hunting with Luther on the upper Loup. I'm sorry I can't be with them.

Mother writes July is dry in Nebraska, gardens drying up, crops still look fair. Not a week later a letter from the young nurserymen says, "Nursery eaten up by grasshoppers, not a leaf left and not much bark. Cleaned us out this time, quitting business, out of funds. Respectfully, Your Friends, Willis and Edwin."

We at this point hear rumors of a fight in early August between the Pawnee and Sioux.

Luther visits us here and brings sad information about the Pawnee and Sioux.

"The Quaker, Troth, who came as Pawnee agent in 1869, was replaced by another Friend, William Burgess, and his judgment, where the Pawnee are concerned, if anything is poorer than any of the other agents the Pawnees have had. The man he sent as trail-agent knew no more about the Pawnees' enemy than himself. New here, from Pennsylvania, twenty-three years old. But showed himself a man all the way.

"Well, I saw the boys after they got back from the fight. Co-rux-ta Puk (Fighting Bear) told me part of the tribe were ready to start when more than half were not. The new "Grandfather" told them the Sioux would not be allowed to attack them, and they were not to fight the Sioux and that it would be all right for them to go ahead of the others. Young Lester Platt[11] went along with John Williamson and the first group of Pawnee. After news got around that the Sioux were out, no other Pawnee came out.

"Somehow the agents of Red Cloud's Ogalallas and of Spotted Tail's Brules neglected to notify officials and the Pawnee Agent that they, at about the same time, were permitting both Sioux bands to go into the Republican country to hunt.

"Agent Burgess got wind that the Sioux Agents had also let their tribes go south to the hunting ground. He shot messages off to the Sioux agents and to the Sioux chiefs. He pleaded with Fort McPherson officers to see that the Sioux chiefs were brought in to smoke a peace pipe with Pawnees he was sending with Baptiste Behale to the fort. Not a Sioux came within two hundred miles of McPherson.

"But the Quaker's agitation alerted the military. Major Russel and troops were dispatched on a forced march. They almost made it. The Pawnees tell me they're sure the Sioux broke off from chasing them because they saw the troops approaching.

"Ti-ra-wat La Shar, Sky Chief; Co-rux-ta Puk, Fighting Bear; Sa-ka-ru La Shar, Sun Chief; Nick Koots; Co-rux-ah Kah Wahdee, Traveling Bear; Ke-wuk-co La Shar, Ruling His Sun; John Box—are dead.

"About fifty-five buffalo were killed when they got to the Republican Valley. They dried the meat, then crossed over to Beaver Creek and killed three or four hundred buffalo. On the west Beaver, white hunters told Williamson they had discovered Sioux off in that direction. He turned the Pawnee southwest along Sappa Creek, and they ran out of buffalo. The Pawnees decided Williamson was being buffaloed by the hunters to scare the Pawnee away. They followed north along the Driftwood and took more buffalo. Their hundred pack horses were nearly loaded. More white hunters told Williamson a large band of Sioux were close.[12] He tried to get the Pawnees downriver where he believed they might have a chance to make a stand protected by timber.

"Fighting Bear—you know his temper—reared up and argued with Williamson. He told Bukskariwi[13] he was favoring the hide hunters and trying to keep the Pawnees from getting more buffalo. He even bragged that if there were Sioux, the Pawnee had whipped them before and they'd beat them again.

"Williamson's advice was good: that they could kill buffalo with their bows and arrows, but to fight the Sioux who had good government-issued arms and ammunition, they needed guns like the seven-shot repeating Spencers they had in scouting. The upshot was that the Pawnee traveled up the north site of the Republican, past the mouth of Whiteman's (Frenchman) Fork onto the plains west of that river. They had found and killed a few buffalo and started skinning when the Sioux rode down on them.

"The women and children ran for the other end of the ravine; their pack horses loaded with meat from six hundred buffalo were slow. Some packs were cut off and women and children rode these horses away. The Sioux were on every side.

"Ralph Weeks told me he and Williamson rode out to meet the Sioux, supposing them to be a few, escorted by soldiers. The Sioux began firing. Williamson's horse was killed from under him just as they reached the ravine.

"The Pawnee men stood and fought to hold the Sioux off until the women and children could get away.[14] After getting across the Republican and some distance east, a troop of cavalry from Fort McPherson, under Major Russel, came up. They tried to get the women and children to come to the north side. Young Lester Platt crossed over and guided the troops to the ravine. He said it was a carnage, dead children lay among the dead horses. Bodies of men and women had been stripped, scalped, and hacked and some, probably not dead, had been put on a pile of travois poles and burned. Woman and children captives were carried away.

"The troops took charge of the Pawnee, brought the wounded back on travois to the army surgeon who treated and took charge of them. The able men were sent in boxcars to Silver Creek. Williamson was sent with troops to bury the dead, two and a half weeks later.

"John Williamson reported about one hundred dead, but when he and the troops went to bury the dead they counted sixty-five on the field. You know a lot of the wounded got away but never made it back, and some are still straggling in. Besides, women and children were carried off by the enemy—I don't know how many.[15] Traveling Bear and his wife and children are dead.[16] Sky Chief, Nick Koots—"[17]

Luther's voice trembles at mention of Nick. They were close friends and Luther credits Nick with saving his life more than once. Good Pawnee friends—fine men, as fair and square as you and I consider ourselves. While I mourn the Pawnee deaths, I'm also very angry that they were so needlessly sacrificed by bigot fools in offices of Indian agencies.[18]

Luther comes with me to John Talbot's, a saloon midway between Cheyenne and Fort D. A. Russell, a mile out of town. Bill Hickok has been around Cheyenne for some time and we often get together there for target work. This time John beats Bill Hickok, and I beat them both. Lute is a good shot with a rifle, but I usually beat him with a pistol.

Leaving to go to Denver, Luther expects to meet Professor Marsh, who was with the group of students I guided two years ago. From Denver, they will go to Greely, Colorado, where Luther will take a crew of four men, wagons, and teams east of that place to dig and gather fossils for Peabody Museum. He expects to work there a couple of months and then has agreed to go into livery business at Columbus with Charley Morse, Phonsie's husband.

32

1874, and a happy New Year to All. Mary, Stella and I are in Columbus
for a few days. Stella is enjoying play with her cousins and I have a long
talk with Luther.

"Frank, it is too bad about the Pawnee. Of course they're still mourning
those killed in the massacre, but the tribe has hit bottom; they've
completely lost heart. You know I worked last year with a crew, surveying
the reservation into sections. The plan is to sell half of the reservation
and raise money to make the rest into separate wheat farms each with one
family house. It's these Friends, Quakers, the Pawnees' agents—first Troth
and now Burgess; the Nebraska Indian tribe's superintendent at Bellevue,
Sam Janney, has been replaced by Barclay White;[1] these corn, bean, and
buffalo-meat Indians will starve to death. They can't have the least idea
what to do with wheat, even if they get some raised.[2]

"The Pawnee learned long ago that Quakers' ideas aren't cut to fit
Indians, and will not go along with their impractical schemes. Spotted
Horse[3] and Lone Chief came up from the Wichitas last fall and tried to
get the Pawnee to go south. Just lately they found the tribe so gloomy that
they dared hold a council and urge the tribe to leave the reservation. Old
Peta La Shar faced them down, made them admit the Wichitas haven't
even any reservation of their own; that there is no more game there than
they find here. He reminded them how sick with ague and malaria the
Pawnees were that went there in 1870; that many had died."

"Old Peta intends to keep the tribe together."

"Yes, but failed. About a third of the tribe slipped away. The chief sent
messengers after them. Spotted Horse and Frank White came back and
went to Burgess. There are some—Old Peta for one—who say something
passed from Spotted Horse's hand to Burgess's hand. I believe he took a
bribe and overrode old Peta's demands that the Pawnees return to the
reservation. Only a few came back, saying the others couldn't find their

194

ponies and would be back when they did. Of course they went on."

The train whistles and the conductor bawls out "Boooard." We wave good-bye. I'm troubled about the Pawnees' problem. I suppose they'll be scattered on separate farms and one day the Sioux will pounce on the lone families and kill and scalp them all.

Luther writes he will join Grinnell on an expedition to the Black Hills. For some years the winds blowing from that direction have whispered "gold." The government is sending General Custer on an exploratory expedition through that almost unknown land. With him will go the Seventh Cavalry; three companies of mounted infantry; Indians, Arickaree and Santee Sioux as scouts under "Lonesome" Charlie Reynolds; scientists, miners and geologists, including George Grinnell, who has gotten Luther to go as his assistant; newspapermen from Minneapolis and Chicago with a photographer; professors, civilian teamsters, packers, and so on.[4]

Both Sioux agencies on the White River called for army protection.[5] Every post is alerted. In the first days of March the Sioux Expedition left Fort Laramie; cavalry and infantry headed for Red Cloud and Spotted Tail Agencies.

On detail to Fort Laramie, I meet with "Lonesome" Charlie Reynolds when he fetches down General Custer's mail, including the newspapermen's dispatches. He says they discovered gold in the Black Hills!

Meanwhile, General Sheridan moves troops to garrisons at Red Cloud's Agency: Camp Robinson, Camp Sheridan, and Camp Hartsuff in the headwater region of the north Loup, to reassure and protect new settlements north and west of the Pawnee reservation, it is claimed.

Non-treaty Sioux and northern Cheyenne visit the reservations and make the more or less confined Indians restless, more discontented, and harder to handle.

Nebraska and Kansas have something other than Indians to worry about. This time it's winged raiders. Rocky Mountain locusts, gray-green grasshoppers, were first a haze before the sun and then gray clouds that filled the sky. They swept in, in unbelievable swarms.

Horses became unmanageable from hits of the countless insects settling to earth, a writhing, creeping carpet, devouring leaves from trees, grass, garden, even the root vegetables, consumed into the ground to the end of the root. Clothing was riddled. It was impossible to keep them out of the houses. Everything at all chewable was grist for the living mill. Harness and leathers, too, caught the destroyers' imprint. Paint was chewed from wagons and finish from tool handles. Holes were bored into the earth and eggs deposited after which drifts of dead insects formed. Hogs found them edible, dogs tried them, perhaps coyotes feasted on them.

People face famine. There is little left of food for men or farm animals.

Those who pushed west beyond settlements, to get better choice of waterway and land, are harder hit, if that is possible.

Grasshoppers are nothing new in Nebraska. The Pawnee were all aware of what they could do, especially in a drouth year.

Newspapers at first gloss over the plague but reports of destitution pile up.

The governor appoints a committee to set up some kind of plan for taking care of the people. Churches and other organizations send men east to solicit aid, eastern relatives send barrels of flour and foodstuffs along with wearables and, sometimes, money. Many are selling claims, giving them away, or just walking off. "Going back home to live with the folks" is not said with humor. One reason they have no hope for another year is that there are enough grasshopper eggs in the ground to raise another scourge when summer comes. Interest is too dear to borrow money to buy seed on that gamble.

Politics comes to the front. The man who organized the first settlement toward the west on the Republican River, Silas Garber,[6] was nominated for governor by the Republican Party, and was elected. He promises a new state constitution.

After the massacre of the Pawnee last summer the Spotted Tail Brules and Red Cloud's Ogalallas were shoved onto their reservations and agents Seville and Howard said under no circumstances would those bands be allowed off the reservation to hunt again. But they did go out hunting last winter, and they're hunting again this summer.

The Pawnee are not being allowed to hunt. Being no troublemakers, they, not the Sioux, are deprived of the freedom to go after meat. They must stay and work their farms. After the Pawnees' crops were destroyed, agent Burgess telegraphed the Washington office which decided to jump on this chance to "take the tribe away from bad influence of white people."

Luther says, "The man from the Washington Indian office came to the reservation with Barclay White (Indian Superintendent at Bellevue) and ordered a council. They railroaded things to the specifications of the top office, up to a point. The chiefs were told to put their marks on the paper.

"The Skeedee's Lone Chief stood, straight and solemn. His grim eyes examined the men who had just professed great friendship for the nation. Baptiste Behale, the interpreter, told me that Lone Chief stood silent before them and not one challenged him. Finally he spoke.[7]

" 'Pawnee Chiefs have touched the stick that talks (the writing pen) many times. Three fathers (generations) back, my great-grandfather traveled (south) in the canoe on the Kiz-par-uks-ti (Wonderful River; the Missouri) with three other Pawnee Chiefs for a treaty of peace and friendship [1818, at St. Louis].

" 'Seven snows pass. Again a treaty. Peace and friendship for the white man's Big Medicine Trail. [1825, at Fort Atkinson. The Pawnee agreed to refrain from molesting white people traveling the Sante Fe Trail.]

" 'Eight more snows. The Great White Father would buy with much gift some earth that At-i-us Ti-ra-wa gives to all. [The 1833 treaty at the Grand Pawnee village; all territory south of the Platte River in return for annual payment of $40,000 in goods for twelve years, and $1,600 of goods given at the treaty-making.]

" 'Again when I was a beginning warrior, the Great White Father sends a man to talk of more earth. The Father [white man] sits on a log by the kizu [river]. Three chiefs sit at the other end. They keep coming closer. They crowd. He moves; twice. The next time the chief asks, 'My Friend, will you make me more room?' The white man says, 'I can not give you more room. I am near to falling off the end.' He is told that is the way it is with the Pawnee, because the Nation ceded too much ground at first. Yet the stick is touched again. [At this time, 1857, by the Table Rock treaty, the Pawnees gave up all of their remaining land except a reservation, which, against their wishes, was located on the Loup River, where they knew they were too accessible to their ancient enemies. The tribe was to receive $40,000 a year for five years, then $30,000 a year in perpetuity plus other benefits and protection from the Sioux.]

" 'We have given all the Great White Father asks—the earth that has taken back the bones of our fathers. He has given it, as At-i-us Ti-ra-wa gives to all. The White Father then drove us from it, and we are forbidden to roam any more where the grass grows over the dust that long ago was Pawnee flesh, holding it to earth's breast. Now we are told our own bones may not lie in this land that our Fathers are part of—that this little land under our feet, must be given to the Great White Father?

" 'Was the Great White Father's tongue twisted when he gave promises so the chieftains would touch the stick that talks? Ah-h-h. Did not he agree each time before the chiefs would touch the stick, that the great *Ki-[or Kiz] ra-ru-ta* ('filthy water') the Republican valley of the buffaloes was forever the Pawnees hunting ground? Forever, he said. He promised many forevers. The Great White Father's promises are as the bird's eggs when the little ones have hatched: only empty shells and so easy broken: and always there are more.

" 'The Great White Father was not troubled that his tongue was forked when he spoke many times to my people. Perhaps it may now be untrue that we must touch the stick? Perhaps he will not be troubled now that we do not?' "

Lone Chief quietly sat down. Peta La Shar, head chief of all Pawnee bands, long known for his patient but positive friendliness and peaceful leadership of the tribe, spoke. He left no doubts in any minds of his

opposition to removal. Old Peta faced the connivers; called their hand
and spelled out the ruin he foresaw if the Pawnees accepted removal from
their last stronghold.

Another Chief talked in mournful tone. "My heart is bad, my mind is
very poor. I am full of sorrow that the Great Father in Washington now
would tear Pawnee from this land he promised to them, and their
children, for as long as the grass grows and the river flows. How is it that
he must send us away to another land to help us, when he can not do as
he promised he would do for us here?"

The agent, the superintendent, and the Washington official took it
from there: the chiefs touched the stick.

The Pawnee tear down their earth lodges and the timbers are sold.
Leaving the children with the old and infirm who stay to care for them,
the rest of the nation set out. Many whites gather around and some escort
the tribe to the Loup River ford. A shot rings out! Commotion centers
where many whites on horseback are jammed around the old chief. Some
are leading a horse supporting the rider at each side out of the stream and
up the bank. It is the chief—Peta La Shar is hurt—was shot. He is
brought back to one of the lodges, left standing for those who stayed
behind. The women wail.[8]

A white physician is brought from Columbus, attends the chief,
pronounces his wound painful though not serious, no damage to bone or
ligaments. Faces lighten, spirits lift. John Williamson leads them south
and the north wind—only the north wind blows south—blows cold.

Peta La Shar's heart went with his troubled, fated people. Lone Chief,
the Skeedee, very distressed now, refuses to leave his friend and brother
chief. He and Peta La Shar's circle of close friends stay; in all, about five
hundred people remain.

Not for many days does the head chief of the Pawnee Nation stay. His
wound rapidly worsens, and Peta La Shar soon sleeps the long sleep in his
fathers' land. Peta's mourning for Sun Chief, massacred last August with
the hunting Pawnee, had been the more bitter for loss of his successor.

1875. Mild winters, the last two or three, not cold enough to kill
grasshopper eggs. This winter breaks early. People are mostly living on
hope, and even that wears threadbare. Barrels and boxes of clothing and
food, with some seed, keep coming from eastern relatives and
organizations. This spring the federal government distributed to the needy
great lots of clothing not usable for the army. Also, rations were given to
nearly fifty thousand persons. I suppose it was about the same in Kansas.
The Grange (Patrons of Husbandry) educational and social organization is
making every effort to help provide seed to farmers.

Waterfowl, migrating northward up the Great Plains flyway, stop to rest, dare not dawdle long in the drouthy land. Homestead farmers stir the dust and plant what seed they can get. Much broken ground stays untilled and unplanted this spring, and twice as much as is planted is abandoned.

OMAHA DAILY HERALD May 11, 1875: Sixty-nine delegates assembled in the new [but already crumbling!] sandstone capitol to draft a new state constitution. They met this morning in an atmosphere of gloom. Hard times are everywhere. The principal item of news is the hatching of grasshoppers across the state.

Economy is the watchword. A resolution requiring the Secretary of State to furnish each delegate with $3 worth of postage stamps was voted down; in lieu of hiring a chaplain the convention decided to ask ministers of the various Lincoln churches to open the daily session with prayer; a shorthand report of the proceedings was dispensed with as too expensive, therefore, there is no verbatim report of the convention. Another resolution adopted, directs that the committees use nothing but pure, unadulterated English in drafting the various sections of the Constitution. . . .[9]

Texas trail herds reached Ogalalla, the present Union Pacific's Texas trail's end June 10. Shoved west from Schuyler to Kearney for a season or so, then to North Platte, now it's at Ogalalla where loading pens and chutes are ready to ship the herds not sold to grazers (local buyers) soon known as ranchers. The strings of horses used by the drovers' men are sold to the cavalry and some to the ranchers. The trail drivers, liking to celebrate at the end of the long trail and finding the little way-station town offering but small opportunity for satisfying their thirsts spilled east and west, by grabbing boxcars to North Platte—tamer now than in railroad construction days—or "wild and woolly" Sidney.[10]

In September Luther writes that Mother tried to save her garden from the grasshoppers and draped sheets over as much as she could. Now she is patching ribboned rags together to have sheets, and the insects got the garden.

His letter says the last of the Pawnees,[11] children and the old and infirm, were taken from the reservation in wagons to join the tribe moved south.

This fall the government is taking still another crack at getting the Sioux to cede the Black Hills region. Miners and prospectors have gone in and brought out gold.

The government's attempt ran into a stone-wall refusal: neither to cede nor sell anything. The Indians did relinquish hunting rights south of the divide between the Niobrara and the Platte River. The non-treaty, non-reservation Indians took off deeper into the wilderness.

The Washington government issued notices in mid-December to all non-treaty Sioux to report to reservations, warning that any Indian not complying by the end of January 1876 would be considered hostile. By the time the message was grapevined to the distant bands, time was already counted out, even for those Indians who might have obeyed.

On the last day of January the Sioux and the northern Cheyenne nations are dumped in the lap of the War Department.

33

1876. I'm transferred to the Sidney Barracks post. Here I see gold seekers[1] rushing up the Sidney Trail to the Black Hills.

The trail runs about a hundred and fifty miles through lonesome country. Since the Allison commission failed last September, and the Indians refused to either cede or sell the Black Hills, the military no longer bothers to arrest and evict the illegal miners.

Whiskey runners keep the agencies' trouble pot boiling, and the troops busy.[2] Non-reservation Indians visit the reservations in great numbers, especially at ration issue times. They steal horses and beef issue cattle, and foray along the freight trails. These Indians kill, loot, and take what they please. Two mail carriers to the agencies were killed.

Two years ago last October (Oct. 23, 1874) northern Indians visiting Red Cloud Agency chopped the flagpole down after imprisoning agent Seville. No flag has flown over that agency since. This year the flag is to be raised on Washington's Birthday.[3]

General Crook,[4] commander of the Department of the Platte, goes through on his way to Fort Laramie to mount a campaign against the hostiles.

Crook takes advantage of March's bitter weather when Indians are unable to travel much until snow-melt bares forage for ponies; sends Colonel Reynolds to the Little Powder River. Reynolds attacks and captures a village, sets it afire and skedaddles with his captives and the horse herd. Warriors give him a running fight, soon a fighting retreat if not a rout, in which the Indians' horse herd is said to have changed hands so many times that General Crook had the remaining ponies killed to prevent their recapture.

In mid-May Generals Terry and Custer go up the Missouri, and then the Yellowstone rivers. General Gibbon marches from the west; and Crook jumps off from Fort Fetterman, working northward toward the headwaters of the four rivers, Tongue, Big Horn, Powder, and Rosebud.

General Crook gets into it up on the Rosebud, June 17, with Crazy

201

Horse. He claims a victory but he got out of it as fast as he could after a long, hard battle, and went back to his supply camp.

About a week later military men are stunned by news that on June 25 at the Little Big Horn, General Custer and five companies of the seventh Cavalry are all killed.[5]

I go to Columbus on business. Talk is all on the Custer fight, and I'm asked why I don't get the Pawnees up there. I'm persuaded to telegraph, offering this to General Sherman. He answers that there is no law authorizing use of the Indians.

I no more than get back to Sidney than a dispatch comes ordering me to report to General Sheridan in Chicago. I go to Chicago, see part of the fire ruin of five years ago.

I report to General Sheridan at his office.

"Major North, you are to go to Fort Sill.[6] From there I've arranged your transportation to the Wichita Agency where you will enlist one hundred Pawnees. Have them furnish their own horses. You and your brother will march them across country to Sidney, Nebraska. There they are to be issued clothing, guns, and equipment. You will be furnished rations at posts along your way."

"But General, I believe the Pawnees are not with the Wichitas, and I don't think we should go by way of Fort Sill to arrive at their agency."

"Major North, I know where the Pawnees are. You go to Fort Sill."

I telegraph Luther before I leave Chicago. After traveling a night, I talk to the conductor and learn from him I should leave the train at Coffeeville, Kansas, to go to the Pawnee Agency. I wire General Sheridan at a layover station. His answer comes within an hour, and I am told to finish this trip as he routed me, leaving the train at Cado to go on to Fort Sill, about 150 miles by stage. We travel around and through the Wichita Mountains.

Somehow I manage to sleep. I'm awakened with a thud. A heavy weight begins to rise off me and I discover the other passenger—a 200-pound Delaware Indian—had fallen on me when our stage upset. He crawls out and helps lever it up so the mules can pull it onto its wheels and we proceed. I'm hurt and shook up. The stage arrives at Fort Sill during the next night. I am stiff and sore.

Although everyone here knows the Pawnee are on their own reservation north of the Cimarron River and west of the Arkansas River, I am obliged to carry through on the general's orders. Lt. Col. John P. Hatch sends me by ambulance to where the Wichitas may be found, also the Pawnees if they are with the Wichitas, and they are not. I return to Fort Sill. Luther is just off the stage.

Again I telegraph General Sheridan. He authorizes Colonel Hatch to furnish transportation. We get some sleep and start back to Cado to get on a train to Coffeeville. Here we face a hundred and twenty overland miles to the Pawnee Agency by a rented team and light spring wagon. We are three days crossing the Osage country. At the Arkansas River we have to ferry. I am suffering asthma and seem to have the ague.

Reaching the Pawnee Agency about midnight we find no place to sleep. Charles Chapin[7] from Columbus, an agency employee, offers us his bed. I'm getting very sick and accept his kindness. My malaria fever breaks in the night and I sleep. Awakening, I feel rested. Lute reports:

"The Pawnees found out we are here. About the time the birds began to twitter I heard them, and told them you had been sick and had just got to sleep. I said I knew you wanted to see them as soon as you could and if they would be quiet and let you sleep you would talk to them. I haven't heard a peep out of them since."

I get up and peek around the curtain. There our friends are waiting. I hurry to dress and go out.

"*Ati puta!*" ("Grandfather") they call, "Pani La Shar" ("Pawnee leader").

I walk closer. "Luther, what is wrong here?"

They crowd around us, as Luther says in low voice: "I'd guess they're starving."

We shake hands and call them by name and ask about members of their families and hear, to our grief: "Dead." "Dead." "Dead."

Shaken by ague and fever, the Pawnees tell an awful story of destitution, disease, and death. These people have only been here two years, a third of them only a year.[8]

I tell the people why we are here, and ask the men who are interested in enrolling as scouts to come to the Council House. Their spirits revive but in the faces of many we see death lurking.

At the time set, we place a table out of doors. Luther calls the boys forward—all crowd up wanting to get their names on my list. I look them over. Many appear sick, but they beg, "Oh Father when I'm north again I'll feel well then." All want to go, but I tell them I can only take a hundred this time.

Most of the horses brought south with the Pawnees have been stolen, perhaps some have been butchered for meat. The Pawnees cannot mount their scouts.

My list is nearly full when a tall boy steps up. Failing to place him I ask his father's name.

"Fancy Eagle," the lad says. I recall La-tah-cots-Kah La Haroo, Fancy Eagle, a Skeedee of the Wolf band of the clan Too-heets pee-ott, doctor and magician; the son of La-tah-cots-te Wetit, Sitting Eagle, one of the greatest doctors and magicians the nation ever had.

"Grandfather, make for me a paper name?" The boy means he wants to enlist, but the boy is so young.

"Have you won your name? When were you born?"

"Me, Ahre-Kah-Rard. Beyond the Kiz-katuz (flat, shallow water, the Platte River) toward the Ki-ra-ru-ta (filthy water, Republican River), seventeen snows back, at the time the winter hunt began, I was."

Ahre-Kah-Rard. I write the name which means Antlers, or of the deer family. I will take this Eagle.[9]

Witnessing the enrollment and the touching of the pen are Baptiste Behale; Eagle Chief, a Skeedee who was my first sergeant on the Powder River Expedition eleven years ago; Tec-La Shar cod-dic, Curly Chief of the Kit-ke-haki band; Ke-Wuk-oo-lah La Shar, Ruling His Sun, of the Pit-a-hau-rats. Too soon my quota is filled and every man and boy who didn't get a paper name is very disappointed.[10]

Eagle Chief[11] honors the enrolled braves in a short speech with good counsel. Curly Chief also speaks a few words then turned to me to beg that if the scouts must be punished I should not tie them on the wheel. He was never a scout, else wouldn't worry about that cruel army punishment made illegal before the Civil War. I promise that my scouts are safe from that punishment.

Actually, there has never been much need for punishment of the Pawnee Scouts. I suppose it is possible some faults may be plainer to others, but when I look I see a man, only a plains Indian, without much acquaintance with white civilization until a few months ago. On a dry, long day's march he saves the last cup of water in his canteen, does his stint of duty at making camp. He then hunts around in the dark for enough twigs or buffalo chips to hear the water for making a cup of tea, which he wakens me to drink. I discover too late he had not any for himself.

Another scout, a tribal medicine man, does his share of guarding, scouting, and fighting, and then while the camp sleeps he spends the night treating the badly frozen foot of a teamster, restoring it by morning to good circulation, color, and use. I'm seeing their tried and true loyalty, their bravery and dependableness. I have authority to dismiss a scout, should he refuse orders. This has never happened. Being a Scout is a high honor, and already is a tribal tradition.

We get a night's rest and drive the light wagon from the agency. Our hundred men walk across the Osage. Now and then one with the ague must lie on the ground until the chills and shaking are over, then he catches up again. I think almost all are sick; looks like some may die.[12]

Nearly as many Pawnees as those enrolled follow along, clinging to a hope that they may fill in for any who become too ill to go on.

I took three days' rations for my hundred men, but it is useless to hope each will use his share for himself alone as long as these poor hangers-on are with us, and some come all the way. When we entrain Luther has to appoint guards to make sure the extras do not get on the train. Meanwhile, I am very sick, and on Luther's shoulders fall the responsibilities of telegraphing General Sheridan for cars here and at the points of change, Kansas City and Omaha.

The cars come and we leave the next day. Things get hazy after that for me, and I'm not aware of what goes on. Lute's voice calls from a far distance, "A doctor for you, Frank." I'm dimly aware of hands fumbling at me. "—Not fit to travel. Put your brother in the hospital—" "Here, Frank, open your mouth for some pills." I swallow and soon the fog closes in on me, again.

I arouse. "What time is it, Lute? Where are we?"

"We've got a few hours layover in Kansas City. I had a doctor for you. He advises that I should put you in a hospital until you are able to travel."

"Oh, I'll be all right when we get to Nebraska," I say. After a while I realize the Pawnees have been saying the same to me.

The next morning we get into Omaha. I'm awake but weak. Luther telegraphs our brother-in-law, Jim Cushing, to have a rig meet me, and for him to be ready to go on with him and the Pawnee to Sidney. I will stop with our folks and get some doctoring until I'm able to go on.

OMAHA BEE NEWS, September 10, 1876: . . . We understand that Major Frank North and his brother, Captain Luther North and 100 Pawnee Indians will arrive in Sidney, Nebraska, in a few days, where they will equip, and, in time leave for the field of action. From the Major we expect to receive favorable news, when he goes after the Sioux fiends, as he is an old Indian fighter, and a braver man never trod the soil of Nebraska. . . .

OMAHA WORLD HERALD, September 12, 1876: Major Frank North and his brother, Captain Luther North passed through on the west bound train yesterday afternoon. A large number of citizens were present at the Depot to shake hands with Frank and Luther and wish them good luck on their journey. The Pawnees were in high spirits and seemed to be anxious to tackle the Sioux Indians. . . .

As the train moves west the boys are alive with excitement. Seeing the landmarks of their old homestead, they begin retelling their legends. Passing Shell Creek, Luther, knowing of Ponca's treachery many years ago, says "Now let's have the Ponca song." Suddenly the whole car is still.

Frank White[13] comes to our seat, saying, "Father, a Ponca is with us. We do not want to make him feel bad by singing that song." The Ponca has lived among the Pawnee several years. He is married to a Pawnee woman, so he is their brother. Some Pawnee, two hundred years ago, lived on Shell Creek, when they were visited by Ponca warriors. Pawnees went out to meet the advancing Poncas, who suddenly threw off their heavy skin robes and commenced shooting arrows. The surprised Pawnees had to fight, but succeeded in whipping the Poncas—ran them back to their own village, and returned to their own to dance the scalp dance with scalps taken from the treacherous Poncas. It was from that battle that the Ponca song was first chanted:[14]

A, Li-hit! Ku's-ke-har-u, Kur-u-u-ras, id-i, tus-ku-ra-wusk-u? Lau-i-luk-u-ru tus. ("Aha, you Ponca! It was [pretended] peace. Did you find what you were laughing at me about? You meant fight.")

The train pulls into Columbus. Everybody and his dog is at the depot to cheer us. Jim comes up to take me to Liz, waiting with a buggy, while Luther shakes hands for both of us. Jim goes with the outfit to Sidney where Lute draws rations, clothes, and camp gear and they take the boys into camp on Lodgepole Creek about a mile east.

In a few days I join my command. Jim comes with me as far as Julesburg to meet Luther with some of the boys. I go on, leaving them to buy horses for the Pawnee Scouts from the trail drovers' saddle horses, which they sell rather than take back to Texas. I figure they'll have a month of rest and good army forage; that should put them in shape.

I have Lute and Jim lead the boys, mounted, out a few miles and back every day to acquaint them with orders and get them used to regulations. Too, Lute has the boys playing ball with the "regulars" of Sidney Barracks. Of course they don't win many games, but it's something for the younger scouts to do.

September 15. A dispatch comes saying General Sheridan is on the train and asks me to meet him during the dinner stop here. I am on hand, present myself and we have a brief talk mostly concerning the scouts, equipment for my command, and so on. He then shakes hands with me and gets on the train. Not a word was said of his blunder in routing me to the Pawnee reservation. He is on his way to confer with Generals Crook and Terry. Crook ran out of rations up in the wilderness and his troops marched on, eating their horses that were dying from starvation.

September 18, 1876. Today the scouts are mustered in by Captain Pollock. I write their names, putting the words "his mark" above and a cross mark in the center of each name, the scout touching the pen. The rolls are backdated to September 3, the day I enrolled them. Our ponies are appraised by Lieutenants Dodge, Pratt, and Clagett from the twenty-third infantry. Some of these nags still look ragged. All mustangs, tough and well broken, they had never eaten grain, and some haven't yet taken to eating it. All lack considerable of being in top shape, but most of them will do.[15]

34

October 14, 1876. Received dispatch from General Crook. Command is to be at Niobrara crossing on the 20th. Broke camp, marched to Water Holes, 12 miles.

October 15. Moved at 8 A.M. Camped at Merchant and Wheelers at 2 P.M.; 18 miles.

October 16. Moved at 8 A.M., left 1 poor horse at the ranch, arrived at Bridge [now Bridgeport] at 2 P.M. Distance, 18 miles.

October 17. Lay over here today. Had 2 horses shod and drew 2000 pounds of forage.

October 18. Moved at 9 A.M. Camped at Red Willow, 2 P.M., distance 19 miles.

October 19. Marched at 8 A.M. Had fearful, bad day, rain, sleet and snow. Camped at Snake Creek. Distance 16 miles, had a wet, cold time of it. Not much wood [for fire to dry clothes].

October 20. Marched at 7 A.M. Lute took the lead with the Skeedees. I told him to hoop [hurry] them up and we made the 28 miles to Niobrara in 7 hours and did not go off a walk. The day was bad, a cold wind and some snow. One poor horse died today. Camped above Clifford's ranch; not much wood.

October 21. No orders to go further and here we are. Adam's team returned this morning to Sidney. I sent two teams for wood and moved camp up river a half mile. Wrote home today. Have no forage. Am anxious to know what I am to do and to get some feed for horses.

October 22. Started one team to Robinson after forage and one after wood. Wood came at noon and then sent team to camp above ours and traded some bacon for beef. At 4 P.M., just as we were at dinner, 2 men came in from Robinson with orders for us to move at once for Robinson. After dinner we loaded on one wagon and started. Made poor time. After going about 10 miles met my team coming back; divided

load and went on. Shortly met L't Elting coming after me to go and join
General Mackenzie to attack Red Cloud. Took 42 men and Lute and lit
out, rode all night. Left Cushing to go on to Robinson. . . .[1]

Lieutenant Elting tells me it is rumored at Camp Robinson that Red
Cloud is about to leave the reservation to join the hostiles. Red Cloud
agreed to the reservation and promised not again to make war against the
government. He has never broken his promise,[2] but could be he's decided
to take a hand. He had moved his village about thirty miles from Camp
Robinson, as far as he can go and stay on the reservation, when Colonel
Mackenzie took over command of Camp Robinson in August. Much troop
movement to and from Camp Robinson must have disturbed Red Cloud.
Colonel Wesley Meritt and part of the Fifth Cavalry came through
Robinson in July, on the way to join Crook. Going on, Meritt learned
several hundred Cheyenne Indians had left their reservation, going north
to join the hostiles. He intercepted them, and after a skirmish in which a
young leader, Yellow Hand, was killed, chased them back to the
reservation.[3]

In October, Crook's troops of the *horse-meat march* reached Camp
Robinson and bivouacked in three temporary cantonments.

The guide, Billy Hunter, leads on. We've covered more than twenty
miles. In the next mile or so we joined Mackenzie and took a breather.

Colonel Mackenzie tells me our objective is to surround two villages,
Red Cloud's and Yellow Leaf's,[4] and disarm them.

We ride on. Before dawn, Mackenzie calls a halt. Here the trail forks.
He separates forces, putting half under Maj. George A. Gordon, who is to
proceed to the Yellow Leaf village, which, Billy Hunter says, is about a
mile downstream from Red Cloud's village. I detail half our Pawnee
Scouts, in charge of Luther, to go with Major Gordon.[5]

General Mackenzie's specific orders: "Not a shot shall be fired unless the
Indians first open fire; surround the entire village before daylight; separate
their horses from them; demand surrender and disarm them; fight only if
all else fails."

General Mackenzie orders me with my scouts ahead along the lefthand
trail. Billy Hunter went with Major Gordon and Luther. Todd Randall,
who has a Sioux wife, guides us. The Pawnees suddenly freeze, hearing a
rooster crow. Randall says we are near Red Cloud's village—that since he
came to the reservation he's taken a fancy to keeping chickens. We
chuckle at the unexpectedness of the familiar sound. A crack of light
wedges between earth and sky as, with my scouts, I sit my horse on top of
a high cutbank with the stream at its base, and look down on Red Cloud's
village.

I back off taking three scouts along, leaving the rest as lookouts, and hustle back to General Mackenzie. He sends his troops to surround the village and I hustle back to my scouts; General Mackenzie and staff come with me to the elevation. Randall is sent to the brink of the cutbank, where, making a megaphone of his hands, he calls on Red Cloud to surrender, informing him he is surrounded by soldiers. Only echos return.

Some women and children come out of the tepees and run for the brush, maybe to hide. I lead the Pawnee Scouts through the village, the objective being to round up the Indian ponies. We cut loose those we find tied in the village and run them out of reach of the Indians, to be herded under the scout guards.

The general dismounts his cavalrymen, marches them into the village where all the male Indians are held under guard while they are disarmed. There is no resistance.

Randall tells the women to take horses to carry their belongings, and break camp immediately. Choosing to act as if they do not hear, the sullen women stand about.

General Mackenzie orders Randall to repeat the message in Sioux, louder. There still is no response. "Tell them," the general takes out his watch, "I will give them exactly five minutes to begin taking down their tepees. After that, we will burn them down."

The women make no move and the time runs out. The soldiers light fires. Little curls of smoke shock the women out of their trances and they beat out the fires and do as they had been ordered to do.

Luther says things happened in about the same way at Yellow Leaf's and Swift Bear's camp. Not a shot was fired in the whole proceedings. We fetch them all to Camp Robinson; some, feeble or ill, riding travois, all the rest, except the able men and warriors, riding the band's horses.

October 23, 1876. Camp Robinson. Just finished a ride of a hundred miles with less than two hours rest, and am tired enough. At daylight we had Red Cloud completely surrounded; he surrendered all arms, himself and warriors with their families.

Our Scouts charged through the villages and rounded up the horses. Lute went with Major Gordon; they surprised and captured Swift Bear's and Yellow Leaf's village. In all, we got 722 horses.

While we are having our meal, Moses E. Milner looks me up and eats with us. The old guide is stormy about Wild Bill Hickok's murder up in Deadwood. He thinks gamblers dry-gulched him. (Don't ask me how Moses got the "California Joe" handle. I never asked, so I don't know.)

General Mackenzie sends for me.

"Certain men close to these Indians say there is talk of stampeding the horses taken from them, so they will go back to the camp and the Indians

may get them again. Can you, and half of your command, start with them
to Fort Laramie at once?"

I can and I will, I say. I call out the scouts I couldn't take with me
because their horses were too weak. Of these I take fifty men, and leave
our horses to feed and come with the outfit at an easier rate. With fresh
mounts in the herd, we get aboard some, and roust the whole herd out.
The boys head them out on the Fort Laramie trail, and move along at a
steady gait.

> October 24. Have been busy all day with the ponies. At 5 P.M. [yes-
> terday] got orders to take 50 men and run the captured herd through to
> Laramie. Drove to Running Water. Stopped 2 hours then started on.

Getting down on the Running Water (Niobrara), the lead boys take us
to a campfire, doused just before we get there. They had heard the horses
and the boys hazing them along and naturally supposed an Indian attack
was near and challenged, "Are you after a fight?"

One Pawnee understands and speaks some English. "No-o-o-o, no want
fight. Me good man," Corporal Koot to-we-coots La Shar drawls as I ride
up. Two men hold guns on the boys. I explain myself and my scouts.
Soldiers escorting this wagon train gather around. The fires are rekindled
and coffee brewed, a welcome cup on this night. The wagon master asks
us what he could expect from reservation Indians, he being fearful of
attack. He was one who had challenged the scouts, the other being a
news reporter from New York City.[6]

We rest a couple hours, the scouts relieving each other on the horse
herd guard. I snatch an hour's sleep by the fire. A sentry rouses me saying
a rider was halted and is asking for me. I have him brought up.

"General Crook sent me—I left camp Robinson about four hours ago.
General Crook held a council with Red Cloud and Yellow Leaf Indians.
He deposed Red Cloud from head chieftain of the Sioux Indians. General
Crook then turned the captured Indians loose, on their promises. But the
reservation agent expects the warriors will borrow ponies from other
Indians and try to overtake you and the herd to get back their ponies. I
brought along some dispatches the general wants you to have telegraphed
from Fort Laramie."

"Tell General Crook that I think, since we are warned, we'll keep the
horses out of the Indians' hands and run them through to Fort Laramie."

I ordered saddles switched again to fresh mounts and we hightail it
down the trail. All day we drive on, making short stops for pasturing,
watering, and changing to fresh backs. At 8 P.M. we drive the herd into
the quartermaster's corrals, glad to call it a day.

"I have not enough men to guard the horses to pasture them. You can detail your men to take charge of them during the day, and corral them at night under my guards."

It seems a fair arrangement, since we are to remain here until my outfit comes.

October 25. Moved before day and hooped the ponies through to Laramie. Arrived 8 P.M.

On the second day scouts tell me they're missing some of the ponies as they take them from the corrals.

"All right, men. Now watch it close, notice the animals you turn in tonight so you can describe some, if you find them missing in the morning." After the herd was taken out again, a scout comes to me. With a quick move of his hands he tells me about how many are gone and describes the markings of some of them.

I look up the quartermaster to ask if I am to be held responsible for the captured horse herd?

He hums and haws, he will not lay it on the line. I tell him I will not require further guarding by the soldiers, that I'm putting my men to night-guarding the herd as well as pasturing them, and I'm sure there will be no further disappearance of stock. Scouts are getting orders to shoot to kill anyone attempting to steal a horse, and they're pretty good marksmen.

Horses are wanted for freighting, cattle ranching, homesteading, and going to and from the mines. There's no telling who got away with the horses, and not much chance of ever tracing them. My guess would be a soldier saw a chance to filch them out of the corrals to sell for easy money. I myself turned down a rancher who offered me $500 for certain horses. He may have known the horses; they're not all scrawny, Indian's ponies.

October 26. Ft. Laramie. Got some mail from home and am glad to hear Mary and Stella arrived at Columbus all safe and well. These ponies are terrible bother.

October 27. Still in camp and herding the ponies. . . .

October 28. Lute and Cushing came today. They came through all safe and sound. Nothing happened today.

Lute reports: "California Joe came back to our camp that evening before you left. He was looking for you. Talked to me a little and left, and we started to come here. We were about ten miles down the trail when Lieutenant what's 'is name caught up. He said, 'California Joe was just murdered.' I told him I guessed that was a mistake as I was talking to him just before I left. He said, 'It happened on his way from your camp back to his own. He was shot in the back.'"

"The gang he was so hot at must have thought they had better shut him up before he got some of 'em caught in a rope over a tree limb."

General Crook is at Fort Laramie. He orders me to choose a horse for myself and one for my brother. Each of the scouts is to have a horse. Then we are to take out seventy to take along on the coming campaign as reserves, and I am to select two hundred as mounts for some of Red Cloud's captured warriors, now enlisted by Crook as scouts.[7] Militarily it's probably brilliant strategy, but I'm not anxious to turn my back on them. Red Cloud and his warriors haven't actually made war on whites since 1868, they've been next door to it.

> October 30. Am very busy making muster rolls. Have had several call[er]s. Captain Dean Monahan; Lt. John G. Bourke and Lt. Albert D. King, 3rd Cavalry; Captain James T. Peale, 2nd Cavalry; and Lt. Thomas F. Riley, 21st Inf.

> October 31. Mustered this morning by Lt. W. P. Clark, 2nd Cavalry, had mounted inspection in the evening. Two men were absent and I am some mad.

> November 1. Tied one of the absent men up [not cruelly] and made the other carry a log in front of my tent for an hour.

I dismiss the two Pawnee at the end of their hour. I think this will end absences that I don't permit. The two are of younger scouts.

> November 2. Sale of ponies began this morning. Had nearly all my men on duty and worked myself about sick. The ponies sold for about all they are worth.

> November 3. Nothing of importance today. I still have two herds of horses . . . to look after.

During the day Lieutenant Clark came to our Pawnee camp near the Laramie River, saying he was organizing all the Indian scouts into a battalion. Captain Randall is up in Crow country to enlist some of their young warriors as scouts. Tom Cosgrove with Shoshones is to join later, near Reno. Sioux braves we rounded up were enlisted by General Crook. I believe there may be a scattering of Cheyenne and Arapahoe with the Sioux.

Clark tells me he aims to place all the Indian scouts under regular officers of the army: Lieutenant Schuyler, the Shoshones; Lieutenant Wheeler,[8] the Sioux; Lieutenant De Lany, the Pawnees; and probably Captain Randall, the Crows (if he gets here with them).

"And just where does that let me come in?" I ask.

"You will have charge of the Pawnees, but under Lieutenant De Lany."

"Nothing doing! I've always been in charge of the Pawnee Scouts, subject only to the orders of the commanding officer of the expedition, and that's how it will be."

"Then I will take this matter up with General Crook."

"Fine, I'll go with you to see the general about it."

November 4. General Mackenzie arrived today with his troops. Got Lute's and my horses shod today and am ready now for a move and here it comes. Lt. Clark, with Gen. Crook's compliments, and says we will move at 8 A.M. tomorrow. Rather short notice but we will be on hand.

We hustle around to get in shape. This is to be another Powder River Expedition—a little different than when we went nearly twelve years ago, under General Connor, in warm weather. My men, sick when they came from the south (two died, two weeks after coming to Sidney), are filled out, look well, seem hardy, and show no sign of the sickness. I think they're ready to go.

35

November 5. This morning winter has set in with cold, blustering wind and snow. Someone "Hello's" outside my tent. Lute unties the storm flap, Lieutenant Clark sits his horse just outside the opening.

"Major North, aren't you going on the expedition?"

"Yes, of course. I've been expecting my moving out orders."

"Well, the general and his staff are already gone and General Mackenzie is getting on the move. You had better fall in if you're coming along."

I surmise somebody has failed to bring an order to me. I order camp struck and packed and loaded and we start out facing rain, sleet, and snow. Toward evening there is no general "Halt" called for bivouac. General Crook chooses a time and a place upstream and just squats there, General Mackenzie does likewise, a mile or so downstream, and I camp at a warm spring. The wagon train is yet below me.[1]

> *November 5.* Moved at 8 A.M., the wind blowing a gale, some snow and rain. Should have gone as far as Bitter Cottonwood but for the Command making camp here.

I receive no message tonight as to when we are to move, nor what place in the column of march we are to be assigned.

This morning a scout comes to tell me the head of the column is moving out.

> *November 6.* Moved early and marched to Horseshoe. General Crook [and Staff or bodyguard] went to Elkhorn. Our teams, [the Pawnee command's supply wagons] followed Gen. Mackenzie to Bull's Bend. I had to send back for them and they didn't come up till late.

> *November 7.* Started at daybreak, came to Wagonwheel. We are in good camp. The boys, Puss and Andrew Murphy [a teamster] each killed a deer. We are living high.

214

We're on the march early, get into Fort Fetterman early afternoon. General Mackenzie was here at noon, ahead of us.

November 8. Reached Fetterman early today and crossed the River and have nice camp and met many friends.

As the Pawnees are still herding the extra horses we need plenty of room for camp. We go on north of Fetterman, beyond the Sioux Scouts' camp to make our camp.

November 9. Today drew rations for 10 days, wood, hay, and about all necessities of life.

November 10. Today drew pants and socks for the men. Nothing new, same old routine of soldier life.

Saturday 11. Rode around a little and did not do much of any business [did not participate in many games or conversations]. Went to Infantry camp and met Dodge, Pollock, Pratt, Claggett and many more friends.

Sunday 12. Business is about the same today as week day, all hurly-burly for the march. Some say we go tomorrow, others say the day after.

November 13. Thermometer 14 below zero. Today drew mitts and some boots and forage for five days, as we expect to leave tomorrow.

Today Lieutenant Clark and a young chief of the Red Cloud bunch of enlisted scouts went to the herd of the Pawnee Scouts' horses, and the Sioux, Three Bears, took out a bay horse, in spite of objections of the Pawnee on guard, who didn't know what to do. Speaking some English, he persuades Lieutenant Clark to come with him to see me, and Three Bears leads the horse to my tent, where the Pawnee Chic-ko-ta Kah calls me out.

"Major North, I've taken a horse for my scout, as his went lame and he needs one."

I walk up and take the rope from the Sioux. "This horse belongs to me and he can't have it," I say.

"But isn't that one of the horses taken from the Red Cloud Sioux?"

"Yes, it is."

"The general said those horses were to be for the Indians and as replacements, and Three Bears wants that horse."

"Well there are plenty in the herd, he can get one of them. This horse is mine and he can't have it," I repeat.

"I will see the general about this," he and the Sioux whirl away.

Lute sends for his gray horse and we saddle up to go see the general. A teamster, or white scout, comes along, says, "Them Sioux are going on the warpath. They're saying they'll clean out the Pawnee and take their horses."

I send word around to the Pawnee scouts to be ready if the Sioux should start a fight. Lute and I ride past the Sioux camp where we see Three Bears haranguing the Sioux braves. We ride up within ten or twelve yards and they stand and stare at us, saying nothing. I touch the high-headed bay with the spur and he begins to prance. Lute does the same, and we dance our horses past them singing the Pawnee war song. It's an act, of course, and well understood by Indians, of readiness. I can understand the Sioux's feelings at loss of their horses. Naturally, they want to get the best of them back, and these two we ride are the best.

The bay is said to have belonged to Three Bears and to be a very fast horse. Aside from whether it was right to take the reservation Indians' horses from them, these animals are removed from any chance of use by the Indians we now are to subdue and bring in.

Finding General Crook in the Sutler's store, Lieutenant Clark comes in, a jump behind us. He skips preliminaries to get the first word.

"General, I went with a Sioux scout to get one of those extra horses you said were for replacements—Three Bear's horse went lame and he needs another, and Major North refused to let me have one."

A clever half-truth, an out-and-out attempt to get me in wrong. The general isn't particularly startled—you might think he didn't hear. Eventually he mildly suggests.

"Major North, did you wish to speak to me?"

"Yes, General, I do have a word to say. No, I did not refuse the lieutenant a horse. But I did refuse to let him have the horse that you, General, gave to me, the choice to be mine, at Fort Laramie."

"Well, Lieutenant Clark, why did you not go and talk with the major, to arrange for taking a horse from those he is holding for the scouts' replacements? The horses I gave to Major North and the Pawnee command are their own, and not to be drawn from by anyone else."

I say, "General, the horses you gave to my men I believe are all the extras we will need. With your approval I would like to turn the others over to the lieutenant's Sioux." The general agrees to this, but I'm still not through.

"General, if you don't mind there is something else. Lieutenant Clark came to me in Laramie with his scheme to take over all the Indian scouts, my Pawnees too, all to be put under officers of the regulars, himself to be their major or captain and myself to be under Lieutenant De Lany. I'm in bad with him because I refused to fall in with his plan."

"I see, I see—" the general comments, and I'm sure he does see what is back of the horse dispute.

"The Pawnee Scouts under Major North and his brother are subject to the commander of the expedition. You, Lieutenant Clark, will refrain from tampering with the Pawnee Scouts and major's organization. Is that clear?"

I find money is being laid on whether Three Bears and the rest of his braves get the bay horse back or not.

November 14. I crossed the River (it's full of floating ice) to see what was to be done, but could get no orders so I sent Lute to break camp as the rest are all moving. I get checks for $200.00 and mailed to Jim, then started off. We came to Sage Creek, twelve miles, have a nice camp but snow bothers some. 14° below zero.

Wednesday 15. South Cheyenne. Arrived here at 1 P.M. Marched 19 miles in five hours. Have a nice camp above the [Bozeman] road, plenty wood, water, feed, just as good as I wished.

Thursday 16. Marched 22 miles, camped on Wind River as it is called now, but when I was here in '65 Bridger called this creek North Cheyenne. Lute was out on a scout but found nothing. The boys killed two antelope and gave our mess two hind quarters. Paymaster came this evening.

November 17. At daylight I never saw a better prospect than we had for a frightful snow storm. I rained some then turned to snow and it was perfectly awful for a while. But we pulled out and came to Dry Fork of Powder River, 25 miles. It was very cold, bad traveling. The boys killed one deer today.

The Sioux and Pawnee are like schoolboys, making faces and insulting gestures at each other. I'm not sure whether they're carrying on the old feud or if they are just entertaining themselves and each other on the march.

November 18. Started early and came into Reno[2] ahead of the Cavalry. This evening we got paid off and the men are making the money fly. They send a good share home. I sent Jim $2289.20.

General Crook speaks to me about the Sioux and a few Cheyenne he enlisted saying the Pawnee treat them unfriendly, that they will not come near nor mingle with them. I give him a sketch of how it's been between them for many generations. "Now, General," I say, "if you are making it an order, I'll do all I can to see that it is obeyed."

"Oh, no—I don't believe we can force friendship on the Indians, any more than we could among ourselves. Yet if they should become more cordial it would be better for all of us, at least during the expedition."

"Well, I'll talk to the Pawnee Scouts. Maybe we can bring them around."

I talk—and the Pawnee listen. Then they talk and I listen: "The Sioux
have only as much love for us as we have for them. The Sioux are like the
Ponca who came visiting many generations ago, with a smile on their
faces and treachery in their hearts; and a bow and full quivers concealed
under their robes. The Sioux make the act of friendliness only for a better
chance to get their captured horses from the Pawnee."[3] The frontiersman,
Tom Cosgrove, got in with his Shoshone (Snake) scouts tonight.

> *November 19.* We lay over here today. I have been busy drawing caps
> for my men, also getting forage and rations as we are to leave in the
> morn. Here is a messenger now saying we will not leave tomorrow. Big
> council today.

General Crook calls all the Indian companies together with their white
officers. Five main tribes are represented.[4] The general talks like a
"Grandfather" which the Pawnee call him:

"Now, my friends, we are all soldiers together. You, as well as ourselves,
are here to serve the great white father. You march along together, and
may be called upon to do battle together. Then should we not all be
friends, at least while we work together?"

On the chance the Indians' aim is to flout an open insult to the Pawnee
Scouts, I gain the floor to call the war/dare dress of certain scouts to
General Crook's attention.

He hears me through and, as is his way, makes no immediate comment,
then goes on with his talk: "Since we are all soldiers, we should always be
brothers from now on, and there are certain times and occasions when we
ought to dress in uniform of the soldier—"

After the general's talk, the Shoshone chief—a son, Tom Cosgrove tells
me, of the Chief Washaki—speaks. A couple of other Indians talk a little,
then the Pawnee chief, Li-heris-oo La Shar (also known as Leading Chief,
enlisted under the name of Frank White), stands to tell us he is a white
man at heart and asks all men to recognize that he is a white man,
following the white man's way, a brother to the white man; a clever way
of saying that, being a white man, that fact lets him out of being a red
man's brother, unless I misread Li-heris.

The Sioux, Three Bears, comes over to Pawnee, directly to Frank
White. They shake hands and Three Bears backs off, pulls up and in high
dignity says, through the interpreter, "Friend, I want to be your brother. I
call you my brother. That you may know my heart is right toward you, I
give you my horse."

Three Bears surprises us all. None can doubt Three Bears' sincerity, at
least for the moment. Frank White climbs off his perch, and accepts
Three Bears' friendly advance and gift with matching friendliness.

November 20. Snowing this morn. I guess all are glad we are not to go today. I sure am.

Striking up quick acquaintance, the Pawnees and Shoshones, strangers before, find much to chatter about. They talk by use of sign language, known to all American Indians. But for satisfying conversations, Tom and I help them out, interpreting when we can. The Shoshones are related to the Comanches who live in Indian Territory and who are known to the Pawnee Scouts. Our last day in camp speeds by.

Last evening, General Crook⁵ sent out Sioux scouts. They come in today with a young Cheyenne captive. He is questioned, says he was with a small group camped on the upper Powder River and that the Sioux Crazy Horse, with his people, is camped on Rosebud River near the big bend where the Sioux and Cheyenne fought General Crook last June.

November 21. Moved early for Crazy Woman and found it a long road to travel over. Our teams did not arrive till after dark. Have a very comfortable camp with the Snakes, the Shoshones.

November 22. Had a terrible time getting anywhere. First, last night got orders to move with pack animals for the northwest; got all ready to go at day light, then got orders to wait a couple of hours. Turned out our horses then got orders to go with teams. But before unpacking any mules I rode to headquarters and there the order was changed to packs again, and the mountains and Cheyennes are the objective. Sent five men ahead on a three day scout. We started after them at 11 A.M., found good grass, wood, and water. Gen. Mackenzie in command.

Early in the forenoon a Cheyenne scout comes in and says the camp which the captive, 'Beaver Dam,' is from has started to join Crazy Horse and that a sizable Cheyenne band's village is back in the Big Horn about at the head of Crazy Woman Creek, rough, rugged country to cross. General Mackenzie's field quartermaster, Captain Lawton, and the wagon master, John Sharp, with some of the Pawnee Scouts are working ahead to smooth out the worst crossings.⁶

November 24. Moved early, about 12 miles. Two Sioux scouts who had been sent out last night came in and said they had found the village. We camped in a ravine and waited till night then moved on, traveled all night.

The way here would be rugged in daylight even without deep snow covering dangers for horse and man. Steep-sided ravines, canyons so narrow and crooked only one horse and rider get through at a time—the column strung out straggling.

Through the night hours we climb in the moon's uncertain light, up and over and down dark canyons. During a rest stop I ask Luther to step aside and try for a count of our men. By and by he reports he saw a number of Pawnee sick at the stomach.

I saw men sick when we came up into these mountains with Connor in 1865. It's an effect of altitude, and we are miserably cold, and tired—some fall asleep with their mount's reins looped over their arms. When the word "Advance" comes down the line, the next man must arouse the sleeper. With some, the sickness could be from anxiety, fear, and uncertainty. Whatever the cause, they've got something else to think of now. The scouts tell me they hear drum beats and singing as of dancing. Soon the sounds are clear to all ears.[7] Tom Cosgrove says his Shoshones believe the village is scalp dancing a victory. General Mackenzie sends the word along the line to "Catch Up," each man to take his place. We are close to the village.

A halt is signaled. Commanders of companies are called forward. General Mackenzie, in a low voice, raps out brief orders. We wait for daylight. The Pawnee Scouts throw saddles off their ponies and strip off coats and caps but wear pants and shirts. I change from the mule I've ridden all night—surer footed on the mountain passes—to my horse. Lute's gray is saddled for him. "Mount up" is signaled, I mount and glance back; I don't see Lute. I send Ahre Ka-rard to fetch him. He comes back without Lute. I dismount and with several scouts look among the rocks. In this last minute Lute stumbles out of his sleep among the rocks and mounts.

We gallop along the left bank of the creek a couple hundred feet below. The rock ledge narrows, allows only single passage in places and this creek is the only passage into the valley. About halfway to the village this trail gets more treacherous. General Mackenzie, riding along the opposite side, sees this trail ends around a bend and has Ralph Weeks, one of my scouts, to call his order that we cross over. We pick our way down, are slowed in a boggy bottom. The Shoshones under Lieutenant Schuyler and Tom Cosgrove turn up the mountain.

The charge is on! The village lies before us and people are already riding and running from it. I lead in, Lute at my elbow, and my Pawnee Scouts well up. A brush-lined dry wash lies between us and the nearest lodges. We plunge into the thicket. An Indian in a blanket jumps up at Lute's right front, swings a rifle on Lute. The Indian and Lute shoot at almost the same time. Lute had to make a half turn in the saddle as he shoots to his left. The young Indian is killed and the Pawnee count coup in passing.[8]

The Sioux start their war-whoop, then all the Indian scouts whoop together, including the Pawnees with their familiar yipping cry. Lieutenant

McKinney and his fourth Cavalry company ride to the right after a group of Indians running toward the canyon. The Cheyenne send lead flying; I see McKinney go down and some of his men. The troops jump from their mounts, run for the ravine, and let loose enough lead to quiet everything.

Companies of cavalry are fighting all around. I lead my Pawnee Scouts charging through the village to the south end then to the west. The village is abandoned. The Indians go up into the rocks. Those in the first tepees ran among the lodges in the upper village where many horses were tied. Most of the women and children escaped on horses while the men delayed their attackers; it was such a group that killed Lieutenant McKinney.

The Shoshones found the mountain they climbed ended in a cliff. We hear their shooting at the Cheyenne who are holding out behind a rocky ridge.

I send a group of Pawnee Scouts to make their way along a swale and try to work up into the mountain behind the Cheyennes. They climb part way up then come out in sight of the cavalry who blast away at them, taking them for hostiles. The Pawnee take cover, climb down and return.

General Mackenzie is shot at but his rabbit foot must be in the right pocket. He sends for me and Lute. We ride across through two or three lively volleys, and report. Two soldiers come on foot; both are hit, one killed.

"Major, do you think it possible to drive those Indians from their vantage point, to stop their shooting our wounded mens' hospital hill?"

"I'll see what we can do, General." I blow on a pocket whistle. A half dozen or so Pawnee Scouts report. I explain what the general and I ask, and hand them the job. They strip clothing, tie bandannas around their heads, change from boots to moccasins, and are soon out of sight up the mountain side. After while there is no more shooting from that spot.

Skirmishing at long distance continues all afternoon. The Cheyennes' loose horses, left behind, are in the open valley to the west. Warriors have not left the rock ridge breastwork. The general hopes to secure the horses, believing loss of their ponies might convince these Indians they had better surrender.

A few Shoshone scouts sneak up the Red Fork, and when near the horses, run out of the aspen and willow brush to stampede them. The Cheyennes shoot one of the scouts, kill some of their mounts, and force them back. The man is bad hurt—a body shot.

Sioux jeers are hard for the Shoshones to swallow. Three Bears gets eight warriors to go along with him to fetch the horses. They don't make it to the horses. All come back riding double, leaving four of their mounts killed.

Now the Pawnees want to try for the horses. The Cheyennes are shooting from only about a hundred yards and they've got the range. I tell them I don't want them to go and get laughed at. Luther overhears this. He demands permission to go. I scowl, say nothing, and he knows I don't like his offer, but it doesn't hold him.

"Frank I can bring that herd in with one man."

"I'll choose Pete Headman."

He lays his hand on my arm and leaves. Pete Headman was with Lute when he was knocked out when his horse slipped on ice near Prairie Dog Creek south of the Republican. Pete is solid, cool-headed and ten years older than most of the scouts. Pe-isk-e La Shar, meaning Boy Chief, has been in Lute's companies several times.

Lute and Pete leave their carbines, take revolvers, and each carries a blanket over his arm. They scoot along the stream bed as the others did, laying low on their horses, behind willows and aspens fringing the banks. Through my field glass I next see them in a flat run toward the scattered herd. Swinging their blankets and yelling—(I'm sure, though I don't hear them), the herd is hard to start.

But they're getting them together, are moving them. Lute runs aside at one animal—strikes at it to start it. The horse goes down from a Cheyenne shot. Lute's horse stumbles, falls onto its head. Lute still rides— his horse is up, the other is dead. Several animals have fallen from Cheyenne bullets intended for Lute and Pete. All are running, pass through the village, head southeast across the open space for the buttes and hills. General Mackenzie is pleased, gives about one hundred head to the Pawnee.

Leaving our horses, Lute climbs with me up a hill. We crawl onto the top, take advantage of shallow depressions to lay there and try to clear the Indians out of their stronghold on the mountain—a long shot, sixty to eighty rods. Some dozen soldiers join us and a couple white scouts.[9]

General Mackenzie gets the officers together.

We fail to come up with any workable plan. Likewise, as at first the ending of the left trail around and above the village prevented me with my Pawnee Scouts, we are powerless to further punish the Indians to effect their surrender. Our scouts have found no way into the mountain but by the way the Cheyennes took, a narrow, very steep defile. The wonder is that the women and children disappeared by that way so quickly while the men held off the troops; since then they have been sharpshooting at us from in the rocks, and we've driven them no further all day.

Two other considerations: to try to capture the large horse herd or to destroy their village and property. Actually, there is no choice, both the horse herd and the Indians being beyond our reach.

"We take no pleasure in contemplating this duty [destruction of the village] which it is apparent at this time must be implemented; for, we saw many of these poor savage people with their children run naked from their beds into the rocks. It is, however, incumbent upon me to leave no stone unturned to bring about the capture or subduing of this people.

"Major North, you, with your command, will move into the village to begin the work of demolishing and destroying—"

I lead my scouts across the stream that cuts down where the village is; we are under fire of the Cheyennes. The troops, supposedly covering for us, can be of little benefit and we will take our chances. Four horses are shot from under us by the time we reach the first lodges. We dismount and head the animals back out of firing range.

Dodging between the lodges, we begin at the end nearest the Indians, setting two lodges afire. The hope is that, seeing their lodges burning, these people will hurry down to surrender and save their property.

From the tepees, Bill Rowland, who talks Cheyenne, bellers "General Mackenzie's demands to the Indians to "come down and surrender." He is heard, I think, and is answered with a fusillade of lead. We set fire to more tepees. Night is near, it will be soon dark. We cannot delay, but pile up buffalo robes, garments, about two hundred Indian saddles, cradle boards, camp items, clothes, weapons, ammunition, besides an abundant winter supply of dried meats in bales. Much is found that these Indians took from Custer's seventh Cavalry.[10]

I have the Pawnee drag up logs to build a fire. The temperature never got above twenty-five degrees below zero all day and as night comes down it grows colder. Luther and I drop down on a log about ten feet from the fire. No one has eaten since this time last evening. There's plenty of buffalo jerky in this camp and while coffee is brewing we chew on some and on our ration-cracker. The boys set a quart tin cup of coffee[11] on our log for us. From up in the rocks we've heard the occasional boom of a buffalo gun. We hear that gun now and a stray mule comes up just in time to catch the bullet and drop dead back of the fire.

"If that fellow lowers his sights he will make us move," Lute almost gets the words out of his mouth when a bullet hits the tin cup of coffee between us. We scramble off the log and it doesn't take us long to throw parfleches of dried meat into a wall to stop the bullets.

Snow is beginning to sift down. I detail guards for the night, to change every hour—an hour is plenty long enough, considering conditions. No one will sleep cold, with plenty of buffalo robes under and over us.

Saturday 25. Had a hard night's march. At 7 A.M. struck Little Wolf's and Dull Knife's village of Cheyenne, 173 lodges, and had a fight which lasted all day and part of the night. We are encamped in the village to-night and bullets are dropping all around us. We have burned all the lodges. Eighteen dead Indians are lying around us at some distance on

the field. One Lieutenant and four men killed on our side and 17 soldiers and one Snake Shoshone Indian wounded. A stray bullet just
killed a mule within 30 paces of Lute and me. [12]

This morning we wake up and push a snow counterpane ten inches deep
off our robes to get up. We get ready to leave; the scouts fashion travois
under Lieutenant Wheeler[13] who has charge of taking the wounded and
dead men along.

November 26. Snowing this morn for all out. . . . Got orders to burn
everything left in the village and move out. We camped tonight on
south branch of Powder River, saw no Indians today.

November 27. Moved early, came to the main Powder River where we
camped. One horse gave out today. Our scout came in today, nearly
famished.

November 28. Got out of camp at 8 A.M. and came to branch of Crazy
Woman. One of the wounded died last night. We are bringing all the
dead and wounded along on travois. Gen. Mackenzie distributed the
ponies this eve. We got 60 head. The Gen. thinks we got enough out of
the village to make up for loss in horses. The Sioux had a regular
knockdown over their division. The Gen. gave each of my five men
who were on scout an extra pony each and one to Peter Sam for one he
had killed in the fight.

November 29. Here I am in my wall tent again and it feels like getting
home. Got a letter from Mary, glad to know they are all well. Must
close this and write to my dear ones.

November 30. Wrote home this morn and went down and mailed letter. Got orders to send scout to Clear Creek. Sent Pe-isk-ke La Shar
[Boy Chief], and two other men. They came back in a few hours and
said a horse gave out. I reduced the lad and sent Lute with four men at 7
P.M. Hope they will have good luck.

36

Since General Crook ordered the scout to Clear Creek to see if the Indians have come out of the mountains on that side, the general speculation is that Crook will move for Tongue River.

Friday, December 1. Drew ten days' rations today and am ready for another ten days. Lute came in at 3 P.M. and did not see anything. Had a long, tiresome ride for nothing.

Saturday, December 2. Here we are, back to Reno. No one seems to know where we are going. I don't much care so I can have feed for my horses. We are only getting half forage now.

Here the remains of Lieutenant McKinney and the dead soldiers are given burial with a short service.[1] The wounded men, after terrible suffering in spite of the near-miracle work of Lieutenant Wheeler and his aides who took pains to lift each travois over rough places, rest in Fort Reno's small hospital under a surgeon's treatment.

The Shoshones leave us to return to their reservation. Tom Cosgrove buys my bay horse to race him there. I sell, instead of running chances of having him stolen or of not having forage for him.

Sunday, December 3. Camp tonight in our old camp on Dry Fork of Powder River. Tomorrow we break off for the Black Hills. Wrote home tonight.

Monday, December 4. Got our wagons all loaded, ready to move, when I learned accidentally that we were not to move. I never saw such an outfit in my life. No one knows five minutes before hand what is to be done. 40 teams started for Fetterman today. I sent some mail home.

December 5, Tuesday. Got no order this morn about moving, so turned out our stock and about 10 o'clock A.M., saw the Headquarter teams moving out so of course we were bound to follow. Came ten miles and camped near Pumpkin Buttes, came over a fearful road.

December 6. Moved this A.M., at 8 and came 25 miles over a most fearful road. Our ration wagon upset and did not get to camp till 9 o'clock. Some of the teams were out all night.

December 7. Started this morn, marched 20 miles in rear of every-thing, came along at a pretty good gait, finally passed all but Headquar-ters' teams. Have a nice camp, plenty wood and water. Teams very late again. Baatz[2] [teamster] came into camp late at night on a mule and said he had left the wagon as he could not find our camp. Sent him back with three men and they came in with the wagon about 9 o'clock.

December 8. Moved at the usual hour, came only five miles, camped in our permanent camp on the Belle Fourche River. No feed to men-tion. . . .

We have been camped here a couple days. A party of prospectors go through on their way to the Big Horn Mountains to look for gold. I warn them it's dangerous to go there since our battle with the Cheyennes.

"Just camp here tonight and in the morning you can turn around and go back," I urge.

"Hell man, there ain't any gold left in the hills. It's up in them there mountains, and we're going after it. We can take care of ourselves—any one of us kin whip fifty Indians."

They went on, but in the night one of the fellows came to our camp and the scouts on guard brought him to me. He's half naked, barefooted, and terribly churned up—I suppose they've met with Indians all right. I call for Le-Herris-oo La Shar and Red Hawk[3] to come and see what they can do for him. He begins to thaw out and we catch some words, "—killed the others—got away—ran for Army camp—five Indians—killed everybody—"

I report to General Crook. He orders me to send a scout detachment to the miners' camp to investigate and punish the Indians if at all possible, the man to guide the detail.

The boys are bringing the fellow around. I believe he may be able to go along as soon as the ten scouts and Luther can get ready and mounted. I hunt up warm socks, boots, and clothes for the man, we get hot coffee down him, set him on a horse, and he rides away between Lute and Big Hawk Chief.

The forenoon is nearly gone, no word from Lute. I expected them back before this. I take twenty-five men and light out to find the detail. We meet Lute coming, in the second mile out. He found the miners' camp stripped of everything—provisions, guns—they had a pretty good supply of arms and ammunition that was taken. One man had been shot through the leg, had pulled the blanket over his head. The Indians had split his head open—hadn't scalped him, but had left the axe under the man's head. There was no sign of the three other men. Lute followed the trail south for some miles but as our horses are weak had to give it up.[4]

Three more surprises today: one at a time, the three miners straggle into our camp. The general sends a detail to bury the dead man, and gives the four men jobs with the command so he can clothe and feed them.

December 19. Today got eight days' forage and they say it is all we will have on the trip. Got orders to move camp in the morn.

December 20. Moved this morn. at 8 A.M. came five miles, have a good camp near HdQts. Drew 11 days' rations today. Had quite a visit from officers this evening, Col. Dodge and five others.[5]

Lute, with a detail out grazing our horses, finds elk in a blind canyon. They kill several, bring in meat and we feast.

No scouting parties have turned up traces of Indian bands.

December 21. Cap. Pollock and Dodge called today and brought pretty good news. We are to move back tomorrow for Fetterman. The Sioux Scouts leave us and go across the country [to the Red Cloud reservation].

December 22. Sure enough, for once the rumors were right. We moved on the back track in a snow storm and came up near the Burning Buttes. Tonight is fearful cold. We are comfortable.

December 23. Moved this morn. I really think it was too cold for any one to be out, but we came 16 miles, all the same, and camped in the sagebrush. No timber, not much water.

December 24. Came ten miles today. Camped in our old sagebrush camp. No wood or water and not much feed. We can melt snow to cook with but our poor animals have to go without. It is so cold we can hardly keep from freezing. In fact, Jim Cushing [brother-in-law] froze three fingers, badly frozen. Tonight is Christmas eve and Oh, what a Christmas it is with us, nearly frozen and so far from home and loved ones.

December 25. Today was Christmas, but I can say there are not many in our camp that have enjoyed it. Mercury froze up solid last night and would freeze today if we had any to freeze. We came 25 miles and camped on a dry creek, no water, but plenty of wood.[6]

December 26. Got out early, came one mile and watered all our horses with a bucket and tincup. We came by a cutoff and reached Wind Creek about 2 P.M. Camped in our old place, lots of wood, water and grass. Marched 18 miles. Lost half of our stovepipe today and it nearly broke us up in housekeeping.

December 29. Got out pretty early and came to Fetterman. Have a good camp and hay for our horses and wood for the men, no grain here so I don't want to winter here.

December 30. Lay in camp today. I was busy as a bee all day getting supplies and muster rolls, Lute and I worked like good fellows to get them ready. Also made out clothing receipt rolls for Lt. Clark.

December 31. Mustered this morn. at 10 A.M., by Lt. Robinson. He done the business up in short order. Did not inspect the arms at all and I guess it was well for some of us he did not. . . .

1877, January 1. Happy New Year to All. We are leaving Fetterman today. Very bad traveling—ice, snow and wicked cold. Only go eighteen miles to Wagon Hound Creek to camp. We are comfortable, but no feed for our stock.

The going is so bad and our horses are getting so weak that we are six days on the way to Fort Laramie. The old fort never was so welcome a sight to me. I'm having asthma too much to be able to walk as the others do, to keep warm.

January 5. Today came to Warm Springs to camp. I left the camp, took Abraham[7] as orderly and came on into Laramie. Found good, long letter from Mary. Stayed at the Rustic Hotel, rode 30 miles today.

January 6. Went out this morn and selected a camp site. The boys came in with the Command about noon and we are in camp below the Fort. All well and comfortable. Find Harry Coon[8] nearly well.

January 7. Our tent blew down last night and I caught cold, have been sick all day, have hardly left my tent. We all promised to go to Bill Reed's for dinner but I was too sick, and Lute went away with Hunter.

I'm ordered to move my command to Sidney. We get the mules shod. I get Jinks shod, buy a horse and saddle, drew grain, hay, rations, and wood.

January 11. Moved at 8½ A.M., in a driving snow storm. Five miles. Lute and Ralph Weeks stayed behind to bring the mail. They got in about dark but no mail from home.

January 12. Moved at 9 A.M. about 15 miles. Camped on the Platte near an old road ranche. Brujah's hay team camped near us. They [Ft. Laramie] were supposed to bring grain down to us but they will not overtake us in time.

January 13. Came thirteen miles today, camped two miles below Nick Janis'es Ranche. If the river was passable I would go over and see the old fellow.[9]

January 14. Moved at usual hour, came 17 miles. Left one horse at Horse Creek Spark's Ranch. Had a hard time crossing the creek, ice very smooth, camp tonight near old Fort Mitchell.

Midafternoon I sent Lute and two scouts, Big Hawk Chief and Matthew Simpson (both Pawnees), after game, and tell them where we will camp. I have the boys kick the snow away and kindle a fire on a hill. As the kindling begins to flame the three come in, but didn't get the game. Fun twinkles in Lute's eyes as he says: "Coming to the top of a hill we found it a straight down, cutbank. We backtracked to find a way down, and decided to try a ravine though it was steep, and slippery. Big Hawk Chief goes ahead, leading the little spotted mule he bought at Fort Laramie and is so proud of. We walk to be safer, and lead our horses. About a hundred yards from the mouth of the ravine, we come to a jump-off—where water from cloud bursts or snow melt had washed a fall, and gullied the ravine. The hillside is very steep and slick with ice and snow, but I said, 'It's already so dark down in the canyons that if we have to go back again to hunt still another way down, we won't find our way out of the canyons tonight.'

"Big Hawk thinks we can make it, and starts climbing along the hill, leading his mule. The other Pawnee, Matt, starts along the other side and I wait at the head of the wash.

"The spotted mule loses his footing on ice, falls flat-sided—is slipping down toward the ravine. But Big Hawk Chief hangs onto the bridle reins, wraps his arm around a jack pine—his hold breaks the mule's fall—swings it around, tail toward the ravine, where it stops a half minute. As the mule scrambles to get his feet under him the bridle reins pop, giving way. He slides over the edge, tail first, and out of sight. Big Hawk Chief eases himself down to the bank, looks down, then up to me with most woebegone expression, saying: '*Oh-ho-Atius-way-te-op-pits-kah-hah-kits-au-wuck!*' ('Oh my Father, broken in two is the spotted mule.')[10]

"Big Hawk bustles down that side, while I take Matt's way. We file up the narrow gully over dead trees and trash carried down by water. The mule fell about fifteen feet and was trapped feet up, his saddle wedged across a log that lay across the ravine, the ends wedged so that it didn't rest on the bottom; neither did the mule!

"Big Hawk climbed up beyond the animal's head, picked up his head, and by his own strength the big Pawnee hoisted the mule, saddle, log, and all and upended him onto his feet. You know, Frank, if that mule's ears were any larger, Big Hawk couldn't have lifted him."

January 15. Moved this morn in a bad snowstorm, through Scotts Bluff; distance 15 miles. Camped at Coad's ranch. Left two horses to-day, played out. New Moon.

January 16. Came about 13 miles, camped about three miles from Chimney Rock on the Platte.

Some of the boys and Luther go over to the rock and climb over it. Tonight they discuss the Pawnee folk tale about a party of horse-snitching Pawnees, chased up on the rock by the Sioux and held there several days. The story is that the Pawnee tied the horsetail-hair ropes they had brought along to take horses, and escaped by climbing down them. These boys are questioning the folk tale, saying those ropes would not have held to let a man down two hundred feet. Maybe the people up there without food and water lost most of their weight—or had become spirit people— who knows?

January 17. I started out early this morn, took one wagon with me, went to Platte Bridge's where I got 2331 pounds of corn which made our horses smile, came on and camped at foot of Court House Rock, distance 12 miles.

January 18. Today came to last water on Greenwood Creek. Left one horse, distance 11 miles.

January 19. This morn I took Bob White[11] and we came through to Sidney stopped at the Gilt Edge, met many friends. Reported to the Commanding Officer, Major Sumner.[12] Am very tired after my ride. Jinks trots too hard for a pleasure horse.

I ride out and meet my command about a mile from town. The town is alerted and ready to welcome us. Everybody is out, all bundled up, but their smiles match the bright sunshine and snow sparkles. We are escorted through the center of town. The Scouts carry the scalps on willow poles and sing their tribal war songs.

Below the barracks about a mile we make winter camp downstream.

January 20. Went out a mile this morn and met the Scouts and came in with them. Made quite a display of scalps.

January 21. I have been writing all day for the men,[13] telling their people all about the fight and all the news we could think of. Wrote 27 pages of letter paper and am tired out. It snows hard all day. Mr. Potts stays with us tonight.

January 22. Got a letter from home today with pictures of Mary and Stella. They are both looking real well. Turned in our teams today and got some orders about camping.[14]

Our winter camp is snug and our needs are supplied. There is plenty of duty to keep the boys busy and interested. They've a good-sized herd of horses to care for.

An occasional hunt, always with a white officer, makes them happy though they have to go over to the Republican, and often to its forks, before they get anything. We insist on careful camp policing (housekeeping), give attention and inspection to routine details, with an eye toward fixing good habits for civilized living.

Lute, Jim, and me take turns with train passes on furloughs home for a few days. I've saved something and we will build us a house in town this summer. Our daughter is eight years old, good company for Mary.

One day, visiting with some of the officers of Sidney Barracks I state that I believe my Pawnee Scouts can stampede their led horses when the troop is dismounted. Lt. Charles L. Hammond takes me up on it and arranges a contest, a sham battle to decide it.

An excursion train sits on tracks: its occupants, and the town people, come out to watch the fun. The Pawnees yell and whoop and holler and do a lot of shooting and Troop H retaliates, all with blank cartridges. They make a tremendous noise. The Indians flap their blankets at the horses—whirl them and set them go at the herd. The horses edge away from a falling blanket but none take to their heels.

So the boys ride in and try to lead or drive the horses away. This is where it gets to be a scramble and some get yanked off their saddles and de-horsed. The fourth Cavalry contingent hold their horses, and their ground, and the Pawnees don't get the job done. But they had a lot of fun, got a few powder burns, and made more friends. The horses haven't gained much since they came in off the winter campaign, too often without forage, many times without grain, and obliged to turn their tails to arctic blasts while they pawed snow away to get at a little grass under it. After all they endured last winter, they're too smart to leave a sheltering shed and bunkers full of hay with corn twice a day.

A few days later at the barracks, Lute and I see a drill with sabers. We have no use for sabers—Indians don't fight toe to toe. Lute says Custer and the seventh didn't carry sabers, and I've not seen any carried since the Rebellion.

This drill is interesting and showy with flashes of sabers in the maneuvers of arms and hands and horses. Suddenly a young cavalryman loses control of his mount which bumps hard into another horse. The big sword in the young recruit's hand runs through the other man, killing him at once.

February and most of March blow away. I'm still keeping a tight rein on my Pawnee Scouts. If this village was wild in the boom days of the railroad's construction, it isn't any tamer now. The town is full of saloons and dance halls. Whiskey and gambling don't add up to much peace. Sometimes, gun battles rage and no one is bad hurt, as happened the

other night when a gambler had the lower tip of his ear shot away by a
teamster who wasn't even scratched. But it's a good thing the saloons have
two doors—they're empty in seconds when the shooting starts. The town
caters to the freighters of the ox and mule trains that load here for the
Black Hills and Deadwood, also to the Sidney to Black Hills stages.
Several men have been killed in town since we came back to camp.

For some weeks Indian chiefs have been leading their people into the
agencies. Dull Knife came into Red Cloud Agency with his people, who,
after Mackenzie's attack, had wintered with Crazy Horse.[15] Touch the
Clouds brought a thousand Sioux to Spotted Tail's Agency. The head
count of newly arrived Indians is more than 4,500, and Camp Robinson is
expecting Crazy Horse with about a thousand Indians to come in within a
week or so.

The wild Indian sees he is through with the free-roving life. The road
builder and the hide hunter did what the armies could not do.

We ride out with Captain Woodson and his pack of greyhounds. When
we find antelope on a south slope the hounds are unleashed. The antelope
prick up their big ears in study of the greyhounds. Two or three trot
toward the approaching dogs then all kite off, and you would think the
dogs were standing still. Soon, all are out of sight, are in sight again going
over a rise, and out again. We ride on and the hounds begin straggling
back. They're quick, but I think there are few living things that can run as
fast and as long as antelope.

In the following days several officers offer to use their influence to
secure a commission as lieutenant in the regular army for me, and I could
ask that favor of quite a number of others I've served with and under.[16]
Lute, too, has had offers of that kind. We discuss it, recognizing that what
success we've made has come through leading the Pawnees in scouting.
With the Indian wars finished we cannot count on the Pawnees being
called on for more scouting. For my part, since I have better health in this
part of the country, I will stay on as post interpreter and guide if I'm
retained, and Mary and Stella would move here again. My asthma is too
bad to let me stand stirring up field dust. Lute says he's seen enough army
to last him the rest of his life.

I'm handed a telegram:

Headquarters, Military Division of the Missouri, Chicago, Ill., April
12, 1877. Col. Robert Williams, Omaha, Nebr. [The telegram had
been very promptly repeated to Sidney Barracks.] The Lieutenant General desires steps taken to muster out the Pawnee Scouts at Sidney Barracks, as soon as it can be done. If the Indians desire, transportation
can be furnished them by rail to Fort Dodge; but if they prefer to return
to their reservation with their plunder and ponies, subsistence will be

furnished them from Post on their route, for a reasonable period.

[Signed] R. C. Drum,

Assistant Adjutant General

I immediately write to General Sheridan, marking at the top of the letter: "Personal. Sidney Barracks, Nebr., April 13, 1877. Lt. Gen. P. H. Sheridan, U.S. Army. Comd'g Military Div. of the Mo., Chicago, Ill."

My Dear General: I enclose copy of a telegram received yesterday by Col. Gordon, Comd'g this Post. If we are to be mustered out of the service there are several points upon which I wish for advice and in-structions from you. Under your instructions of last August I went to the Pawnee Reservation, enrolled 100 Indians and brought them to this Post, where they were regularly enlisted and mustered in.

In the campaign of last winter we captured about 100 ponies; these, with the hundred we had when we started out, about fifty more which the Indians have bought since we came back here last January make a herd of some 250 ponies belonging to my men which they, of course, desire to take home with them; to do so they must necessarily march from here. In his telegram, General Williams says that "transportation will be furnished the Indians by rail to Fort Dodge; or if they prefer to march home with their plunder and ponies, subsistence for a reasonable period will be furnished them from Posts along the route of travel."

What I desire to ascertain from you is this: Are not my men—the same as other regularly enlisted and honorably discharged soldiers—entitled to travel pay and rations, or commutation of rations, from here to their homes, and also will they not be entitled to the 40¢ per day each for their ponies during the time they shall be on the march home? The men desire, when they are sent home, that I and my 1st lieut.—my brother—accompany them, as the country through which they must travel is quite thickly settled all the way. They wish us to be with them, and for the protection of their interest on the road I think it necessary that we go.

If the war with the Indians in this Department is over, I suppose there is nothing to do with my Pawnee but to muster them out; but they came up here with the expectation and hope of remaining in their old country for some time, and are much disappointed indeed that they are so soon to go back. If there is, or is to be, any thing for us to do that can be done by Indians, I know that no better men than mine can be found, and I doubt if any as good.

I would also like to know what, if any, position I will be retained in after I take my men home. When you sent for me last August, I was on duty at this Post as post guide and interpreter, and would very much like to be stationed here again.

Hoping that you will kindly give this your attention, and issue any instructions you may deem necessary to secure my Pawnees everything to which they are entitled, I am, General, very respectfully, Your Obed't servant,

[Signed] Frank North

The reply came back from division headquarters at Chicago, through department headquarters, Omaha, Nebraska, April 16, 1877: Major North is informed that the Pawnee Scouts will muster out at Sidney. If they elect to march overland to their homes, subsistence for a limited period will be furnished them, but no travel pay for men or *per diem* for horses will be allowed. The commanding general, Department of the Platte, will direct Major North and his brother to accompany the Pawnees to their reservation, giving them transportation back to Sidney.

My letter writing didn't get much for the Pawnees. They've sent most of their pay home, will be without travel pay and any allowance other than rations, and we won't find posts to get rations along a great part of the way. The Pawnees are disappointed to be going back so soon, and I am more sorry than I'll let them know. They are so well here, though almost all were affected by disease when they arrived, and three died shortly after arriving.[17]

From Headquarters,
Department of the Platte, *In the Field*

Camp Robinson, Nebr.
April 19, 1877.
Captain[18] Frank North,
Comd'g Pawnee Scouts,
Sidney, Nebr.

Dear Sir:

The muster out of the Pawnee Scouts was ordered by Lieutenant General Sheridan. There is no longer any necessity for the employment of scouts, nor is there any appropriation on hand from which to pay them, for reason I regret that I shall not be able to retain you in service.

I think it only just and appropriate to thank you for your excellent behavior during the time of your stay in the military service under my command; and to say that the soldier-like conduct and discipline of the Pawnee Scouts is the most eloquent testimony that could be adduced to prove your fitness for the position you have held as their Commanding Officer. I remain, Very Respectfully, Your Obedient Servant,

[Signed] George Crook,
Brigadier General.[19]

A communication comes from: Headquarters, Department of the Platte. Assistant Adjutant General's Office, Omaha Nebr., April 25, 1877. Commanding Officer, Sidney Barracks, Nebr.

Sir: The Department Commander directs that you at once muster out
the Pawnee Scouts, in compliance with endorsements on papers which
were transmitted from this office through your Headquarters, April 19,
1877, copy of which is enclosed. He also directs me to inform you that
an officer of the Paymasters Department will leave this city for your post
tomorrow for the purpose of paying off those Indians. Very Respectfully,
etc.,

[Signed] Robert Williams
Ass'nt. Adj. Gen.

In the last days of April we lead the Pawnees to Julesburg and to
Ogalalla. South of the river the horses stampede and some get away. The
boys track some to old Fort Sedgwick before they catch them and bring
them back in three days, and that plays hob with our ration supply. We
have no rations for our last camp south of North Platte before reaching
Fort McPherson.

We reach McPherson before noon, get our rations, and settle into camp
below the fort. Along in the late afternoon the sheriff from North Platte
drives up with a settler from south of the town with a warrant for arrest of
all the Indians—says they had killed a cow yesterday when they were
herding their horses on a river island; says he's going to have the price of
the cow or he'll prosecute the whole bunch of Indians.

This time I have all I can do to hold my temper. The fellow couldn't
have known a white person was with the boys—probably thought he saw a
chance to rook the Indians.

"Well Mister, these boys didn't kill your cow," I tell him and say to the
sheriff: "Go ahead, arrest them all, and we'll all go back to town with
you." (I guess he figures feeding this many men for a few days would put
things pretty badly out of balance for him and the county.) He tries to
squirm out.

"Well, I don't know what to do. Can't you and him get together
somehow to settle this? We don't want any trouble you understand?"

"No, I don't understand. These men are not killing people's stock and I
don't propose to pay for the cow, nor that they should, even if they had
the money. I'll see that justice is done after being accused of such a thing,
if it is within my power to get a just hearing."

Some of the boys understand some of this and some of them understand
a lot more English than they talk. They tell me they would rather pay for
the cow than take the horses and everything back. Pawnee Puk oot, Old
Horn, says, "We want to get home. I will give this man one of my
horses." He talks in English.

"You ought not to pay this man anything. If you pay, the white man
will tell that you are guilty of killing a cow—if one is dead—and if he is
lying, if you pay he will think you have a guilty conscience about

something so you are paying, and he will still say you killed his cow, because you pay him its price," I tell them in their own tongue.

"I will take the horse or forty dollars and call it settled," the man says to Old Horn.

Between them the boys dig up forty dollars. I hate to see them part with it, but they hand it over and the men leave.

We take out southward along the old Military Road through Cottonwood Canyon, then follow the Medicine to the Republican River. Several of these men were with us in 1869 and recall incidents of that expedition.

Pawnee Puk oot comes up to ride beside Lute and me. "Father, I have done a bad thing," he says, and then talks so fast I can't get a word in edgewise, telling us he killed the cow. "You know, Father, I am not a good shot and I did not think I could hit her."

It seems when the herders for that time took the horses onto the river island south of North Platte, the boys began making fun of the little rifle he had bought at Sidney. Old Horn defended his thirty-two caliber rifle, with no means of proving its worth, when a cow came out of the willows. He was told to shoot at the cow and see if it would even hurt her. Old Horn refused, afraid he might kill her, but was told he couldn't even make her feel it. Old Horn pointed the gun in the general direction of the cow and pulled the trigger. They were all confounded when the cow dropped dead. The bullet had struck in between her eyes. All were scared and they argued what they should do and decided to drag the carcass into the river, thinking she would go down in the quicksand.

The owner had found where the cow was dragged. So the man knew what he was talking about, after all. Pawnee Puk oot's doleful face and story, ending as it did, set us to laughing.

An afterthought occurs to me: those boys were without rations; they killed the cow—unintentionally, to be sure—but they could have butchered out the beef. Their awareness that, by civilization's standard, they were in the wrong, troubled them enough to overcome their natural urge.

We cross the succession of corridors between the rivers—the Republican, Prairie Dog (Short Nose), the Solomans, Smoky Hill, and Arkansas, while the sun grows warmer every day. We have seen no buffalo. Only three or four years ago there were still millions on these plains. Since then I suppose the missing number are accounted for in the ricks of buffalo hides I've seen along the railroads, anywhere within a mile or so of loading stations, and the bleaching bones where the buffalo died on the prairie.

Now we see occasional herds of cattle and new settlements and homesteads, though still a long way apart. I'm thinking the Texas Trail drive will have to swing west through Colorado, to get beyond settlement.

After crossing the Saline River I'm feeling bad. There are still several miles to Hays, Kansas. I'm outright sick by the time we finally camp, well out away from town, with the horse herd held back. In early evening while I concentrate on trying to breathe, Lute tells the boys not to bother me. Some of my men go into town to look around. In a store window they saw a weather forecasting box from which a little figure of a man ran a circling course into another opening while a little woman figure holding a broom ran after the first and both disappeared to come out again and repeat. All gazed a while and sauntered on, but Red Willow was spellbound and stayed to watch as long as there was light. The boys came back to camp without Red Willow.

Lute sends the sergeants to bring Red Willow back. The men learn Red Willow had been shot. Stunned, not knowing what to do and unable to find Red Willow, to know if he had died or yet lived, they come back and talk it over among themselves, not wanting to disturb me. This time they saddle up and quite a number go into town. Threatened, and told to get out of town and stay out—"No dirty Indians wanted around here," they came back and this time come to us.

Hearing the story, I forget about trying to breathe and it takes care of itself. I get up and Lute and I ride into town, look up the sheriff, introduce ourselves, and give a short explanation of presence here. The sheriff is decent enough, says a deputy shot the Indian in front of the store on "suspicion he would attempt to break in"—the flimsiest excuse for shooting an Indian I have yet to hear. We see Red Willow, still laying on a floor mat where he had been half dragged, and dumped. I get a doctor who treats my boy, and we move him into a kind of hotel hospital, but Doc says he's done for, may live a few hours. I send Lute for his two closest friends. They come and one of us stays with one of the boys beside Red Willow until he leaves us.

It's a sad funeral and Red Willow's grave is made outside of the town's cemetery, Indian graves not being permitted in it, but a clergyman reads a Bible text and the orthodox burial service ending with a prayer.

All are very quiet as we get ready to start marching again. A little man rushes up to me as Lute and I ride up to mail a letter.

"Oh Major, I know you will appreciate having a copy of this issue of my publication. I'm happy to present this week's copy—"

I glance at the paper, *Ellis County Star*, Hays Kansas, May 24, 1877, and skim over the story of Red Willow's shooting by "our brave deputy sheriff. . . ." The *brave* deputy sheriff skipped town the same night, the sheriff said, adding, "and good riddance," though I'm not sure just how sincere the sheriff is. He seemed real anxious to treat me right, but who had sent the boys out of town when they went to find Red Willow? I read on, ". . . the comrades of the wounded man mounted their ponies and came into town single file, and it was then that the lights went out and our citizens went for their side arms. . . ." He's tried to make out that the Indians act like the trail-driving cowboys! "They, the Pawnees, said, 'Pawnee kill white man—Pawnee bad Indian, when made mad by white man—Red Willow die—heap trouble'. . . ." The lying cur of a rabblerouser! "As to the necessity of shooting the Indian we shall not venture an opinion at this time. However our citizens certainly owe Major North a debt of gratitude for holding the revengeful and bloodthirsty redskins in check." Not a Pawnee has made any sign of threat. They are scared and bewildered by this brutality, and they have no glimmer of an idea of how to protect themselves, let alone take "bloodthirsty revenge."

We go on, a somber-faced troop. We're heading for the north point in the Arkansas River, Big Bend. Hours before we get there, I'm fighting for breath and mighty glad to camp. Lute doesn't want me to try to go further, as I was very sick last fall in this country. By morning I'm better and we march on, reach Arkansas City and malaria fever with asthma stops me. I will not try to go further. The rest of the way has not much if any settlement. The boys can follow along the Arkansas River to the Bear Creek Reservation, and they have rations to see them home. We call in the sergeants, discuss it with them to be sure of how they feel about assuming the responsibility and leadership. I judge they can go on alone. In the morning, feeling better, I talk to the troop—unexpectedly, a hard thing for me to do. We shake hands with each man, call them by name, and see them mount and ride away.

One hundred men came, ninety-six are returning. Yet not a Pawnee Scout died in combat. Still, surely it is as they say: Tirawa has protected Pani La Shar—and the Pawnee Scouts. Great God of All, whom the Pawnee call Tirawa; will You just hold Your Hand over the Pawnee and all the red people from now on—Amen.

37

Mustering out in early June we return home to Columbus. Jim, Lute, and I sit down to thresh out a cattle ranch proposal Cody had suggested when stopping by from his theatrical tour west. I describe the spot I saw in the sandhills in 1870 when I guided Professor Marsh to the fossil grounds of northwest Nebraska, on the Dismal River's south fork—the greatest grass country I've ever seen, with plenty of watering places. This is my choice for a ranch location.

My brothers know of no place to match it. There are two things against the location. There are ranches adjacent to the sandhills, but the huge world of sandhills is avoided as a desert. People have attempted to cross the region and were never seen again. It is the sameness, without landmarks or features to see any place apart, that muddles a traveler, confuses and loses him.

It has been commonly supposed that there is little water in the hills, but the Niobrara (called Running Water) River fringes the north sandhill border, runs nearly four hundred miles to join the Missouri River. All other Nebraska streams north of the Platte River flow out of the sandhills. I saw the Dismal and its south fork, besides many ponds that I am sure are springfed. I'm sure a cattle ranch would have water.

Last year Capt. Jim Cook[1] and a ten-man crew brought 2,500 or 3,000 head of Texas cattle up the trail, crossed the Platte River between Ogalalla and Alkali. Cook hired Aron Baker to guide them through the sandhills to the Missouri River Whetstone Bottom.

We consider everything as close as we can. James has the best head for matters of this kind. He and Luther know, as I do, of many men making good profit in ranching stock, and we conclude we may as well go into the partnership with Cody, providing he makes a satisfactory agreement. I communicate our decision to Cody and we are to be notified when the trail herd is expected at Ogalalla, and agree to meet it.

I get a carpenter, and Mary and I plan our new home. Mary wants a pantry, cupboards, and sliding doors, and bay windows so she can have

house plants. I order gingerbread trim, doo-dads and shady porches—I've
rested out under the sky enough.

I get wagons, teams, supplies, and hire some men to go along to help
make our ranch headquarters. Across country we journey west about a
hundred and seventy-five miles to the valley where the South Fork Dismal
sprouts from a spring. We cut cedar logs and hew and notch them, put up
fifteen- by thirty-foot walls for two rooms.

It is soon roofed over and while two men put windows in and finish it,
the rest of us start a cedar pole corral.

Two sturdy poles for posts are planted deep and tamped in every twelve
feet, just close enough together to hold cedar poles stacked as high as we
want the corral walls, about eight feet. The posts are bound together with
rawhide or wire. It's a sizable lot, to corral more than a few head of stock.

Lute returns from his trip with mother to Ohio and New York, visiting
our relatives. He, with Jim, meets Cody and me at North Platte. We go to
Ogalalla to buy stock. Several large herds from Texas are being held south
of the South Platte River and up on the bench. Lute asks:

"Frank, how do you think the cattle across the river compare to the
numbers of buffalo we found south of the river, when we were here
hunting in 1870?"

Lute's question recalls tens of thousand of buffalo on the Plains. Now,
few buffalo roam the prairie; the animals we see are cattle.

I believe there were ten times as many buffalo in sight then, I say. We
discuss the end of buffalo[2] as we cross the river, where we are told forty
thousand cattle await buyers. We look the cattle over, but are not
permitted to ride among them, lest something "spook" the animals, the
main parts of which look to be horns and legs and high-ridged backbones.

The next morning we buy fifteen hundred head, our choice; then we
find ourselves with a bear by the tail, unless we manage to hire some of
these marvels on horseback commonly called "waddies." We hire four
capable men and a pair of brothers. Nineteen-year-old "little" Buck Taylor
is six feet, four inches tall and weighing about two hundred and twenty
pounds. The older, Baxter, weighs about the same, though a runt, being
an inch shorter than Buck. Both Taylors are top broncobusters, and the
best of cowhands.[3]

In about ten days our cattle are branded with NC[4] and on our range,
where we close herd them around our headquarters, until they get so
they're at home. Our cowhands teach us many tricks of this trade.
Everybody works: daily riding our range, putting up hay and a sod stable
and more corrals.

In odd moments we get acquainted with the sandhill cranes, make
friends with the trumpeter swans nesting on the muskrats' house in the
lake above the spring. Lute rows the skiff to take bread to the swans. They

get quite tame, and when the little ones hatch, it isn't long before they meet us to get their bits of bread.

Our nearest neighbor is John Bratt,[5] ranching at the head of the Birdwood Creek, about forty miles southwest at the edge of the Sandhills.

I go with a four-horse team and wagon down the Birdwood and east to North Platte where I get supplies loaded. Starting the boys back with the wagon, I take the train for Columbus for a few days with Mary. Our house is coming up in fine shape and we hope to be living at 1002 West 14th Street by Christmas. After visits with our families I go back to the ranch.

Two men ride our range every day in opposite directions, working clockwise so that as one man is leaving his half the other is beginning to ride it. One day Lute rides near the North Dismal, finds horse tracks and, following them, discovers a band of Indians in a camp of several lodges; he gets away unseen, and runs in to tell us.

A man is out after our horse herd when Lute comes in, but doesn't show up until after supper and without the horses.

I'm pretty sure the Indians are some of Spotted Tail's people, probably came from their new Rosebud Agency. I think I had better notify General Crook in Omaha, where he commands the Department of the Platte, of loss of the horses and of these Indians being off their reservation. Lute will go to North Platte tomorrow to telegraph a message.

"Yes, I can make it through the Hills in one day," Lute says. "While I was riding the south range I found a way that I think will take me through the Sandhills without having to go so far around, west by the wagon trail."

Buck Taylor, Billy Jaiger, and I ride out maybe ten miles with Lute, and he goes on while we turn back.

An hour or so after our return, Indians sit their horses on the north hill and when we stand out, watching them, make signs that they wish to talk. I motion them to come and wait for them to approach while the boys cover me from inside.

I neither understand nor talk Sioux, but I can give the sign talk a good limbering up. The Indians, about eight times as many as we are, come up, and make signs that they are friendly and want to talk in my house.

"No friends of mine come to my house in war paint. You are dressed in war paint. You did not come as friends after stealing my horses yesterday."

"We do not have your horses," they declare, not bothering to deny they stole them—only that they don't have them. Besides the horses that are missing we have about forty head in a small enclosure. The Indians are trying to determine how many men are out of sight with gunsights trained on them. That unknown number—our ace-in-the-hole—turns their mischief-bent hearts to water and they ride away.

Intending to send a dispatch to Fort McPherson, I say to Billy Jaegers:

"Billy, Wes Rhone is to start from North Platte with the wagons in the morning. If Luther got through the hills yesterday, he will be with Wes. I'm sending you to North Platte. You're to meet them at the Birdwood forks where they will camp tonight. You'll travel twice as fast as the wagon." I ride along with Billy—start him down the wagon trail and warn him: "Now, Billy, you stick to our road, pass the first camp place by Birdwood Creek; go on—Lute camps by West Creek inlet."

On the second day, around half-past eight p.m., Lute comes in—says they'd been seeing tracks all afternoon, and coming near the camp at the head of the Birdwood after dark, heard someone yell and an answer that seemed from close in front of him. At first he thought some of the ranch boys were coming to meet them, but they couldn't get answers when they hollered. Then Lute got alarmed, thinking Indians may have raided the ranch, and that the tracks seen might be of one who had escaped the Indians and was lost. By that time he was untying his saddle horse from the back of the wagon and hit out on a high lope and didn't let up until he saw our lamplight from a hilltop, about a half mile away.

Of course we conclude Billy got lost somehow—he's a tenderfoot. A thunderstorm roars in soon after Lute comes. It would be the old hunt for a needle in a haystack, blindfolded, to try to find a man lost and afoot. So we wait until near daylight when Lute and Wes go back to the head of the Birdwood, and from there Wes circles west and southward as Lute moves east and gradually south meeting Wes. Soon they begin seeing footprints, unmistakably plain in the wagon road. The afternoon had nearly passed before they came near enough to holler at Billy. Then he was helped onto Lute's horse to ride double.

They started back, but Lute soon saw Billy was too weak. About that time Lute brought down an antelope. With what roots of sand cherry and soapweed they could gather to make a fire, they broiled meat. Billy ate about two pounds of meat and Lute thought that was enough for then, though he wanted more. They brought him on in. Billy had been lost three days.

In spite of my instruction, as soon as I disappeared over a hill he had left the road to take Lute's trail, had gotten off his horse to shoot at antelope. The horse jerked loose at sound of the shot and kited off with everything Billy had tied on the saddle. He soon found he was lost, became frightened and finally delirious, but had gotten nearly clear of the Sandhills before the boys found him.[6]

*   *   *

We have a housewarming in our new home with a Christmas tree and family dinner, with Mother at the head of the table and Mary and I at the other end. The young people have a separate table and the little folk have a table their size. I'm mighty proud and happy to have them all together, even Mary's Uncle Sam Smith and family. It's different than the way Lute and I spent last Christmas.

I get the bobsled out. Not even Santa Claus has more fun than I do, hauling all the children around town in it, besides all the children's sleds hooked on for a ride. Mary pops dishpans of popcorn, and gets a whole bunch of children all mixed up with taffy pulls.

1878. Happy, happy New Year to everybody. I have a last romp with Stella and Mary, take my big dog—a friend's present—and get on the train to North Platte. In the smoker the conductor says, "Major, dogs are not allowed in the passenger cars. I'll just take him to the baggage car for you," and reaches for his collar to take him from where he lay by my feet. The dog makes a short deep-throated growl, shows a little of his fangs without bothering to raise his head, and the train man backs off, saying that he "guesses no one objects if the dog stays." I think he should make us a good ranch dog, being Great Dane and Newfoundland.

One night a wolf howls, unusually close. Next morning the dog is gone. We never see him again, not even his collar.

Days fly by in a blur and only special days are remembered. One such time was our first roundup. Although we have daily circled our range, throwing back animals wandering too far, the roundup proves its value when we cut out and drive home a bunch that had roamed away from our range.

The roundup starts after a careful inspection of stock on our home range, looking for stray or unbranded stuff. These were driven, along with whatever was found away from the home range, south into the Platte valley. Other men are rounding up from other directions, though no further than a wide circle that can be worked from the first crack of light until noon. All cattle found are put into tight herds of a size to cut from, and these are held by as many men—twenty, more or less—necessary to hold the herd together. Most outfits have their own cookwagon and cook. We arranged to throw in with the Bratt outfit for our first roundup. As men come in off the circle, they go to the cookwagon.

After dinner a man ropes a fresh horse and is ready for his assignment, made by the captain or boss man of the roundup on his range. On another day and a different range, another boss man who will send a couple of men from one outfit or men "repping" for a rancher who didn't send an outfit (either a small ranch or one so far from this part of the roundup that not many animals of his brand are expected to be found here) to cut out that outfit's brand (cattle).

This part of working the cattle must be done with care not to disturb the close-held herd. A cutting horse is edged into the herd, circulating around until his rider finds a brand he wants to cut out and points the horse at that specific critter. After that it is up to the horse. Dodge as they will, few critters can outdodge, outguess, or escape the trained cutting horse.[7]

After all of one brand has been cut from the herd, the same is done with another brand and so on, until only cattle belonging on this range are left. These are driven in the opposite direction from the way the roundup will go the next day. Each brand owner holds his cut, day and night, and works it, branding and castrating as necessary after the herd cutting is done for the day. He continues with the roundup with his outfit and men, as long as he expects to find critters of his brand in the days' gather. If he collects a large herd he may send it to his home range whenever he decides to.

After our first roundup we have more than five hundred calves to work. Working a cow and calf herd is organized disorder in the midst of complete confusion. The cows bawl and run to get to their calves. The little fellows lose their mamas and the mamas lose the little ones. Men working this bunch have to be mindful of a mad mama's horns.

These are wild cattle. Other than when they were branded and the male calves castrated, their contact with man has been distant. Groups nurse their calves and the calves lie down fairly close. Like buffalo calves, they blend into the smallest clump of bunch grass or slight hollow. A cow or two—very often a dry or barren cow—or even steers stand guard over the nursery while the nursing cow feeds or goes off for water.

Cattlemen tell me gray wolves, the buffalo wolf, is coming back. They had nearly disappeared as the buffalo were killed off. Now with cattle in the country they are found and some are shot. Along toward fall one of our men, Al Pratt, jumps a gray wolf with seven nearly grown pups, four of them black like the big dog I brought to the ranch. Our man shot two of the blacks and brought them in. It was plain our dog had sired them— even to markings. I suppose the wolves killed him.

A few weeks later one of Bratt's men, Bill Burke,[8] killed two of the gray pups and just a little later Jim Carson[9] killed another gray pup. That leaves two black ones and the old female. No cattlemen will rest until the three are hunted down.

Bill Burke came to me at the roundup, told me he remembered me. I didn't know him and didn't place him until he told me where he first saw me. It was in 1865 when I stopped with my scouts at his father's place west of Fort McPherson where they were digging a ditch to irrigate from the river. This boy of John Burke's is one of seven sons. Their sister is married to John Bratt.

After driving a Texas trail herd to the Rosebud Agency, some of the waddies stole a bunch of horses from the Indians. They fetched them to

North Platte where they sold them and skipped out. On their way the fellows rode in to our ranch for dinner; had left the horses away from the house, which didn't cause any questioning. Nobody drives a herd of horses or cattle up around anyone's place, so we're unsuspicious.

A couple days later our man goes to bring our horses up but doesn't find them. Lute and Al Pratt get out after them—find moccasin prints in the trail of the cowboys' herd and find about a third of our horses off in a further valley. Bringing these in, we get good horses saddled, take coats, grub, blankets, and rifles and revolvers with plenty of ammunition, and light out north cutting across the Hills to the Dismal's North Fork.

A camp wagon and three men from the Middle Loup Rankin ranch are here. The Indians are about two hours ahead of us, they say. They were here with our horses, demanded to eat, got it, and went on. The Indians are carrying Winchester rifles. The three Rankin men, having only revolvers, didn't challenge the Indians' possession of the NC brand horses.

We eat here, then take up the trail, stay overnight at the Rankin Ranch on Middle Loup River, and in the morning discover we had passed the Indians only a half mile from where they left camp early this morning a couple miles downstream from the ranch.

The Indians have our best horses; there's no use to try to catch them. The horses we have are already fagged out. Returning to the ranch I send Albert Pratt and the foreman of the Rankin ranch men, Jim Lawson, who saw the Indians at camp with our horses, to the Spotted Tail Agency (Rosebud).

The men get back, report the Rosebud agent called a council. They stated the case and accused the Indians of having our horses.

Old Chief Spotted Tail actually acknowledged that the horses were taken by his men. It seemed the Indians' horse herd had been repeatedly raided by lawless white men. In the new location the agency has no protection of a military post. A bunch of Indian trackers declared the trail of the stolen herd stopped at a ranch on the Dismal fork, that they found horses (the loose, ranging NC horses), and took them and only recovered their own number.

The agent called it "recompense through reciprocal robbery." Whatever it is called, it leaves the NC ranch holding the bag, so I will refer the matter to the Department of the Interior.[10]

Early in the winter we round up our beef and ease our grass-fat steer herd toward the railroad for shipment to Chicago. They make up enough to replace and buy half again as many. Besides we have as many calves, a right nice gain for the first year of stock ranching.

At the Sherman House where we stop, we see a newspaper. Headlines scream: "Cheyennes leave Territory, Dull Knife and Little Wolf murder their way north."[11]

Lute and I decide we had better get back to the ranch. The Cheyennes have gone through by the time we return. But the Rosebud Indians, not at all discouraged by their agent's willingness to make excuses and wink at their mischief, went down along the Platte, raided the big ranches, and got away with some horses. The North Platte guards, Lieutenant John Bratt commanding in my absence,[12] took out after the horse-lifting Indians, recovered the horses, and chased the Indians away. They were heard trying to get into our stable during the night, but had to leave without getting any more of our horses.

None of the ranches around the sandhills escape a raid. After the Indians ran off the saddle horses on the Stearn-Patterson ranch, they came back and nabbed the team of work horses. That was when these two decide to leave the ranch until the owners return, and they come, afoot, to our ranch. Bratt's winter cabin was abandoned too, and that sets us out alone for the winter.

Lute and Al are at the ranch to guard our horses until I get back from a trip to town. At North Platte I find a telegram from the folks at home. Mary is seriously sick. I send a dispatch to General Carr, at Fort McPherson, about the Rosebud Indians' devilment, and ask if he can send some soldiers to get this business stopped before we have to let the Indians take it all back. Then I write a note to Lute, hire a man to take it out to him—and jump on the train to go to Mary. Knowing the Cheyennes were in the country and the Sioux more or less on the loose, I was anxious, returning from Chicago, to get to the ranch—didn't stop off at home as I had intended. Now that the beef shipping is over, if the Indians are controlled we won't need to have more than a couple of men at the ranch this winter, and Lute can spell them now and then. The cattle out in the hills take care of themselves. I'll stay home with Mary.

In just a few days Mary is much better. I stay home until she is able to be up in a chair, tell her I must go, must take that wagonload of supplies to the ranch, and promise her if I can come right back, I will.

The boys meet me about twenty miles from our ranch. Lute never got my note, and no soldiers showed up. No wonder he got uneasy and decided to do some investigating. By late the next day a detail of soldiers come, escorted by a dozen cowboys, out of a job in the winter, after the beef roundup and shipping is done.

After the soldiers come, the two men return to the Stearns-Patterson ranch. The Dismal River country is quiet. Indians are seen now and then, but no more horses are reported missing.

Our cowhands want to ride into town to spend a few days before winter sets in. After they get back Lute and I go home for the winter, he to go out a couple of times to see that they're getting along all right.

1879. Winter passes. Roundup time again. We get a good crew together, take our own wagons this time, and begin at the North Dismal. Several thousand head of cattle are brought out of the hills and into the valley, where we work west. We have a "rep" with us from the Newman and others from small ranches between the Running Water (Niobrara) and the north edge of the Sandhills. A big new outfit has a spread at the mouth of the Dismal about sixty miles east, the Olives from Texas, but they're not in this roundup. I may have to send a "rep" to that one, if our cattle are found to have drifted down in there through the winter.

The roundup proceeds west—Bratt, Wheeler-Paxton, the Van Tassels Cattle Company, Bosler Brothers, Powers Brothers, and then Sheedy are all big ranchers with thirty to forty thousand head of cattle each. Numerous small ranchers like us, some smaller, are represented in this roundup. Until we get further west, we are made aware by the numbers discovered of different brands that, besides the large Newman and Hunter-Evans outfits on the Niobrara, there are now a surprising number of small ranches started. I think we are the only completely Sandhills ranchers, but others are bound to find out what a great country it is for cattle.

There is much talk of a band of horse thieves operating from northwest Wyoming and Dakota Territory, and down through Nebraska. I suppose the Indians up there are being regularly plundered—I guess I understand their "recompense through reciprocal robbery." Doc Middleton[13] seems to be the big cheese of the horse thieves. I hope never to meet him, nor his men, nor his work. I've lost enough horses to thieves.

At the head of Birdwood Creek, in a rainstorm, the held herd stampedes. Lute is on herd at the time. The night is pitch black. Suddenly the cattle get up and light out for no reason. Those with the herd try to ride with them to turn them, but the cattle run through a narrow, grassy, two or three mile long ravine. It is too narrow to turn the herd in and the boys come to camp—all but Lute. They say he was on the other side where the ravine bank was steepest. He doesn't show up, and hours pass. I'm getting ready to go on out to try to find him, when Lute walks in.

His horse ran up a sandhill on the ravine side, and at the top jumped or stumbled into a blowout and fell, throwing Lute out of the saddle. The horse ran off. Cattle followed the horse up the hill and Lute was in a bad place, but he managed to rattle his slicker and make enough noise to make the cattle split around his pit. He thought after the cattle had run by some of the boys would hear him yell, but he never got an answer. The cattle were a mixed herd—cows, calves, and steers—and they didn't run far.

Every man has a tale to tell about a stampede. It seems an all-steer herd is the most dangerous. One of the older ranchers tells of a stampede of steers that ran more than twenty-four hours and were still traveling, breaking into a trot now and then—not a bit ready to bed down. A steer running like that would be forty to sixty miles away in that time. But he will be awful slow about putting on fat afterwards, if ever.

At Blue Creek we have always before left the roundup to follow back down the Platte valley, turned north up the Birdwood, and from there, over the Sandhills to our Dismal South Fork. This time, pulling out of the roundup at the head of the Blue, I decide against the long trip back to our ranch. I think we should find water through the Sandhills, even though no one has ever gone in and returned with any information.

This year we have mostly steers—good travelers. We move to one of the numerous little lakes heading the Blue and fill everything with water. We are heading the long way through the hills—which may make it more of a gamble.[14] After traveling steadily since daylight with only rests for the horses and wagon teams (the sand makes heavy pulling), Lute, going ahead, finds a lake—and cattle!

Here we camp. In the morning we begin rounding up more than seven hundred head, some six to seven-year-old fellows with horns yards long, and showing "Bar-7," Rankin's brand. The boys call them regular old "mossy-backs." About half are up to three years old and have had no contact with a man and are unbranded. We have to play a ring-around-the-rosy to keep the wild doggies from running off the flat holding ground. All night the boys are singing and circling to hold the bunch, and prevent their starting a stampede of the whole herd. Some of the three-year-old bulls do break out, are speedily roped and tied.

We shove out early for the Rankin ranch, get there in a couple of days, and make the Rankin manager, Mr. Stemm, our friend when we deliver all showing the "Bar-7" brand—about half the gather—to him. We brand the rest and drive to our ranch. Finding water was no question in any part of the trip of about seventy miles, besides the extra trip to the Rankin ranch.

We have company at the ranch, Bill Cody with a bunch of friends, including Dave Perry, out for an outing. Of course, Cody didn't forget to come supplied with liquid refreshment, and the same with Perry and, I think, most of the other fellows. But they are a lot of fun. We tell Cody he waited until we scared the Indians away to come, but he always has a good answer. Besides all the jokes and horseplay, the building of a great and rich cattle kingdom is projected, and pushed further with every bottle of refreshment gurgled down. I think if Cody's bottles had lasted long enough, he might have projected the greatest cattle kingdom ever on earth.

The time comes to go to Ogalalla to buy our yearly replacement stock. Getting down to the Platte valley, Cody's friends elect to return to North Platte while we go on to where the Texas trail herds are expected. It's a big drive this year; in all 100,000 Texas cattle come up by the Western Trail.

We buy two thousand head, take delivery right away, herd them north, then brand them.

38

With autumn and cooler weather it's beef roundup time, and I get back to the ranch. We get a good beef gather and ship again to Chicago. Lute and I go with our shipment. The market is good, and those three-year-old mavericks we found in the hills by the lake up our take.

We go to the theater where Cody is on stage. I can't say much for the play, "The Prairie Waif," but a stunt Cody does while he is trick shooting is really something to see, and he doesn't have to take a back seat to anybody. Sighting with mirrors, he shoots an apple off a girl's head with the gun aimed backward over his shoulder![1]

An old man is lost from a hunting party on the Dismal about ten miles below us.[2] We join in hunting him and have the camp moved to our ranch. At one place he had shot two deer, and what coyotes left of them is found. The tracks lead away so I suppose the man's directions got switched. The hunt continues from where the tracks were lost, and no further trace is found. Finally the search must be abandoned and the men go back to their homes in the Republican Valley.

A week or two later the sixty-three-year-old man's son and some of the men here earlier return and search several days. A man goes once more toward the north river, follows an antelope trail up a sandhill and over, and there finds the old man's body.

As we reconstruct it, he had gone up the hill to look around, being lost, had then sat down for a rest. A buck deer came up the hill behind him, jumped on him—they get pretty aggressive about this time of year—and trampled him to death.[3]

Getting ready for winter means putting up as much hay as we can at the main ranch and at our winter headquarter place,[4] where we keep a couple of men to turn cattle back from the unwatered part of the hills. Nebraska has another mild, open winter, and a lot of new-come homesteaders.

Lute found four critters killed in one day by wolves. They're doing a lot of running of cattle, slashing and hamstringing. Often critters are not

eaten. Every man on the range carries a rifle in the saddle boot. Lute says
he will hunt those wolves down this winter.

They're wise, never return to eat the second time from a kill. I think
they can't be poisoned. Someone sees them several days running, always
three—the old gray wolf and her black shadows, and coyote scavengers
near. Then they're gone, no reports of them for some time until they're
seen in another neck of the hills. Few ever get a shot at them—they're too
clever.

Siberian wolfhounds were brought in on the Middle Loup to get the
three wolves. One day the dogs got led out on a chase. The wolves took
off for rough country. The rancher's horse was soon winded. He saw the
wolves go over a hill, the dogs after them. The next thing he saw was the
wolves on their haunches, watching him from hills. Down in the valley,
the dogs, widely separated, were ribboned piles of hide and bloody gore.

Luther stays on the ranch this winter, and I go home. Asthma attacks
me hard all fall—choked me down while we were in Chicago marketing
our cattle. As I get over the worst of this attack I propose to find some
place where asthma won't bother. Mary thinks I'm sick because I'm
restless.

The truth is that I'm restless because I'm in such a battle to breathe.
Maybe that asthma treatment place at Ceres in Stanislaus County,
California, might be helpful. I should be able to make the trip now. Lute
will go part way with me.

So, I board the train. At Ogden, Utah, I write:

December 10, 1879. Editor [Columbus] *Journal,* [Columbus, Nebraska] Dear Sir:—Having promised my many friends on leaving home,
that I would let them know from time to time how I was getting along, I
can think of no way half so good as through your columns, i.e., provided you agree with me. Brother Lute, of course, will tell you of our trip
up to the time he left me at Cheyenne.

I always hate to part with friends, but never did I leave home and
friends under such circumstances as now; being very weak, it was doubtful in the minds of many if I could stand the trip, while on the other
hand, should I improve and find a climate adapted to my case, I was to
locate and never return. Well, such circumstances made it a hard step
for me to take. But I am started, and hope to find the relief sought for.

I felt quite well on leaving Cheyenne, but the snow sheds and tunnels on the way over here were bad for me, and I find myself worse than
when I left home. The first shed we passed through I really thought I
would smother before reaching the end. The road is very much upgrade
and the engine was just more than throwing fire and smoke, which,
with the dust from the roadbed, made it very disagreeable. I soon got to
know when we were nearing one, and would at once place a wet towel
over my face, which would prevent me from inhaling the coal dust and

smoke.

At Evanston, I met our friend, W. B. Doddridge, Superintendent, Union Pacific Railroad, and accepting his invitation, I remained with him one day and had a nice visit. Mr. D. is the same sociable fellow he always was; promotion does not have the effect to make him forget friends and acquaintances.

From Evanston to this point the scenery along the Union Pacific is the finest; most wonderful of all nature's doing is the Devil's Slide. Having called the attention of some passengers from the East to this wonder, one of them at once declared that it was not the work of nature but had been built by human beings, *"the absurded idea!"*

On reaching this place the first acquaintances I met were Mr. Martin and Mr. Hale of Madison. They are both at the Hot Springs doctoring for rheumatism. The springs are nine miles from here, reached by both the California Pacific and Utah Northern Railroad.

The weather has been very bad ever since I came here, either snow or rain, and I have not been able to go out much. I shall spend a few days at the Springs, and the same time at Salt Lake City, then "HO" for the west! Until then, Adieu. Very Truly, Frank North.

I write again from Virginia City, Nevada:

December 29, 1879. Dear *Journal*—I have delayed writing some time, in hopes to write something encouraging about myself, but up to the present, I can't see that I am in any way benefited. At Ogden I tried the hot springs for one week and am satisfied that they can do an asthmatic no material good. I believe them to be, however, an almost certain cure for catarrh or rheumatism. I visited the great city of Saints twice during my sojourn at Ogden, and find it very much improved since my visit there in 1870.[5] The two tabernacles and the temple are wonderful structures. The temple now looms up fifty feet above the two stories of the ground foundation, and is said to be only one-fourth as high as the plan designates. The walls underground are fifteen feet thick, and above ground nine feet and nine inches; are built of a bluish-cast granite susceptible of a very fine polish. It is now twenty-five years since the structure was first commenced, and at this rate it will be many years before completed.

The city can boast of one of the nicest theatres in the West. I had the pleasure of attending the play by the Juvenile Pinafore Troupe, where one hundred Mormon children participated. I don't see much to the play, but produced as it was by these children it was really immense, many of the youngsters not being more than four or five years old; they did not make a balk or blunder during the whole performance. I found many old friends and acquaintances there, among whom was Judge Alex Pyper and his brother, Jimmy, both well known by many of our Columbus people.

The cooperative mercantile establishment is another attraction visitors could surely see. It is simply immense, three hundred feet in length, one hundred wide and four stories high, and employs over one hundred clerks. I could say much more about this wonderful city, but space forbids.

I left Ogden Christmas night at eight o'clock. The night was a beautiful one, and my anxiety to take in as much of this new country I was about to traverse forbade sleep, and I took my seat in the rear end of the car and watched for points of interest. After an hour's ride we stopped at Corrine, the once noted place for gambling in all its various forms; the town is very dull now since the freight for Montana, Idaho, and northern points was transferred to Ogden.

I notice at this point the one thing our Columbus people are now agitating, viz water power. Right here, on this dry plain, are mills and manufactures driven by water obtained through an immense canal which is supplied from Bear River. Why can't the Loup Fork play Bear River a while and do for Columbus what the latter is doing for Corrine?

Next we came to Promontory. Here I got out and tried to find someone who could tell me the exact spot where the last spike was driven, but as much as I wanted to see this, I was doomed to disappointment; it being such an unseasonable hour (11 o'clock at night), there were few people around. From here I took a short nap, but was awake again at the Humboldt Wells, and from there down the Humboldt River, I took a good look at the country. There is said to be three hundred thousand head of cattle grazing in the valleys of this stream and I saw a great many . . . Very Truly, Frank North.

At Carson City, Nevada, a news reporter looks me up. This is his write up as published:

Dec. 30, 1879. The TRIBUNE, Carson City, Nevada. Major Frank North was in this city yesterday and during his short stay the genial Scout and a Tribune reporter had a pleasant hour "talking Injun." Major North is now the oldest Scout on the Plains in experience; the Commander of the Pawnee Scouts, and partner of "Buffalo Bill." He is at present enroute to California to seek relief from a severe attack of asthma.

Major North said the Utes were a tribe with which he had never had dealings. He knew them, however, to be what are called first class Indians. From all he could learn, a general war would be inaugurated this winter. Like most persons familiar with Administration and Peace Commission, he viewed the whole thing as a farce. He thought its labors would end in nothing, and then the only alternative would be war. In case of war he expected to again call his Pawnees into service, and take a hand in the conflict.

In his Command he has every confidence. It is, he says, composed of the best braves of the tribe, and are, without exception, of the finest warriors among our American Indians, and on every occasion they have shown their fidelity to the whites; never yet showing the least treachery in their dealings with our people. Should war with the Utes be declared, as now seems likely to be the issue, the Pawnees will be an important factor in the campaign.

To the question whether in all his twenty-four years among the Indians he had ever known a difficulty to arise between them and our Government in which the Indians were to blame, he returned the negative answer. In not a solitary instance had he ever known of an outbreak but our Government was the aggressor. He said that the great source of difficulty was in the appointment of Agents. Not only were poor men frequently appointed, whose course with the Indian wards could not but create strife and discontent; but even men of probity at first succumbed to the temptation to steal and thereby began trouble. A man from the east is sent out to take charge of the Indians, at a salary of fifteen hundred dollars per annum. This seems wholly inadequate to keep his family, and almost invariably the result is theft. For this reason the Major is a warm supporter of the policy to hand over the care of the Reds to the War Department which is compelled to keep a detachment at each reservation anyhow. This policy would save the Government a large sum of money . . . put an end to the trouble between Agent and Commission, as well as remove the temptation to steal.

The only objection the Major admitted against the plan is the inclination of many Commanders to precipitate an Indian war with the hope of valorous conduct and a speedy promotion.

Referring to Buffalo Bill, he [Major North] said he had a letter lately from him which contained information that he would desert his [stage] troup in the event of an Indian war. "What in hell is that long haired cuss doing here, when there is an Indian war in the west?" is the question the letter makes the people ask each other, as they view the scouts on the stage [who are] holding the same supposition [while] scalp-raising forty times an evening. . . .

January 18, 1880. Ceres, Stanislaus County, California. Dear Journal: I have really been more negligent in my correspondence than I ever thought I would but I shall plead want of time and health . . . several letters home . . . suffering asthma . . . could hardly hold the pen, and very little better now.

I arrived here on the 16th, went at once to Dr. Eugene Lee's where I have been since. Will . . . remain two or three weeks . . . if no better shall return home. Doctor Lee is suffering with asthma. He tells me this is his first attack in two years . . . have not seen Dr. Thomas Lee, but am told that he is suffering from the same complaint.

I can't say I am stuck on California. Of course climate is very different here from most places, while at the same time it is almost as disagreeable . . . as any. . . .

*   *   *

1880. Meadowlarks have been talking spring for some time. I get back
to the ranch, have been away all winter. We commence roundup again. A
rep is with us from over on the Niobrara. We gather thousands of cattle
out of the hills and drive into the Platte valley, as usual.

It's a big roundup this year, the largest we have had. Aside from the
familiar brands of the large ranchers, the number of brands seen for the
first time this year indicates that homesteaders are someday to be
cattlemen.

Cody, mostly a silent partner of the ranch, joins the roundup with a
wagonload of whiskey and cigars, antidotes against snake bite and other
accidents, he says. Naturally the cowboys and their bosses do their best to
help him have a good time for, as John Bratt says, "Nothing is too good
for 'Colonel' Cody." Ever the flamboyant showman, he "ginned" the cattle
too much, having fun with roping and cutting, and was not of much help,
the others said.[6]

The roundup proceeds west: Bratt, Wheeler-Paxton, the Van Tassels
Cattle Company, Bosler Brothers, Powers Brothers, Sheedy—all are big
ranchers with thirty to forty thousand head of cattle each. This year the
increase of small ranches is astonishing in number of outfits; each with a
string of at least six horses besides the bed roll and cookwagon teams.

I wouldn't guess how many cattle are gathered in. It is real work. It
takes good men and horses to stay with it. Both rest when they get a
chance, if there's no foolishness to pull off: sun-fishin' (the horse), or a
varmint to slip in a bedroll (pranks exchanged between cowpokes).

This year there is talk that cattle ranching will not last. Reasons
mentioned are: homesteaders are raising cattle; too many cattle can be
expected to glut the market; and the new fence material called barbwire
which only needs posts a rod or so apart upon which to stretch and fasten
the wire strands.

The Sandhills aren't crowded yet, though several are edging in. Hinman
Brothers have built up a spread at the Birdwood forks. On the Dismal
North Fork, Stearns and Patterson located eight miles north of our ranch.
There are no barbwire fences in the Sandhills yet, and I hope to never see
a fence in this Sandhill country.

Lute gets a lot of appreciation for bagging the three wolves that were
the meanest marauders in the hills. Men demand to know how he did it.

"I hunted them every day, day in, day out. Finally found them over on
the North Dismal. They had pulled a critter down. I took a too distant
shot at them, then killed the cow they had hamstrung and half gutted. I
kept on, finally saw them when I was resting, crawled near and got a shot
at the old she-wolf and a few minutes later got a crack at one of the black
ones and soon at the other one. Both ran off, but I trailed and killed one;
the other either died or left the country. I skinned the black wolf—nailed

a seven-foot hide to our ranch house logs."

The cattlemen believe the three wolves killed more than a hundred head of cattle on our ranges, probably more than two thousand dollars worth, you bet.

Finished with the summer roundup, we go down to Trail's End—Ogalalla—to restock. We buy two thousand head of yearling doggies and drive them onto our Sandhill range and into our big cedar post corral to brand them.

Within the first two days we get about five hundred branded and turned out to close herd. After this very hot day, we are down at the lake past bunk time, cooling off and soaking off a layer of dirt churned up in the roping.

Bax and Buck Taylor stretch on the warm sand, drying off. We hear a cracking, crunching sound that I don't understand. Buck and Bax leap up on the horses and are gone. I hurry onto my horse, though I don't know what took the boys off so fast.

Coming up to the corral, the full moon shows the yearling critters' heads lined up above the top logs, which are giving way. The yearlings climb over the top. Weight of the stampeding calves flattens the corral side.

Lute comes from the other ranch in time to run along side of the leaders with Bax and Buck. The yearlings race, tails up, across the mile wide flat for the hills. We crowd them and turn the foremost—gradually set them to milling.

"Something scared 'em," Bax says as we ride round. Lute is the only one in clothes and on a saddle.

"Sing, damn it," Buck called. We sing with voices somewhere between a bullfrog's and a screechy pot-scraper's. Gradually the whirl slows. All are still scared—ready to go at the snap of a finger. None of us dares leave yet. The boys gradually loosen the circle, edge out to give these little buggers room to bed down, and around the circle may be hears strange, crooning lullabys. None of us think of laughing. These critters are explosive, here and there jumps start into runs, quickly headed by watchful men and horses.

Buck finally eases back, leaves slowly—does not dare run his horse for fear pounding hoofs would set the calves off again. He gets clothes for himself and Bax, and with care not to let a garment flap, hands me something too.

The moon travels into the west, pales and slips on down. We are in the darkest hours of night. Steadily the humming, sighing, yawning, singing continues. Not a doggie has acted like he wants to fold himself down to rest. They're still awfully skittish and it's still touch and go. We hang on, still making sounds supposed to pass with the calves for a reassuring lullaby. Dawn, sunrise, and full day come before the yearlings finally give it up and lie down; still in sight of the cedar pole pen. They stay down several hours—pretty well worn down, a sorry looking bunch of doggies. They had around a ton of horns knocked off, and are bruised, sore, and lame. We have to kill several broken legged or bad hurt, and a half dozen or so had been killed under the corral wall when the stampeded weight hit it.

We never are able to get these critters corralled here again, and so the branding job is slow. Each animal has to be roped and thrown. When it's all done we can't account for forty head. Lute and Buck Taylor backtrack them toward the Platte River and find the runaways, on their way back to Texas, I suppose. That night, two of the realest cowboys this country will ever see made the difference, I believe, between a possible total loss and a very small one, besides preventing a run that would have ruined the cattle.

October and snow came almost together to begin a long winter of snow on top of snow. This year we do not see the ground until six months later.

Cattle north of the Platte drift with the wind, into towns, into railroad cuts, canyons, creeks, and streams or crowd under protecting bluffs where they smothered under the powder-fine snow that drifted deep over all.

In January, Lute and Bax Taylor are caught in North Platte by a blizzard. When it subsides John Bratt rounds up all the men he finds around the town to help them drive his starving herds away from the valley and into the sandhills, where they would stand a chance of finding sheltered spots of grass stems still standing above the snow on hill sides opposite the winds.

Twenty-five or thirty fellows met at the ranch on the Birdwood. Lute said they tried all day to move ten thousand head from the valley, but the snow was two and a half to three feet deep between the streams and the foothills. The cattle wouldn't budge, and they had to give it up. A couple of days later the weather moderated and the cattle followed ridden horses into the hills.

Here in the Sandhills our cattle do not drift so bad, as the hills break the wind's wallop as well as the drift of snow, but it's an awfully hard winter—a long while to depend on what cured-on-the-stem hay-grass was long-stemmed enough to stand above the snows. After that is skimmed off, the doggies will have to chew the top crusts off the snow drifts.

1881. Roundup this May and June is a sober get-together. We pull out of it in good shape. Our loss is slight compared to many who, at the end of the roundup, find themselves with no herd to drive home. Herds are terribly shrunken at the best, expecting our own, though we have lost a higher percentage than usual. The Sandhills saved our herd, and we make a good profit on a stronger market.

Lute hustles in, excited over "tracks" he wants us to see. Stella, now twelve years old, and Jim's boy, Edd, are here for a few days. We get on horses and go along. Lute takes us over the hills, stops us, and carefully moves behind hills and through a sandy ravine to show us what he tracked —buffalo! A herd of more than thirty. I had supposed for some years now there were none in the country.

We dash at them, split them into two bunches and Edd (who had never seen a live buffalo and wants to kill one) and Lute take after one bunch and Stella and I chase a calf out of the other herd and nearly run it down, but I have no rope on my saddle, and not wanting to kill it, we let it go. We find Lute and Edd where Edd killed a prime young cow and they are butchering it out. The buffalo herd is never seen again. I suppose the Sioux from the reservation found and killed them.

This fall Luther gets as much hay put up as he can manage. A few haystacks might tide a herd of starving cattle through to grass. Since last winter's losses, men who stay in this business will have to come to some such provident ways with stock. Free range and Texas cattle were the beginning of ranching, but free-ranging cattle was a bust last year.

Winter 1881-82 is fierce and cold enough, but not so many bad blizzards, and less cold wind. Some cattle starved this year where the snow stayed deep in the valleys. But they weren't driven by blizzard winds as last year when spring melt showed creeks and rivers choked with dead critters.

Here in the hills our cattle fared very well—no loss worth mention. Spring comes on with another roundup time. I've not been out to the ranch a great deal these past couple of years, but I can't stay out of a roundup, though I've learned to avoid the working center dust. In the rounds of talk I mention that because of my poor health I'm thinking of getting through with ranching. Soon John Bratt catches me off aside.

"Major, are you just discouraged like everybody else, or have you actually decided to quit?"

"Well John, if by 'discouraged' you mean have I taken heavy losses, or am I going broke, or failing, it's not for any such reasons that I've decided to stop ranching. These tough winters haven't hurt the NC ranch—in fact, each winter brings a better profit. But I'll unload one of these times. I am not able to continue, and I must relieve my brother from the double load he's carried. He is ready to get out of ranching, too."

"But it is a three-way partnership, isn't it?"

"Yes, Cody is our silent partner and will agree with our decision."

"Have you set your asking price?"

"No—as yet we haven't gotten that far," I say, and he is called away by his foreman.

Along in the afternoon, Mr. Bratt rides over to where I sit my horse, talking with the Bar-7 foreman, Stemm, and Bill Paxton.

"Now about your ranch. You've done all right in the Sandhills, and I'm going in, since my range borders the hills. What do you consider you would have to have to turn the NC range over to me?"

Of course I have to hedge. I'm surprised that in spite of his heavy recent years' losses he wants to buy deeper into the ranch business.

"The valley combined with a Sandhill range should work right well for you, John, if you're going to buy in. Would you care to make me an offer?"

"Why yes, I believe I will. For the entire NC ranch and range, $60,000."

I only chuckle and promise to think about it. Before we pull out of the roundup, John Bratt manages to run across me.

"Well Frank, we can get together in North Platte to finish our deal."

"I haven't agreed to any offer I've had, to date, John, but I'll take $80,000 for the ranch and range."

"I'll give you $65,000—"

I see we can't get together.

Arranging to ship early we order cars, but the herds close, everything without calves not old enough to wean; and ease them down the trail to the railroad. These cattle are in good shape early in the season—only late June—grass fat. We graze them along so as to keep them marketable ahead of very hot weather. Too, I don't want them on hand as an item to consider with the ranch deal. Lute and Al Pratt ride our cattle train, hit a good market, get back and start the haying.

One of these days John Bratt rides up. He's had a good look at the Sandhills, has seen a few of the spring-fed lakes and the rich grass covering. There's a gleam in his eyes.

We invite our neighbor to sit in to dinner with us. The boys eat, pick up their hats, and go about their work. I ask Luther to stay.

After some conversational maneuvers, Mr. Bratt announces, "Now, Major, I've come to make you my best bid: for the NC ranch, range, cow and calf stock, and the brand, $70,000."

That's a good offer. I'll have to encourage him—a few minutes of "thinking" to show my willingness to consider his offer.

"Well, John, I've had some pretty good offers (I don't mention these were his own) but if nothing better comes along I'm prepared to winter through again."

"You must think you're selling a gold mine in these hills!" he says with some heat.

"No, no, nothing like that—only just about the best range to be found in all the Plains, and I've seen a good share of the Great Plains."

"Seventy-five thousand is my top offer and I want immediate possession

—the whole thing just as she is, except your personal belongings and saddle horse."

"Mr. Bratt, you've just bought the NC ranch." I shake hands with him on it, and we complete the deal in North Platte. We each get $25,000 out of it, besides the yearly profits from cattle marketed.[7]

39

My friends are campaigning—boosting me for the legislature, all over Platte County. The October 12, 1882, *Columbus Journal* prints a contribution written from Lindsey, Nebraska, in my behalf, a "light verse," to be used with an old tune.

> And Major North, that man of worth
> Who faced the Sioux in battle
> When he goes there, you may declare
> Legislative Halls will rattle.
> For I'm sure a man who made Sioux run
> And preserved our habitation—
> This Great old Scout will tell Bill Stout
> "No more wings or appropriations!"
>
> CHORUS—Then hip, hip hurrah!
> Three cheers I say
> For our noble leader, etc.

Here's some more in a later issue of *Columbus Journal*, October 19, 1882:

. . . Since Major North was mustered out of the service, he has lived in Columbus. He has been engaged in a cattle enterprise up on the Dismal River, but in summer, last, he sold his cattle, and, while not now actively engaged in any business, he expects to go into something at home.

The voters of Platte County, in giving their franchise to this brave man, cannot go amiss, for certainly a man who won fame, and the confidence of his superior officers on the Indian campaigns, cannot be found wanting when the interests of his country are at stake. Give him your votes, send him to the legislature and not one in this country will ever have to repent the election of Frank North. He will stand by you in all trials, and in every instance where the interests of the people are op-

posed by any power whatsoever. You can be assured that he will stand
shoulder to shoulder with the people and fight their battles to the end.

After election day when the ballots are counted, I am elected by a
popular majority. It means a new and very different frontier on which to
serve. Lucky am I that brother James will give me pointers, as he was first
elected six years ago and has served in the senate.

Christmas this year was one of our very happiest. All of the young
cousins get together. Their jolly Uncle Luther provides the bobsled and
goes skating with them. Mother is at the head of the table as three
generations sit down to Christmas dinner. Mary is pleased that I've
disposed of the ranch and cattle.

Happy New Year to All, 1883. We plan that Mary will come with me to
the Capitol City to enjoy the inaugural ball, receptions, teas, and other
social events. She's had a dressmaker busy sewing fancy stitches and fine
seams in stylish wearables. Stella and her grandmother will keep our home
fires burning the few days that Mary will be with me in Lincoln.

I've a bout of asthma to whip by the time I am due to report in
Lincoln. It seems to me I've worn out an awful lot of wind trying to
breathe it in, and then to push it out.

February 3. Mary feels bad today. I call our family doctor. He drives up,
hitches his horse to the gatepost, and spends an hour or so with Mary—
leaves pills and medicines. I am careful to dose Mary by the clock. Mother
comes and takes over the household.

Three days get by, each more anxious than the last. The doctor comes
daily—changes medicine and pills, but he isn't changing Mary's sickness,
and she is worse and weaker.

February 6. Our doctor is back for the second time today. He asks my
consent to calling a doctor from Omaha to come and see Mary and
consult with him. Of course I agree.

Lots of visitors today—good friends, concerned for Mary. But I wish
they'd wait until Mary is better—she needs rest.

The Omaha doctor, a specialist, comes. The two doctors are with Mary.
Terrible anxiety gnaws at me. Finally the doctors come out, close doors
behind them, and sit down with me.

"Major," our doctor says, "I'm sorry I cannot bring you a more
encouraging report—we know of no real medical help for Mrs. North.
Now if—" he rambles among learned medical terms awhile, then says,
"Actually, we see but little hope for her. We believe she is presently
nearing termination—a matter of hours."

My senses reel with that blow. After that my only awareness is keenly of
Mary, until she draws her last breath.

February 9, 1883. Mary is gone—she is dead!

The friendly clock is silent—I ask it nothing—it tells me—it constantly screams *that* fateful hour and minute.

Time stands still—waits on rituals—yet gives not another day of life to Mary. I'm vaguely aware that the sheet-covered form laid out in an emptied bedroom is placed in a casket—that I follow Mary's casket from our home to the Episcopal Church, and somehow from there to an opening in our Pioneer Cemetery.

Duty calls me to serve in the legislature—a somewhat stabilizing experience for me. One term is enough—I must be out where far distant horizons invite me, and where, riding out alone, the deep-down ache fades for awhile, replaced by the tranquility I find in the great open stretches of the Plains.

As Mary and I had planned for our young daughter, Stella enters Omaha's Brownell Hall School for Girls this fall. Although Mother is cheerful, the house is cold and empty. Stella comes home for Christmas[1] —too soon must return to school.

Cody, wintering at his Scout's Rest ranch, a short distance northwest of North Platte, stops over to see me. I am glad to see him, and Mother welcomes him like one of her sons. Ah, it's good to sit down and talk with him. Of course our reminiscences examine past years' doings, and down to the present. Cody tackles me head on.

"So now, what do you intend doing with your time?"

"Well, I'll do something. The buffaloes all 'went west,' I won't be called on to guide any hunting parties. The Pawnees are all gone from Nebraska. Probably there will be no more Indian wars. Six years now since Lute and I took the scouts to Indian Territory. I'm all done with ranching. I sometimes wonder if I haven't already outlived my time."

"Horse feathers! Why you're not even forty-five years old. You're doing too much lonesome thinking. How about you coming along with me this spring when I take the Wild West Show on the road? I can think of a hundred ways I can use you—keep you too busy to do much thinking. Better yet, how would you like bringing a bunch of your Pawnee men along? I think we could manage to give them a decent wage—you could lead them much as you did in your scout organization.

"That's where I need you, to drill all these people, animals and equipment you and North Platte men have been collecting since the Old Glory Blowout celebration last July 4. We have only weeks left us to get it ready to go on the road."

I fail to get up much ambition for such a thing, but time hangs heavy. I can't see myself as a showman, but the Pawnees, now . . . I write a couple of letters. In answer, a group of my Pawnee friends show up.

We go to North Platte, and they're on the payroll. I'm caught up in a whirl of churned up confusion, action, movement to settle my restlessness, all of it interesting, hard work. Time flies, and so do we, putting thousands of odds and ends together right down to the first run-through of our program.

If that one had been public the audience would surely have ran us out of town. I didn't laugh—then. I was most sure I would never get it hammered into something that might work, to say nothing of entertainment.

We shake it together for a re-run. It drags this time, but it catches step and proceeds. I take new hope for tomorrow. Overnight everyone seems to have gotten some idea of their parts as the day's first rehearsal goes off—not smooth, but off. Again we do it all the way through. This time all is falling into place.

Tomorrow the show boards the Union Pacific's special show train of box and passenger cars for a run to Columbus and a dress rehearsal there before the first real ticket show at Omaha.

Bill Sweeney has put together a band. He leads the show members to the depot where the town gathers to see us board.

Arriving at Columbus the stock must be unloaded, fed, and watered in the railroad's stock pens.

Bill Sweeney and his band begin to warm up—and draw a crowd. Fred Matthews unscrambles his stagecoach and four-horse team as the first event scheduled. As the driver is a hometown man, some of our most prominent citizens accept the honor of riding in the stagecoach.

Painted Indians behind conveniently planted brush jump out to attack the stage, but scare the mules. They race around the grounds. Fred Matthews manages to control and stop his mules. The local officials leave the stagecoach with considerable more haste and noticeably less dignity than when they entered.

Bill Sweeney and his cowboy band's lively and loud music drowns out possible words of anger, and the show goes on.

I go to Omaha and to Council Bluffs with the show, then Luther goes to Springfield, Illinois, with it. I stay at home in Columbus several months.

As the show is scheduled to play the New England states this summer (1884), I arrange for Mother and Stella to come east for a visit with relatives—I intend that Stella shall get acquainted with our families and all her cousins, also with her mother's people too. That trip to bring Stella back to get acquainted with her kin was in our plans for the future, before Mary passed on. Mother and Stella arrive in New York. I plan to have some time with them, later.

July 4, 1884. The Wild West Show is playing in Hartford, Connecticut, now. We've had a long stand here and this is our last show. Everything is being loaded on the railroad cars as fast as each act and scene is ended— the props and gear packed, everything in its place, and placed on the cars.

All the Indians stand at horse with me, each division waiting its cue. Fred Matthews, who used to be one of my officers of the Pawnee Scouts, drives the stage once around the sawdust ring, then I send in the "attack" Indians. Besides the Pawnees, some Sioux, Cheyenne, and Arapahoe joined the show and all whoop their own tribal war cry, swinging war clubs and tomahawks.

Next, I lead in with the Pawnees. We chase the Indians and the stage, careening around the ring. On the second time around, the Pawnees shuck their uniforms, down to not much more than their "G" strings, as they did when preparing for real battle. Yelling the Pawnee battle cry we race on. About halfway around the ring, with most of the excited audience standing, seeing we're about to overtake the "attack" Indians, my saddle turns, flips me off under the racing horses. I'm trampled by several hooves, stepped on and stumbled over. I cannot escape them.

The act is aborted—signaled out of the ring as the band plays lively music, and the clowns come on. I'm brought to a hotel where a doctor finds several broken ribs, says extent of my injuries will become more evident in a few days; bandages "abrasions, contusions, and concussions" and, as I object to entering a hospital, demands a nurse for me. I ask Bill to send for Mother, the best nurse.

Our act was next to the end—the Indian war dance is the last act, while the stage and horses are loaded on the train cars. Most of the show people are already in the train's sleeping cars and in bed.

Knowing I am hurt the Pawnees stay, waiting near the hotel. The doctor finally gives Cody consent for two Pawnees to enter a few minutes. My friends are fetched in—they stand stiff—I sense they're frightened and I'm wrung with compassion for them.

"Grandfather"—it's their title of respect for me. The Pawnees are beside the chair in which, unable to lie down, I'm braced and pillowed.

"Yes," I say. (I've been given something for my pain and I'm confused— feel I am drifting away.)

"Grandfather, do you know us?"

The boys think I'm not conscious, test me further.

"Rattlesnake and White Eagle," I tell them in their own tongue.

"Grandfather, you never lied to us. You never deceived us; are you going to die?"

Now I realize my good, loyal friends are stalling the whole show train, loaded with people, buffalos and other wild animals, and horses, by refusing to desert me. I have little breath—can't argue with them, but I try for a strong voice to reassure them—to send my friends on their way.

"No, I'm not going to die—go on with the show and I will come in thirty days." I'm pretty bad hurt—may have to take a month to recover, but I don't believe I'm bad enough to die.

The Pawnees bid me goodbye and leave. I ask Cody to send to Columbus, Nebraska, for Bill McCune[2] to come to stick along with them as they know and trust him, until I can get back.

Mother arrives, has a conference with the doctor, rents rooms and moves me "home."

Stella is with us, and Luther comes to help Mother while I begin the uphill mend. Asthma had let up on me considerably the past couple of years, but as I begin to recover from the injury, the disease jumps on me with all fours and I have some tough bouts. Nevertheless, I promised my Pawnee friends I would come in thirty days. The doctor forbids and Lute and Mother object, but I get up and go to Albany, New York, where the show is playing. Still weak, I just straw boss awhile.

I leave New Orleans March 5, 1885, doing some advance work for Cody. On the way to St. Louis I catch a cold and know, by the time I arrive there, I am in for a bad time. I want just to go home—dare not try traveling alone. I wire for Luther.

Luther comes but insists we wait as the doctor advises, until I'm better. I tell him I haven't time to wait. He surprises me by consenting to get us on the way. I'm mostly unaware of the miles and the hours, thanks to medications administered by Luther. He gets us to Nebraska, and I was never so glad to be coming home, and never before so tired.

A few days pass, I know now I shall never recover, and the fact doesn't at all bother me. Quite detached, I'm thinking I've had a wonderfully good life, busy and full of interests, dear friends, and good fortune along with never falling down on a job I found at hand to do. Best of all, my one and only Mary was my wife, and mother of our children—the dear young lady by my bedside. As I cross my last horizon to go to Mary, my last sun has set.

> Columbus Journal, Tuesday, March 17, 1885. At 10 a.m. today, in the opera house the funeral of Major Frank J. North was held, the Reverend Dr. Doherty, Episcopal, from Omaha officiated . . . borne . . . along the long, straight road to Pioneer Cemetery[3] . . . to his grave beside his wife . . . Survivors: daughter, Miss Stella, fifteen year old student of Brownell Hall School for Girls, Omaha; mother, Mrs. Jane Townley North; brothers, James E.; Luther H.; sisters, Mrs. Charles Morse; Mrs. Jim Cushing and eastern relatives.

APPENDIX

North Platte Telegraph, Saturday, September 7, 1909

BUFFALO BILL HOLDS IMPRESSIVE MEMORIAL SERVICES
IN CEMETERY AT COLUMBUS
Dean Beecher Also Takes Part

Columbus, Sept. 3—With all the pomp and solemnity that attends a royal funeral, or a man who has spent his life in many different countries, a memorial ceremony was held over the grave of Major Frank North here this forenoon, and the chief figure in the proceedings was Colonel Wm. F. Cody, for many years a friend and partner of the dead man.

Twenty-five different nationalities marched from the grounds where Colonel Cody's Wild West Show was holding forth, to the cemetery. Many original members of the show, which was organized here twenty-six years ago, were present. Though the memorial service was read over the grave of Major Frank North, it also included Fred Matthews and George W. Clothier, who before they died were also friends of Colonel Cody and famous men on the Plains.

Dean Beecher of Trinity Cathedral, Omaha, read the services and offered up prayer. After all the guests had joined in the Lord's Prayer, Dean Beecher called upon Colonel Cody, who eulogized his three departed friends.

Among those who headed the long procession were: Captain Gus G. Becher, L't. George Lehan, and a daughter of Major North. These men had fought with the dead soldier many years ago, and they revered his memory in the way that Cody expressed it over the grave of Major North.

Never before, it was said, has the little cemetery *at the end of the long straight road* been so crowded with people. Long before the procession arrived which was nearly 11:30, hundreds were at the gates of the place awaiting the visit of the old Scout, Major North's friend and partner, William F. Cody.

With slow marching steps the horse and carriages wended their way to

267

the cemetery and then as silently as if it were the burial of a soldier, they all dismounted without a word to even the men that were there to hold the horses. All the costumes that adorn twenty-five different nationalities, as well as a band of be-feathered and painted redskins, marched, four abreast toward the grave. From the way things were done, at the sign of Johnny Baker, the whole affair might have been rehearsed for a week. Every man seemed to know his part. (Mr. and Mrs. Fred Garlow, the latter a daughter of Col. Cody were among those who rode in carriages to the cemetery.)

The mere rustling of leaves was the only noise that broke the heavy silence until the voice of Dean Beecher reading the Psalms, made it sound like an outdoor church. All stood bareheaded, and Johnny Baker, who is the stage manager of the aggregation, gave the signal for all to stand by the grave. Captain Sweeney's Cowboy band then played, "Nearer My God to Thee."

Captain Devlin's troup of Zouaves then fired three rounds over the graves of the dead soldiers and Colonel Cody placed flowers on the graves of his departed friends. Adding additional interest and soldier-like solemnity to the occasion, one of the cavalrymen then sounded "taps" over the grave and many a tear was furtively wiped away, as others had known Major North and respected him for his valor and goodness. It was a great day for Columbus.

His long, white hair caught in the wind, dressed in his civilian attire, Buffalo Bill looked a picturesque figure of old, and when he began his eulogy of Major North all ears were strained to catch every word.

"Major Frank North," said Cody, "whose gentle spirit; calm judgement; marked magnificent qualities; personal daring and equitable disposition, makes me apologize for my inability to pay a fitting tribute to one of the truest friends I ever had.

"In the camp, on a hunt, on the trail, in lonely bivouac; in the dangers of the day's scout or terrors of the night prowl, in the loneliness of the ambush or attack that precedes the savage warfare, in the surprise, charge or retreat; Major North was a man one could rely upon, and facing of dangers seemed to please.

"He was a man on whom you could stake your life. My friends, you must imagine the emotions that fill my heart and soul, for my tongue can not do justice to the memory of my dear departed friend and partner. *He was one of the loveliest characters that God ever created, one of the bravest products of frontier days;* a man of whom it may truly be said that his like is seldom seen.

"Peace to his ashes, and may his story go down the ages to illuminate the pages of the days that tried men's souls in the settlement of the great West!" Cody brushed away a tear when he had finished this part of his short eulogy of Major North. After that, the showmen and others went back the same slow way they had come.

"He was a man worthwhile, and a man I love to see honored," said one among the crowd.

NOTES

CHAPTER 2

1. Florence is located on the site of the Mormon winter quarters of 1846-48 where many perished from the rigors of a harsh winter and deprivations, as is evidenced in the Mormon Cemetery there. Departing trains of Mormon emigrants who survived until spring were staged out here for Salt Lake City. After the Mormons' makeshift, tent/log/sod village burned, the new town was surveyed and platted and incorporated as Florence.

2. *The Fighting Norths and Pawnee Scouts,* by Robert Bruce. Published with the cooperation and approval of the Nebraska State Historical Society, State Capitol Tower, Lincoln, Nebraska. Copyright 1932.

    Grenville M. Dodge, 1831-1916 (boxed excerpt p. 2): ". . . Major General Grenville M. Dodge, Commander Department of the Missouri, 1865. In *The Indian Campaign of 1864-1865.* Written in 1874 and published with other papers in 1911: My acquaintance with Frank North began in 1856. . . ."

3. Abraham Lincoln successfully defended the railroad company. My version of this event is a small, intentional anachronism, telescoping three years to allow narration of the entire incident, its cause and outcome.

CHAPTER 3

1. *Bellevue, Larimer and Saint Mary: Their History, Location, Description and Advantages,* by C. Chaucer Goss. Published by John Q. Goss, Bellevue, Nebraska, 1859, and reissued by Bank of Bellevue; by cooperation of

Sarpy County Historical Society and Nebraska State Historical Society, 1956. "In 1856 . . . the Presbyterian Board of Missions in New York . . . sent Rev. Edward McKinney . . . and family . . . in fall of that same year [to Indian Territory]. He erected a log house up on the plateau [above Traders Point and the steamboat landing] . . . D. E. Reed, sent out by the Board as Superintendent of the School . . . in 1847 . . . All the interest of the Mission gathered about this house, while that of the Trading Post and Agency Indian centered at the bottom." (p. 5)

2. The Indian name of Sun Chief is variously spelled. George Bird Grinnell, in *Two Great Scouts* (The Arthur H. Clark Co., Cleveland, 1928), spells it Sa-kur-e-a-le Shar. (Shar in or on a Pawnee name denotes chieftainship.) Grinnell quotes Luther North (p. 217): "Sun Chief was a nephew of Peta Le Shar" (the head chief of the Pawnee Nation in the 1850s and 1860s).

   In *The Fighting Norths and The Pawnee Scouts* (published with the cooperation and approval of the Nebraska State Historical Society) pp. 4 and 29, Robert Bruce gives the name of Sun Chief as La-Roo-Chuck-a La Shar, expressing the Pawnee pronunciation. Others give the Pawnee for Sun Chief as Sa-quele-ah-la Shar, and La Noo Chuck oo La Shar. Sun Chief was killed in a massacre by the Sioux in 1873 at Massacre Canyon, near Trenton, Nebraska. A granite memorial marker on a hill overlooks the site.

3. During the first half of the 1800s there were at least three chiefs by the name Peta La Shar, among the Skeedee and Chaui (Great) bands of Pawnee. In Bruce's *The Fighting Norths* (p. 4), the picture of the heroic young Peta La Shar, son of an equally heroic sire, Knife Chief of the Skeedees, is a reproduction of a portrait done by artist Dr. King in Washington, D.C. The Pawnee was visiting the Capitol, where he was lionized for his rescue, four years before, of a young girl of an enemy tribe whom the Skeedees were about to sacrifice to the Morning Star (see George Hyde, *Pawnee Indians* [University of Denver Press, 1951], p. 130), to gain blessings in crop yield and hunting. The young man was emulating his sire's similar noble deed of the year before; both believed human sacrifice wrong and brought an end to it. (The story of his sire's rescue of a Spanish boy, brought to St. Louis by Manuel Liza, was published in the *Missouri Gazette,* 19 June, 1818.) The caption under this picture pertains to the Peta La Shar known by both Frank and Luther North, though the picture is of the earlier man, member of another band. It reads, "Petah La Shara (18____-1874), Chief of the Chaui (Grand) Pawnees; a picturesque and famous Indian, well known to the North families and mentioned several times in the Captain's reminiscences. Also written Peta La Shar, Pe-ta-Na Sharo and Petalasharu. The old line of chieftainship terminated with the death of Sun Chief (La-Roo-Chuck-a La Shar), his son

... line now extinct."

4. *Pioneer Hero Stories and Folk Tales,* by George Bird Grinnell: "I owe much of my interest in, and knowledge of, the Pawnees to my long intimacy with the late Major Frank North, who from his extended intercourse and close connection with this people—a connection which lasted more than thirty years—was unquestionably better informed about them than any other white man has ever been; and with Captain L. H. North, Luther, his brother, who was for many years associated with Major North in command of the Pawnee Scouts." (p. 20)

"Major Frank North was undoubtedly more conversant with the spoken Pawnee tongue than any other white man has ever been. Since his death (1885) there is no one who is so familiar with the language as M. J. B. Dunbar, who has devoted much time to its study and has made himself acquainted not only with the vocabulary, but also its grammar . . ." (p. 213)

5. William Duncan Strong (anthropologist, Bureau of American Ethnology), in "An Introduction to Nebraska Archeology," Smithsonian Misc. Collections, vol. 192, No. 10 (20 July 1935), gives the dimensions of Pawnee caches as up to six feet across at the mouth, wider at the bottom, and five feet, more or less, in depth. They were dug in the earth floor around the inside walls of the lodge, and often outside. Those outside of lodges were covered with poles and bark and coarse grass and leaves, then camouflaged by a heap of dirt, which also prevented changes of temperature and food spoilage. The inside caches required less covering, and the low pallets or beds were arranged around the walls above the inside caches. Early pioneers managed much of their winter store of dried vegetables as did the Pawnee, and made pits for keeping of cabbage heads, turnips, and other root crops, covering them with straw, then with tarpaulin or canvas or grain sacks, and dirt or fodder and hay over the whole.

6. The site for the proposed Neapolis was between that of the earliest fort on the west side of the Missouri River, Fort Atkinson, and the later Fort Calhoun.

CHAPTER 4

1. See *The Second Bank of the United States,* by Ralph C. H. Cottrell, copyright 1903; and *Bank and Politics in America from the Revolution to the Civil War,* copyright by Bray Hammond. These authors agree the panic of 1857 followed a period of marked prosperity, increasing land values and a great surge of construction and investments in public conveyance and freight transport.

2. Nebraska's Territorial Legislature allowed banks "to incorporate without financial backing," according to Marvin F. Kivett, Director, Nebraska State Historical Society and Museum, Lincoln, Nebraska, "and many such banks issued 'wild cat,' bank notes not worth the paper they were printed on."

3. Became Russell, Majors and Waddell, the greatest Overland bull-freighting firm of the time, with 1600 yoke of oxen and 1500 employees, and established Nebraska City.

4. Coleville subsequently was renamed Columbus.

5. *Our Own History, Columbus, Nebraska,* by Martha M. Turner (Art Printery; Published August, 1936, by the author with cooperation of Platte County Historical Society, Nebraska): "The American House (hotel) opened November, 1858. The Columbus Town Site Company erected the hotel at a cost of $7,000.00 which was opened shortly before November 22. Frank G. Becher was installed as manager."

6. Reference to the initial trip of Western Stage Company is in accordance with the *Omaha Times* of October 7, 1858. Mr. Hagerty drove horse cars many years in Omaha. In 1846-66, Fred Mathews drove mail stage west from Columbus; served as lieutenant, Company C, Pawnee Battalion, command of Major North, and drove stage in Cody's Wild West Show in Indian attack act.

7. The *Omaha Times,* November 11, 1858; see also Hyde, *Pawnee Indians* (University of Denver Press, 1951).

8. Poisoning wolves was cheaper than using ammunition, and the hides were better preserved. Wolves living about fringes of the buffalo herds were even more numerous than the buffalo.

CHAPTER 5

1. E. B. Branch was superintendent of Pawnee and Otoe Indians under Commissioner W. F. Dole, who was succeeded by Alfred Cumming.

2. John Rickley, of the group who first pioneered Columbus, Nebraska. Born March 19, 1815, in Berne, Switzerland, he emigrated to America, to Ohio, and later, to the frontier, bringing his family and saw and grist mill in the spring of 1857. He was a merchant and built the second store in Columbus to which he added a lean-to room for a post office. He was the first postmaster, and held various town offices.

3. Known as Big Island until renamed Grand Island after Fort Child, soon renamed Fort Kearny, was placed almost opposite its western end. Grand Island is sixty miles long but narrow.

4. Known as Pawnee Spring, it was renamed Cottonwood Spring for a huge tree that was a landmark on the Oregon Trail.

5. A son was born in 1859 to the Nelson Boyers at Cottonwood Spring, and a daughter in 1860 (after the county was organized and named Shorter in honor of Congressman Wm. B. Shorter of Tennessee, but soon changed to Lincoln County), the youngest son, Frank Boyer, related, when interviewed by this writer, May 13, 1940. The third child born in the area was to the Charles McDonalds: William, born June 14, 1861.

6. Christopher (Kit) Carson served as Indian agent at Taos, 1853-61. He then joined the Union Army at the outbreak of the Civil War.

7. "Elder" Moses F. Shinn, born January 3, 1809, learned tailoring, became a speculator and financier at Council Bluffs. As chaplain of the Iowa Legislature in 1858, he prayed:

> Great God, Bless the young and growing state of Iowa; bless our senators, representatives and officers . . . Give us sound currency, pure water and undefiled religion.

When preaching at the First Methodist Church west of 13th Street, near Douglas Street, he acquired the reputation of being able to outshout mule and ox teamsters in the freighters' yard next to the church. In December 1856, the First Methodist Church of Omaha was dedicated by Elder Shinn; the year before he had built Cottonwood Church in Council Bluffs.

In 1859, after gold was discovered in Colorado, Elder Shinn, forseeing a great surge of prospectors and gold diggers, placed a ferry across the river, fifteen miles below the joining of the Loup with the Platte. Elder Shinn died in January 1885, in Omaha. Near relatives in eastern Nebraska are Mrs. George G. Barker, 5308 Cumming Street, Omaha, and Mrs. Julius Steinberg, Bellevue Boulevard, Bellevue, Nebraska. Mrs. Steinberg was, between 1955 and 1962, the informant of this writer. See also the *World Herald,* May 17, 1959.

CHAPTER 6

1. John M. Thayer, Major General of the Nebraska Militia; senator, 1867-71, one of the first two of the new state's senators; governor, 1885-89.

2. Lt. B. H. Robertson. Company K, Second Dragoons, stationed Fort Kearny, under command of Col. Charles May.

3. Livestock killed was a cow. Poncas were later found to have killed the animal.

4. Not until 1880 did Indians enjoy rights in the courts of law. A band of Poncas brought the corpse of Chief Standing Bear's son back to his Nebraska homeland for burial and were arrested near Omaha. A. J. Poppleton and J. L. Weaver represented the chief and his band. The chief

pleaded his own and his tribe's case in remarkable oratory. The decision that Indians were human beings still stands, and the Poncas were released. Not until a congressional act of 1924 could Indians vote. In Arizona and New Mexico, Indians did not receive voting privileges until 1948.

5. Present Nance County, Nebraska, was the site of the Pawnee reservation. A tract of fifteen by thirty miles along the Loup River was assigned September 24, 1857.

A hundred years later (April 20, 1959) the Pawnees, who were banished from their reservation seventeen years after it was granted them, began their multi-billion-dollar land payment claim hearing. A two-man Indian claims commission sat in the Douglas County Courthouse, Omaha, Nebraska, to hear the claim involving twenty-three million acres, or 40 percent of Nebraska and northern Kansas land ceded in 1833, 1848, 1857, and 1875. Action was started in 1947 in behalf of approximately eighteen hundred Pawnee whose tribal home is near Pawnee, Oklahoma. Of the four tribal officers on hand, George H. Roberts, of Pawnee, Oklahoma, president of the Tribal Council, is the son of the last surviving Pawnee army scout, the youngest to serve under the North brothers in 1876-77. Enlisting as Ah-re Kah-Rard, meaning Antler, after his first (successful) combat, he was, according to Pawnee tradition and custom, privileged to change his name. This he did, choosing Fancy Eagle, the Indian name of his father, La-tah cots kah La haroo, a magician and doctor. His grandfather was Sitting Eagle, La-ta-cots-te-wa-tit, ". . . one of the most famous doctors and magicians in Pawnee history." (Bruce, *The Fighting Norths and Pawnee Scouts*, p. 630.)

Ah-re Kah-Rard or Fancy Eagle, known as Rush Roberts, survived the Sioux's massacre of his buffalo-hunting people in 1873 near Trenton, Nebraska, where a granite shaft overlooks the site.

Rush Roberts was the father of fifteen children by two sisters, daughters of Kah-he-yee, a Skeedee, Almighty Chief. His sons had chieftainship rights from both parents. George H. Roberts, Good Chief, has been conspicuous in his efforts to preserve tribal history and perpetuate hereditary customs.

CHAPTER 7

1. The grist mill owned by John Rickly had been lost in a flood, though the sawmill continued operation.
2. A mochila remained in the custody of the Pony Express rider until it was placed in the hands of the succeeding rider. It consisted of nearly square, strong, pliable leather that fitted over the saddle pommel and had mail

pockets secured to each side before and behind the rider's legs.

3. "The Sower," a bronze figure in the act of hand broadcasting grain, tops Nebraska's state capitol.

4. Fremont's report of his 1842 exploration gives the Loup River as "430 yards wide with a broad swift current of clear water, in this respect differing from the Platte which has yellow muddy water derived from limestone and mearl formation. The Fork Loup was difficult as the water was so deep that it came into the body of the carts and we reached the opposite bank after repeated attempts, ascending and descending the bed of the river in order to avail ourselves of the banks. We encamped on the left bank of the Fork on the point of land at its junction with the Platte. . . ."

CHAPTER 8

1. Judge Gillis, appointed Pawnee agent, traveled by boat up the Missouri River in the company of Indian Superintendent A. M. Robinson. They were joined at Bellevue by Samuel Allix, former teacher of the Pawnee, and an old trapper of the American Fur Company, William G. Holius.

2. The Pawnee school was a crude log house which the Mormons, who had founded Genoa Village, had erected. The roof leaked and partially collapsed, but was repaired and still used for the school. Later a brick school building was built.

3. *The Thunder Ceremony of the Pawnee*, by Ralph Linton (assistant curator of North American ethnology, Department of Anthropology), published by Field Museum of Natural History, 1922, Leaflet No. 5, pp. 9-10. "In winter, gods were thought to have withdrawn from earth. The first thunder in spring was thought to be notification that they had once more turned their attention to it. . . . The first thunder was thought to be the voice of Paruxti, a deity who was the messenger of Tirawa and combined in himself the essence of the four servants of the Evening Star—Wind, Cloud, Lightning and Thunder. He passed over the land in a storm and as he spoke the earth awakened, and life was kindled anew. Returning to his lodge in the west, he kindled new fire and offered smoke to the great heavenly gods, informing them that he had visited the earth, and that all was well. The gods then turned their attention earthward, and prepared to receive the prayers and offerings of men."

4. Peta La Shar. See Chapter 3, footnote 4, history of Pawnee chiefs of this name in two bands of the tribe.

CHAPTER 9

1. This tale of the disappearance of the warriors is unsubstantiated. Howev-

er, lack of verification does not disprove the incident which was reported by Luther H. North (Collection, Nebraska State Historical Society, Lincoln).

One possible explanation is suggested by an article in the *Omaha World Herald* by staff member Tom Allen:

> DEVIL'S CATTLE TRAP OF 1880 IS STILL A DEADLY QUAGMIRE
> Lyman Nebraska—A long forgotten hell's half acre of frontier lore is still very much alive in Scotts Bluff County.
>
> The Devil's Cattle Trap is no ghost. It heaves and sucks and frequently regurgitates the whitened bones of its victims.
>
> It is a geological freak, a quagmire of ever-changing boils containing an apparently bottomless goo of white, chalky, alkaline mud. It is said to be the grave of hundreds of frontier cattle.
>
> The area known by old timers as simply "the bog," is 1½ miles from the Wyoming border and seven miles south of here on what is otherwise a rich wheat and sugarbeet tableland. Most county officials and area residents have forgotten its existence.
>
> Bob Brammeier, the young farmer-rancher on whose land it is, wishes he could forget it. Two years ago it almost claimed the life of his son Jonnie, now three. "I was away and he crawled under the fence. He was in up to his chest when Mom and Dad heard him and pulled him out. I've had some steers get in but . . . they managed to get out and I keep it fenced off . . ."

CHAPTER 11

1. H. H. Sibley, born 1811, Detroit, Michigan. In 1834 established an American Fur Company trading post near Fort Snelling and erected a stone house; married in 1843; was a delegate to Congress in 1849, where he worked for creation of Territory of Minnesota. In 1855 became a member of the territorial legislature. He was active in the constitutional convention preparing for statehood, after which he was elected the first governor of Minnesota. He led three expeditions, from 1862 to 1865, to subdue Sioux uprisings, and was commissioned brigadier general by President Lincoln.

2. *Pawnee Hero Stories and Folk Tales,* by George Bird Grinnell (University of Nebraska, 1961).

> Their [medicine men's] guild was entirely distinct from that of the priests. A priest might be a doctor as well, but not because he was a priest. The doctors were primarily healers. Their function was to fight disease. Like many other savage nations, the Pawnees believed that

sickness was caused by evil spirits, which had entered into the patient and must be driven out if he was to recover. In their treatment of injuries the doctors were often singularly successful. Major North has cited for me a number of instances in which men whose hurts had refused to yield to treatment of the United States Army surgeons, had been cured by Pawnee doctors. . . . As might be imagined, however, the Pawnee treatment of disease was less efficacious . . . in the case of more serious complaints, the dancing and rattling which constitute so large a part of the doctor's treatment, tend to aggravate rather than to check the disease.

. . . As the doctors had to fight evil spirits, it is not surprising that they should have summoned magic to their aid; but this magic probably served its more important purpose in impressing the other Indians with a belief in the doctors' powers. Some of the performances which took place at the doctors' dances were marvelous, and most of them were quite inexplicable to those who saw what was done. That they should have imposed on the Indian spectator is perhaps not surprising; but it is further to be noted that clear-headed, intelligent white men, whose powers of observation have been highly trained, have confessed themselves wholly unable to explain these startling performances, or to hazard a guess as to the means by which they were accomplished. That these things happened as detailed is well authenticated by the testimony of many perfectly credible witnesses.

Other masters of mystery are provided with mechanical aids of one kind or another—some apparatus (page 376) which assists them in imposing on their audiences, by concealing certain objects, or certain acts, by means of which they cause things to appear different from what they really are. The Pawnee doctors had nothing of this. Their dances were conducted by naked men in a ring surrounded by spectators. The floor of bare earth, packed hard and worn smooth by the tread of many feet, afforded no apparent opportunity for concealment or trickery. (p. 374)

Major North told me that he saw with his own eyes the doctors make the corn grow. This was in the medicine lodge. In the middle of the lodge the doctor dug up a piece of the hard trodden floor of the lodge, about as large as a dinner plate, and broke up between his fingers the hard pieces of soil, until the dirt was soft and pliable. The ground having thus been prepared, and having been moistened with water, a few kernels of corn were buried in the loose earth. Then the doctor retired a little from the spot and sang, and as the place where the corn was buried was watched, the soil was seen to move, and a tiny green blade came slowly into view. This continued to increase in height and size until in the course of twenty minutes or half an hour from the time of planting, the stalk of corn was a foot or fifteen inches in height. (pp. 379-80)

Similar . . . was a feat performed with a cedar berry. The berry was passed around among the spectators for examination, and was then planted as the corn had been. Then after a few moments, the doctor approached the spot, put his thumb and forefinger down into the soft dirt, and seemed to lay hold of something. Very slowly he raised his hand, and was seen to hold on the tips of his fingers the end of a cedar twig. Slowly his hand was moved from the ground, the twig growing longer and longer. When nine or ten inches high, it began to have side branches. The doctor still holding the top-most twig of what was by this time a cedar bush, continued to lift his hand slowly, until it was about three feet from the ground, and then let go of the bush. Then presently he took hold of the stem close to the ground, and seeming to exert a good deal of force, pulled up the bush by the roots; and all the people saw the bush and its bunch of fresh and growing roots. (p. 380)

Enough has been said of these mystery ceremonies to indicate that they were very remarkable. The circumstances under which they were performed would seem to remove them from the more common-place tricks of professional jugglers. And I have never found anyone who could even suggest an explanation of them.

3. The root *pomme-de-terre* (fruit of the earth) grew abundantly in areas of the Loup River. The Pawnee dug the bulbs, roasted them in hot coals or stewed them, or dried and pounded them into a meal or flour for breadstuff.

CHAPTER 14

1. Frank North served in 1864 as lieutenant, in 1865 and 1869 as captain, and as major in 1867. Luther was his captain in 1867.

2. Red Hawk, Koot-tah-we-coots-oo-pah, commonly known as "Roan Chief," was over seven feet tall, spare and muscular. A photograph taken while in Buffalo Bill's Wild West Show, probably in 1885, leaves the impression that he would have been ready at a moment's notice to start trailing an enemy. Born near Fremont, Nebraska, about 1849; died at his home five miles south of Pawnee, Oklahoma, in 1919. He was of the Chaui band, and married into and became one of the chiefs of the Pitahauerat band. Two sons, Clyde Roan Chief and Harry Richards survived him.

Information is from caption under picture in Robert Bruce's *The Fighting Norths and Pawnee Scouts* (published with the cooperation and approval of the Nebraska State Historical Society, Lincoln, Nebraska), p. 59.

CHAPTER 16

1. The Overland Trail was selected by General Dodge as a route by which mail stages would bypass that stretch of the Oregon-California Trail believed then most infested by hostile Indians.

2. The August 7, 1864, "massacre" occurred a half mile east of the Plum Creek stage station and three quarters of a mile from the Thomas ranch where Lieutenant Bowen, with a small detachment of the Seventh Iowa Cavalry, watched a hundred Cheyenne Indians attack the wagon train. The soldiers were too few to go to the aid of the train of ten wagons, but sent a messenger to Fort Kearny for reinforcement. Not until late afternoon could soldiers come to the scene. Col. Samuel W. Summers and 2nd Lt. Francis J. Comstock with seventh Iowa Cavalrymen buried the dead: Michael Kelly of Saint Joseph, Missouri, and five men hired to drive wagons loaded with machinery and corn; Thomas Frank Morton and his wife, Nancy Jane, 19, from Iowa; Charles Iliff and wife Mabel, and a boy (probably a relative), William Fletcher; Smith and partner from Council Bluffs. Mrs. Morton and the boy with the Iliffs survived in captivity. Traced to the Big Horn wilderness, they were ransomed the following spring and Mrs. Morton was returned to her parents in Sidney, Iowa. She became the wife of George W. Stevens and the mother of three children, and died in 1912. Mrs. Stevens wrote her memoirs, published in 1937. A granite marker was dedicated at the massacre site after Phelps County, Nebraska, obtained the historic area in November of 1930.

   Northwest several miles from the Plum Creek stage station is the town of Lexington, known in its beginning as Plum Creek Village. In 1867, only a few miles west of this place, Chief Turkey Leg and his band wrecked and plundered a Union Pacific combination construction-freight train. William Thompson, an Englishman, though scalped, survived, found his scalp and took it in water to Omaha in hopes a doctor could regraft it. This was unsuccessful and his wound healed without it.

3. Fort Cottonwood Spring was renamed Fort McPherson. When the fort was abandoned, the name was retained for the National Cemetery of Nebraska.

4. Jack Morrow, a bull-train boss, took squatter's rights on the "flats" on the south side, and back of, the bluffs overlooking the main trail through the Platte Valley, where he established a trading post. Known to be a squaw man, Morrow became notorious for extortion from travelers. Once an

immigrant came to his post leading a fine-looking horse. Old Jack knew that horse would match one he had back in his pasture. For that reason he paid a stiffer price in trade than he ordinarily would have, anticipating a fancy price for the matched team. The immigrant left. Jack Morrow sent for the horse that Indians had snatched from an immigrant train. That horse was not found, and never was. Old Jack had just paid, for once, for a horse his henchmen had stolen.

The late William McDonald, born at Cottonwood Spring, June 14, 1861, and interviewed during the 1930s said: 'Jack Morrow had a squaw. Later, he got rid of her and got a white wife who was a good friend of my mother's. He was a notorious character and in his time was one of the two wealthiest men in the state."

5. Charles McDonald and his wife, Orra, arrived at Cottonwood Spring January 15, 1860, according to their eldest son, William McDonald, born June 14, 1861, in that place. The following is from this writer's interview in 1939 with William McDonald.

It wasn't long before father had a corral stockade seventy-five by one hundred feet, built east and west. My mother, in traveling ten miles one way, counted twelve hundred wagons. I remember seeing wagons in endless lines all day long, every day [in season] passing our ranch.

Ben Gallagher set in to supper October 30, 1863, [from the book]. He was the first sutler at Fort McPherson. He sold out, October, 1866, to Woodmen and Snell, and came to North Platte and opened a store. He had a ranch at Cottonwood, and later was one of the firm of Paxton and Gallagher.

We often saw stagecoaches come in all shot up. There had been an Indian uprising in 1864 . . . ranches burned between Fort Kearny and Denver, and what few people there were in the country got to a well-fortified place as fast as they could. I was still a small tot when that occurred. My mother took me and went, in August 1864, to Omaha on the stage. She stayed two months during which time there were no coaches running out this way. But she came back on the first stage allowed through and had no trouble whatever.

The next stage was attacked several times and had a horse killed. They [the driver and men riding the stage] cut the tugs to the dead horse and had a running fight with the Indians, to the John and Judd Gilman ranch and stage station, twelve miles east of Fort McPherson. The stage had expected the soldiers to meet it and escort it to Cottonwood Spring. Cody [William F.] based his last show on that battle.

The Sioux objected to so many travelers through their territory. General Mitchell tried to make a treaty with the Indians. He held a big pow-wow two miles from the fort, the Sioux to the west side and

Pawnee to the east. Sam Watts interpreted. The Indians made nasty signs across at each other. The Pawnee hated the Sioux, which was mutual, and the general failed in his treaty. Immediately after the pow-wow . . . a company of fifth Iowa Cavalry was sent from Fort McPherson to build Fort Sedgwick. Cy Fox was a private who went.

We used to have jerked buffalo, dried meat that a man put in his pocket and could chew on all day. It was good and it was strengthening. A piece of meat three-fourths by four or five inches would be cut for drying. It dried as hard as sole leather, and dark colored. If it was an old bull it made some real chewing. It was tough.

6. Cyrus (Cy) Fox came in 1864 to Cottonwood Spring, Nebraska Territory, with the fifth Iowa Cavalry, Company C. They were sent to guard mail stages and travelers on the Oregon-California Trail and were to build Camp Tone McKean with barracks, officer quarters, stables, and all buildings.

When this writer interviewed Mr. Fox, December 5, 1938, the old soldier, at ninety-three years of age, was a great figure of a man, powerfully built, still markedly erect, and decay of age seemed remote. His step was firm and brisk, his wit sharp and his laughter hearty. Excerpts from the interview follow:

The unwritten law was about the only law there was around here. Lots of devilment was laid to the Indians that they didn't know anything about. Not that they didn't do that kind of thing, but white men did, too.

This country the Indians tried the hardest to hold. When immigrants came through in the spring of 1865, we had to hold them until there was a pretty good bunch. It took three or four hundred men to go through Indian country safely. One couple was uneasy, and say, they were impatient! We had them in camp about a half mile from Fort McPherson for about two weeks. I had to stand guard over them at night to keep them from pulling out. I . . . talked to them, told them there was nothing in sight yet to make up a company. They seemed pretty satisfied. I went back to my officer and reported that I didn't think they would need a guard that night, and I left them unguarded.

In the night . . . they hitched up their four milk cows and left.

The next morning we were ordered to Julesburg . . . an Indian scare-out . . . the call came for soldiers from Fort McPherson, and we rallied to the call. On the way we saw a burnt wagon. The cows had been driven off and things taken and the wagon destroyed. The three little children and the couple were there in the ashes.

We had two or three real good times—we'd had twenty or thirty families there. We had them about a month. We'd clear off a place on the ground and dance every night. The boys [soldiers] could kick up more dirt than a windstorm.

One time we went to O'Fallons on stage escort. We always had to lay over four hours to escort the east-bound stage to Cottonwood Spring. That time, we had a good time with a family camped there that had been at Fort McPherson.

We felt no sympathy for the Indians. No. They had no sympathy for their victims, and they murdered whole trains of people. As old Murphy [Capt. Edward B. Murphy] used to say, "Lice make nits and nits make lice."

While soldiers in the Indian War felt and thought much as Mr. Fox expressed it, yet the attitude of the mountain man/guide/scout toward Indians was in the order of wary tolerance. Many became squaw men, and adapted to Indian life. They, and scouts of the next generation, such as Frank and Luther North and William F. Cody, practiced a live-and-let-live policy.

7. John Burke, a tireless worker, served the fort many years under various contracts. Peter Burke, youngest of nine sons and one daughter, himself about seventy years of age when this writer interviewed him in December 1938, mentioned contracts for furnishing hay, cordwood, logs for building, and garden truck and milk. His father logged out crossties for much of the railroad from Omaha.

When the Union Pacific came, his father took a contract for freighting to the fort from North Platte. Mr. Burke hauled heavy army wagons into the river, lined them up, securing them with logs, and built a corduroy bridge over the wagon base. This would sway in high water or under a heavy load, and the mules—three and four teams to a wagon—would crowd away from the sides. The hired teamster would sometimes panic or fail to control the teams and a load would tip into the river, drowning or injuring animals, tearing up harness and breaking wagons.

John Burke lost his life at this bridge, repairing it after a flood. Mrs. Burke then said to her youngest son, Peter, a student in Nebraska City, "Petie, you will have to quit school and take over the hired hands in the freighting." All of his brothers and the one sister were married and ranching. Peter Burke, at fifteen, fulfilled the contract himself, alone, after letting his hired help off because of their inept handling of the mules.

Mr. Peter Burke presented the land which Curtis, Nebraska, occupies, a part of his ranch of the original "flat-iron" brand. The cemetery just south of Maxwell (Pleasantview), was a part of his mother's homestead, which she gave for the purpose when selling her land.

The Burkes first squatted on the place west of the fort, were attacked and burned out by the Indians more than once, and had to run to the fort, losing stock and home. Their hired wood- and log-cutters were obliged to carry both gun and axe, some losing lives as well as stock to the Sioux and Cheyenne.

Parts of "Burke's Bridge" wagons still appear in this area of the Platte River, also the canyon logging road.

8. Veteran of twenty-two years of early telegraphy in Indian country, Mr. Searle was a pioneer Nebraskan and an early settler at Ogalalla, Nebraska, where his name continues in businesses he founded.

9. August 7, 1864. Cheyenne Indians raiding along the Little Blue in southeastern Nebraska Territory attacked the Eubank's Road ranch stage station killing a number of stage men and settlers. Mrs. Eubank saw her husband killed and scalped, and she and her baby son, one-and-a-half years old, and three-year-old daughter, Isabelle, were carried into captivity with Laura Roper, age sixteen. Mrs. Eubank survived more than a year of barbarous slavery.

She was carried to Wyoming and sold to Chief Two Face, and later rescued by Fort Laramie soldiers. Her testimony may be read in the Special Senate Report, 39th Congress. The woman's statements doomed the two Indians, Two Face and Black Foot, who were hanged. Mrs. Eubank was returned to relatives in Laclede, Missouri, and died in McCune, Kansas, Crawford County, April 4, 1913.

William Joseph Eubank was the infant. The child survived captivity and was rescued by the army. He grew to manhood in Kansas and Colorado, married, raised a family, and died in 1935 at about seventy-three years of age. Mrs. Jack Lingelbach of Omaha was a granddaughter, and Arthur Eubank of Gordon, Nebraska, was a grandson.

Miss Laura Roper, sixteen-year-old daughter of William Eubank, Jr., was visiting the Eubanks at their farm-stage station and was captured with the others by the raiding Cheyenne along the Little Blue, near present-day Oaks, Nebraska. Mr. Eubank, his four brothers, a sister and his father, and sister Dora, 16, and brother-in-law John Palmer and a neighbor, Mr. Kennedy, were killed as were about fifty other settlers during August 1864.

Miss Roper and Isabelle were not taken north, but a few weeks later Major Wynkoop, first Colorado Volunteers, effected a rescue of them and another child and brought them to Fort Lyon, Colorado, September 11, 1864. Miss Roper was returned to Fort Kearny and went to Pennsylvania. She married and spent the rest of her life in Oklahoma. In 1929, Mrs. Laura Roper Vance returned to visit Nebraska where she told the story of her own and the Eubanks' kidnap before the Nebraska Historical Society.

The fate of little Isabelle Eubank was a mystery until 1959. Don Danker, archivist of the Nebraska Historical Society, was preparing to publish a diary written by Mrs. Mollie Sanford, who after her marriage went from near Nebraska City to Denver, and discovered the clue in Mrs. Sanford's memoirs. She had written of hospitably caring for a young woman and two children who had been rescued, and of adoption of little Isabelle by a Dr. Bondsall.

Mrs. Eubank never learned what became of her daughter. Her son, William, never found any trace of his sister though he lived in Kansas and in Pierce, Colorado. Perhaps the child's mental derangement from the Indians' torture, her condition when rescued as described by Major Wynkoop in his book, *A Small Remnant*, explains in part why her family never found her. (Also see: *Official Records, Union and Confederate Armies*, Vol. 84, pp. 612, et. seq.)

The two chiefs who were hanged were found some time later to have been working to deliver Mrs. Eubank to the officers who had them hung. The two chiefs had bartered for the woman from her captors and were within hours of getting her back to her own kin when captured and brought to Fort Laramie, where they were summarily hanged.

CHAPTER 17

1. From the religious song *Rejoice All Ye Believers*, composed by Lauretius Laurenti in 1700, translated by Mrs. Sarah B. Findlater in 1854, music by Henry Smart, 1836.
2. Platte Bridge Stockade was named in November 1865, by order of Maj. Gen. Pope, to be "Fort Casper in honor of Lieutenant Casper Collins, 11th Ohio Cavalry, who lost his life while gallantly attacking a superior force of Indians at this place." The young lieutenant was the son of Col. William O. Collins, eleventh Ohio Cavalry. Fort Collins, Colorado, was named in the elder's honor. See *The Bozeman Trail*, by Hebard and Brinistool (1922), and *The Indian War of 1864*, by Capt. Eugene F. Ware (University of Nebraska Press, 1961; reprint), pp. 120, 216-17.
3. Brig. Gen. P. E. Connor on March 30, 1865, took command of the District of the Plains. *The Fighting Cheyenne*, by George B. Grinnell (Charles Scribner's Sons, New York, 1915), p. 195. Also *The Indian War of 1864* (Ware, Crane & Co., 1911; reprinted., Bison Book, St. Martin Press, 1963), p. 402.
4. Grinnell, *The Fighting Cheyenne*, p. 161. Also *Official Records of the Union and Confederate Armies*.
5. Grinnell, *The Fighting Cheyenne*, p. 195 footnote: "Connor's orders to Cole and Walker are in the Official Records, vol. 102, pp. 1045-49. Connor orders Cole to kill all males (hostiles) over twelve years."

CHAPTER 18

1. George B. Grinnell, *The Fighting Cheyenne*, p. 196, provides a vivid word picture of this beautiful area (Lincoln, 1885) or, see *Transactions and Reports, Nebraska Historical Society*, vol. 11, p. 206.
2. From the religious song *Ten Thousand Times Ten Thousand*, by Rev. Henry Alford, music by John R. Dykes.
3. Ski-ri Taka, the Pawnees' symbol of war. The name was conferred on a leader who had covered himself with glory and was a very high honor. The new name bestowed upon Frank North was a truly stupendous honor, acclaiming him, a white man, as their Pawnee chief (which is the meaning of Pani La Shar). As North had no chieftainship ambition, he consented to accept the title as Pawnee Leader.

CHAPTER 19

1. The two companies of sixth Michigan left to garrison Camp Connor stayed at the wilderness post an entire year before General Carrington came in 1866, leaving a contingent from his force to relieve them.
2. In military parlance General Connor's act was a precipitation, an unwise or rash and headlong rush.
3. George B. Grinnell, *The Fighting Cheyenne*, chap. 16, p. 200, gives an excellent version of this incident.

CHAPTER 20

1. The cannon shot heard was from the 1865 Sawyer Road layout crew defending against Indian attacks which occurred near the Bozeman Road crossing of the Sioux City to Virginia City trace. An escort was subsequently supplied by General Connor.
2. By the mid 1830s much of the trans-Missouri River country had been seen by army expeditions following the paths of fur trappers and traders along waterways, but shunning the inland wildernesses. Governeur Kemble Warren, West Point graduate and topographical engineer, assigned briefly in 1855 to Fort Pierre, was probably the first to cross from there south to the Platte River. Ordered in August to join Gen. William S. Harney at Fort Kearny to serve with the general's punitive expedition in September 1855, against the Brule Sioux following the Grattan incident, Warren found insufficient time to go by boat down the Missouri River to a point from whence he might go west over land to Fort Kearny. After consulting an American Fur Company agent, Warren, with a few half-breed Dakotas and another white man, braved the unknown but direct route. In slightly more than two weeks he gathered much essential infor-

mation. See Governeur K. Warren, "Explorations in the Dakota Country in the year 1855" (Washington: A.O.P. Nicholson, Senate Printer, 1856), p. 21.

3. The east wing of the Powder River Expedition, Colonel Cole's division, traversed northwest Nebraska's and South Dakota's Bad Lands, a nightmarish region of rock of weird forms and regions of sand.

4. The mountains near the juncture of the Tongue River and the Wyoming-Montana state line now known as Wolf Mountains were earlier called Panther Mountains.

5. Cole's complaints of terrain and hardship are strikingly similar to those Warren penned eight years earlier, in July and August 1857. During his third topographical survey he traversed virtually the same route as Cole's. See G. K. Warren, "Preliminary Report of Explorations in Nebraska and Dakota in the Years 1855, 1856, 1857" (Government Printing Office, Washington, D.C., 1875).

6. The brothers, Nicholas and Antoine Janis, variously spelled Janisse, Janic, etc., married Ogalalla women at Fort Laramie and reared large families. Antoine, the older, died at Pine Ridge Reservation, probably 1897. Nicholas died about 1905. They were of French descent and their language was French. Their boyhood friend James Bordeaux, born in Saint Charles County, Missouri, as were the Janises, hired them and their brother-in-law, Sefray Iyott, and Leon Palladay and brought them to the country of the upper Platte River where they were employed by the American Fur Company until Bordeaux sold Fort William trading post to Fremont to be used as a military fort. The older Janis brother moved with his family to Colorado, and after 1868 and the treaty the Sioux-related people came back around the Platte. Grinnell believes (see footnote, p. 126, *The Fighting Cheyenne*) that when the Ogalalla Sioux were moved from Fort Laramie to the Missouri River Whetstone Agency, Iyott, called Jarrot in the reports, was appointed agent of the Upper Platte in 1864-65. From the Whetstone agency the Janises subsequently moved to the Pine Ridge Reservation where, according to Grinnell, they remained. Nicholas was often employed as a Sioux language interpreter, and as a guide. (Information from Grinnell, *The Fighting Cheyenne*, Scribner's Sons, 1915. Also the Nebraska State Historical Society Elia S. Ricker Interviews: with Mrs. Nicholas Janis, Tablet 8; with William Garnett, Tablet 22; Ricker Collection.)

7. In the spring of 1864 an expedition under Gen. Alfred Sully marched from the head of the Cannon Ball River to Heart River, where they fought and drove the Sioux south toward the Black Hills and into the region between the Platte and Yellowstone rivers and east of the Big Horn area, where the Sioux began harassing Oregon Trail travelers and settlers.

CHAPTER 22

1. James Murie emigrated from Scotland. He married a Pawnee woman, served as second lieutenant in the Pawnee Scouts in 1865 on the Powder River campaign, and subsequently as first lieutenant and as captain. Rank depended upon the number of scout companies enlisted in any year. Captain Murie died in the Grand Island, Nebraska, Soldiers' Home. His son, James R. Murie graduated from Carlisle Indian School and was interested in the preservation of Pawnee history and lore. *Nebraska History*, No. 4, p. 16; No. 39, p. 112, fn.

2. Luther North enlisted and was mustered into the second Nebraska Cavalry in October 1862. The regiment was detailed to garrison the Pawnee Reservation. The troops, including Luther, left in the spring on the Sully Expedition and participated in the White Stone Hill, North Dakota, engagement and running fight. (Luther North, *Man of the Plains*, University of Nebraska Press, 1961, p. 12.)

3. See, *Gun Collector's Handbook of Values*, Howard-McCann, Inc., New York, 1951, p. 272; also see Harold L. Peterson, *The Pageant of the Gun*, Doubleday. The Spencer carbine was the arm tested, admired, and ordered by Lincoln; he reordered several times before obtaining any. It was also used by some members of Berdan's sharpshooters. The 8.75-pound, 37-inch, .50-caliber weapon took a rim-fire copper cartridge carrying black powder and was a seven-shot. It was much used in the Civil War and in Indian fighting. The manufacturer also made other calibers.

4. The Republican River rises in northeast Colorado and flows east for two hundred miles along the Nebraska-Kansas border, then turns south by east and joins the Kansas River.

5. The area was full of many kinds of game. Traders along the Missouri River brought many beaver furs and hides from the Republican and tributary valleys. Indians knew it as the country in which America's greatest herd of bison wintered, moving from it northward as far as the Yellowstone in summer and into Canada, and in winter migrating south as far as the Arkansas River, sometimes as far as Texas. See Dr. W. T. Hornaday, "The Extermination of the American Bison," 1887 Annual Report of the Smithsonian Institute; also see, Marie Sandoz, *The Buffalo Hunters*.

6. See Harold L. Peterson, *The Pageant of the Gun*. The Ballard was a breechloader, single shot, and its action was by lever. It was made in several calibers and took a rim-fire cartridge.

7. Robert Bruce, *The Fighting Norths and Pawnee Scouts*, pp. 33, 34, (Quoting Luther North) ". . . My boys said afterward that the Indians didn't stop for the first and second volleys from the carbines, but broke in all directions at the third. We moved slowly down to Driftwood Creek (the dry wash at the time) finding some of our enemies in possession . . . My

boys were so well mounted that they could easily have ridden away if they had been willing to leave me to my fate; but with odds of some 15 to 1 against them, they jumped off their horses, formed a circle about me, fought it out and saved my life—which took cast iron nerve. Is it any wonder that I have always stood up for the Pawnee Scouts?"

8. Between the forks of the Platte River General Dodge laid out the city of North Platte, which in 1866-67 was the end of track, the railroad reaching that point in November 1866. The "Hell on Wheels" tent city of several thousand railroad laborers spent the winter here. With spring the population nearly deserted North Platte, and Sidney became the next tent city.

9. Luther North Collection, Letters, Nebraska State Historical Society.

10. Robert Bruce, *The Fighting Norths*, p. 17. Caption under picture: "Crooked Hand, of the Too-Heets-Pee-Ott clan, Skeedee (Loup or Wolf) band, The Great Pawnee Warrior."

"Never a chief or an army scout, but personally known to the Norths . . . Simon Adams, Us sah Kip pe re La Shar, son of Crooked Hand, lived in 1926 in Oklahoma, and was totally deaf." The son's name has no connection with his sire's name. The hereditary or surname system was not used among the Pawnees until after their removal to Oklahoma.

Robert Bruce, *The Fighting Norths*, quotes Capt. Luther H. North, p. 18:

Crooked Hand, Ska dicks, though never one of our scouts, was among the greatest of Pawnee fighting men, and several times made his prowess felt, particularly by the Sioux. . . . I believe . . . he had a broken leg in a fight with the Cheyennes in 1852. . . .

I not only knew him very well, but considered him one of my best friends. Crooked Hand was about 5′7″ in height, and unlike most of the old time Pawnees, wore his hair long. It was also fine and wavy, instead of straight and coarse. . . . He was active and swift in his motions, quick spoken, good natured and humorous, but also quick tempered—and in battle a raging savage. I was at the Pawnee Reservation the day when Crooked Hand killed six Sioux with his own hand and three horses were shot under him; and personally saw him on his return to the village that evening.

He was covered with blood, and a Sioux arrow had been driven through his neck from the front as he was facing one or more of his antagonists. It had gone into his throat on one side of the windpipe, and about half the length of the arrow protruded from the back of his neck. The old Indian doctor at the Reservation had to cut off the iron head before he could pull it out. Crooked Hand was laid up for sometime and his throat probably never healed; but he lived ten to eleven

years after the fight and killed some more enemies of his people. . . .
As near as I can tell he died in 1873, in the prime of life, at about forty or forty-five years of age. A letter written by J. Sterling Morton in
the early '60s states that he was born with a deformed hand . . .
notwithstanding which he seemed to have done very well.

At one time when he had plenty of scalps, some white man said, "I
suppose you are not afraid anymore, as you have been so lucky in battle?" Crooked Hand answered, "Every enemy I kill brings me so much
nearer my own death. Who knows but that I have killed enough, and
will be the next?" There is a rare bit of philosophy in that reply from a
savage warrior.

I've heard it said among the Pawnee that their greatest warrior,
Crooked Hand, had killed more than one hundred of the Pawnee's
enemy, but was a good friend of the white man. At the scalp dance
when he had killed the six Sioux [and was wounded, yet appeared]
. . . wearing a robe made of the hide of a black and white steer and
fastened around the border of the robe were seventy-one scalps that he
had taken.

11. The men appointed by North were Corux-to Puk, Fighting Bear; Tee-
rah-wat La Shar, Spirit or Sky Chief; Ska Lah Tah La Shar, Lone Chief,
and Peta La Shar, Man Chief.

12. The temporary boom towns, tents, and ramshackle buildings that came
with the railroad grading and construction crews were called "Hell on
Wheels."

13. Rails were laid past Platte City or North Platte, ending at O'Fallons Station in 1866, which shortened hauls of passenger and mail stage coaches
and ox- and mule-drawn freight trains by nearly four hundred miles in
one year—a year ahead of the congressional deadline.

14. Information from Silas Seymour, "Incidents of a Trip Through the Great
Platte Valley, to the Rocky Mountains and Laramie Plains, in the Fall
of 1866, with a Synoptical Statement of the Various Pacific Railroads,
and an Account of the Great Union Pacific Railroad Excursion to the
One Hundredth Meridian of Longitude" (D. Van Nostrand, New York,
1867), pp. 82-109. Reprinted in Nebraska History, Vol. 50, No. 1, pp.
27-53.

CHAPTER 23

1. Nebraska History, Vol. 41, No. 3. "Henry James Hudson and the Genoa
Settlement," p. 201, edited by Marguerette R. Burke (granddaughter of
the early German settler at Cottonwood Spring, and of an earlier settler
of Columbus, a Swiss immigrant, John Rickly).

Henry James Hudson was born in London, England, in 1822. He became a convert to Mormonism several years before emigrating to America with his wife in 1851. In 1856 Hudson, with others, delegated by the church to establish colonies, visited Nebraska Territory. In May of the next year he helped found a settlement of 110 Mormon families where Genoa is now located.

After the colony was abandoned in 1859, Hudson removed to Columbus, Nebraska. He was a member of the Nebraska Legislature for one term, 1871-72, and held a number of public offices, among them, postmaster, justice of the peace, county commissioner, and county judge. (Margaret Curry, "History of Platte County, Nebraska," Chicago, 1915. I. 60, 281; Mrs. Albert J. Galley, MS Notes.)

2. The so-called death warrant, and information on the murder and hanging are from Andreas, "History of Nebraska (Platte County)" Western Historical Co., Chicago, 1882.

3. Miss Marguerette Burke (see fn. 1, this chapter) informed this writer that she remembered the "hanging tree" which stood for many years. On a later visit to Columbus she missed the tree and learned it had been removed.

4. A member of the Arnold family, with whom Frank and James North moved to Columbus.

5. James Murie: See Chapter 22, fn. 1.

6. C. E. Morse, born about 1840 in New York State, moved with his family to Illinois in the 1840s. Went to California about 1859, returned and settled in Columbus, Nebraska. There, on December 24, 1868, Capt. Charles E. Morse was married to Maj. Frank North's sister, Alphonsine North.

7. Fred Matthews, born 1831 in Canada, died 1890, is buried in the Pioneers Columbus Cemetery not far from the graves of Major and Mrs. Frank (Mary) North.

8. Gustavus G. Becher, born Pilsen, Bohemia, died 1913 at Columbus. Emigrated to America in 1847 with his parents, and came to Columbus in 1856. He served as an officer in the Pawnee Scouts after which Gustavus became a real-estate dealer and in 1895 was elected to the legislature.

9. Big Hawk Chief (variously, Black Hawk Chief; see L. H. North, *Man of the Plains*, p. 42), Koo-tah-we-coots-oo-lel-e-hoo La Shar, a Pawnee Scout, "One of my favorites," quoting Capt. Luther H. North in Robert Bruce, *The Fighting Norths and Pawnee Scouts*, p. 35.

The Pawnees were great runners, and 40 miles a day was easy for them. Early in July, 1870, I took some horses from the Pawnee Agency, Nebraska, to Fort Harker, Kansas. (This refers to the voluntary return of some horses stolen from the Cheyenne of Indian Territory in the fall of 1869, by a raiding party led by Big Spotted Horse. At that time the Indian Bureau was under Quaker influences; and attempts were made to adjust such matters by the Golden Rule. Between 30 and 40 horses remaining from that herd in the early summer of 1870 were taken by L. H. North and a few Indians (Pawnee) to Fort Harker where they were turned over to another agency and returned to the Cheyennes.)

The agent sent 7 Indian boys to drive them. They were mounted on the going trip and seven days on the way; but we returned the 250 miles in five days, with them all afoot.

I rode a mighty good horse, but he had about enough the last day. We would start around 5 o'clock in the morning, and by 9 be about 25 miles on the way; then lay down during the head of the day, taking another 25 mile jog in the evening. No matter how hilly it was, they would make those 25 mile jaunts in four hours.

[Ibid. p. 35, feats by Big Hawk Chief (quoting Luther North)]. In '76 or '77 . . . he (Big Hawk Chief) ran from Pawnee Agency to the Wichitas, a distance of about 120 miles, inside of 24 hours. The Wichita chief wouldn't believe it, and when the Hawk was ready to start home, asked if he could run back in the same time.

When he said he could, the skeptical chief sent a relay horse ahead about 60 miles, and told the Pawnee that he would go along. They left at sunrise, the Wichita Chief mounted and Big Hawk Chief afoot. Before reaching the relay horse, the old Chief's first one gave out.

Big Hawk went right on, and the Wichita Chief saw no more of him on that trip. Reaching the Pawnee village before sunrise, less than 24 hours after their start from the Wichitas, the Chief found the great runner asleep in his own lodge. They said he came in during the night . . . making the 120 miles in about 20 hours—up and down hill, across country with numerous streams and other natural obstacles. . . .

. . . While at Sidney after coming down from the Dull Knife Expedition, another man and I timed him (Big Hawk) both with stop watches. He ran the first half in 2 minutes flat and the second in 1.58, or the mile in 3.58—so much faster than ever done before that we didn't believe the track was right, and had it remeasured with a steel tape. I had him run again. To this day no man has ever equaled it. . . .

10. See George B. Grinnell, *Two Great Scouts*, Clark Co., Cleveland, 1928, p. 141, gives the number of attacking Indians as about a hundred; nine soldiers of Fort Sedgwick were killed.

11. T. A. Larson, *History of Wyoming*, University of Nebraska Press, 1965, p. 41. "People were excessively prone to aid and abet deserters," reported Captain Henry Mizner, commanding officer at Fort John Buford (tempo-

rary name of Fort Sanders) in July 1866. "These ranchmen," Mizner asserted, "concealed deserters and bought horses, mules, arms, clothing and other government property from them."

L. H. North, *Man of the Plains*, University of Nebraska Press, 1965, p. 54, reports this incident, pointing out, "for the remainder of the time we were with him, there was a Pawnee Indian Scout on guard over the tent of the head of the United States Army, and there were no more horses stolen from the staff officers."

12. Granite City was a railroad construction camp eighteen miles west of present Cheyenne, Wyoming.

13. Fort Sanders, briefly known as Fort John Buford, was about 18 miles south of where Lander, Wyoming, is located.

CHAPTER 24

1. T. A. Larson, *History of Wyoming*, 1965, University of Nebraska Press, p. 39.

2. Ibid.

3. Ibid, p. 40.

4. Ibid, p. 41. Early in 1867 L. L. Hills, chief of a surveying crew, was killed by Indians east of where General Dodge located Cheyenne a few months later. In west-central Wyoming, on Bitter Creek, Indians three times attacked a surveying party, killing two men, and in the final attack killed Percy T. Brown, chief surveyor.

5. Chap. 16, this book, fn. 7, on John Burke of Cottonwood Spring.

6. Bruce, *The Fighting Norths*, p. 30; also Nebraska State Historical Society Collections: Frank North and Luther North diaries, letters, papers, clippings, and mss.

7. Bruce, *The Fighting Norths*, "Record of this engagement will be found on p. 429 of Heitman's Historical Register and Dictionary, of the United States Army, Vol. 2, in which the date is given as August 17, 1867; the place Near Plum Creek, Nebraska, and the troops engaged—Pawnee SCOUTS." The official report, General Orders No. 39, Headquarters, Department of the Platte, Omaha, Nebraska, August 27, 1867. By command of Bvt. Maj. Gen. C. C. Augur, Department Commander, H. G. Litchfield, Acting Assistant Adj. Gen., and endorsed by William H. Bisbee, Capt., 27th Infantry, Aide-de-Camp. Also, George B. Grinnell, *The Fighting Cheyenne*, p. 254.

8. G. B. Grinnell, *The Fighting Cheyennes*, p. 258. "A runner—"; Robert Bruce, *The Fighting Norths*, p. 30 (center of page) gives slightly different version: ". . . When he (Frank North) entered the tent where the chiefs were assembled, Turkey Leg . . . recognized him, and through his interpreter asked Frank if he had some prisoners." The *Omaha Weekly Herald*,

September 26, 1867, printed a melodramatic account of the exchange of
prisoners. For this in part, see L. H. North, *Man of the Plains*, p. 75.

9. That the buffalo came from under ground, originally, was a traditional
belief of the Pawnee Nation, according to Grinnell.

10. George B. Grinnell, *The Fighting Cheyenne*, p. 259.

11. See, T. A. Larson, *History of Wyoming*, p. 42. Also fn. 5.

12. Ibid., p. 43.

13. Bruce, *The Fighting Norths*, pp. 28-29, presents L. H. North's version.
"I'll bet," quoting L. H. North's comment, "the Sioux and Pawnees were
never that near together before without a battle. About 150 of them were
warriors, and I presume that if they hadn't had a lot of women and children along, we would have mixed anyhow. Of course I don't know how it
would have finished, but there would have been another entry in the official records under the head of indian engagements, anyhow. That was
another illustration of my brother's way in meeting an emergency."

14. The *Omaha Weekly Herald*, October 17, 24, 1867. "The Union Pacific
sponsored this excursion of newspaper men and railroad officials to end-
of-track. Thomas Clark Durant, vice president of the railroad, organized
the Credit Mobilier, the construction company which built the U.P.
Oakes Ames, Congressman from Massachusetts [1863-73] was also an organizer of Credit Mobilier and a director of the U.P. He was censored by
the Forty-second Congress for his part in the financial manipulations in-
volved in the building of the Union Pacific. Ames and his associates
brought about Durant's removal from the management shortly after the
railroad was completed.

"George Francis Train [1829-1904] was promoter, author and eccen-
tric. He was chief of publicity for the new railroad, boomed townsites,
and built many a paper city. The Ebullient Train reported on the progress
of the excursion in telegraphic dispatches and often referred to it afterward in speeches. By his count, the excursionists killed eighteen buffalo."

15. L. H. North, in *Man of the Plains*, p. 64, states: ". . . My brother's wife
and our sister, who was sixteen years old, were in the thick of the chase
and had as much fun as anyone. I think this was the only buffalo hunt
that either of them ever took part in."

16. *September 30, 1867.* Report of Maj. Gen. C. C. Augur, Commander
Dept. of the Platte, Omaha, Nebraska [slightly condensed].

THE UNION PACIFIC AND PAWNEE SCOUTS

The rapid extension of the Union Pacific Railroad has opened up a
new and attractive country, and towns spring up as if by magic along
its route. Besides being of great national importance, the railway is
very essential to the interest of the Department [of the Platte, Army]

in moving troops and supplies at a great saving of time and expense. I have therefor [sic] endeavored in every way possible to assist in its construction, deeming its completion even to the Black Hills [of Wyoming] as equivalent to a successful campaign.

During the entire summer [1867], the 30th Infantry, parts of the 4th and 36th, four companies of (the 2nd) Cavalry and four of Pawnee Scouts have been escorting engineers and commissioners and protecting grading and working parties. . . . The 200 Pawnee Indian Scouts authorized for this Department were all enlisted from the Pawnees and organized into four companies of 49 each under Major [Frank] North. . . .

They were officered from men, most of whom speak their language, and mounted on common Indian ponies. I have never seen more obedient or better behaved troops; they have done most excellent service. Should it be necessary to carry on war another year against the hostile tribes, I respectfully recommend that Congress be asked to permit me to organize three battalions of 400 each from the friendly tribe in this Department. It opens to those people a useful career, renders them tractable and obedient, educating and civilizing them more effectually than can be done in any other way.

They are peculiarly qualified for service on the Plains; unequalled as riders, know the country thoroughly, are hardly ever sick, never desert and are careful of their horses. I have never seen one under the influence of liquor, though they have had every opportunity of getting it. As the season for active operations closes, they can be discharged to go home and look after their families for the winter. This they prefer. I propose to discharge my Pawnee Scouts early in December.

CHAPTER 25

1. *Omaha Weekly Herald,* August 19 and 26, 1868, J. J. Aldrich, "Diary of Twenty Days Sport Buffalo Hunting on the Plains with the Pawnees Accompanied by Major Frank North U.S.A. and an escort of forty U.S. Pawnee Soldiers, Captains Morse and Matthews and four Private Gentlemen." The article names the "private gentlemen" as G. H. (Henry) Magee, a Chicago lawyer in later years; Sumner Oaks, son of the proprietor of the St. Charles Hotel which opened in Omaha in the spring of 1868; F. W. (Wayland) Dunn, editor of the Chicago Christian (Baptist) Freeman and later a teacher at Hillsdale College, Michigan, died in 1872.
2. *Omaha World Herald* feature.
3. George B. Grinnell, in *Two Great Scouts,* p. 155, verifies the incident of

the siege and shooting of the Indian with the small flag.

4. *Omaha Daily Herald,* letter to the editor by "One of the Whites," one of the news correspondents with the hunting expedition, in answer to "Blue Cloud."

5. Ibid.

CHAPTER 26

1. James Henry (Jim) Galley, born in England, was a driver with a bull-train freighting to Salt Lake in 1859. He returned as far as Columbus, Nebraska Territory, and settled. Galley enlisted with Luther North in the second Nebraska Cavalry; then became a merchant. The Galley name is carried on in Columbus. He became blind in later years and was still living on the same city block with Luther North, according to a letter written by L. H. North, December 7, 1928, to Dr. "Diamond Dick" Richard Tanner; the letter is in Luther North Collection, Nebraska State Historical Society, Lincoln.

2. "Lots of fun" was a frequent expression in this era of Maj. Frank North's life. It expressed his pleasure in good conversation, dancing, which he greatly enjoyed, and when in camp or bivouac such entertainment as individuals might offer in the way of elocutions, recitations, theatricals, and music when someone had a jew's harp, a harmonica, or, more rarely, a stringed instrument. "Lots of fun" also stated admiration for excellency in target shooting or marksmanship on the hunt.

3. The American House was the frame hotel constructed in Columbus in 1857-58. At the time North made mention of it in his diary, he and Mary held a lease on and were operating the hotel. Notice issued by the Internal Revenue tax collectors for the year was found in the Maj. Frank North Collection, Nebraska State Historical Society, Lincoln.

4. Willow Island was a railroad station twenty miles west of Plum Creek Station, now Lexington, Nebraska.

5. Lone Tree, named for a huge cottonwood landmark tree by the Overland Trail. Immigrants camped and built fires under the tree, and its base became so charred that it finally fell in a windstorm. Central City marks the site.

6. Luther North Collection, Nebraska State Historical Society, Lincoln. A letter Luther North wrote on Nov. 25, 1874, to his uncle, John Calvin North, describes his adventures in recovering his two horses, one a gift four days earlier from his youngest sister Alphonsine and her husband. Sioux Indians had broken into the stable on the Pawnee Reservation and stolen the horses and took them to the Whetstone Agency near Fort Randall on the Missouri River.

7. "I talked Nebraska strong," Frank North noted in his diary, Jan. 24,

1869, while visiting relatives in Ohio. His statement was representative of the early pioneers in Nebraska Territory. Seeing great possibilities in the land, and longing for nearness of kin and friends, they "talked Nebraska strong" by letter.

8. McPherson Station was north of Fort McPherson about three miles. About 1879 the Union Pacific bought the Kansas Pacific Railroad on which was also a McPherson Station. This Nebraska station and village was becoming widely known as Mac's well. Big John McCullough, 6 foot 5 inches, came in 1866 as a meat hunter for track layers. He then tended the railroad station's pumps and woodyard, opened a store and saloon in a sod building, and married the sister of the section-boss's wife, Miss Mary Ann Gallagher, while Luther North, who was engaged to marry her, was away trying to recover his stolen horses from the Indians. Apparently the abrupt marriage was a severe blow to him, as nearly thirty years passed before he married in 1898.

The "Maxwell" (error of spelling) sign was affixed to the railway depot but referred to Mac's well—the well in the hotel-saloon which Mac built just south across the rails. The well was located in his Irish wife's kitchen where immigrants and travelers came to pump and freely use water. The railroad station did not furnish water to the public. See *The Saga of Brady Island* by Mary Jane Meehan collaborating with Mary Francis Rielly, 1967, p. 28.

9. Robert Bruce, *The Fighting Norths and Pawnee Scouts*, quoting Luther North: "Traveling Bear, Co ruxa Kah Waddee, was about 6 feet tall, very muscular, weight about 200 pounds. He had a frank, open countenance, was outspoken, and looked straight at you with his brown eyes (unusual in an Indian). Though apparently rather serious, he was generally pleasant; but in battle a whirlwind—and I do not think he was ever afraid of anything.

"In 1867 when we had some Union Pacific officials hunting near Fort Kearny the Bear shot an arrow entirely through a buffalo—a feat that he probably never duplicated. The only other Indian I ever heard of nearly equalling it was Two Lance, the Sioux Warrior. . . . I never heard of any white man even killing a buffalo with bow and arrow—much less shooting an arrow through one."

Fighting Bear lost his family in the 1873 Sioux massacre of the buffalo hunting Pawnee, near the Republican River and present day Trenton. A granite memorial marker at the head of the canyon overlooks the site known as Massacre Canyon.

10. Big Island was McCullough Island.

11. Lt. Gustavus G. Becher born 1844 in Pilsen, Bohemia. Came to America with his family at age of three, and to Nebraska Territory where his father was one of the Columbus founders. Dealt in real estate and had a

term in the legislature. He served several times as an officer of the Pawnee Scout organization. Died 1913.

12. Bvt. Brig. Gen. William Myers was stationed in Omaha as chief quartermaster of the Department of the Platte.

13. Fort Harker was in Kansas, near the old Sante Fe Trail crossing of the Smoky Hill River.

14. The Glasgow steamboat was on the Missouri and Mississippi rivers from the early 1860s until it sank somewhere off Louisiana more than a decade later.

15. At this time Major North's bouts with asthma—"tissic" he calls it—appear to be more frequent and severe.

16. The baby girl was named Stella. His daughter was in her midteens when her father died in 1885, two years after her mother's death. Her grandmother, Mrs. Jane North, and "the best brother a man ever had" (the Major's words), Stella's uncle Luther North, maintained the home until Stella's marriage to Edwin H. Chambers, telegrapher and depot agent. To them was born only one child, Helen Marguerite, who died of diphtheria at five years of age. Stella North Chambers lived past ninety years and died in 1960, almost totally deaf.

17. Although he resided at Columbus, Charles Whaley was the Pawnee agent, 1867-69 and was succeeded by J. Troth. George H. Hyde, *Pawnee Indians,* Denver University, 1951, p. 217.

18. Brady was about ten miles east of Maxwell, Nebraska, earlier called McPherson Station, a stagecoach, freighters, and after 1866, passenger station. The village took the name of the island lying south, in the Platte River.

19. Wanting the support of the Pawnee chiefs in disciplining and teaching the young Pawnee Scouts, Frank North laid his problem before the Pawnee Council. He explained that, since the young braves were enlisted in the army as scouts they must stay until permitted to leave, either by coming to him for a paper of permission or until they were dismissed and sent home.

CHAPTER 27

1. Correspondence, dated May 31, 1869, from Gov. David Butler of Nebraska, to Gen. C. C. Augur. Records of United States Army Commands: Selected Documents, Hq. Dept. of the Platte. Letters Received, 1867-69. National Archives and Records Service (NARS) Record Group (RG) 98, MS Microfilm at Nebraska State Historical Society. This body of records is hereafter cited as NARS RG 98.

2. C. C. Rister, *Border Captives, the Traffic in Prisoners by the Southern Plains Indians,* Norman, Okla., 1940, p. 162, states that the Alderdice baby

was strangled by the Indians along the way to the Republican Valley.

3. Gen. C. C. Augur, information and excerpt from letter to Gov. David Butler, June 1, 1869. NARS RG 98.

4. Bvt. Maj. Gen. Eugene Asa Carr, assigned to command of the Republican River Expedition by General C. C. Augur, commanding officer, Department of the Platte, Omaha, Nebraska, June 7, 1869.

5. Pawnee House of the Genoa Pawnee Reservation was a brick schoolhouse built after Frank North had started leading the Pawnee Scouts. Andreas' *History of Nebraska,* p. 1125, gives Pawnee House as built in 1864, a two-storied building of 42 × 125 feet.

6. Bvt. Brig. Gen. Benjamin Alvord was chief paymaster of the Department of the Platte (Collins, p. 293).

7. Following his experience in the 1865 Powder River Expedition, Major North enlisted each company from a single Pawnee band. A company of Skeedees had captured a number of ponies from Indians; North returned these "spoils of war" to them. It was these with possibly others the scouts had bought or bartered for that he had taken the responsibility of shipping to the point nearest to the Skeedee scouts' home reservation.

8. The river was at near flood stage and the ponies were of those North had been ordered to buy (belatedly) by Colonel Litchfield when he came to muster in the Pawnees. With horses scarce, North was obliged to purchase the best "Indian ponies" available. After twelve or fourteen hours jammed in freight cars, the best of the poor lot of ponies was hardly up to swimming the Platte river.

9. From Fort Kearny Major North was ordered to proceed south with Company C, to find the Republican Valley Expedition and join General Carr's command. (Ruggles to North, June 11, 1869, NARS RG 98.)

10. Alfred Sorenson, "A Quarter Century on the Frontier, or The Adventures of Major Frank North," as told by Maj. Frank North. Manuscript in the archives of the Nebraska State Historical Society, from which Sorenson wrote a serialized biography that appeared in the *Omaha Weekly Bee,* starting December 6, 1886.

11. William Frederick Cody (Buffalo Bill), was assigned to General Carr in the 1868 winter campaign south from Fort Lyons, Colorado, into Texas against southern Plains tribes. Upon his being placed in command of the Republican River Expedition, Carr requested ". . . Particularly that the scout be retained with the regiment. . . ." From letter, Bvt. Maj. Gen. E. A. Carr to Bvt. Brig. Gen. G. D. Ruggles, May 22, 1869, NARS RG 98.

12. Letter, L. H. North to J. C. North, Nov. 28, 1874. MSS., Letters, and Papers of Luther Hedden North, 1874-1935, Nebraska State Historical Society. Hereafter cited as letter, L. H. North to J. C. North, Nov. 28, 1874, Nebraska State Historical Society.

13. Diary entry June 23, 1869, Maj. F. J. North.
14. Luther H. North, *Man of the Plains* University of Nebraska Press, 1961, p. 110. ". . . We sent the wounded man back to the fort with the train. The weather was very hot and his arm had no care in the five days it took them to get there.

". . . When the surgeon said the arm would have to be amputated, the man said he might die, but would not have his arm cut off.

"Then he was put on a train and sent home. The arm by this time was in an awful condition, badly swollen and full of maggots, but one of the Pawnee doctors took charge of him, and when we got home that fall he was all right, except that his wrist was stiff."
15. Report of Operations (Carr to Ruggles), June 30, 1869, to July 20, 1869, NARS RG 98.
16. As written in booklet carried in 1869 by Frank J. North.
17. The Pawnee had their own recipe for making a wiener-frankfurter type of delicacy: a strip of tender meat (the buffalo calf veal or loin meat), placed with water in a length of intestine, both ends tied, and then roasted in hot coals or on heated stones, producing the *co-wis* or *kawis*. Information, *Nebraska History*, Vol. 39, No. 2, p. 36, fn. 104.

CHAPTER 28

1. Report of Operations, June 30-July 20, 1869, NARS RG 98 Nebraska State Historical Society. "On the 4th of July believing that the Indians were near, I [General Carr] sent Bvt. Col. W. B. Royall with three companies of 5th Cavalry and one of Pawnee Scouts, amounting to about one hundred men with three days rations to follow the trail."

In General Carr's orders to Colonel Royall were, "You will try to surprise and kill as many warriors as possible and capture their families and animals."
2. The semicircular North Fork in eastern Colorado is roughly forty miles in length. The army obviously followed the stream's contour. This country was not strange to the Pawnee or to the Sioux and Cheyenne, it being part of the buffalo's favorite grazing ground.
3. A. Swanson, "A Quarter Century of the Frontier . . ." p. 136-37; also Diary, Maj. Frank J. North, entry July 7, 1869. Items in Nebraska State Historical Society, Lincoln, Nebraska.
4. General Carr reported "a number of Indians attacked . . ." Report of Operations, Carr to Ruggles, June 30-July 20, 1869, NARS RG 98, Ms, Microfilm. Nebraska State Historical Society.
5. Although unseen at the time and unknown by Pawnee Scouts or white men for many years, a second Cheyenne horse and rider tumbled in the Cheyennes' charge on the army camp. G. B. Grinnell, *The Fighting*

Cheyenne (New York, Scribner's Sons: 1915), p. 299:

"... During the Cheyenne charge on Carr's camp the horse ridden by Yellow Nose fell with him, and Yellow Nose was thrown and lost his horse. No one noticed the occurrence, but a little later, as the Cheyennes were returning to their camp, they found with them a loose horse. Yellow Nose was out for two nights then came into camp." Also, cf. Luther North, *Man of the Plains* (University of Nebraska Press, 1961), p. 111. "... A spring twenty feet from my tent and about the same distance back from the river ... had cut a channel two-three feet deep. ... After many years the Cheyenne had become friendly with the Pawnee, (and) told them one of the men that was in the charge was thrown from his horse and fell into the spring. He lay there until everything was quiet, when he crawled down the channel to the river, then down the river until he was clear of the camp."

6. Major North, Diary entry, July, Friday 9, 1869. "(Gus) Becher's Battleground," did not refer to Colonel Forsyth's fight of 1868 which occurred on an island in the Arickaree River approximately seventy-five miles south of the place North refers to. On July 6 the scouts under Lt. Gus Becher attacked and killed three of a small group of Cheyenne warriors. The place was nearly midway between Yuma and Sterling, Colorado, but perhaps twelve or fifteen miles east of a line between the towns, in sandhill country.

7. Report, Carr to Ruggles, July 20, 1869.

8. Letter, L. H. North to his uncle, J. C. North, Nov. 28, 1874, from Nebraska State Historical Society's Letters and Papers of Luther H. North: "... The next morning we left the Republican River and started north towards the Platte River, and traveled forty miles before we found any water, and when we did find it we found ourselves on the Indians' trail again and with a better prospect of catching them than ever before, for of course they had seen us turn back and thought we were going straight to Fort McPherson. I want to tell you right here, one of the Indians' failings. When he knows that an enemy is after him it is impossible to take him unawares, but let him think himself safe and he is the most careless being on earth."

9. Capt. George F. Price, *Across the Continent with the 5th Cavalry* (New York, 1883), p. 138, gives version of Cheyenne youth on fleet steed; see L. H. North, *The Plainsman*, (University Nebraska Press, 1961), p. 115.

10. George B. Grinnell, *The Fighting Cheyenne*, p. 306. Also, George B. Grinnell, *Two Great Scouts*, p. 197.

11. G. B. Grinnell, *The Fighting Cheyenne* (an excerpt from the Cheyennes' story of the Summit Springs battle as they told it to Mr. Grinnell): "... Tall Bull ... stabbed the Orange horse behind the foreleg. There in the ravine was where he expected to die." Alfred Sorenson, MS interview of

Major North about 1880, published *Omaha Bee,* May 1886: excerpt p. i40 of MS, in Nebraska State Historical Society. ". . . Major North and his brother, Captain Luther North, with a party of Pawnees and several soldiers surrounded one of the ravines into which a number of warriors and a squaw and child had fled for safety. One of the warriors, as was afterward learned, was the noted . . . Tall Bull to whom the squaw (woman) and child belonged. He and they were mounted on . . . orange colored horse, with silver mane and tail. Reaching the ravine he placed the squaw (woman) and child out of danger, and he . . . killed his horse . . . rather than see him fall into hands of his enemies. . . . One of the Indians climbed the bank nearest the soldiers, and raising his rifle slowly over the bank poking it up sufficiently to take a sight he fired directly at Major North but missed him. Major North marked where the Indian had dropped his head out of sight—aimed his gun at the spot. . . . He saw the rifle coming up . . . soon the Indian raised his head to take aim. Major North fired. The Indian dropped without shooting, directly below where he had climbed up."

Also, letter, L. H. North Collection, Nebraska State Historical Society, Luther North to his uncle, J. C. North, Nov. 28, 1874. Written five years after the Summit Springs event, his remembrance of that happening was yet fresh, unimpaired by forgetfulness of age, as some writers have accused in efforts to portray the fifth army scout, Wm. F. Cody, as the hero-killer of Tall Bull.

Moreover, Luther North was the only man present, exactly at the scene, besides Major North, who has left written word of the Tall Bull incident of the battle: ". . . and in fifteen minutes the fight is all over . . . and that big Bro. of mine had killed the chief, my sergeant [Corux a Kah Waddie, Traveling Bear] . . . killed four in this fight and was presented with a medal for his bravery. . . ."

Another paper, purportedly written by Major Walker, was discovered by Mrs. Nellie Snyder Yost. The penciled, faded and yellowed script was deciphered by her as well as was possible. In his narrative he says that he and his detachment, in crossing an unnoted bog or seep from the spring "foundered in the mire, but were soon crossed over the low ground."

He also states: "The Indians had the two women by the hair trying to pull them onto their ponies, and they were resisting. We were so close to them that I feared a stray bullet from my troops might kill them." This seems improbable.

12. Robert Bruce, *The Fighting Norths,* p. 19 ". . . Traveling Bear was specially mentioned in General Augur's order (number 48) of August 3, 1869, for bravery and gallant conduct in the battle of Summit Springs, Colorado, about three weeks before. He, and a white Corporal Kyle, 5th Cavalry, Co. M, received medals for that action, though it should be said in

explanation of an apparent discrepancy between this reference and General Augur's order number 48 that either the General or his adjutant confused the names of Mad Bear, Corux to Chodish, and Traveling Bear, Corux a Kah Wadde, but the latter rightfully received the medal." Also, cf., George B. Grinnell, *Two Great Scouts*, (Cleveland, 1928), p. 200; Luther North, *Man of the Plains* (University of Nebraska Press, Lincoln, 1961), pp. 119-20. Sgt. Traveling Bear was the medicine man who treated and saved the teamster's frozen feet as told in chapter 26.

13. Bruce, *The Fighting Norths*, p. 14-15. "At the battle of Summit Springs, July 11, 1869, I was struck by a spent ball which Captain Cushing picked up; it fortunately hit a square Government buckle, leaving a large black and blue spot—painful but not serious. That was fired by one of the Cheyennes we were driving out of Tall Bull's village. In the same fight an arrow clipped me over the eye, but luck was again with me and there was no permanent injury." Also, cf., Luther North, *Man of the Plains*, pp. 118-19.

CHAPTER 29

1. *Nebraska History*, Vol. 15, January-March, 1934, p. 54. Leon F. Palladay testified before a government commission in 1879 that he was forty-seven years old, living then at the Pine Ridge Agency, and had spoken the Sioux language for thirty-five years. He had been an interpreter with Spotted Tail's band of Sioux. Obviously, since the Cheyennes and Sioux interassociated, Palladay very well could have understood and even talked the Cheyenne tongue also. There is no record that the major mentioned his belief to any one that it was Tall Bull he had shot. After the command reached Fort Sedgwick, the interpreter, Leon Francois Palladay questioned the Cheyenne women prisoners and reported the woman who with her child had appealed to Major North for mercy said the major killed Tall Bull.

2. Early frontiersmen and tradesmen who knew the Cheyenne's restless habits called the tribe kites, because they were always flying off to somewhere else.

3. This northward march is known as "the Niobrara Pursuit."

4. No Cheyennes visited Nebraska again until the march of Little Wolf and Dull Knife with their people from Indian Territory (Oklahoma) in 1878.

5. Birdwood Creek flows into the North Platte River through Springdale and Birdwood Precincts in Lincoln County, Nebraska. From Plat Book of Lincoln County, Neb. (Rockford, Ill., W. W. Hixon Co.)

6. Forty-two horses unfit for further military service were given to the Pawnee on the condition they would be transported to the reservation with-

out expense to the government. This decision was made on August 14, 1869, by a two-man board composed of Colonel Royall and Major North. Proceedings of the Board of Officers, August 24, 1859, NARS, RG 98.

7. James C. Mitchell for whom Jim North had worked at Florence before coming west to Columbus.

8. The command traveled south from Fort McPherson through Cottonwood Canyon, then turned southwest and followed an old wagon road, used by wood and tie chopping details, for about seven miles along a ridge, turned left through a canyon "evidently the head of a small branch of the North Fork of the Medicine Lake Creek." The canyon was followed about three miles when the command reached running water and camped. Journal of the March of the Republican River Expedition consisting of B, C, and M Troops of 2nd Cavalry, A, B, E, F, I, L and M Troops of 5th Cavalry, Brev. Brig. Gen. Thomas Duncan, commanding; A, B, and C Troops of Pawnee Scouts, Major Frank North, commanding under Gen. Duncan NARS, RG 98.

9. The old stockade has not been identified. General Carr described it when he visited the locality on June 14, 1869. He wrote, "Reached the Republican River striking the bottom at a point about five or six miles below (east of) the mouth of the Medicine Lake Creek. An old and decayed defensive stockade was found on the north bank of the river at this point—by whom built or when, was unknown." ("Journal of the March," June 13, 1869, NARS, RG 98.)

10. North's and Cody's acquaintance, begun during General Carr's Republican River Expedition of 1869, with daily association in this later campaign under General Duncan, developed into friendship. That it was of lifelong endurance, withstanding adventures shared and even a business (that of a ranch partnership) without a ripple ever being known to come between the two dissimilar men, who yet had much in common, was proof of its quality. Cody, in 1909, staged a dramatic memorial appearance at the old cemetery of Columbus, Nebraska, and his graveside eulogy for his old friend yields the secret of their fine friendship.

11. Nelson Buck, with his surveying party of eight or nine men, had been killed on Beaver Creek, a southwest tributary of southwest Nebraska's Republican River. The Dunkin Expedition passed a destroyed camp where a tripod, tools, and camp equipment lay broken. Days later, an army detachment accompanied by young Buck seeking his father delivered a dispatch to Colonel Dunkin, still in the field, informing that the Nelson Buck surveying party was missing, and no word of them since leaving Fort Kearney in first week of August 1869—two and a half months earlier. Belatedly sure the destroyed camp was that of the surveyors, Dunkin ordered an officer and detachment to escort young Buck to

the site (near present Danbury, Red Willow County). There he identified his father's broken tripod and other articles.

12. The woman was questioned through the interpreter, John Y. Nelson,
whose Sioux wife was her cousin, and through a Ponca Indian serving
with the Pawnee Scouts. The Ponca talked to her in Sioux and translated her statements into Pawnee which Frank North translated into
English. She said that the band was led by Pawnee Killer, Whistler, and a
head soldier named Little Bull. She had lost her way in the fight and was
trying to walk to Spotted Tail's camp to the northward. Questioned later
at Fort McPherson, she stated she was Pawnee Killer's mother and Whistler was responsible for the hostility of the band. ("Journal of the
March," October 3, 1869, NARS, RG 98.)

13. Sky Chief, Tira Wahut La Shar, variously Tee rah Wat La Shar, head
chief of the Kit-ke-haki Pawnee band and brother to La Roo La Shar Roo
Cosh, Man that Left His Enemy Lying in the Water, the valiant hero
who bravely rode through the hostile Sioux warriors to get aid for Frank
North, Morse, and four or five scouts surrounded by numerous Sioux
near Mud Creek in 1868. Sky Chief was an outstanding orator. Upon
recorded occasion he evinced a judicial mind: his logic in addressing the
court in behalf of the four young Pawnee indicted and found guilty of the
McMurty murder; his concurrence with Peta La Shar and Eagle Chief in
bringing the problem of the Skeedees' use of meat from the other three
bands' cache to Frank North. His sound reasoning, no doubt, was a factor substantiating Peta La Shar's determined keeping of the peace, not
only with white folk, but also among the nation's bands. Sky Chief was a
victim of the Sioux in the Massacre Canyon affair in 1873. Information
from Bruce, *The Fighting Norths*, p. 20; *Omaha World Herald*, Aug. 4,
Nov. 5, 1869, reprinting from *Omaha Daily Herald* of Aug. 4, Nov. 5,
1869.

14. The Pawnees—Yellow Sun, Horse Driver, Little Wolf, and Blue Hawk—
were tried in the United States district court in Omaha for the murder of
Edward McMurty. All four were convicted. Upon conviction, Horse
Driver and Yellow Sun attempted suicide and Blue Hawk escaped as he
was being led from the courtroom and made his way back to the reservation. He was located there by North but refused to return to Omaha and
was supported by many members of the tribe. It was only after soldiers
were sent from Omaha that Blue Hawk consented to go back to jail. The
United States Circuit Court of Appeals reversed the decision on grounds
that the state of Nebraska should have tried the Indians because the murder was committed off the reservation. *Omaha Weekly Herald*, November
17, 24, 1869; May 11, 1870.

Luther H. North, *Man of the Plains*, pp. 129-30, adds to the information, "No record has been found indicating the Indians were tried again.

However, Little Wolf died in jail and the others, shortly after their release. Several years later, another Pawnee, Shooting Star, confessed to
the murder of Edward McMurty." *Omaha Weekly Herald,* November 17,
24, 1869; May 11, 1870, Luther North to Robert Bruce, February 9,
1929; Luther North Papers, Nebraska State Historical Society.

15. Frank North's attacks of asthma are becoming frequent and more severe.
"O, how I suffer," he wrote in his diary entry of November, Tuesday 16,
1869.

16. Bruce, *The Fighting Norths,* p. 34. "Officers of the Pawnee organizations
were paid through the Quartermaster's Department, the scouts, being enlisted men, were paid the same as in the regular service by army paymasters. Although the North brothers were not commissioned, the commanding officer recognized their rank and title. One time, in 1870 Major
Carr detailed L. H. North's company and a 5th Cavalry troop (1st Lieut.
E. M. Hayes) to make a 3 day scout south of the Republican River. After
Carr gave his instructions Hayes asked which of the two officers would be
in charge. The General replied, 'Captain North, of course.'"

CHAPTER 30

1. General Philip Henry Sheridan, thirty-nine years of age in 1870, went to
Europe to study the military tactics of the German Army campaigns of
the Franco-Prussian War, and returned during 1871.

2. The Yale college group under Prof. O. C. Marsh was the first to visit
Nebraska in a purely scientific or academic study. George B. Grinnell
was a member of the party and his friendship with Frank North began
then. Eli Whitney, Jr., was also in the party. Bruce, *The Fighting Norths,*
p. 34.

3. Consult James C. Olson, *History of Nebraska,* pp. 194-199; William D.
Aeschubacher, "Development of Cattle Raising in the Sandhills," *Nebraska History,* Vol. 28, pp. 41-64; "Development of the Sandhill Lake
Country," ibid., Vol. 27, pp. 205-221; Norbert R. Mahnken, "Early Nebraska Markets for Texas Cattle," ibid., Vol. 26, January-March, pp.
3-25; April-June, 1945, pp. 91-103; Everett N. Dick, "The Long Drive"
collections, Kansas State Historical Society, Vol. 17, pp. 27-29; James
H. Cook, "Trailing Texas Longhorn Cattle Through Nebraska," *Nebraska History,* Vol. 10, pp. 339-443; "The Texas Trail," ibid., Vol. 11, pp.
229-240.

4. See: James C. Olson, *History of Nebraska,* p. 195; also, cf. Nellie Snyder
Yost, *The Call of the Range* (Denver: Sage Books, 1966), pp. 40, 67, 69,
70, 388.

5. Ruby E. Wilson, "Interviewing in 1940 Mr. Charles Stamp, North Platte
pioneer," unpublished, MS copy in writer's possession. "That same

[1869] summer Jack Omohundro, trail foreman, brought the first large herd of Texas cattle into this Platte River country and it was the start of the cattle industry in this country. Keith and Barton, east of town, bought a thousand head. Brown and Russell, west of town, bought about five hundred, and the rest sold in smaller lots. As I had been laid off the Union Pacific roundhouse, I got a job helping to heat the irons to brand Keith and Barton's stock. Jack Omohundro was the only one of the trail-driving crew that stayed, and he tended bar for Lou Baker, and I then tended bar for another man not twenty feet from where Jack worked. There wasn't much to do in the daytime (I didn't work at nights as I was just a kid then, and an older man tended bar at night), so I got pretty well acquainted with "Texas Jack."

"Ned Buntline, pen name of Edward Zane Carroll Judson wrote up Omohundro calling him 'Texas Jack, King of the Cowboys.'"

6. Major North's guest was twenty-four-year-old James Wolcott Wadsworth (1846-1926). He served, 1881-1907, in U.S. House of Representatives. His son, James W. Wadsworth, Jr. (1877-1952), was U.S. senator from New York, 1915-27, and later a member of the House of Representatives.

The elder Wadsworth's father, James Samuel Wadsworth, 1807-64, was educated at Hamilton, Harvard, and Yale colleges, studied law with Daniel Webster, and was admitted to the bar in 1833. He served in the Union Army as brigadier general. In 1862 he was military governor of the District of Columbia. He ran on the Republican ticket as a candidate for governor of New York. His opponent, Horatio Seymour, won. He participated in the battles of Fredericksburg, Chancellerville, Gettysburg, and the Wilderness. He received wounds from which he died two days later within Confederate lines.

The father of General Wadsworth, James Wadsworth, 1768, graduated at Yale 1787. He went with his brother William to the Geneseo Valley of western New York in 1790. There they bought large acreages of land the value of which so increased that James was reputed one of the richest landholders in New York. A consistent philanthropist, he fostered establishment in 1811 of normal schools, and in 1838 procured enactment of the New York School Library Law. He founded and endowed a library and scientific institution at Geneseo.

The father of James Wadsworth, also James Wadsworth, 1730-1817, was brigadier general of Connecticut militia, 1776; commissioned major general, 1777, and ordered to New Haven to organize defense of the coast towns; appointed judge of Common Pleas of New Haven County; 1783-86 delegate to Continent Congress and member of the executive council, 1785-1790.

Research does not reveal what the North-Wadsworth connection may be. Jane Townley North periodically corresponded with New York relatives and friends. She made several trips to visit there. Other members of the family also visited in New York. Luther more than once, also Frank and wife and baby; his mother and daughter were visiting there at the time he was injured during the Indian's act in Cody's Wild West show in Connecticut. Stella's plush autograph album, the 1883 Christmas gift of her father, was extensively autographed by relatives and friends on that occasion. The special guest of Major North's who participated in the buffalo hunt may have been a cousin, possibly once or twice removed.

7. A. T. Andresa, *History of Nebraska* (Chicago, 1882), p. 1099. Con Groner was an early sheriff of Lincoln County Nebraska, after several years of employment with the Union Pacific railroad. He is still something of a legend in Lincoln County. As the outstanding, early day peace officer of Lincoln County, Buffalo Bill persuaded Groner to take part in the Wild West show as the "Cowboy Sheriff."

8. Wetmore and Grey, *Last of the Great Scouts* (Grosset and Dunlap, 1918), pp. 325-28; Chauncey Thomas in a last interview with Cody, shortly before his death:

"'Who was the best revolver shot you ever knew?' I asked.

"'Frank North, white chief of the Pawnees. He was the best revolver shot, standing still, in the air, from horseback, or at running animals or men, that I ever saw,' and again those dark eagle eyes of the old Scout lit up like an excited boy's. . . ."

9. Robert Bruce, *The Fighting Norths*, p. 40 (quoting Luther North): ". . . Captain Cushing (called Jim). In the North genealogy, prepared during his life-time is the following item: Cushing, Sulvanus E. Born March 30, 1835; married December 24, 1868, Sarah Elizabeth, daughter of Thomas J. and Jane Almira (Townley) North, of Tompkins, Co., N.Y.; resides at Columbus, Nebr. The Captain was over six feet tall, weighed about 220 —a giant in strength as in size. . . . He became a farmer near Columbus, and afterward entered business here. . . . Later, Cushing moved to Wenatchee, Washington, where he died October 1, 1904."

10. A letter to Stella (North) Chambers dated April 28, 1949, from Black Hawk, Colorado, signed by Clarence Reckmeyer, an earlier friend of Luther North, indicates that Wm. H. Harvey (Billy), after leaving Nebraska, had prospected for metals in Colorado with a man named Creede who died, whereupon Harvey assumed the name of Crede and later struck a rich silver mine. A tantalizing, strange, and curious letter.

11. See Chapter 24.

12. This horse, a gift to Luther North given by Charles Morse and Luther's youngest sister, Alphonsine, after they were married on Christmas Eve of 1868, was the one that had been stolen by Sioux Indians and taken north to the Whetstone Agency. Luther was leaving to recover the horse at the time Frank North made his first, January 1869 visit to eastern relatives.

Luther's choice of a name may have been from a poem, "Mazeppa," by Lord Byron, or, possibly, from the character "Mazeppa" in a popular play of the time, in which the actress Adah Isaacs Menken, in delicately tinted tights resembling, and even rumored to be, bare flesh, was bound on a steed which galloped up a specially constructed incline.

13. Luther was ever the story-teller as evinced by his reminiscences, much of which were published in his *Man of the Plains* (Nebraska University Press, 1961). Frank was known to have granted one interview while commanding Pawnee Scouts and only two subsequently. In general conversation he talked seldom and very little of his own adventures and experiences but spoke freely of the scouts and Pawnees.

14. Texas cattle were immune to the fever-carrying ticks which they hosted in great quantities. From the trail, ticks spread to domestic livestock. Laws were passed to give settled areas wide clearance of the longhorn droves.

15. General E. O. C. Ord succeeded General Augur in command of the Platte Military District. Until 1876 the scouts were not again in service.

16. This explanation of origins of the Arikaree Indians is over-simplified.

17. Wetmore and Grey, *Last of the Great Scouts*, p. 195. Kit Carson Cody died at five years of age. "Little Kit was laid to rest in Mount Hope Cemetery, April 24, 1876" (p. 228).

CHAPTER 31

1. In September 1868, Col. George B. Forsyth with Lt. Fred H. Beecher and a command of fifty scouts were attacked by a large band of Cheyenne Indians on a sand-bar in the Arickaree River. A bullet broke Forsythe's leg, a very bad wound. The lieutenant was killed as were several other men. They finally succeeded in killing the Indian leader, Roman Nose. The command endured nine days, they were pinned down by Indians on the river banks and surrounding hills. Capt. L. H. Carpenter with a detachment of the Tenth Cavalry, scouting toward Denver from Fort Wallace, Kansas, was found by a courier who brought orders to go to the rescue of Colonel Forsyth. The place is known as Beecher's Battleground, though the sand-bar has washed away. A stone shaft marks the place.

2. Spotted Tail bickered about the location of his reservation at Whetstone Agency northwest of Fort Randall until, in 1871, he persuaded the government to change it, moving him and his Brules to the White River in northwest Nebraska. In the same year Red Cloud was relocated about thirty-two miles east of Fort Laramie. This was a temporary arrangement and in the next year Red Cloud's reservation was also permanently placed in northwest Nebraska, near present-day Crawford.

3. Nellie Snyder Yost *The Call of the Range* (Denver: Sage Books, 1966), p.

106. Dr. W. F. Carver, a dentist from Illinois, also drifted to the Medicine Creek in 1872 and built a dugout on the creek. Claiming to be the "Champion Buffalo Hunter of the Plains," by 1873 he boasted he had killed "in the neighborhood of 30,000 buffalos."

Carver made regular visits to North Platte . . . to fix a few teeth. He was partner of Cody in the first year of the Wild West Show and later headed on his own show. He conceived the idea of teaching horses to dive from great heights into water, and trained the first of them by jumping them off a high bank into a deep spot in the Medicine, near his dugout. Dr. Carver's Diving Horses and the Diving Girls (his daughter and others) who rode the horses off the forty-foot-high boards into tanks showed in numerous big cities and were famous for many years.

4. Ibid., p. 105. W. H. Paddy Miles, real name William Herbert Palmer, was the son of a Georgia plantation owner who lost his holdings during the war. Paddy, after a serious infraction of the law, left his clothes on a Georgia river bank and disappeared, hoping the authorities would conclude he had drowned. He drifted north, reached the Medicine in 1870, and decided to settle down. While looking for a location, he came upon a likely spot on the creek where a white wolf, his foot in a trap trailing a broken chain, lay dead.

Paddy made himself a dugout there, called his place the Wolf's Rest Ranch, and became an official of Frontier County at its organization a year later. He was also a participant in the great buffalo hunt for the Grand Duke Alexis. Of that event he said, "None but those in high places were supposed to speak to Duke Alexis, but I thought while in Frontier County I could. I thought I had a right to speak genteely to any person, and no man stood above me. . . ."

5. A granite shaft erected near present-day Hay Center, Nebraska, marks the site of the Grand Duke Alexis of Russia hunt site of 1872.

6. Ruby E. Wilson, "Pioneer's daughter, Mrs. Ray (Mamie Watts) Langford describes her parents' hosting of the Duke Alexis Hunting Party" (a 1940 interview). Unpublished MS, of which a copy is in possession of Lincoln County Historical Society.

When the Grand Duke Alexis of Russia came for a buffalo hunt he was a guest of the United States Government. It was a great honor to entertain a duke and especially the Grand Duke of Russia.

In spite of all the precaution taken by officers and men at the fort, and all the preparations made, they were still short of outfits. Nobody wanted the government to make a shabby appearance, though it was perhaps the most elaborate hunting party in its preparation, equipment and personnel of any this part of the country ever saw. My father, Russel Watts, and Isaac Dillon and others sent their outfits. An outfit is the mess wagon with a cupboard in the back end of the wagon and the necessary things, stove, utensils, equipment, dishes. The cook drove the wagon but did not care for the team or look out for any of the fuel. With father's outfit he had sixteen cowboys with a string of three to six horses for each man when working the round-ups. [It is probable only the cooks and flunky—the man who cared for the team and rustled up the fuel—were sent to the grand hunt.]

When they returned it was still January. They were the coldest, the most tired and the most elated bunch of men you ever saw in your life. Think of it . . . not a sight of a house any where, sleeping on the ground with their quilts and a tarpaulin for protection. Heavens! It would kill us now-a-days. All the animal carcasses they brought with them were frozen solid.

They came in late in the afternoon and mother prepared the meal for them. The meat was frozen but Mother fried it to prepare it as quickly as possible for the hungry men. After dinner the Duke asked Mother how she prepared the meat, and when Mother told him it was fried, he wanted to know in detail, so he could have more prepared as she had done.

The next day Mother held a dinner party for my father, the Duke and Army Officers including General Sheridan. She again fried the meat to the pleasure of all. All were elated over the hunt and every one was in high spirits. Before the Duke left town, Cody and my father held a banquet in the Duke's honor, inviting all the leading citizens. The banquet was held in that old frame building, then the new Union Pacific Depot. The hotel part, at the time, was owned by M. C. Keith. The Union Pacific Chef baked the meat, but the men said it was not as good as that Mother had fried.

While the Duke was with us he no doubt had observed there was to be a new-comer in my father's home. When he returned to Russia he took with him a number of buffalo hides, one of which he had tanned and returned to Mother for a floor robe for the baby. On the under side of the robe was a solid pattern of beautifully colored beads in a Russian art design. With stove heat, and wood for fuel, the robe came in good place for my baby brother. . . . The hunt was the most talked of affair in North Platte and the country around for years. . . .

7. From Nebraska State Historical Society, Maj. Frank North Collected Papers, a letter written twenty-five years later by one of those "chaps," Erwin P. Jaques:

> Geneseo, Ill. July 24, 1897—Editor, *Forest and Stream*: . . . It was early in the spring of 1872 that I and another boy, Willis Lawbaugh, landed in Columbus with . . . our enterprise. . . . We were given our pick of [Major North's] farmlands for our nursery on surprisingly favor-

able terms, plus horses, plows and so forth when needed. . . .

. . . We heard many stories of adventure on the plains during the summer, one of which was of the Major's ride of 102 miles on horseback in one day. Mrs. North showed us a bear-skin rug, the original owner of which the Major had killed with one shot from a .32 cal. revolver. The story was that he came suddenly upon the bear in a narrow defile in the mountains with only a small pocket revolver at his command. He opened fire with this when the bear turned and ran away, but only a short distance before it fell dead, the bullet having found the heart.

She also entertained us with the story of a buffalo hunt in which she took part, herself. During the summer of '72 the Major was in the employ of the government as a scout, and spent the greater part of the time in Wyoming, coming home every few weeks as opportunity offered. The station was two miles east of his farm, and when the train slowed up at the Loup River bridge he would jump off and walk over or ride a pony which had been previously tied there, by his man, for that purpose.

He was a great hand to ride, and I have often seen him crossing the prairie at breakneck pace, carrying his daughter, Stella in his arms. The Pawnee Indians, whose reservation was twenty miles up the river, used to flock there in great numbers, eager to shake hands with him. Coming down the river, they would stop at our shanty, and their eager question, "Is the Major home?" proved they held him in high esteem.

In the spring and fall the river used to be lined its length with swarms of wild geese. We boys each had a double barreled muzzle loading shot gun, and we used to have high old times worrying them, bringing one down occasionally and giving a good many more a bad fright. I remember what supreme satisfaction it was to me to get a chance to show off before the Major, who was visiting at our shanty, by bringing a goose down from a passing flock. I supposed he would be amazed at such a revelation of skill, and he did indeed seem to be. Such is fame and such is conceit. Another circumstance that pleased me greatly happened one day as the Major's brother, Lute and myself were seated on the bank of the river. Lute had his needle gun with him, which I was examining, when a flock of geese lit upon a sand bar some 400 yards up the river. At the suggestion of Lute, I trained the needle gun on them and fired. The bullet fell short of the geese by about 100 yards, and in the meantime they took wing again. When about eight foot above the water one of them was struck by the ball, which had glanced up and come down again.

Though I saw just what had happened, I hoped Lute had not, but a merry twinkle in his eyes revealed that he was onto the "how" of it, yet, such is the power of success that I was still very happy.

At that time, Major North was a sufferer from asthma, and his brief visits to the heavier air of Nebraska usually brought on an attack of the disease. This led him to move his family to Wyoming that fall.

Our nursery flourished nicely till the fall of the first year when grasshoppers raided and nearly ruined it. This was followed by another raid in '73 which completed the ruin. This broke up the enterprise. The Major promptly remitted the rent and we organized for a big game hunt on the upper Loup River that winter. A quarter century has rolled by since then, and great has been the change wrought by passing years. . . . [Signed] by E. P. Jaques.

At the time this letter was published George B. Grinnell was editor of *Forest and Stream*. Grinnell was the young Yale student of fossils in the group Major North had guided nearly thirty years earlier, to northwest Nebraska.

8. George B. Grinnell, *Pawnee Hero Stories and Folk Tales: Forest and Stream* (New York, 1869), reprinted by University of Nebraska Press (1961), Introduction by Maurice Frink; "A Summer Hunt," pp. 270-302. The incident of the Pawnee children and the flock of wild turkeys is told on pp. 288-90.

9. James C. Olson, *History of Nebraska* (University of Nebraska Press, 1955), p. 179. In 1872 George Hunter and E. S. Hill settled on the site of Indianola.

10. The surveying crew Luther worked with at the reservation were platting the reservation into sections from which small individual allotments were to be made. See, George E. Hyde, *Pawnee Indians* (Denver University Press, 1951), pp. 237-38, 240-44.

11. Young Lester Platt, nephew of Elvira and Lester Platt, Sr., Friends, or Quakers. The elder Platt was ousted from the reservation and forbidden to trespass after the second agent disgraced himself and assistants with the Indian Bureau. Platt owned a trading post near the reservation. Elvira came back to the Pawnee school many times and completed a long career there in teaching.

12. It was learned the Sioux had camped, one band on the Stinking Water and the other band, one ride to the west, on Whiteman's Creek (Frenchman). A band of Ogallalas discovered the Pawnee in August and plans of attack were made. Trail agent Antoine Janis knew this, saw them paint in preparation, but made no objection.

13. Bukskariwi, a Pawnee name referring to the young man's brown wavy mane, hanging to his shoulders. John Williamson was also called Whiteman Leader, "Chaikstaka laket," according to Hyde, *Pawnee Indians.*

14. The number of Sioux warriors was between 1000 and 1200. On the Paw-

nee side Williamson in his report gave the number of men as 250 men and 100 women and 50 children, all mounted.

15. The women and children carried off into captivity—actually taken back to Red Cloud and Spotted Tail reservations—were subsequently recovered.

16. Traveling Bear, Corux ah-Kah-Wahdee, considered by the Norths the greatest tracker and trailer among the Pawnee Scouts, was cited for bravery and gallant conduct at the battle of Summit Springs, July 11, 1869. His family, wife, and four children all were killed and he was reported dead, and was left for dead by the troops. He regained consciousness about twilight; seeing a Sioux warrior scalping a dead Pawnee near him, he waited until the man stooped above him, then lunged and threw his arm about the Indian's neck, took the Indian's knife and killed him. The Bear was badly wounded, and though he made his way back to the reservation he only lived a couple of months. Robert Bruce, *The Fighting Norths*, p. 39.

17. Nick Koots; see Chapter 22. The name meant "bird" in Pawnee. This Pawnee was Luther's striker or batman in the Pawnee Scouts. Luther tells many incidents of this boy's faithfulness. Bruce, *The Fighting Norths*, p. 33. Nick Koots was also one of the tribe's great runners.

18. Galen E. Baldwin settled early in 1872 near the mouth of the Blackwood Creek, nearly opposite the Driftwood flowing into the Republican River from the south. His memoir, written in 1923, further illuminates the massacre of the Pawnee. Excerpts from the hand-written manuscript:

> . . . I went back to my old home in Iowa . . . had left my wife and family and sister Maria Talkington who had just come with her husband, and the three other men that first came there to Hitchcock County, near the mouth of Blackwood. About six days before the . . . Massacre Canyon battle, six Indians came to our place.
>
> . . . While the men were working up the creek, the Indians robbed us of everything they could carry. They took a Sharps .45 caliber, 120 grams of powder and two forty-five shooters. They also threatened to take away my small son. When my wife and sister saw them coming they thought they could reach the timber a short distance . . . but the Indians saw them and rode their ponies after them, driving them back as one does cattle. When they got back, my wife thinking they would kill them all anyway, refused to go in the house and sat down on the dugout bank with her arms around her three children, preferring to die in the open. One of the Indians, seeing earrings in my wife's ears reached over and jerked them out. All at once she saw that the Indians were quite excited . . . pointing to the bayou and then to my son and saying "Pa?" My wife jumped upon the bank and screamed. The

Indians saw the men running to the dugout and got on their ponies and rode off. I dread to think what might have happened if the men had not come when they did. My wife sent a man to North Platte to wire me to notify the soldiers of the raid. The soldiers reached our place the day of the Sioux-Pawnee fight. . . . My wife and sister stood on the dugout and could see the smoke and hear the guns of the battle. I guess the Sioux were using my Sharps rifle too. I reached home three days after the fight. I was in North Platte in 1874, I had Mrs. Baldwin move there for the winter. I was freighting to the Red Cloud Agency and met a Sioux and he told me they lost only six men in the battle.

Mrs. Olive (Baldwin) Spears, excerpts from manuscript of interview, July 13, 1939:

. . . Mother's ears were badly injured, one entire lobe was torn away and the other torn, but she never let those Indians know she was afraid. A few days before that we saw the Pawnee, a large hunting party, I would guess them about three hundred, with their squaws and families, their pole rigs fastened to their ponies with their camp goods. They passed along that old rutted trail—I can still see that old trail, it was so deep rutted, the buffalo had made several paths, just numerous ones, going to the river and that old trail was the one used for a road. I suppose the Pawnee had camped along the creek and followed the buffalo trail west toward hunting grounds. They were surprised in a canyon. No, we didn't talk to them, we weren't within speaking distance of that trail, and they went along and didn't molest us or pay any attention to us. They didn't even stop to beg. The Pawnees never seemed bad about bothering a lot.

When the Pawnee came back they were in a great hurry and retreating just as fast as they could. They were mourning but didn't stop, except one old Chief came to the house. He couldn't talk but a few words of English, but he managed to make us understand he was mourning for his squaw, he called Pawnee Mary. We never knew who this was but always believed it was possibly a white woman, maybe she had been captured or rescued from some Sioux tribe, as the Pawnee were a friendly tribe. Mother often remarked how sincerely that old Chief was mourning, as a white man would. He said, "Me, Squaw killed," pointing west, "Pawnee Mary killed" and of course, we could see the Pawnee had been in a battle, and we had heard the guns and the battle going on over west of us. We were frightened, of course, for we never dreamed we wouldn't eventually be attacked. Father had been gone. . . . He came home after the battle and he went over to the battlefield.

Mr. Eleck (Alex) Baldwin, son of Galen and brother of Olive, excerpts from manuscript of interview:

. . . A squaw came down to our place. Mother gave me a plate of grub to take out to the squaw, buffalo meat and corn bread. She had an arrow broken off in her side. We heard that some white hunters cut it off, and she went over on an island in the river and died. Some years later my Uncle, Laff Talkington visited us. He and my father's sister, his wife, were with us (1873) and he was one of the men who came when my mother screamed. I mentioned, during his visit, that I had seen the squaw's hair moving with lice. My Uncle said it was not lice I had seen, but maggots from head wounds. Father had let me go with him, over to the battle ground, and he counted sixty-three dead. They were buried later. We always theorized that the Sioux had been on a scouting expedition and spying on the Pawnee and maybe waiting for them to come on across the river, when they ran onto our place. . . .

CHAPTER 32

1. George E. Hyde, *Pawnee Indians*, p. 234, fn. 128. William E. Walton was licensed as the Pawnee trader when the Friends took charge. It was Mr. Walton who told George E. Hyde that President Grant sought advice of his friend, Benjamin Hollowell, an educator of the Quaker faith and headmaster of the Alexandria, Virginia, academy. The result was appointment of Hicksite Quakers to take charge of the Nebraska Indians. According to Mr. Walton, also a Quaker, Jacob Troth, a personal friend of Mr. Hollowell, was an "honest and honorable man, but a visionary with a head filled with impractical theories."

2. Olson, *History of Nebraska*, p. 205 (3)". . . There were no satisfactory alternative crops from which to choose—spring wheat was generally unsatisfactory, winter wheat was still in the experimental stage. . . ." This statement applies to 1878-89, some years after the Quakers had conceived the idea of making the Pawnee producers of wheat for market. Also see p. 206, ". . . Wheat found little favor among Nebraska farmers until about the turn of the century. The soil and climate of Nebraska seemed to be unsuitable for spring wheat and for such varieties of winter wheat as most of the farmers were willing to plant. The Mennonites who came to the south-central part of the state in the Seventies and Eighties got good yields from the Turkey Red winter wheat they brought with them from Russia, but most farmers were slow to adopt it. Moreover, the millers looked with disfavor upon the hard winter wheat because their equipment was designed for processing of soft spring wheat. . . ."

3. Hyde, *Pawnee Indians*, p. 230, names Big Spotted Horse as the youth of the Kit-ke-haki band who in 1852, with a left-hand shot, killed the Cheyenne wearing a Spanish coat of mail. Growing up, he had become "very proficient in the Pawnee art of abstracting desirable horses from enemy camps." It seems this "art" consumed most of his time and the remainder was spent in gambling, at which he persisted, but was not proficient. It was in such forays that he, with the Kit-ke-haki Lone Chief, made friends with distant cousins, the Wichitas, and at the Pawnee villages began to talk of these people and the wonders(?) he and Lone Chief, the Kit-ke-haki, claimed were there. The Pawnee tribe was clutching at straws and sent an investigating party in 1870. Many of these, suffering fevers and ague, died before they could return. However, multiplying harassments by white men, who boldly cut hay and hard timber from the reservation, which the Pawnee were powerless to prevent and the agent would not; plus years of frustrating, impossible demands of officials; the massacre of the hunters, along with periodic raids of enemy tribes moved closer; drouth and grasshoppers which made total failures of the last two or three years of corn, bean, and melon crops; and finally, being denied the privilege of going to make meat had reduced the tribe to depondency.

4. George E. Hyde, *Pawnee Indians*, p. 255, fn. 131.

5. *Nebraska History*, Vol. 39, No. 3, pp. 194-95. Military authorities, aware of the trouble at the Red Cloud and Spotted Tail Agencies, discussed stationing troops there as early as January 1874. General Sheridan was also unwilling to dispatch troops until April or May because of the severity of the weather. Moreover, neither the agent nor the Indian Bureau had yet requested military assistance. Events in early February made military assistance necessary. See also, Vol. 22, No. 1, "Red Cloud and the U.S. Flag," pp. 77-88; George E. Hyde, *Red Cloud's Folk, A History of the Oglala Sioux Indians*.

6. Silas Garber settled and organized Red Cloud, Nebraska.

7. Hyde, *Pawnee Indians*, cf. p. 253, Lone Chief speaks.

8. Either the shooting was accidentally self-inflicted or the murderous intent of a white man. There was no investigation.

9. Olson, *History of Nebraska*, cf., p. 183; *Nebraska History*, Vol. 30, cf., pp. 317-47; ibid., Vols. 11-13; Addison E. Sheldon, ed. "Nebraska Constitutional Convention, Sheldon, "The Land and the People," Vol. I, cf. pp. 386-524.

10. Olson, *History of Nebraska*, pp. 194-95, ". . . Between 60,000 and 75,000 Texas Cattle were driven into Ogalalla in 1875; by 1876 the number had jumped above 100,000 where it remained until 1880.

    "The trail into Ogalalla was an extension northward from Dodge City, Kansas, of what was known as the Western Trail, which, as settlers

moved west into Kansas, replaced the old Chisholm running from San
Antonio to Abilene. The Western Trail started at Bandera, Texas,
crossed the Red River at a point known as Doan's store, then pushed on
to Dodge City, the Santa Fe's boisterous shipping town on the Arkansas
River. Some of the longhorns were left there, but most of the younger animals were driven on to Ogalalla. From Dodge City the trail angled north
and west to Buffalo Station, about sixty miles west of Hays on the Kansas
Pacific. The next stop was Ogalalla. The last leg of the journey was the
most difficult, principally because of the lack of water. Streams were few
and far between at best, and the drovers frequently found that many of
the smaller streams on which they were depending had dried up. The last
day's drive, some thirty miles from Stinking Water Creek to the South
Platte, was almost the worst of the whole journey for the trail weary cowhands. . . ."

Norbert Mahnken, "Ogalalla, Nebraska's Cowboy Capital," *Nebraska
History*, Vol. 27, p.85. ". . . Gold flowed freely across the tables, liquor
across the bar, and occasional blood across the floor as a smoking gun in
the hands of a jealous rival or an angered gambler brought an end to the
trail of some unfortunate cowhand on the stained boards of 'Tuck's saloon'" Apparently an oversight on the part of Ogalalla's initial hosting of
the Texas Trail's End cattlemen and that was abundantly amended.

11. The last contingent of about 500 Pawnees on the Nebraska reservation
had planted and harvested fair crops, despite grasshoppers. None were so
disabled that they could not do some job in harvesting, drying, and preserving and packing the food south to rejoin their tribe. The Skeedee's
insistence that they were staying on the reservation was defeated by the
agent and Indian officials. Hyde in *Pawnee Indians*, p. 260, states that
agent Burgess had bought twelve wagons and teams to transport the people and their belongings. In addition, some Pawnee individuals owned
wagons and there were a few other vehicles described as carriages or bug-
gies. Also, Hyde states that a herd of cattle were driven along from which
beef rations were issued once a week.

Yet two more graves were made in the Pawnee's reservation cemetery
before the last Pawnee left their reserve. The wife of Eagle Chief, the
Skeedee's head chief, went to tend her corn, drying much as was done in
rural homes as late as fifty years ago, by cutting sweet corn from the cob
and drying in racks covered by several layers of mosquito bar netting. She
was shot as she approached her work and died quickly. Young boys
herding the Pawnee horse herd were attacked by fourteen men dressed as
Indians but believed to be white men trying to take the Pawnee horses.
One boy was killed, it was said, "in sight of the agency." The raiders escaped and the agent did nothing but report to Washington.

CHAPTER 33

1. Roger T. Grange, Jr., "Fort Robinson, Outpost on the Plains," *Nebraska History*, Vol. 39, No. 3, p. 206. . . . The Sidney Trail supplied agencies and military posts; it also became a major route to the Black Hills following the discovery of gold there by the Custer Expedition in 1874. Soldiers from camps Robinson and Sheridan were called upon to check the illegal influx of miners into the Black Hills. Although the soldiers frequently removed parties from the hills, there were far too few troops to cope with the situation.

2. Ibid., p. 207. The agency became a "mighty tough place" according to George Colhoff, an employee at the Yates Trading Company (post trader). It was a road agent's rendezvous with men like Black Doak, Fly Speck Billy, Lame Johnny, Paddy Simons, Tom Reed, and Herman Leisner frequenting the agency between their attacks on the stage coaches traveling the Sidney-Deadwood and Cheyenne-Deadwood trails. See also footnote 20 of Interview by Judge E. S. Ricker with George Colhoff. Tablet No. 17, MS, Ricker Collection, Nebraska State Historical Society.

3. See George E. Hyde, *Red Cloud's Folk*, Norman, Oklahoma, 1937; General Orders No. 13, February 21, 1876, Fort Robinson, Nebraska Selected Post Orders, 1874-97, U.S. Army Commands, Records of the War Department, NARS, RG 98.

4. George Crook, born September 23, 1829, near Dayton, Ohio, died Chicago, Illinois, March 21, 1890, was graduated from West Point in 1852. Served against the Indians. Rose to rank of major general. In 1888 he took command of the Department of Missouri in which position he died. He championed the cause of the Indian in the case of the Ponca chief, *Standing Bear* vs. *Crook*, and was instrumental in arranging the case against himself, according to James T. King in *Nebraska History*, Vol. 50, No. 3, p. 240. Also see, James T. King, "George Crook, Indian Fighter and Humanitarian," *Arizona and the West*, 11 (No. 4), Winter 1967, pp. 337-38; Marvin F. Schmidt, ed., *General George Crook, His Autobiography*, Norman, Oklahoma, 1960, chapters 1 and 2.

5. *Nebraska History*, Grange, "Fort Robinson—" Vol. 39, No. 3, p. 209. Before the Omaha Military Headquarters had heard of Custer's defeat, the Indians at Red Cloud Agency were discussing it. Frank Yates, one of the traders at the agency, was a brother of the Captain Yates who fell with Custer. When the rumors were reported to him he went to Camp Robinson where officers rejected the possibility of such a disaster. They telegraphed Omaha, but no word had yet reached officers there.

6. Originally established as Camp Wichita in 1869, at the foot of the Wichita Mountains in Indian Territory, the military post subsequently became

Fort Sill.

7. Charles Chapin returned to Columbus where he still lived in the early 1930s.

8. Bruce, *The Fighting Norths*, p. 43, reports about a third of the tribe dead in less than two years after the tribe had been in the south country. No Pawnee mortality figures for 1875 to 1900 agree. The tribe went down to 600, its lowest census, when it began to rally.

     George B. Grinnell, *Pawnee Hero Stories and Folk Tales*, p. 397. ". . . The full history of the plot to eject the Pawnees from their northern home may never be recorded, for there are few white men who know the facts. If it should be written there would be disclosed a carefully planned and successfully carried out conspiracy to rob this people of their lands. This outrage has cost hundreds of lives, and an inconceivable amount of suffering, and is another damning and ineffaceable blot on the record of the American people, and one which ought surely to have had a place in Mrs. Jackson's 'Century of Dishonor'."

9. Brummett Echohawk, full-blood Pawnee writer-artist, "Last of the Pawnee Scouts," reprinted from the *Tulsa World Sunday Magazine*, by the *Omaha Sunday World Herald Magazine*, July 17, 1958 (excerpt): "Fancy Eagle [the youngest Pawnee Scout to serve with the North brothers in 1876-77 and known then as Ah-re Kah Rard, Antlers] who was 14 when he escaped the Sioux massacre, near the Republican River, and near the present town of Trenton, Nebraska; but was to see more tribal misfortune. The West was becoming settled. And in 1874 'papered' words of the Great White Father uprooted the Pawnees and marched them to Indian Territory. It was another 'Trail of Tears' as experienced by other Indian Territory tribes. . . ."

     Rush Roberts had changed names after his scout service, as was customary, and was also known as Leading Chief. His later tribal name of Fancy Eagle, under which Echohawk knew him, was the name of his sire who died in the 1873 massacre.

10. The Norths, after returning to Nebraska, corresponded with George B. Grinnell in hope of having the Pawnees' plight investigated and relieved. Mr. Grinnell and John Dunbar later visited the reservation and induced others to look into conditions, and got a change of agents, none of which materially benefited the Pawnee.

11. Eagle Chief, whose wife was killed in the last month's residence on the Nebraska reservation, was one of the chiefs who came, in 1866, to the Norths' hay field to have Major North settle a tribal dispute. Eagle Chief died about 1884, in Pawnee, Indian Territory.

12. Two of the enlisted Pawnee Scouts died within two weeks after arriving at Sidney, Nebraska, before they were formally mustered.

13. Frank White was also known as Traveling Chief (not to be confused with

Traveling Bear), Li-heris-oo La Shar, meaning Leading Chief. Not a tribal chief, he was yet a man of force and character. George Roberts, son of
Ah-re Kah Rard, Rush Roberts, the youngest scout on the 1876-77 Powder River Expedition with the Norths, states about 1930 that this Indian
served more than once under the Norths, and that his last Indian name
was We-te-roo-tooks-tu Koo. Frank White died after 1907.

14. Information on the Ponca story and the Pawnees' Ponca song, variously
interpreted, George B. Grinnell, *Pawnee Hero Stories and Folk Tales*, pp.
305-6; Robert Bruce, *The Fighting Norths*, pp. 42-43; Nebraska State Historical Society, the Luther H. North collections, papers, letters, documents, MS. (of his own reminiscences, may be termed an autobiography); also collection of Major Frank North, much like his brother's; also
see Hyde's interpretation of story and song: Ponca-Pawnee Indians. Also
cf. Grinnell, *Two Great Scouts* (Cleveland, 1928), p. 248.

15. Maj. Frank North failed to make allowance for the mustangs' slowness to
comprehend that grain was horse food. His ponies did not recover weight
and strength in the allotted time. Therefore ponies began giving out before half the distance from Sidney to Niobrara was covered. His weak
mounts, the best available, continued to be a nagging worry to him
throughout the expedition.

CHAPTER 34

1. Born in New York City, Ranald S. Mackenzie was graduated at head of
his class from West Point in 1862. He served in the Civil War and commanded a division of cavalry at war's end. Relieved as commandant at
Fort Sill he was transferred to the Department of the Platte to participate
in General Crook's Powder River Expedition. Six companies of the
Fourth Cavalry were ordered north with General Mackenzie. He later
served in the Southwest and held the rank of brigadier general when he
died in 1889.

2. Red Cloud became an intimate friend of Captain George Cook of Agate,
Nebraska, and was often a guest at the Cook ranch. Red Cloud came to
trust Mr. Cook as he did no other white man. And Mr. Cook came to
know and understand the simple greatness of the once savage leader, who
died in 1909. See Hebard and Brininstool, *The Bozeman Trail, Book 2*,
pp. 175-205; George E. Hyde's *Red Cloud's Folk*.

3. William F. Cody, army scout attached to Col. Wesley Merritt's com-
mand, gained great publicity for his killing of Yellow Hand, *Nebraska
History*, Vol. 39, Roger T. Grange, Jr., "Fort Robinson, Outpost on the
Plains," p. 210.

4. The name Red Leaf is also given as Yellow Leaf. The village on Chadron
Creek was first occupied by Swift Bear who was joined by Red Leaf when

Red Cloud also moved away from the agency to the edge of the reservation.

5. George Alexander Gordon was graduated from West Point in 1850 to the
   fifth Cavalry, and served in the second Cavalry during the Civil War;
   after Civil War service with distinction and plains war engagements, he
   took breveting as major and lieutenant colonel. Mustered out in 1871,
   he was reappointed major fourth Cavalry in 1873. He commanded Fort
   Sidney and died in 1878.

6. Bruce, *The Fighting Norths*, pp. 46-47. The correspondent was probably
   Jerry Roche, who accompanied the Crook expedition and wrote the only
   contemporary newspaper account of the Dull Knife fight. A vivid account of the meeting of Major North and the encamped wagon train in
   the darkness, including "An Indian Scare," dated Fort Laramie, Wyoming Territory, October 27, 1876, was published in the *New York Herald*,
   Saturday, November 4, 1876.

7. General Crook enlisted 88 Sioux warriors for scouting.

8. Col. Homer W. Wheeler, "The Winter Campaign of 1876-77" (The
   Frontier Trail, Los Angeles, California, 1923): Clark's original idea was
   to organize two companies of Indian scouts, Lt. William Philo Clark,
   acting as major of scouts, to command them all. Had this plan been
   carried out, I was to command one of the companies. . . ." Warriors
   from hereditary enemy tribes would have been arbitrarily thrown together. North knew the plan wouldn't do.

CHAPTER 35

1. This apparent disorganization of the Crook command bothered Major
   North and continued to do so throughout the campaign. He was apprehensive about the scattered and separated segments of the command.

2. Cantonment Reno, established October 12, 1876, about three miles
   from Fort Reno, established in 1865 as Camp Connor and abandoned in
   1868. Cantonment Reno became Fort McKinney in 1877, honoring the
   lieutenant killed in Mackenzie's fight with the Cheyennes.

3. Several Pawnee in this company of scouts were veterans of the Sioux attack upon the hunting Pawnees, when woman and children along with
   men were killed at "Massacre Canyon."

4. Tribes represented were Pawnee, Sioux, Arapaho, Cheyenne, Shoshone
   commonly called Snake. Individuals of other tribes, such as Bannock and
   perhaps Piute, may have been present. The Crows did not arrive to participate in the Dull Knife battle. It was about a month later when 76
   Crows under Major Randall came, according to Grinnell, *The Fighting
   Cheyennes*, p. 355.

5. General Crook detached General Mackenzie with ten companies of cavalry and the Indian scouts to attack the Cheyenne village reported by the scouts. General Crook was to follow as rapidly as possible with eleven companies of infantry under Col. R. I. Dodge, four companies of dismounted artillery, and one retained company of cavalry. Major North left his wagons and thirty Pawnee Scouts under Lieutenant Cushing with Crook. (Major North made no diary entry for November 23.)

6. Two Sioux and two Arapaho scouts had been sent out the previous evening. Credit is given the Arapaho who came in with this information. However in both of the North brother's collections of letters, papers, manuscripts, clippings, and documents reposing in Nebraska State Historical Society archives, mention is made of the Sioux as discoverers of the Cheyenne village.

7. Grinnell, *The Fighting Cheyennes*: ". . . I have pointed out that the troops that attacked Dull Knife's village supposed they had surprised it, but the Cheyenne account of the fight and the events immediately preceeding it show that the proximity of the troops was known to the Indians days in advance of the attack. They might readily have escaped and undoubtedly would have done so except for the obstinacy and arrogance of Last Bull— at that time chief of the Fox Soldiers, police or marshalls of the village and responsible for safety of both, who seems to have cowed not only the chiefs of the tribes but also the owners of the two great medicines of the Cheyennes, and the chiefs of the other soldier bands" (p. 355).

"I have received the story of the fight from many of the people who were in the village; Two Moon, nephew of old Two Moon; Little Hawk, a son of old Gentle Horse, a famous Cheyenne of the old war times; other men and many women. . . ." (pp. 357-61). Grinnell relates that young hunters saw and reported the troops, after which four men were sent to keep the troops under surveillance, which they did for two days and nights, stole horses at two separate times from under the troops' and Indian scouts' noses, even mingled with some and took fried hot cakes to eat. These four returned and reported to the Cheyennes, "four languages spoken in the camp" (military), which was a poor count as actually two or three other tongues were there—English, Bannock, and perhaps another.

"Two Moon said: 'If they reach this camp I think it will be a big fight.' When the chiefs learned the soldiers were near they wished to move camp . . . but Last Bull . . . said, 'No we will stay here. . . .' Before sundown they built a 'skunk'; that is, a pile of wood for a fire to dance by. . . ."

The story relates that a man going down by the creek to look at his horses discovered they were being " 'driven away . . . whipping them . . . I think the soldiers are there, for further down the stream I heard a rumbling noise. . . .' " Yet the Fox Soldiers allowed no one to leave, or to move up into the mountains, as many wished to do. "Early in the morning a chief, Black Hairy Dog, untied all his horses and took them up on a hill. . . . 'Get your guns. The camp is charged, they are coming. . . .' " The Cheyenne were not surprised, nor were they prepared when the troops charged.

8. The young Indian killed was identified by Bill Rowland, who had charge of the Cheyenne scouts, as one of Dull Knife's three sons, about 20 years of age. Bull Hump, another of Dull Knife's sons, also participated in the battle.

9. Frank Grouard (see Joe DeBarthe, *Life and Adventures of Frank Gouard*, Univ. of Oklahoma Press, Norman, 1958) claimed he killed Little Wolf, a Cheyenne chief, in this battle. Bill Hamilton, mountain man since 1842, was employed at various times by the army as a scout, guide, and interpreter. He was about 57 years of age at this time and lived until 1908.

10. Grinnell, *The Fighting Cheyennes*, p. 353, ". . . Dull Knife's following had taken active part in the Custer fight. One of the articles found in the village was a roster book of a first sergeant of the Seventh Cavalry, giving many details about the troop. The book had been captured by an Indian who had filled it with his drawings. It came into the possession of then Lieutenant, later Colonel, Homer W. Wheeler, and was deposited in the Museum of the Military Service Institution at Governor's Island, New York. Years later it passed to a dealer, from whom it was purchased by John Jay White, of New York, and finally was given to me to take to the Cheyenne reservation to see whether I could identify the artist who had illustrated it. Bull Hump, the son of Dull Knife, and Old Bear, both of whom had been in Dull Knife's village, recognized the book as the property of High Bear, who had drawn the pictures."

11. Bruce, *The Fighting Norths*, pp. 51-52 (quoting Luther North): "The quart cup mentioned was common in those days; a tin cup with handles on the side, like the smaller cups still seen. Even the Indians had many of them. I am inclined to think that the one which figures in this story had just been picked up in the Indian village by one of our men."

12. Grinnell, *The Fighting Cheyennes*, p. 367: ". . . the camp had burned, but about ten lodges on the other side of the creek from the main camp were left unburned. That night, Two Moon went to these lodges and found two robes, then another. He put these on his horse . . . someone down the stream uttered a yell and . . . firing began from all directions. He and his party rode back to the breastworks."

13. See Luther North, *Man of the Plains*, p. 218: ". . . He must have been a genius to have succeeded in getting them out safely," Luther North declares of Lt. Homer W. Wheeler's excellent work in transporting the

wounded men down the mountains and through the passes on travois. The dead were fetched on pack mules.

CHAPTER 36

1. Besides Lieutenant McKinney, six soldiers were killed and seventeen wounded.
2. Frank North hired C. C. Baatz as a teamster, October 26, 1876.
3. Red Hawk, Koot-tah We-coots-oo Pah, first named in Chapter 14, note 2, and Chapter 21.
4. It was determined that five Indians had made this attack. They were believed to have followed Crook's command from the Dull Knife battle ground.
5. Bvt. Col Richard Irving Dodge, lieutenant colonel twenty-third Infantry, commanded the infantry in this campaign. The author of *The Black Hills* (1876), *Hunting Grounds of the Great West* (1877), and *Our Indians* (1882).
6. Much hardship was endured from November 22, 1876, when the command was divided and General Mackenzie with the cavalry and scouts started after the Cheyennes, leaving tents with the wagon train and taking minimum supplies, sleeping on the snow, the thermometer never being higher than 14 below, according to Luther North.
7. "Abraham Lincoln" was the English name chosen by a Pawnee to be enlisted under, as was their privilege. The Pawnee name is unknown. The 1876 enlistment of Pawnee men included a number of English names: Bob White, Harry Coon, Ralph Weeks. Eddie Crooked Hand (not to be confused with the great older warrior called Crooked Hand, Ska-dik; see chap. 22): Andrew Murray, Frank White, Sam Moore, Pete Hedman, Martin Prichard, Jonas Woodruff, Peter Sam, Matthew Simpson, and James Wood. Others, commonly called by an English name, were enlisted by their Pawnee names. The majority were known and enlisted only by Pawnee names.
8. Harry Coon participated in Mackenzie's capture of the Red Cloud and Swift Bear-Red Leaf villages, went to Fort Laramie with the Pawnee command where he became very ill and, unable to go with Crook's movement northward, was left in care of the fort surgeon. This Pawnee, long years later in 1898, wrote an eloquent letter to Luther North, now in the Nebraska State Historical Society Luther North Collection (papers, letters, documents, MS, and clippings):

   > Pawnee Okl. Terr., Sept. 20, 1889. Lute North, Columbus Neb.—
   > Dear Friend. I had intended of writing of you before, but thought would wait until we arrive home, which we did four days ago. I hardly

know how to excuse myself to you and other friends, in not stopping
on my way from Genoa to Omaha City exposition, and bidding you
all a last farewell, especially your old kind mother and my old school
teacher.

In visiting Genoa one of my objects was to visit the graves of my
two sisters who died with measels over 30 years ago [See chapter 12],
as well as to see the old reservation where I was raised, once more. Although I met some kind Friends there—I felt very lonesome and Sad
on account of my feelings, as my thoughts were full of the past.

Where my sisters graves were is now cornfield what few graves I did
find were open and robbed of what little—if any trinkets were found
on the dead. Among the places I visited was the old school where I
and other Pawnee Children got their schooling. [The large brick
"Pawnee House" which replaced the original log building put up by
the Mormons and used for the agency school house.] Other buildings
has been put on to it—but the place looked familiar to me. I stayed at
Genoa 2 days—and at Omaha city 3 days did not see to it all. The
pawnees I understand were invited to attend—the exposition, but
upon learning it was a kind of a show—they wanted pay for showing
themselves in the old way. As the exposition paid no Indians—they
did not go. Altogether we had a very present [pleasant] overland trip.
Stopped 2 day on the Platte River—where the Pawnees lived [near
Fremont], to get some flag roots and to see once more the mysterious
Bluff or Bank where the Spiritual animals are supposed to live in a
cave under the water—This very time the Pawnees still reverence that
place and have Doctor songs and talks about it now. [According to
Grinnell, *Pawnee Hero Stories and Folk Tales*, pp. 98-120, the place
was called by the Pawnees "Pahuk, where the Nahurac were."]

They [Pawnee in Oklahoma] were very glad to see me and we are
just now being feasted by friends. It took us altogether 20 days from
the Omaha Agency [which he and group also visited] to get here.

I find that they had splendid crops down here had lots of rain—
what Pawnee Country now needs is a railroad. While the Pawnees are
a sad people still they are getting used to the new conditions of life.

James Murie [Jr., the son of the Scotsman immigrant who married a
Pawnee woman, of the Skeedee band, and served several times as an
officer with the Pawnee Scouts. The son, educated at Carlisle Indian
School, was especially interested in perpetuating history of his mother's people] is now clerking in a bank here if he will stick to it now he
will be all right—as it is an honored position. I told him so—and poor
Ralph Weeks our friend—Well he is doing nothing—although he has
been somewhat busy—has an increase in family—a girl baby—I
understand—has invited me and family to feast with him. There is a

story about Ralph among the Indians—how he nearly roasted himself from the effect of heat at a bear dance this summer. It seems the Bear dancers invited our Ralph to come and dance with them and to wear the Bear Robe during the dance—all the rest [of him] being naked, this being an honored position Ralph ex[ac]cepted the invitation.

It is an old custom that whoever wears the Robe must not put it off during the dance and must keep moving about as a bear. Well on the day of the dance it got very warm [hot] and the dance was in the Dirt lodge. When the dance commenced the door and inside was jam and crowded with people—it shut out air except through where the Smoke goes out. That day it was suffocating—but the dance went on—Everybody was ringing wet with sweat—even onlookers. They say poor Ralph stood it as long as he good [could] finally he gave it up as bad medicine. Exhausted—sat down and took the Bear Robe off nearly roasted.

It seems James Murie presented the Bear dancers this big Bear Robe —sometime this spring and he got from the Superstitious Indians— some ponies and money for it.

You know I was telling you that the Pawnees say they once lived in dirt lodges just below the mouth of Loup River on the Bank of Platte River. I find that 2 bands did live there—Chowees [Also known as Grands], and the Pita ho rats about 150 years ago. The Kit ka hawks or Republicans at that time—living and roaming over on the Republican River—The Skeedees away up the Loup River—Well I must close—hoping to hear from you—Your Friend Harry Coons. [Capitalized words and punctuation about as the original.]

Weeks, mentioned in the letter, was also educated at Carlisle Indian School. He was the scout with Mackenzie, who called the order to Major North to cross the creek just before attacking the Dull Knife Village.

9. Nick Janis (variously spelled) married a Sioux woman, raised a large family, was sometimes employed as interpreter at the Spotted Tail Agency, or guide; see chapters 19 and 24.

10. Information from Nebraska State Historical Society, Collection, papers, letters, and MSS, Frank North and Luther North; also of Luther H. North, *Man of the Plains*, pp. 225-26; cf. Robert Bruce, *The Fighting Norths*, p. 54.

11. Bob White, a Pawnee Scout whose tribal name is unknown, held the dubious designation of "camp cook" on the 1876-77 campaign. He served in 1869 on Carr's Republican Valley Expedition, and possibly at other times under his Indian name.

12. Maj. Gen. Samuel S. Summer at the age of eighty-nine was still living in

Brookline, Massachusetts. His statement, from R. Bruce, *The Fighting Norths*, p. 27:

> Recollections of the North Brothers: I first met L. H. North in the summer of 1869 when he was Captain of a company of Pawnee Scouts forming part of a battalion . . . under command of his elder brother, Major Frank North, then attached to the 5th U.S. Cavalry. . . . Those Scouts participated in the Battle of Summit Springs, Colorado, July 11, 1869. . . . The Pawnees had a very important part in that affair, one of the most brilliant and successful of Indian warfare. . . . By that decisive victory, peace was brought to the western frontiers of Kansas and Nebraska and—Colorado.
>
> I met the North brothers again in the winter 1876-77, when the Pawnee Scouts, who had returned from the Powder River Expedition after the Dull Knife fight, reported at Sidney Barracks for the winter quarters. Frank North had his command in good order, and their behavior was very satisfactory. The Major was an exceptional man. He, and William F. Cody (Buffalo Bill) were close companions; they formed a class by themselves, and had no superiors as scouts and plainsmen in their day.

13. Major North's diary entry date, January 21, 1877, further demonstrates his interest in his men and consideration for the Pawnee families. Mail service came from Big Bend, Kansas, to the Pawnee Agency, and some Pawnees of around twenty years of age had acquired, under Mrs. Platt's tutoring, passable reading and writing ability, so the letters would be deciphered. Letters went to the families of the three men dead of illness.

14. This is the last diary entry Major North is known to have written.

15. Grinnell, *The Fighting Cheyennes*, chapter 27, pp. 346-68. Although some participants complained, there is also evidence that the Dull Knife people were hospitably treated by Crazy Horse Sioux.

16. Frank North had served under or with Samuel R. Curtis, 1864; Brig. Gen. Robert Mitchell and Fort Kearny Post Commander Captain Gillette, early 1865; Maj. Gen. Grennville M. Dodge, commander, Department of the Missouri, Gen. Patrick E. Connor, 1865; Gen. C. C. Augur, commander, Department of the Platte, and under direct command of Col. W. H. Emory; Lt. Col. Thomas Duncan, Maj. Gen. E. A. Carr and Maj. W. B. Royall; also, in association with Col. Wesley Merritt and Capt. Geo. F. Price, was escort and guard for Lt. Gen. Phillip H. Sheridan, various periods; Gen. George Crook, commander Department of the Platte; actively campaigning in the field with Gen. R. S. Mackenzie, Col. Gordon, Maj. Gen. S. S. Sumner, and many more.

17. A memoranda in the booklet in which the major wrote his diary yields the names of the Pawnee Scouts who died of disease soon after arriving

back in Nebraska: "Sept. 25. Died, Ku wuck oo Kah la ha of typhoid fever, 11 P.M. Oct. 3, 1876. Died . . . 11 P.M. Stee te kit tah us hi la [or ta]
rick of congestion of lungs . . . Oct. 12 at 4 A.M. Died, Ke wuck oo had
de (or dc)."

18. After the Civil War and shrinking of the military forces, numerous career
    officers reverted to lower ranks. Most of them received brevet commis-
    sions recognizing their wartime ranks, and were addressed by the higher
    title. This courtesy was extended to the leaders of the Pawnee Scouts,
    though their designation varied, dependent upon how large the scout
    command was at the time. When Frank North commanded a battalion of
    scouts he received the majority equivalent. General Crook, in this letter,
    addressed him as captain as he was commanding a company of one hun-
    dred men and his brother, Luther, was then first lieutenant. A brother-
    in-law, Sylvanius Cushing, who had served as captain at times, now was
    second Lieutenant. Those orally addressing Frank North would have
    called him "Major." Not all of the commanders of Indian scouts during
    the Indian wars were actually army officers. Often, as in the case of the
    Norths, they were civilians, employed and paid through the Quartermas-
    ter's Department, although by courtesy known and referred to by the mil-
    itary title of their qualification.

19. This letter, handwritten and signed by General Crook himself, while still
    at Fort Robinson, before returning to his headquarters office of the De-
    partment of the Platte, in Omaha, was not a formal, routine communica-
    tion. Ordinarily, such a letter would have been written and signed by a
    subordinate officer. For this reason the letter was long prized by the
    North family. Through Luther North, the letter was mounted and
    framed and entrusted to the Nebraska State Historical Society.

CHAPTER 37

1. Capt. Jim Cook, guide, hunter, soldier, Texas trail drover, and pioneer
   settled in northwest Nebraska near Agate. He became friend of the
   Ogalalla Sioux chief, Red Cloud. Paleontologists found his ranch an important fossil bed.

2. Oldon, *History of Nebraska* (University of Nebraska Press, 1951), pp.
   191-92, "The development of the range cattle industry on the Plains was
   coincident with the extermination of the bison. So long as these shaggy
   beasts occupied the Plains, there could be no room for cattle. Moreover,
   while the bison remained plentiful, the Indian had the where-withal to
   maintain resistance against white encroachment. . . . Extermination of
   the bison occurred after the discovery, in the early seventies, that their
   hides could be used in the manufacture of harness, belting, shoes and

other leather goods. To satisfy the demand thus created, commercial hunters went out on the Plains in gangs, armed with high-calibre, long-range rifles, and in a few short years literally wiped the bison off the face of the earth. Conservative estimates place the kill on the Plains at more than ten million during the years 1870-1875. Moreover, this was simple, wanton destruction. Whereas the Indians had used virtually all of the animal, the commercial hunters took only the hide, leaving the carcass to rot where it fell." Such eminent army men as Generals Sheridan, Sherman, and Mackenzie believed that to end the Indian it was first necessary to exterminate the bison, and urged this policy.

3. Buck and Baxter Taylor stayed on in Nebraska, and a cattle rancher was fortunate indeed to hire them. The younger brother, Buck, joined the Wild West Show, billed as "King of the Cowboys," when Frank North organized the show and put it together at North Platte, Nebraska, in 1883.

4. Early cattle ranchers formed the Wyoming Stock Growers' Association in which brands owned by members were registered.

5. John Bratt came to Nebraska Territory as a common hand in 1866. He had emigrated from England, moved west working as a bull-whacker with a freighting ox train and three years later joined with Isaac Coe and Levi Carter to form the John Bratt Cattle Company. He prospered, expanded, and married the daughter of John Burke of Cottonwood Spring (see chapter 16).

6. See James H. Clark, "Early Days in Ogalala," *Nebraska History,* Vol. 14 (April-June, 1933). Known at the NC ranch as Billy Jaeger, the man's name is given by Clark as Louis John Frederick Jaeger. He joined Buffalo Bill's Wild West in 1883, and was billed as "Billy, the Bear," and also was employed by Cody as a bookkeeper. "Billy" worked for a rancher in Wyoming where he became lost a number of days in a blizzard and was severely frozen. Both legs were amputated below the knees, also all digits of both hands. He later settled in Chadron, Nebraska.

7. Demonstrations by highly trained cutting horses and roping horses are today's rodeo highlights. The horses most used now are quarter horses, bred from the mustang, also called a bronco. The mustang-bronco was the horse of the early American cattle ranching industry.

8. William (Bill) Burke is said to have been the eldest son of John Burke. His sister was Mrs. John Bratt.

9. James (Jim) Carson was a nephew of the famous frontiersman, Kit Carson.

10. An agent, Mr. Schurz, representing the Secretary of the Interior, came to the agency, held a hearing, and ruled in favor of the Indians, allowing them to retain the horses, and Major North failed to recover any payment for them.

11. Marie Sandoz, *Cheyenne Autumn* (McGraw-Hill Book Co., 1953), tells of this episode in Cheyenne history. Also see George B. Grinnell, *The Fighting Cheyennes* (New York, 1913).

12. Major Frank North was the commander of the North Platte Home Guards; John Bratt, secretary, second in command.

13. Luther North Collection: letters, papers, manuscript; the Nebraska State Historical Society,

> Doc Middleton . . . also had the reputation of taking horses. . . . He ranged the sandhills from Niobrara. . . . We often heard of him crossing the South and Middle Loup east of us . . . seen at North Platte but he never came to our place and so far as I know never took any of our horses or cattle. Finally . . . run down . . . shot through the hip . . . captured . . . brought to Columbus . . . overnight, under guard . . . sent word to J. E. (James, called Jim) North requesting him to come. . . . My brother . . . very surprised at the message, curious . . . went.
>
> . . . Doc said, "I guess you don't know me." Three years before, [James North] had made a business trip [in January] to the Black Hills. . . . By Stage Coach from Sidney, Nebraska and took a big buffalo robe for protection. At . . . first station [out from Sidney] a man got on to go to Fort Robinson. The stage was full and this man was obliged to ride outside with the driver. My brother saw . . . he had no overcoat . . . gave him the buffalo robe to wrap around him. . . . He . . . returned it at Fort Robinson. This man was "Doc" Middleton.
>
> The night before . . . he had quarrelled with soldiers and killed one . . . had walked to the station where he got on the stage coach. He told my brother that the buffalo robe kept him from freezing to death, and that this was the reason he never bothered our ranch. This may have been true, but one of our men, Bax Taylor knew Doc in Texas, and said that when he left there he stole one of Bax's horses and Bax swore that if Doc ever came to the ranch while he was there he would kill him. . . . Bax said Doc's name was Jim Cherry and that he knew him well in Texas. . . .

Also, the *Oakdale Pen and Plow*, July 31, 1879. "Doc Middleton, the northern bandit passed down yesterday in charge of U.S. Marshals. He was captured by a posse of five detectives and twenty soldiers. Doc was wounded and on his back, otherwise they would not have got him." Wyoming had no penitentiary so Doc Middleton was sentenced to a term in the Nebraska Prison. He died some years after release, December 27, 1913.

14. Maj. Frank North successfully drove his herd through Sandhills, proved there was water there, and is credited with opening Nebraska's Sandhills to the cattle ranching industry. For this, and for his pioneering leader-

ship in the Sandhills, his name is commemorated in the Cowboy's Hall of Fame in Oklahoma.

CHAPTER 38

1. William F. Cody was challenged at this time by "Yank" Addams, Maine's state rifle champion, to a shooting match, which he accepted. Some weeks later the match was held. Among the spectators was a member of the firm of Smith and Wesson, manufacturers of guns, one which was presented to Cody, who won the match by a narrow margin. Cody afterwards presented this rifle to Luther North, who called it the best gun he ever had. The rifle was in his possession the rest of his life.

2. Story reprinted in Sunday *World Herald* Magazine, July 5, 1959, from A. E. Sheldon, "History and Stories of Nebraska," 1929.

> . . . In the early years of exploration and settlement, the Sand Hills were regarded as a dangerous region. Many stories are told of hunters and explorers who were lost among these hills. In more than one place human skeletons have been found, telling their mute story of a losing struggle with hunger and thirst in these treacherous wilds. . . . Each sand hill seems like each other sand hill. . . . If one climbs to the top of the highest hill in sight, everywhere is a confused medley of hills and hollows extending as far as eye can see. . . . An ocean tossed by a great storm, the waves suddenly . . . changed to sand.
>
> In the Sand Hills of Thomas County, in 1891. . . . A German family named Haumann settled near Thedford . . . nine or ten children. . . . On May 10, . . . eight year old Tillie and four year old Retta went about a mile and a half to the neighbor Gilson's where an older sister worked. . . . They reached Mr. Gilson's safely and about four o'clock started hand in hand to return home. . . .
>
> . . . About noon of this day, Wednesday, the searching party, Mr. Haumann, Mr. Stacy, Mr. Naseburg and Dr. Edwards, found Retta carrying one little shoe with its sole worn through, the other had been dropped on the trail. Both of the girls had worn new shoes when they left home on Sunday. . . . She had wandered so long without food or water that her mind was affected for many days. She said they saw a prairie fire and went to it in hope of finding someone, but no one was there. [A hallucination.]
>
> . . . On Sunday, May 17, the Dunning search party found the other lost girl. She had taken off her apron, spread it over some rose bushes, laid herself on the sand beneath and died.
>
> Her body was placed on a handcar and taken to Thedford. Her parents did not recognize their child except by her clothing. She was

wasted to skin and bones. Her fair tender flesh burned black by the exposure. All the neighborhood came to her funeral and wept with her family as the worn-out little body was laid to rest.

That country is settled now and fences stretch everywhere across the hills. One has only to follow a fence and he will reach a ranch or road. The Haumann family still live on their ranch near Thedford. [Editor's note—this was published in 1929. A nephew still farms the homestead.]

3. See Luther North, *Man of the Plains* for instances of belligerent deer, pp. 272, 273-74, 276.
4. In 1879 Major North built a sod ranch house, stable, and corral about sixteen miles northwest of the original log house. This sod house was occupied in winters by at least two hands, who were there to patrol the area and turn back cattle that were drifting off the range. Luther stayed alone at this post during six weeks of one winter, seeing no one. Other times he regularly visited the cowhands, fetching mail, newspapers, and supplies, usually staying a few days to break the long winter loneliness at the outpost.
5. No record was found explaining Major North's 1870 trip (mentioned) to Salt Lake City, which probably was a mission for the army or guiding hunters.
6. Nellie Snyder Yost, *The Call of the Range* (Denver, Swallow Publishing Company, 1966), p. 85.
7. John Bratt, *Trails of Yesterday* (Lincoln, the University Publishing Company, 1921), p. 178, paid $75,000 for the North-Cody (NC) ranch. While this amount purchased the buildings, as in many such deals in the history of early ranching where no real ownership of land existed, not an acre of ground was owned or exchanged.

CHAPTER 39

1. An album given by Major North to his daughter, Stella, as a Christmas gift after the death of her mother ten months earlier. In his own handwriting, the following appears on the album's first page:

> My Dear Daughter
> Wait not till tomorrow's sun
> Beams upon the way
> All that thou canst call thine own
> Lies in thy today.
>
> 　　　　　Ever Your Loving Papa

Columbus, Nebraska
December 26th, 1883

2. William McCune responded when called, went and joined Cody's Wild West Show, supervised the Pawnee and all other Indians as long as the Cody Wild West Show existed.

Mr. John N. Baker (not the famous Johnny Baker of the Cody shows, but nephew of William Sweeney, director of the famous Cowboy Band of the Cody shows) recalls his (then) elderly uncle's periodic trips to Columbus, Nebraska, to visit the aging William McCune, after their retirement from the show. The three "Bills" remained fast friends to the end.

3. Other members of Maj. Frank North's family have come to rest in the Pioneer Cemetery. Many fellow pioneers, including some of his Pawnee Scout white officers, lie nearby.